Circular and Bioeconomy Pathways to Global Sustainability in the Age of Intelligent Innovation

Saurabh Agarwal
https://orcid.org/0000-0003-3836-2595
Yeungnam University, South Korea

D. Lakshmi
https://orcid.org/0000-0003-4018-1208
VIT Bhopal University, India

IGI Global
Scientific Publishing
Publishing Tomorrow's Research Today

Vice President of Editorial	Melissa Wagner
Director of Acquisitions	Mikaela Felty
Director of Book Development	Jocelynn Hessler
Production Manager	Mike Brehm
Cover Design	Jose Rosado

Published in the United States of America by
IGI Global Scientific Publishing
701 East Chocolate Avenue
Hershey, PA, 17033, USA
Tel: 717-533-8845 | Fax: 717-533-7115
Website: https://www.igi-global.com E-mail: cust@igi-global.com

Library of Congress Cataloging-in-Publication Data

LCCN: (CIP Data Pending)
ISBN13: 9798337399232
Isbn13Softcover: 9798337399249
EISBN13: 9798337399256

British Cataloguing in Publication Data
A Cataloguing in Publication record for this book is available from the British Library.

Table of Contents

Detailed Table of Contents

In this book chapter the intersection of artificial intelligence (AI) and circular economy is invented, which focuses on durable business models. As the global economy turns to a circular to reduce environmental influence, AI emerges as a major technique that facilitates this transition. The chapter is investigated how AI enables resource efficiency, waste reduction and closed-loop systems in industries. The main subjects include AI-powered forecast maintenance, smart resource allocation and advanced recycling processes. Case Studies Circular Explains the successful integration of AI in professional models, highlighting benefits such as cost savings, enhanced production life cycle management and improved environmental metrics. The chapter ends with the insights of the future AI application, challenges and circular businesses.

This chapter explores the importance of resource management, circular economy, and food sovereignty as strategies for transforming the global agri-food system. Food production contributes approximately one-third of global greenhouse gas emissions, estimated at 17.318 billion metric tons of CO_2 equivalent per year 57% of which originates from animal-based foods, 29% from plant-based products, and

but ensuing circular bioeconomy is a possible strategy for addressing these universal problems. It emphasizes nature driven processes that reutilizes existing reserve into useful materials. Whereas sustainability instigate reduce and recycle of waste to reduce carbon footprint and enhance self-reliant economy. Efficient waste conversion methods transform biodegradable carbonaceous wastes into clean energy using thermochemical processes. Anaerobic digestion, composting, biochar processes convert organic waste into value added product like biofuel, biofertilizers. Sustainable management practices, like spent mushroom waste or nature based solution can guarantee sustainability while valorizing wealth from waste. Biomass waste can be minimized through technological innovations to ensure sustainability and zero waste through circular economy models..

This chapter develops an empirical model to assess the impact of social-economic development, environmental degradation, green and digital technologies on water productivity in G20 countries. Therefore, water productivity is treated as a dependent variable, and it is adopted as a representative variable for water resources sustainability (WRS). While sex ratio, education expenditure, population growth, population density, urbanization, industrialization, capita GDP, per capita CO2 emissions, environmental technologies, renewable energy consumption, inflation, technological advancement, trade openness, foreign direct investment, cereal yield, and DTs are used as independent variables. Country-wise panel data of explained and explanatory variables are compiled to estimate regression coefficients. Log-linear regression model is adopted to estimate the impact of aforesaid variables on WRS. The descriptive result shows a decreasing trend in WRS in G20 countries during 1990-2022. Thus, G20 countries should take effective policies to increase WRS to increase sustainable development.

This chapter is an attempt to establish the understanding of how CI methods and optimisation approaches can enhance the capacity in WM. Water safety and potability emerge as an international subject that requires better methods in identifying, assessing, and forecasting the quality of water. It explains how the water quality that is measured by pH, conductivity, hardness and turbidity data sets is analyzed through several computational intelligence based machine learning algorithms to provide an overview of the water quality. The approaches to enhancing the efficiency of water treatment and decision-making regarding the usage of the resources in sustainable water quality management are discussed here. In this section, we use machine learning on real world application where we predict water potability using water quality proxy data sets.

Bioeconomy refers to managing the flow of materials within nature to build a sustainable economy. The goal is to combine scientific progress with effective policies and frameworks to create systems that are both cost-effective and eco-friendly. Moving towards a circular bioeconomy is essential, as it enables smart systems to handle complexity, variability, and sustainability challenges in bio-based value chains. From precision farming to waste management and closed-loop production, machine learning (ML) plays a vital role by identifying patterns, forecasting trends, and supporting smart decisions. This chapter explores key areas such as supply chain strength, waste handling, predictive upkeep, and lifecycle planning. It focuses on ML tools, digital twin use, and industrial applications to enhance resource flow, improve tracking, and lower environmental impact. Real-world cases show how ML can drive innovation and efficiency in eco-friendly, low-carbon economies.

Green hydrogen produced via renewable powered electrolysis, is seen as a key solution on the clean energy technology landscape as the world transitions to sustainable energy systems powered by wind, solar, and similar technologies. Being the cleanest form of hydrogen, it has enormous potential to decarbonize hard-to-abate sectors such as heavy industry, aviation, and shipping. Green hydrogen production, storage, and distribution are undergoing advancements accelerated by the convergence of artificial intelligence (AI) and Industry 6.0 technologies. Such smart grids powered by Industry 6.0 support seamless integration of hydrogen into existing energy infrastructures, while AI-driven predictive analytics optimize energy consumption during electrolysis, boost efficiency, and reduce operational costs. The possibilities for a more sustainable energy landscape through the merging of innovative technologies including AI, Industry 6.0 and hydrogen offer us a cleaner, smarter, and more resilient future.

This chapter highlights the role of education and capacity building in promoting global bionomically, which integrates ecological and economic principles of stability. This underlines the inclusion of bioeconomic standards in education to develop competent experts. Multi -colored fields such as ecological economy, environmental science and biotechnology are important for developing a skilled workforce. Important strategies include sustainable courses, bioinizing and special courses in renewable energy, and decisions of best practices from large institutions. Vocational education, especially for indigenous communities, is important for coordinating traditional skills with green economy. The chapter promotes progress in accurate agriculture, biotechnology and renewable energy through academic government cooperation. International cooperation is necessary to remove loss of biodiversity and climate challenges. Governments should establish side rivers and public-private partnerships. It is important to achieve stability and balance organic, economic and social flexibility.

Preface

The world stands at a pivotal moment in its pursuit of sustainability. Escalating environmental degradation, resource scarcity, climate change, and socio-economic inequities demand transformative solutions that move beyond incremental change. At the heart of this transformation lies biodiversity—the vast variety of life on Earth that underpins ecological stability, economic productivity, and human well-being. In parallel, the emergence of the circular economy and the bioeconomy, increasingly shaped by intelligent and digital innovations, offers powerful pathways to reimagine how societies produce, consume, and thrive. This edited volume, *Circular and Bioeconomy Pathways to Global Sustainability in the Age of Intelligent Innovation*, is situated within this critical global context.

The book explores how ecosystems and natural capital can serve as the foundation for sustainable economic development when aligned with circular principles and advanced technologies. It provides an interdisciplinary examination of the dynamic nexus between ecology and economy, highlighting how intelligent innovation—ranging from data-driven decision-making and precision technologies to biotechnology and systems thinking—can accelerate the transition toward sustainability. The overarching goal is to advance a bioeconomy that not only supports economic growth but also ensures the long-term preservation and regeneration of the planet's natural resources and life-support systems.

The chapters assembled in this volume showcase innovative approaches across agriculture, biotechnology, ecosystem management, and policy design that are consistent with sustainability principles. Emphasis is placed on practices such as precision farming, genetic resource conservation, bio-based and circular innovations, and nature-based solutions that enhance productivity while safeguarding biodiversity. The book also underscores the indispensable services provided by natural systems, including water purification, air quality regulation, climate stabilization, and the conservation of biological diversity—services that are often undervalued yet essential to global sustainability.

A defining strength of this volume is its interdisciplinary perspective. By integrating ecological science, economic theory, technological innovation, and policy analysis, the book offers a holistic understanding of how biodiversity can be valued, governed, and leveraged within circular and bioeconomic systems. It fosters dialogue across disciplines and sectors, encouraging collaboration among researchers, policymakers, industry leaders, and civil society to address complex environmental, social, and economic challenges in an interconnected world.

Ultimately, this book imagines a future in which biodiversity is recognized not as a constraint on development, but as a key driver of resilient, inclusive, and sustainable economic growth. We hope it inspires optimism and action by deepening appreciation for natural capital and demonstrating practical pathways toward ecological balance and economic progress. In doing so, this volume seeks to contribute to the development of models capable of sustaining the planet—Mother Earth—and its people in the age of intelligent innovation.

ORGANIZATION OF THE BOOK

Chapter 1: Factors of Sustainable Resource Use: Biocapacity and Circular Economy

This chapter lays an empirical foundation for understanding sustainability within the framework of the circular economy by foregrounding Earth's biocapacity as a critical limiting factor. The authors argue that living within planetary boundaries is central to reducing ecological stress and achieving long-term sustainable development. Using biocapacity as a proxy for circular economy performance, the chapter employs a random effects model across 13 countries to identify key determinants influencing biocapacity. The analysis reveals complex and sometimes counterintuitive relationships among ecological footprints, energy use patterns, emissions, waste generation, and access to basic services. By grounding circular economy discourse in measurable ecological limits, this chapter offers important policy-relevant insights into how resource use, infrastructure, and energy transitions can be better aligned with sustainability goals.

Chapter 2: Sustainable Circular Economy Through Artificial Intelligence and the Circular Age

In this chapter, we turn to the transformative role of artificial intelligence in enabling circular economy transitions. The authors explore how AI supports durable and sustainable business models by enhancing resource efficiency, minimizing waste, and enabling closed-loop industrial systems. Through discussions on predictive maintenance, intelligent resource allocation, and advanced recycling technologies, the chapter demonstrates how AI-driven tools are reshaping production and consumption patterns. Real-world case studies illustrate tangible benefits, including cost reductions, improved lifecycle management, and enhanced environmental performance. The chapter concludes by reflecting on future opportunities, implementation challenges, and the strategic implications of embedding AI within circular business ecosystems.

Chapter 3: Circular Economy and Food Sovereignty Management in the Food Sector: A Socioeconomic Approach to Sustainability

This chapter addresses one of the most resource-intensive sectors of the global economy: food systems. The authors critically examine the environmental and social consequences of linear agri-food models, noting the sector's substantial contribution to global greenhouse gas emissions. In response, the chapter proposes a regenerative and circular approach grounded in food sovereignty, resource reuse, and agroecological diversification. By integrating socioeconomic analysis with technological perspectives, the chapter explores the roles of circular technologies, artificial intelligence, renewable energy, and waste reduction in building resilient food systems. The contribution concludes with actionable recommendations for policymakers, producers, and other stakeholders seeking to transition toward a circular, equitable, and sustainable food economy.

Chapter 4: Economic and Sustainability Perspectives on Organic and Conventional Banana Farming

Focusing on agricultural sustainability at the farm level, this chapter presents a comparative economic analysis of organic and conventional banana cultivation in Tamil Nadu, India. Against the backdrop of soil degradation and chemical-intensive farming practices, the authors examine production costs, returns, and benefit–cost ratios using field data from organic and conventional farmers. While organic farming entails slightly higher production costs and marginally lower yields, the findings reveal superior net incomes and economic efficiency due to premium pricing and improved soil health. The chapter also explores adoption drivers and barriers, highlighting the importance of consumer demand, certification systems, and policy support. This contribution underscores organic farming's dual role in advancing farm profitability and environmental sustainability.

Chapter 5: Towards a Sustainable Zero-Waste Bioeconomy: The Time Travel of Organic Waste

This chapter situates organic waste management at the core of a zero-waste circular bioeconomy. The authors emphasize the growing challenge of biomass waste generation and argue that waste valorization offers a viable pathway toward sustainability and self-reliant economies. By examining nature-based and technology-driven processes—such as anaerobic digestion, composting, and biochar production—the chapter illustrates how organic waste can be transformed into biofuels, biofertilizers, and other value-added products. Case examples, including spent mushroom waste utilization, highlight practical applications of circular thinking. The chapter reinforces the idea that technological innovation, combined with ecological principles, can convert waste streams into economic and environmental assets.

Chapter 6: Water Resource Sustainability and Environmental Degradation in G20 Countries

This chapter provides a macro-level assessment of water resource sustainability across G20 nations, using water productivity as a proxy indicator. Employing a log-linear regression model with panel data spanning more than three decades, the authors examine how socio-economic development, environmental degradation, green technologies, and digitalization influence water sustainability outcomes. The findings reveal a declining trend in water resource sustainability across G20 countries, underscoring the urgency of coordinated policy interventions. By linking water productivity to broader development indicators, this chapter highlights water governance as a central pillar of sustainable development in an increasingly resource-constrained world.

Chapter 7: Computational Intelligence and Optimization for Water Quality Management

This chapter explores the application of computational intelligence and optimization techniques in addressing water quality and safety challenges. Recognizing water potability as a global concern, the authors demonstrate how machine learning algorithms can analyze key water quality parameters such as pH, conductivity, hardness, and turbidity. Using real-world datasets, the chapter illustrates predictive modeling approaches for assessing water potability and supporting data-driven decision-making. By integrating computational intelligence into water management systems, the chapter showcases how advanced analytics can enhance treatment efficiency, resource allocation, and long-term sustainability of water resources.

Chapter 8: Machine Learning and Circular Bioeconomy Transforming Sustainability Through Intelligent Systems

In this chapter, the focus shifts to machine learning as a core enabler of circular bioeconomy systems. The authors examine how intelligent algorithms help manage complexity and variability across bio-based value chains, from precision agriculture to waste management and lifecycle planning. Emphasis is placed on tools such as digital twins, predictive analytics, and smart tracking systems that optimize resource flows and reduce environmental impacts. Through industrial applications and case studies, the chapter demonstrates how machine learning drives efficiency, transparency, and innovation, reinforcing its role in building low-carbon, eco-efficient, and resilient bioeconomic systems.

Chapter 9: Future of Energy Innovation with AI and Industry 6.0: Green Hydrogen as the Next Frontier

This chapter addresses the future of clean energy transitions by examining green hydrogen within the context of artificial intelligence and Industry 6.0. The authors highlight green hydrogen's potential to decarbonize hard-to-abate sectors such as heavy industry, aviation, and shipping. By integrating AI-driven analytics with smart grids and advanced manufacturing systems, the chapter demonstrates how efficiency gains, cost reductions, and infrastructure integration can be achieved across hydrogen value chains. This contribution positions green hydrogen, supported by intelligent technologies and enabling policy instruments such as green taxes, as a cornerstone of a resilient and sustainable energy future.

Chapter 10: Integrating Bioeconomy into Education, Vocational Training, and Research Capacity Building

This chapter underscores the critical role of education, training, and research in advancing a sustainable bioeconomy. The authors argue that embedding bioeconomic principles into formal education, vocational training, and capacity-building initiatives is essential for developing a skilled and adaptable workforce. Special attention is given to interdisciplinary curricula, vocational programs for indigenous and local communities, and collaborative models involving academia, government, and industry. By emphasizing public–private partnerships and international cooperation, the chapter highlights education as a long-term investment in ecological, economic, and social resilience.

Chapter 11: The Contribution of a Touristic Destination's Soundscape to a Holistic Approach to Sustainability

The final chapter broadens the sustainability discourse by examining sensory dimensions of sustainable tourism, with a focus on soundscape. Using the context of Greece as a tourism destination, the authors explore how natural, cultural, and social sounds shape visitor experiences, well-being, and perceptions of environmental quality. The chapter argues that soundscape management is an often-overlooked yet powerful component of holistic sustainability strategies in tourism. By integrating sensory experience with ecological preservation and cultural identity, this contribution highlights innovative pathways for enhancing sustainable tourism while fostering harmony between visitors, communities, and natural environments.

CONCLUSION

The chapters brought together in this volume collectively affirm that global sustainability in the twenty-first century will be defined by our ability to integrate circular economy principles, bioeconomic thinking, and intelligent innovation within the limits of the planet's biocapacity. Across diverse sectors—ranging from resource governance, agriculture, water and waste management, and energy systems to education, tourism, and advanced digital technologies—the contributions demonstrate that sustainability is no longer a peripheral concern, but a central organizing principle for economic and social development.

A unifying insight emerging from this book is the critical role of data-driven and intelligent systems in enabling circular and bioeconomic transitions. Artificial intelligence, machine learning, computational intelligence, and Industry 6.0 technologies are shown to enhance resource efficiency, optimize decision-making, and support closed-loop systems across complex value chains. At the same time, the chapters remind us that technological progress must be guided by ecological realities, social equity, and ethical governance. Living within Earth's biocapacity, safeguarding water and biodiversity, and ensuring inclusive access to resources remain non-negotiable foundations of sustainable development.

Equally important is the recognition that sustainability is deeply human in nature. Education, vocational training, traditional knowledge, community participation, and even sensory experiences such as soundscape in tourism all shape how societies understand, value, and implement sustainable practices. The transition toward circular and bio-based systems therefore requires not only innovation in technologies and policies, but also investments in human capital, institutional capacity, and cultural awareness.

In closing, we envision this volume as both a comprehensive reference and a forward-looking guide for researchers, policymakers, practitioners, and educators. By bringing together interdisciplinary perspectives and global case studies, the book highlights practical pathways toward resilient, low-carbon, and regenerative economies. We hope it inspires informed dialogue, collaborative action, and continued innovation toward a future in which economic prosperity, ecological integrity, and social well-being are mutually reinforcing, ensuring sustainability for present and future generations.

Chapter 1
Factors of Sustainable Resource Use:
Biocapacity and Circular Economy

Manvi Ganotra
School of Economics, Shri Mata Vaishno Devi University, Katra, India

Meenakshi Gupta
https://orcid.org/0000-0002-7866-4961
School of Economics, Shri Mata Vaishno Devi University, Katra, India

Ajay Kumar Singh
https://orcid.org/0000-0003-0429-0925
Department of Humanities and Social Sciences, Graphic Era University, Dehradun, India

ABSTRACT

This chapter highlights that the need for a sustainable model can reduce the ecological stress and ensure long term sustainable development in the age of circular economy. The most effective way of promoting a circular economy is to live within the Earth's bio capacity. Thus, this chapter uses biocapacity as the proxy for circular economy. It examines the determining factors of bio-capacity to promote circular economy using a random effect model in 13 selected countries. Ecological Footprints, Carbon emissions, Renewable energy consumption and population with access to clean fuels and technology for cooking produce a negative implication on bio-capacity. While there is reported a positive impact of solid biofuels, CO2 emissions from fuel combustion per total electricity output and renewable energy, people using at least basic drinking water services, municipal waste, people using at least basic sanitation services and access to electricity on biocapacity.

DOI: 10.4018/979-8-3373-9923-2.ch001

1. INTRODUCTION

The traditional linear economic model is not able to meet the constantly rising market demand for the inputs that mankind requires to survive their livelihood (Abad-Segura et al., 2020, Laumann & Tambo, 2018). This unprocessed waste makes recycling and composting a challenge and ultimately ends up in unregulated dumps or incinerators (Abad-Segura et al., 2020, Schumann, 2020). Furthermore, it has adverse environmental impacts on the system (Abad-Segura et al., 2020; Wastling et al., 2018). 1.5 Earths would be needed to support the current rate of consumption. Also, according to Rockstrom's paper, planetary boundaries are a gauge of how much humans have impacted the biosphere. Further, according to the 2013 Millennium Ecosystem Assessment, stress and depletion are already occurring in fifteen out of the twenty-four ecosystems that support life.

Circular economy (CE) is bringing multiple positive benefits to reduce environmental problems and enhance the sustainability of the system in the long run (Dong et al., 2021). For instance, CE may be positive to reduce the health burden of people and their poverty (Garg et al., 2025). So, efforts are underway to promote the CE to attain sustainable development worldwide (Sharma et al., 2021; Lima et al., 2021; Ashton et al., 2022). Thus, the prime aim of CE is to maintain the process of sustainability in the production system (Mongo et al., 2021). The most important concern of the CE is to address the earth's biocapacity that has been overextended due to human-driven activities. The circular economic model can reduce this stress by minimizing resource extraction, encouraging reuse and recycling, and lowering the waste.

CE is an economic development approach that relies on the ecological circulation of natural materials (Feng et al., 2007). This approach emphasizes the need to adhere to ecological laws. The adoption of CE in India can result in a conservation of more than five hundred billion dollars of the country's GDP. Additionally, it can lead to increased annual savings of more than one billion dollars by reducing CO_2 emissions (Fiksel et al., 2021; Niwalkar et al., 2023). The extractive economy employs an unsustainable approach to utilizing resources, resulting in harm to the resources and the emission of greenhouse gases. Consequently, it poses a significant obstacle in obtaining the 1.5°C objective outlined in the "Paris Agreement." To achieve the objective of net zero emissions by 2050, significant and decisive actions are required. CE is trying to reduce zero waste (Khan et al., 2021). CE can be helpful to achieve net-zero emissions by the 2050s (Khalifa et al., 2022). The predicted cost of this endeavour, estimated to be USD 54 trillion by 2100, will be shouldered by the world economy in relation to the changing climate. This cost will continue to rise as global temperature increases (Macarthur & Heading, 2019; Majeed & Luni,

2020). Sustainable consumption is defined as consumption that results in reduced waste, increased social welfare, and increased resource efficiency (Tunn et al. 2019).

Elia et al. (2017) asserted that a circular economy necessitates a higher consumption of sustainable and reusable resources, which includes green energy sources. Energy is significant to increase the well-being of society (Nguyen-Phung & Le, 2024). Replacing non-renewable fossil fuels with sustainable sources of energy was cited to illustrate one of the ideas that govern the CE (MacArthur et al., 2015). Optimizing energy and material efficiency, generating value via waste products, and implementing biological replication concepts to transition from unsustainable to environmentally friendly resources are key activities in CE (Schroeder et al., 2019). Eliminating waste through design, and replacing non-renewable materials with energy-efficient alternatives are key principles of CE. Ishaq et al. (2022) explained the role of the circular economy to increase the transformation of energy transition. This chapter, therefore, determines the factors of sustainable resource use, bio-capacity, and circular economy in selected 13 countries.

2. LITERATURE REVIEW

CE highlights the development of innovations and frameworks that ensure the continuous flow of materials and enhance the quality of the ecosystem (Schröder, 2020). Multiple studies investigated the role of circular economy in ecosystem services. CE can be positive to increase environmental quality, environmental sustainability, social sustainability, energy transitions, and sustainable development in following ways: Circular economy (CE) policies can be significant to increase sustainable growth and environmental quality (Abad-Segura et al., 2020). CE may provide an alternative solution for environmental problems (Adami & Schiavon, 2021). CE promotes environmental and social justice, and reduces environmental hazard (Purvis et al., 2023; Garg et al., 2025).

In relation to the utilization of raw materials and energy sources, an efficient CE requires a worldwide approach to resource efficiency to handle the situation. For this reason, energy should be derived from renewable sources. CE, energy efficiency, and green energy help to increase environmentally friendly growth. Businesses accountable for generating worldwide resources are increasingly seeking ways to meet market demand by reducing their energy requirements. CE is helping business communities to adopt environmentally friendly technologies and resource saving plans to increase sustainable development (Tsironis et al., 2024). Reliance on renewable energy sources can make the goals of the CE easier to achieve (Majeed & Luni, 2020). Renewable energy consumption may be an alternative mechanism to reduce GHGs and CO_2 emissions (Ishaq et al., 2022). Increases in the availability of renewable resources are beneficial to carbon absorption. When renewable resources are turned into waste (through usage), they do not emit pollutants into the atmosphere in the same manner as products derived from traditional fuels. Thus, CE promote renewable energy (Mutezo & Mulopo, 2021).

A significant contributor to the biobased economy and a substantial contributor to carbon capture, forestation is one of the renewable resources (Majeed & Luni, 2020). CE develops a path of carbon neutrality (Garg et al., 2025). Around one billion individuals do not have access to a steady supply of electricity and renewable power solutions. There has been an annual growth of 1.3% emissions associated with energy over the past five years. Alterations to the structure also make it possible to achieve greater energy efficiency. The relocation of industrial units to locations that are plentiful in renewable resources is one example of such a transition. Existing scholars have made significant contributions to the understanding of energy consumption trends, the onset of critical energy shifts, and the forces that accelerate change (Chen & Kim, 2019). Energy transition is a structural shift in the energy system that is associated with the gathering, conversion, transportation, consumption, and governance of energy resources (Chen & Kim, 2019). Solar, wind, hydropower, biomass, and biofuels are all examples of renewable energy sources. The vast majority of renewable energy sources do not produce carbon dioxide, whereas biomass and biofuels are in the category of carbon-neutral sources (Okafor et al., 2021).

Modern energy technology is sometimes referred to as low-carbon or sustainable energy today. Thus, use of modern and advanced technologies in the production sector including energy sector would reduce environmental issues (Mongo et al., 2021). This is in contrast to the historical transitions, which were predominantly led by technological innovation and the adoption of new supplies of resources. The most recent energy transition is being driven by national policies that seek to restrict GHG emissions and prevent the rise in the world's temperature according to the Paris Agreement. The advancement of renewable sources of energy and improvements in energy efficiency are the primary strategies that can be utilized to accomplish this objective (Kim, 2018).

Sustainable development may be broken down into three distinct dimensions: the environment, the economy, and society. CE framework helps to increase the promotion of all integrated dimensions of sustainable development (Ashton et al., 2022). The cornerstones of low-carbon transition research are linked to these three dimensions. According to what was stated earlier, the new ET was brought about by changes in the global environment.

CE is the result of a number of different forms of sustainability, including the sustainable use of resources, which is supported by low-carbon and renewable energy sources (Kalmykova et al., 2018). Macarthur and Heading (2019) also notified the role of circular economy to mitigate the negative implication of climate change.

Niwalkar et al. (2023) also detected the role of CE in climate change issues. Gallego-Schmid et al. (2020) explored the association of circular economy with climate change mitigation. For instance, increasing resource efficiency through adopting CE can be effective for mitigating climate change impacts (Gallego-Schmid et al., 2020). CE can be active to reduce climate related concerns (Sharma et al., 2021). Yang et al. (2023) argued that circular economy develops a plan and strategies to fight against climate change. CE is found to be an effective driver to reduce sustainability issues in urban areas (Dong et al., 2021).

As the shift to CE continues to progress, there is still no agreement on which policy would be most suitable for adoption. There have been criticisms leveled against certain CE policies and tactics for their lack of resilience (Suárez-Eiroa et al., 2021). Production and consumption involve several key factors: having enough raw materials on hand, providing sufficient municipal water for each person, generating enough waste (excluding major mineral waste) per unit of household good consumption, and managing food waste. The reuse of the same material would be effective for the reduction of greenhouse gas (GHG) emissions. Within the business sector, waste elimination is achieved by the adoption of the CE. In an effort to attain net waste to zero, businesses have tried to close the production cycles in their supply chains (Tiwari et al., 2023). When practices are continuous, the value of goods is kept in terms of labor, materials, and energy. So, things that last and can be recycled keep the business going instead of making waste. The CE effectively utilizes biological materials for various business purposes before returning the nutrients to nature. CE policies are crucial to increase the attention of the business sector to towards sustainable development (Ashton et al., 2022). In this way, the process keeps the energy in the goods and materials (Majeed & Luni, 2020). Therefore, the loop economy was taken into consideration. Selling the utilization of the product rather than ownership can help lessen the environmental load, as well as the costs and externalities that are involved with production (Stahel, 1982).

The term waste management refers to the amount of waste that is recycled, including municipal waste, overall waste (apart from major mineral waste), plastic and wooden packaging, e-waste, biowaste, and waste from construction and demolition (C&D), with regard to recovery rates. It is expected that solid waste may be 3.4 billion tonnes worldwide by the 2050s (Sharma et al., 2021). Thus, solid waste creates many serious problems for improving the sustainability of the environment, economy and society (Sharma et al., 2021). Circular designs extend the product lifecycle and encourage the regeneration of natural systems, which facilitates carbon capture in the soil and reduces externalities, trash output, and emissions (Macarthur & Heading, 2019). In addition to lowering expenses, reducing the production of single-use plastic also lessens emissions, trash creation, and other related externalities (MacArthur, 2013). The circular economy emphasizes the idea that waste can be converted into value. Consequently, it is possible to exercise control over the deterioration of land and the depletion of biodiversity. Due to the fact that the land is required for the provision of the majority of the essential services, its capacity to act as a carbon sink can be enhanced by reducing the rate at which it degrades (Shukla et al., 2019).

This planning must take into account the economic viability of a variety of different solutions. The collection of municipal solid waste has been the primary focus of research over the years. This is due to the fact that it accounts for around 80% of the total expenditures contained within municipal solid waste (Rathore & Sarmah, 2020). CE is a notion that has been around since 1966 (Adami & Schiavon, 2021). There are many concepts of CE. Furthermore, in the year 1991, researchers analyzed the strategy related to economic recycling (Leontief, 1991). Nevertheless, the concept of CE did not become a recognized notion until the year 2013. Within the framework of CE, one of its components is the reduction of waste that is generated during the production and distribution processes. CE possesses the capacity to be an effective method for reducing garbage (Yang et al., 2023).

These wastes contain materials that have the potential to be harmful. CE strategies have a positive impact on solid waste management (Ezeudu & Ezeudu, 2019). Circular economy can be effective to minimize municipal wastage. Municipal wastage can be used for another purpose to increase sustainability. An investigation into the possibility for the generation of biogas from food waste was carried out by Al-Wahaibi et al. (2020) conducting a techno economic analysis. The experimental findings indicate that the aggregated value of gas production is 1550 milliliters per one gram of dry matter. Rolewicz-Kalińska et al. (2020) investigated the relationship between waste collection and CE strategies. It is noted that by the year 2030, the total volume of biogas that might be produced from solid waste might rise to about 9 million cubic meters per year. With this, the yearly generation of renewable energy would reach over 17-kilowatt hours. Considering the investigation's results, the adoption of the CE strategy affects both solid and toxic waste. In the realm of solid waste management, the CE strategy presents several positive application opportunities. Through prolonging the lifespan of goods and components, the CE approach will increase product utility while simultaneously minimizing the amount of trash generated by public and commercial sectors. Ashton et al. (2022) explored the association of the circular economy with justice and equity.

3. RESEARCH METHODOLOGY

The current study examined the impact of energy transition on environmental sustainability in the selected Asian economies.

3.1. Discussion of Variables and Sources of Data

Biocapacity per capita (*BC*) is used as a proxy variable for the adoption of a circular economy (*CE*). The amount of energy transition to renewable sources in each group of nations is similarly represented by renewable energy share in total final energy consumption (*REF*), annual CO_2 emissions per capita (*COE*), CO_2 emissions from fuel combustion per total electricity output (*CFC*), electricity generation from renewables (*EGR*), renewable energy share of electricity generation (REG), renewable energy consumption (*REC*) and solid biofuels and renewable municipal waste (*BMW*). To witness the extent of equitable distribution of resources in the South and East Asian nations, variables such as the proportion of the population using at least basic sanitation services (*BSS*), the proportion of the population using at least basic drinking water services (*ADW*), the proportion of the population using clean fuels and technology for cooking (*ACF*) and the proportion of the population with access to electricity (*ATE*) have been considered in empirical investigations. This chapter includes 13 countries from different income groups. The following countries are: high income (Japan, the Republic of Korea), upper middle income (China, the Maldives), lower middle income (Mongolia, Bangladesh, India, Bhutan, Pakistan, Nepal, Sri Lanka), and low-income (the Democratic People's Republic of Korea, Afghanistan). These countries have been finalized based on the availability of statistical data for the mentioned variables in South and East Asia. Table 1 shows the list of variables and their sources that are considered in this study.

Table 1. Variables and data description

Variables	Symbols	Unit of measurement	Data Sources	Expected Sign
Biocapacity per capita	BC	global Ha./ person	Global Footprint Network	(+/-)
Ecological Footprints per capita	EF	global Ha./person	Global Footprint Network	(+/-)
Annual CO_2 emissions per capita	COE	Tonnes/person	Global Carbon Budget (2023)	(+/-)
Renewable energy share of electricity generation	REG	%	IRENA (2023)	(+/-)
Renewable energy consumption (share of total final energy consumption)	REC	%	IEA, IRENA, UNSD, World Bank, WHO (2023)	(+/-)
Renewable energy share in total final energy consumption	REF	%	IEA, IRENA, UNSD, World Bank, WHO (2023)	(+/-)
Electricity generation from renewables	EGR	Terawatt-hours	Our World in Data	(+/-)
Solid biofuels and renewable municipal waste	BMW	Megajoules per Kilogram	IEA (2023)	(+/-)
CO_2 emissions from fuel combustion per total electricity output	CFC	Megatonnes per billion-kilowatt hours	IEA (2023)	(+/-)

continued on following page

Table 1. Continued

Variables	Symbols	Unit of measurement	Data Sources	Expected Sign
People using at least basic drinking water services	ADW	%	WHO, UNICEF	(+/-)
Population with access to clean fuels and technology for cooking	ACF	%	IEA, IRENA, UNSD, World Bank, WHO (2023)	(+/-)
People using at least basic sanitation services	BSS	%	WHO, UNICEF	(+/-)
Access to electricity	ATE	%	IEA, IRENA, UNSD, World Bank, WHO. 2023	(+/-)

Source: Compiled by authors.

3.2. Tools Used for Analysis

This study first examines the trends of the selected variables. Then it uses a random effect model after performing all initial screening tests, such as the unit root and Hausman test. This chapter compiles a country-wise balanced panel data set during the stated period.

3.3. Formulation of Empirical Model

This model is estimated through the one-way random effects model. Mathematically, the model can be written as:

$$(BC)_{it} = \alpha + \beta_1 (EF)_{it} + \beta_2 (COE)_{it} + \beta_3 (REF)_{it} + \beta_4 (CFC)_{it} + \beta_5 (EGR)_{it} +$$

$$\beta_6 (REG)_{it} + \beta_7 (REC)_{it} + \beta_8 (BMW)_{it} + \beta_9 (BSS)_{it} + \beta_{10} (ADW)_{it} + \beta_{11} (ACF)_{it} +$$

$$\beta_{12} (ATE)_{it} + \mu_i + \epsilon_{it} \quad (1)$$

Here, BC_{it} is a dependent variable, EF_{it}, COE_{it}, REF_{it}, CFC_{it}, EGR_{it}, REG_{it}, REC_{it}, BMW_{it}, BSS_{it}, ADW_{it}, ACF_{it}, and ATE_{it} are the independent variables, μ_i is the entity-specific effects that captures the unobserved characteristics of individual entities that are constant over time, ϵ_{it} represents the disturbance term, and α is a constant coefficient and βs are the parameters of associated variables. While i is cross-sectional country and t is period in equation (1). The description of the variables is presented in Table 1.

4. RESULTS AND DISCUSSION

4.1. Trends in Variables

Bio-capacity Per Capita

Biocapacity per capita (*BC*) is explained as the capacity of ecosystems to replace the resources that humans demand from the surfaces they inhabit. *BC* refers to the ecosystem's ability to generate biological resources utilized by humans and to assimilate waste material produced by humans. Due to variations in climate, management practices, and the parts deemed valuable inputs to the human economy, *BC* fluctuated from year to year.

Figure 1. Trend in bio-capacity per capita in selected countries (National Footprint and Biocapacity Accounts, 2023)

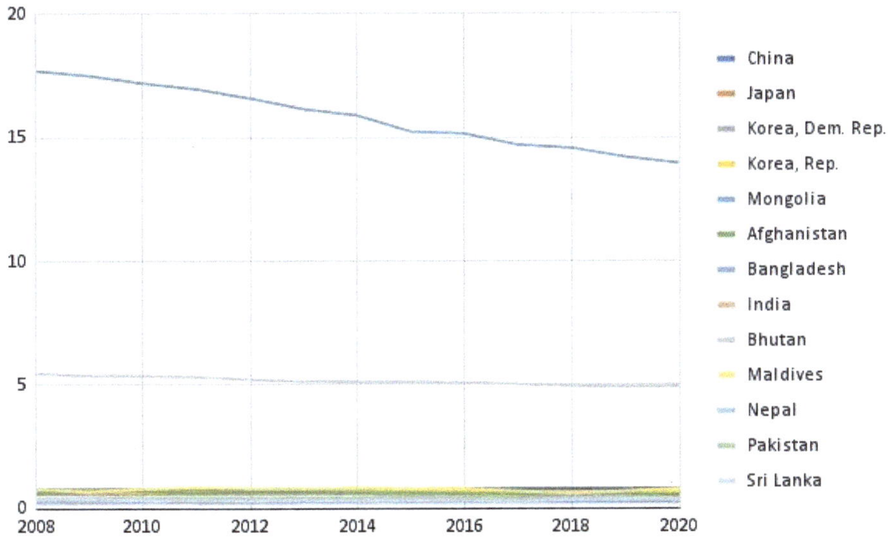

High-income nations, notably Japan and the Republic of Korea, have seen substantial changes in *BC* per capita over time (Figure 1). Japan had 0.641 gha per person as its *BC* in 2008. By the end of 2020, it had increased to 0.624 gha per person, having decreased to 0.623 gha per person in 2013. The Republic of Korea's *BC* per person was 0.71 gha per person in 2008. In 2013, it decreased to 0.67 gha per person. By the end of 2020, it had dropped once more to 0.64 gha per person. An increase in the *BC* per capita has been witnessed over the years in the upper-middle-income nations such as China and the Maldives. *BC* per capita in China stood at 0.78 gha per person in 2008. But in 2020, that number rose to 0.80 gha per person. Maldives, on the other hand, witnessed various fluctuations over the decade. Therefore, the *BC* per capita of the Maldives was 0.8 gha per person in 2008. By 2013, that number increased to 0.81 gha per person, and by the end of 2020, it slightly fell to 0.8 gha per person. The *BC* per capita of Bangladesh was 0.24 gha per person. Therefore, the number increased at a decreasing rate to 0.25 gha per person in 2020. Additionally, *BC* per capita of India increased from 0.340 gha per person in 2008 to 0.346 gha per person in 2020. Nepal's *BC* per capita was 0.367 gha per person in 2008, and it rose to 0.40 gha per person in 2020. The *BC* per capita of Bhutan, Pakistan, and Sri Lanka were, in 2008, 5.46, 0.40, and 0.39 gha per person, respectively, and declined to 4.93, 0.37, and 0.37 gha per person in 2020.

There has been a decline in *BC* over the years, as evidenced by the graph of low-income nations such as Afghanistan and the Democratic People's Republic of Korea. The *BC* per capita of Afghanistan was 0.643 gha per person in 2008. Substantially, it declined to 0.671 gha per person in 2013, fell to 0.582 gha per person in 2017, and then decreased to 0.540 gha per person by the end of 2020. In comparison, the *BC* per person in the Democratic Republic dropped from 0.587 gha per person in 2008 to 0.579 gha per person in 2013. By the end of 2020, it had decreased to 0.537 gha per person.

Ecological Footprints Per Capita

EF is computed by dividing the region's total EF by its population (Chen & Pao, 2024). To assess a region's ecological surplus or deficit, compare per capita EF to BC per person, which is the supply of natural resources.

Figure 2. Trend in ecological footprints per capita (National Footprint and Biocapacity Accounts, 2023)

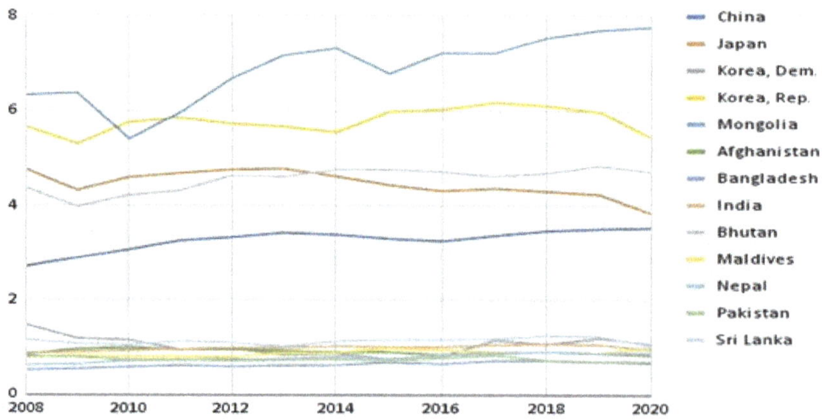

High-income nations, including Japan and the Republic of Korea, have seen a decline in their per capita ecological footprint (EF) since 2013 (Figure 2). In 2008, Japan's per capita EF was 4.75 gha per person. It climbed slightly to 4.77 gha per person in 2013, but by the end of 2020, it had dropped to 3.84 gha per person. Similarly, the EF per capita in the Republic of Korea was 5.6 gha in 2008. It stood at 5.6 gha per person in 2013, but seeing an increase in EF in 2017 and 2018, it again dropped to 5.4 gha per person in South Korea by the end of 2020.

The EF per capita in China and the Maldives has increased significantly over time. In China, annual emissions were 2.7 gha per person in 2008, but by the end of 2020, the figures had increased to 3.5 gha. Comparably, in the Maldives, the annual EF was 0.8 global hectares per person in 2008, and by the end of 2020, it had fallen to 1 global hectare per person.

It is interesting to look at the graph of lower middle-income nations. Every nation witnessed an increase in EF per capita. However, the rate of increase was decreasing, with the exception of Mongolia, where EF increased at an increasing rate. By the end of 2020, Mongolia's yearly per capita EF, which was 6.3 gha in 2008, had dramatically increased to 7.7 global hectares. Over time, Mongolia had a significant increase in EF per person. Bangladesh's yearly per capita EF was 0.5 gha in 2008, and by 2020, it had increased to 0.6 gha per person. Additionally, by the end of 2020, India's per capita EF increased from 0.8 gha per person in 2008 to 0.9 gha per person in 2020. The per capita EF of Bhutan, Nepal, Pakistan, and Sri Lanka were, in 2008, 4.3, 0.6, 0.8, and 1.1 gha per person, respectively, and 4.7, 0.89, 0.71, and 1.04 gha per person in 2020. It is also found that there has been a downfall over the years by examining the graph of low-income nations such as Afghanistan and the Democratic People's Republic of Korea. According to Afghanistan's trend, the nation's per capita yearly EF was 0.85 gha per person in 2008, increased to 0.96 gha per person in 2012, and declined to 0.8 gha per person by the end of 2020.

Trend in CO_2 Emissions Per Capita

Figure 3 depicts the trend in CO_2 emissions per capita in the individual countries. This indicator incorporates carbon dioxide emissions directly from industrial operations like the production of cement and steel, as well as emissions from burning fossil fuels like coal, oil, and gas.

Figure 3. Trend in CO_2 Emissions Per Capita (COE) (Global Carbon Budget, 2023)

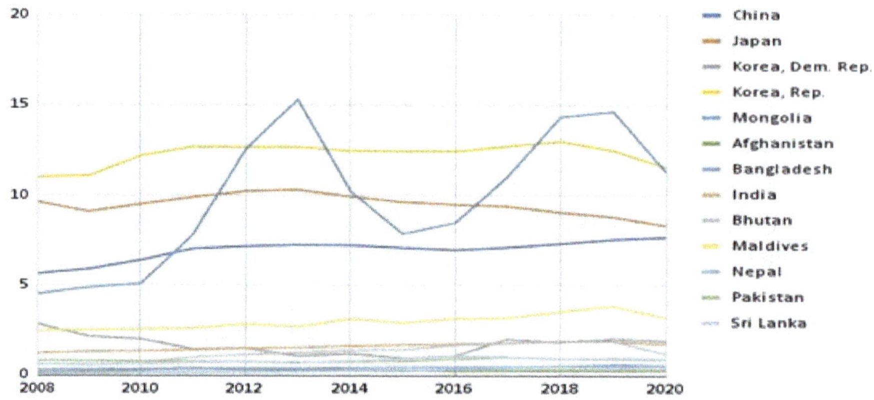

High-income nations like Japan and the Republic of Korea have seen a decline in their per capita annual CO_2 emissions since 2013 (Figure 3). In 2008, Japan's per capita annual CO_2 emissions were 9.6 tonnes. It climbed dramatically to 10.3 tonnes per person in 2013. It had dropped to 8.3 tonnes per person in 2020. Similarly, the COE per capita in the Republic of Korea was 11 tonnes in 2008. In 2013, it increased to 12.6 tonnes per person. Despite witnessing an increase in emissions in 2017 and 2018, it dropped to 11.5 tonnes per person in South Korea by 2020.

The COE per capita of upper-middle-income nations, such as China and the Maldives, has seen an increase over time. In China, the COE per capita was 5.6 tonnes in 2008. By the end of 2020, it increased to 7.6 tonnes per person. In the Maldives, COE per capita was 2.5 tonnes in 2008. It rose to 3.8 tonnes per person in 2019. But anyhow, it fell to 3.2 tonnes per person in Maldives by 2020.

It is interesting to look at the graph of lower middle-income nations. Each nation witnessed an increase in COE per capita at a decreasing rate, with the exception of Mongolia. Mongolia's COE per capita increased at an increasing rate. Therefore, Mongolia's COE per capita was 4.5 tonnes in 2008. It had dramatically increased to 11.2 tonnes per person in 2020. Bangladesh's COE per capita was 0.3 tonnes in 2008, and by 2020, it had declined to 0.5 tonnes per person. Additionally, the COE per capita of India witnessed a rise from 1.2 tonnes in 2008 to 1.7 tonnes in 2020. The COE per capita of Bhutan, Nepal, Pakistan, and Sri Lanka were, in 2008, 0.6, 0.1, 0.82, and 0.5 tonnes, respectively. It climbed to 1.1, 0.5, 0.88, and 1.04 tonnes per person for respective countries in 2020.

There has been a twofold tendency over the years of COE per capita in low-income nations such as Afghanistan and the Democratic People's Republic of Korea. The COE per capita of the nations has seen both increase and decrease over time.

Afghanistan's COE per capita was 0.1 tonnes in 2008. Gradually, it increased to 0.4 tonnes per person in 2011, fell to 0.2 tonnes per person in 2016, and then, finally, increased to 0.3 tonnes per person by the end of 2020. On the contrary, COE per capita in the Democratic People's Republic of Korea decreased from 2.8 tonnes per person in 2008 to 1.08 tonnes in 2013. The number increased to 1.2 tonnes per person in 2014. By 2015, it dropped to 0.9 tonnes per person. By the end of 2020, it had decreased to 1.9 tonnes per person from its peak of 2.04 tonnes per person in 2019.

Trend in CO_2 Emissions from Fuel Combustion (CFC) Per Total Electricity Output

CFC is a measurement of the carbon footprint of energy generation that is obtained by dividing power output by CO_2 emissions from fuel combustion. Mega tonnes per billion kilowatt hours ($MtCO_2/TWh$) are used to report the data. High-income nations like Japan and the Republic of Korea have seen a substantial decline in *CFC* over the years (Figure 4). Japan had 1.22 $MtCO_2/TWh$ as its CFC in 2008. By the end of 2020, it had decreased to 1.11 $MtCO_2/TWh$. Korea Republic's CFC was 1.17 $MtCO_2/TWh$ in 2008. In 2013, it increased to 1.12 $MtCO_2/TWh$. By the end of 2020, it had dropped to 1.11 $MtCO_2/TWh$ in South Korea.

The *CFC* of upper middle-income nations such as China and Maldives have decreased significantly over the years. In China, *CFC* was 2.11 $MtCO_2/TWh$ in 2008, but by the end of the year 2020, that number had decreased to 1.39 $MtCO_2/TWh$. In the Maldives, CFC was 3.18 $MtCO_2/TWh$ in 2008, and by the end of 2020, it had fallen to 2.45 $MtCO_2/TWh$. Mongolia's *CFC* was 3.07 $MtCO_2/TWh$ in 2008. It dramatically increased to 6.52 $MtCO_2/TWh$ in 2020. Over time, Mongolia witnessed a significant rise in *carbon dioxide emissions*. The *CFC* of Bangladesh declined from 1.38 $MtCO_2/TWh$ in 2008 to 1.16 $MtCO_2/TWh$ in 2020. Additionally, *CFC* in India increased from 1.8 $MtCO_2/TWh$ in 2008 to 1.55 $MtCO_2/TWh$ in 2020. Similarly, the *CFC* in Sri Lanka declined from 3.03 $MtCO_2/TWh$ in 2008 to 1.57 $MtCO_2/TWh$ in 2020. Also in 2008, the *CFCs* of Bhutan, Nepal, and Pakistan were 0.05, 1.16, and 1.64 $MtCO_2/TWh$, respectively, and increased to 0.11, 2.01, and 1.68 $MtCO_2/TWh$ in 2020.

Figure 4. Trend in CO_2 emissions from fuel combustion per total electricity output (CFC)

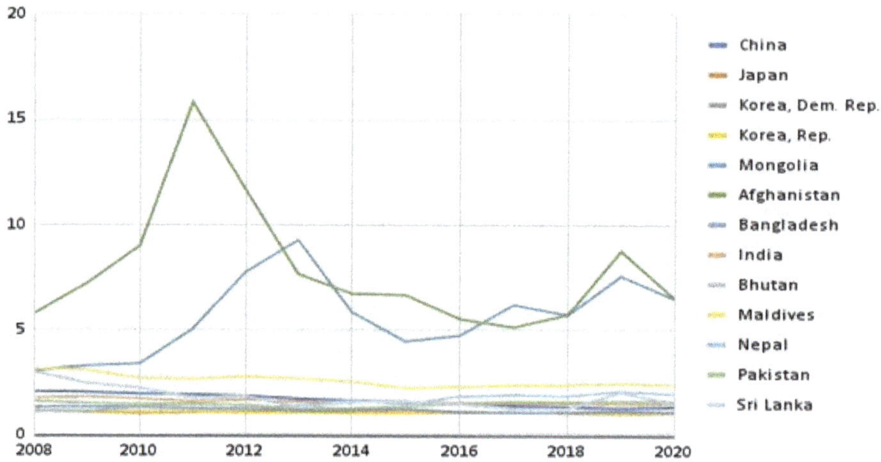

It is noticeable that there has been a decline over the years, as evidenced by the graph of low-income nations such as Afghanistan and the Democratic People's Republic of Korea. Afghanistan's *CFC* was 5.8 $MtCO_2$/TWh in 2008, and it substantially rose to 11.68 $MtCO_2$/TWh in 2012. Gradually, it decreased to 6.56 $MtCO_2$/TWh in Afghanistan by 2020. *CFC* of the Korea Democratic Republic decreased from 3.03 $MtCO_2$/TWh in 2008 to 1.57 $MtCO_2$/TWh in 2020.

Trend in Renewable Energy Share of Electricity Generation (REG)

High-income nations like Japan and the Republic of Korea have seen a sharp rise in *REG* over time (Figure 5). Japan had 8.89% as its total renewable energy share of electricity generation in 2008. By the end of 2020, it had increased to 19.42% in Japan. Additionally, the Republic of Korea's renewable energy share of electricity generation was 0.98% in 2008. By the end of 2020, it had increased to 5.83% in South Korea.

The *REG* of upper middle-income nations such as China and the Maldives has increased significantly over time. In China, the *REG* was 17.49% in 2008, but by the end of the year 2020, that number had increased to 27.63%. In the Maldives, the REG was 0.43% in 2008, but by the end of 2020, it had increased to 5.58%.

By the end of 2020, Mongolia's yearly renewable energy share of electricity generation, which was 0.33% in 2008, had dramatically increased to 9.23% in 2020. Bangladesh's renewable energy share of electricity generation was 2.02% in 2008, and by 2020, it had decreased to 1.47%. Additionally, by the end of 2020, India's *REG* increased from 17.02% in 2008 to 18.44% in 2020. The *REG* of Sri Lanka decreased from 41.93% to 36.75% in 2020. The *REG* of Bhutan, Pakistan, and Nepal were, in 2008, 99.99%, 30.82%, and 99.69%, respectively, and increased to 100%, 32.11%, and 100%, respectively, in these countries by 2020.

Figure 5. Trend in renewable energy share of electricity generation (IRENA, 2023).

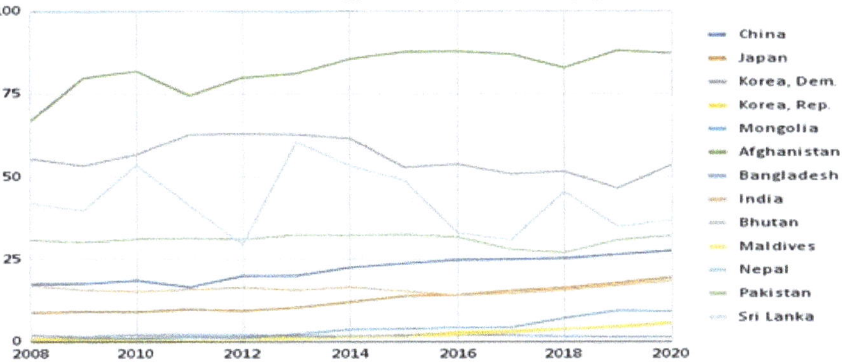

It is perceived that there has been a declining trend in *REG* over the years, as evidenced by the graph of low-income nations such as Afghanistan and the Democratic People's Republic of Korea. Substantially, it increased to 87.12% by the end of 2020. *REG* in the Democratic People's Republic of Korea declined from 55.24% in 2008 to 53.44% in 2020, after reaching its peak at 62.80% in 2012.

Trend in Renewable Energy Consumption (share of total final energy consumption)

This variable captures the proportion of the population consuming renewable sources of energy.

Japan and the Republic of Korea have seen a sharp rise in renewable energy consumption over time (Figure 6). Japan had 4.44% of its renewable energy consumption in 2008. By the end of 2020, it had increased to 8.45% in Japan. Additionally, the Republic of Korea's renewable energy consumption was 1.06% in 2008. By the end of 2020, it had increased to 3.63% in South Korea.

The renewable energy consumption in upper-middle-income nations such as China and the Maldives has seen various fluctuations over time. In China, renewable energy consumption was 14.14% in 2008, but in 2011, that number had decreased to 11.34%. China managed to increase its renewable energy consumption to 14.81% by the end of 2020. In the Maldives, renewable energy consumption was 1.53% in 2008, but by 2012, it had dropped to 1.2%, its lowest point in the decade. Nevertheless, it had increased to 1.28% by the end of 2020, which is still lower than the renewable energy consumption noted in 2008.

By the end of 2020, Mongolia's yearly renewable energy consumption, which was 4.66% in 2008, had dramatically decreased to 2.97% in 2012. But by the end of 2020, Mongolia's renewable energy consumption stood at 3.98%. Bangladesh's renewable energy consumption was 45.2% in 2008. With time, the renewable energy consumption of Bangladesh had decreased to 27.96% in 2020. Additionally, by the end of 2020, India's renewable energy consumption decreased from 39.38% in 2008 to 35.82% in 2020. The renewable energy consumption of Pakistan was 46.63% in 2008. Instead of various fluctuations, the renewable energy consumption of Pakistan stood at 46.6% by the end of 2020. The renewable energy consumption of Bhutan, Sri Lanka, and Nepal was, in 2008, 91.81%, 61.58%, and 90.47%, respectively, and decreased to 88.39%, 49.32%, and 74.54%, respectively, in these countries by 2020.

Figure 6. Trend in renewable energy consumption (% of total final energy consumption) (IEA, IRENA, UNSD, World Bank, WHO, 2023)

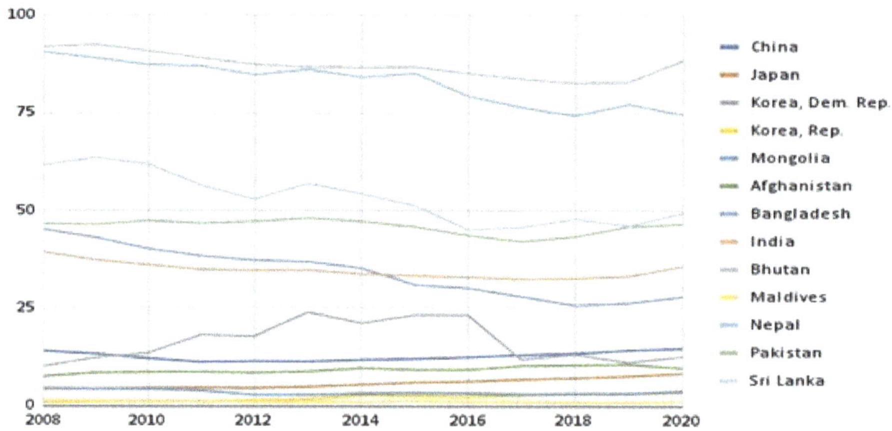

It is reported that there has been an increase over the years, as evidenced by the graph of low-income nations such as Afghanistan and the Democratic People's Republic of Korea. The renewable energy consumption of Afghanistan was 7.65% in 2008. Substantially, it increased to 9.84% by the end of 2020 after reaching its peak point at 10.74% in 2019. Similarly, the renewable energy consumption in the Republic of Korea increased from 10.2% in 2008 to 12.7% in 2020, after reaching its peak at 24.05% in 2013.

Trend in Renewable Energy Share in Total Final Energy Consumption (REF)

The proportion of energy used in a final product that comes from renewable resources is known as the renewable energy share in total final consumption (*REF*). Its mission is to guarantee that everyone has access to modern, affordable, dependable, and sustainable energy. It does not include traditional biomass, which refers to locally available solid biomass resources (such as wood, charcoal, dung, and agricultural leftovers) that are utilized by low-income households without access to contemporary cooking fuels or technologies.

Japan and the Republic of Korea have seen a sharp rise in *REF* over time (Figure 7). Japan had 4.4% as its *REF* in 2008. By the end of 2020, it had increased to 7.26% in Japan. Additionally, the Republic of Korea's renewable energy consumption was 1.1% in 2008. By the end of 2020, it had increased to 3.13% in South Korea. In China, the *REF* was 4.4% in 2008. The number increased to 9.83% in China by the end of 2020. In the Maldives, the *REF* was 0% in 2008. Gradually, by the end of 2020, it increased to 0.33% in the Maldives.

Figure 7. Trend in renewable energy share in total final energy consumption (IEA, IRENA, UNSD, World Bank, WHO, 2023)

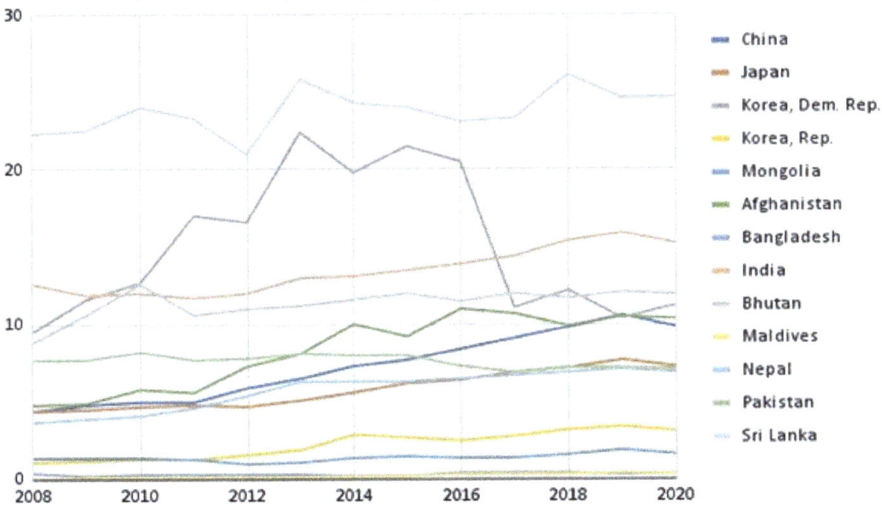

By the end of 2020, Mongolia's annual *REF*, which was 1.4% in 2008, had dramatically increased to 1.63% in 2020 after reaching its peak at 1.9% in 2019. Bangladesh's *REF* was 0.4% in 2008. The *REF* of Bangladesh had decreased to 0.36% in 2020. Additionally, by the end of 2020, India's *REF* increased from 12.6% in 2008 to 15.9% in 2020. The proportion of *REF* in Pakistan was 7.7% in 2008. Instead of various fluctuations, it decreased to 7.1% by the end of 2020 in Pakistan. Similarly, the *REF* of Bhutan, Sri Lanka, and Nepal were, in 2008, 8.8%, 22.3%, and 3.7%, respectively, and decreased to 11.93%, 24.66%, and 6.9% in 2020.

There has been an increase in *REF* over the years, as evidenced by the graph of low-income nations such as Afghanistan and the Democratic People's Republic of Korea. The *REF* of Afghanistan was 4.8% in 2008. Substantially, it increased to 10.36% by the end of 2020 after reaching its peak point at 10.7% in 2017. The *REF* in the Republic of Korea increased from 9.5% in 2008 to 11.23% in 2020, after reaching its peak at 22.4% in 2013.

Trend in Electricity Generation from Renewables

In many regions of the world, renewable energy sources are currently the most affordable way to generate new electricity due to a significant decrease in the expenses of solar energy systems and windmills. It is possible to generate electricity, heat, and cool spaces and power vehicles with renewable energy. Conversely, non-renewable energy originating from finite resources like oil, natural gas, and coal is costly and scarce.

Japan and the Republic of Korea have seen a rapid increase in the electricity generation from renewables over time (Figure 8). By the end of 2020, it had increased to 195.17 TWh. Additionally, the Republic of Korea produced 4.39 TWh of electricity from its renewable sources in 2008. By the end of 2020, the amount had increased to 35.05 TWh in South Korea. Likewise, the Maldives was not involved in electricity generation from renewables by the end of 2013, but by the end of 2020, the EGR in the Maldives increased to 0.04 TWh.

Figure 8. Electricity generation from renewables (Ember - Yearly Electricity Data, 2023)

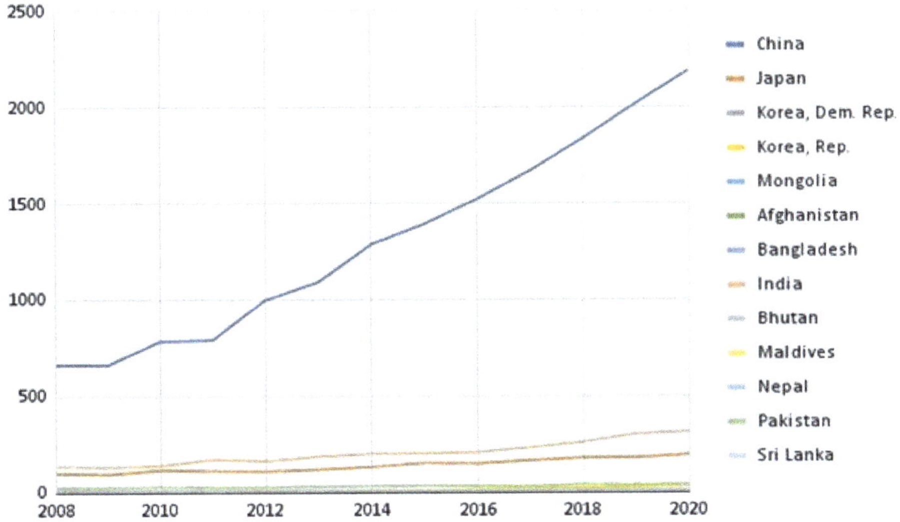

Mongolia's yearly electricity generation from renewables, which was 0.01 TWh in 2008, had dramatically increased to 0.68 TWh in 2020. Bangladesh produced 0.96 TWh of electricity from renewables in 2008. The electricity generated from renewables in Bangladesh had increased to 1.28 TWh in 2020. India produced 138.91 TWh of electricity from renewables in 2008. The number increased to 315.67 TWh in 2020. The electricity generation from renewables in Bhutan, Sri Lanka, and Nepal was 6.89 TWh, 4.12 TWh, and 2.79 TWh, respectively, in 2008. The electricity generated from renewables in the Democratic People's Republic of Korea decreased from 13.93 TWh in 2008 to 12.82 TWh in 2020.

Trend in Solid Biofuels and Renewable Municipal Waste

Non-fossil organic materials are the source of solid biofuels. It provides energy that can be used for cooking, heating, and electricity generation. Examples of these materials include plant biomass, animal waste, and municipal garbage. Municipal waste is waste that is collected and managed by municipalities or on their behalf. Municipal waste is also known as green waste. Garbage from houses, particularly bulky waste, as well as similar waste from commercial and industrial establishments, workplaces, educational entities, and small businesses, is included. It involves cleaning streets, disposing of waste from yards and gardens, and managing the contents of trash containers, as well as waste that, if managed as domestic waste, is used for cleaning markets. Waste from building and demolition projects, as well as waste from municipal sewage networks and treatment, are not included in this definition.

Figure 9. Trend in solid biofuels and renewable municipal waste

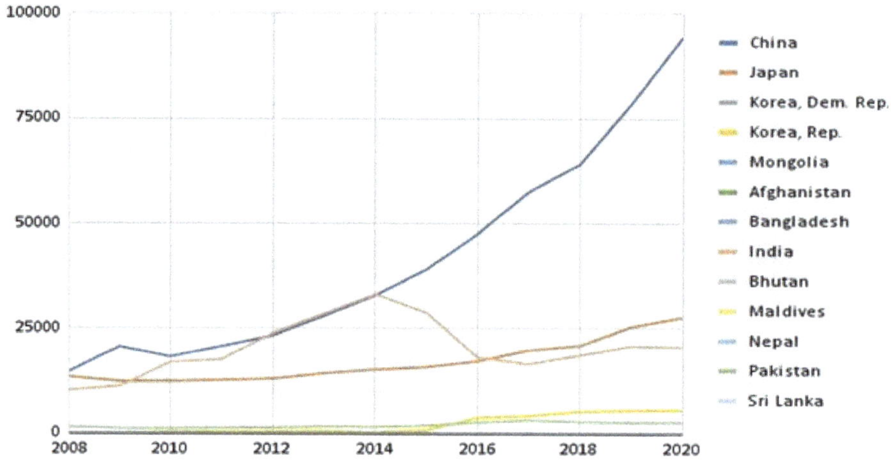

Japan and the Republic of Korea have seen a rise in *BMW* over time (Figure 9). Japan had 13,454 thousand tonnes of *BMW* in 2008. By the end of 2020, it had increased to 27,741 thousand tonnes. Additionally, the Republic of Korea's BMW was 131 thousand tonnes in 2008. By the end of 2020, it had increased to 5,697 thousand tonnes in South Korea. In China, the solid biofuels and renewable municipal waste were 14,715 thousand tonnes in 2008. The number increased to 94,404 thousand tonnes in China by the end of 2020. China's garbage generation and treatment have a far larger carbon footprint than Japan (Sun et al., 2018). In the Maldives, *BMW* was 0 thousand tonnes in 2008.

Each nation experienced growth in BMW, except in Mongolia and Bhutan. *BMW* remained zero in Bhutan and Mongolia by the end of 2020. Bangladesh's *BMW* was 0 in 2008. It increased to 1.752 thousand tonnes in Bangladesh in 2020. Additionally, by the end of 2020, India's *BMW* increased from 10,341.437 thousand tonnes in 2008 to 20,629.934 thousand tonnes in 2020. The *BMW* of Pakistan was 1,598 thousand tonnes in 2008. However, *BMW* of Pakistan increased to 2,819.936 thousand tonnes by the end of 2020. The solid biofuels and renewable municipal waste *in BMW of Sri Lanka and Nepal were, in 2008, 6.00 thousand tonnes and 8.551* tonnes, respectively. At the same time, it increased to 100 thousand tonnes and 10.275 thousand tonnes in 2020. An examination of the graph of low-income nations, such as Afghanistan and the Democratic People's Republic of Korea, reveals no change over the years. The *BMW* of Afghanistan and Korea, the Democratic Republic, remained zero over the past decade.

Trend in People Using at Least Basic Drinking Water Services (share of population)

This variable considers the percentage of users who utilize at least the most fundamental water services. Both users who securely managed water services and users of basic water services are covered in this indication. Japan and the Republic of Korea have seen growth in the proportion of people using at least basic drinking water services (*ADW*) over time (Figure 10). Japan had 98.64% as its *ADW* in 2008. By the end of 2020, it had increased to 99.07%. Additionally, the Republic of Korea's ADW was 98.83% in 2008. ADW has increased by 99.93% in South Korea by the end of 2020.

Figure 10. Trend in people using at least basic drinking water services (% of population)

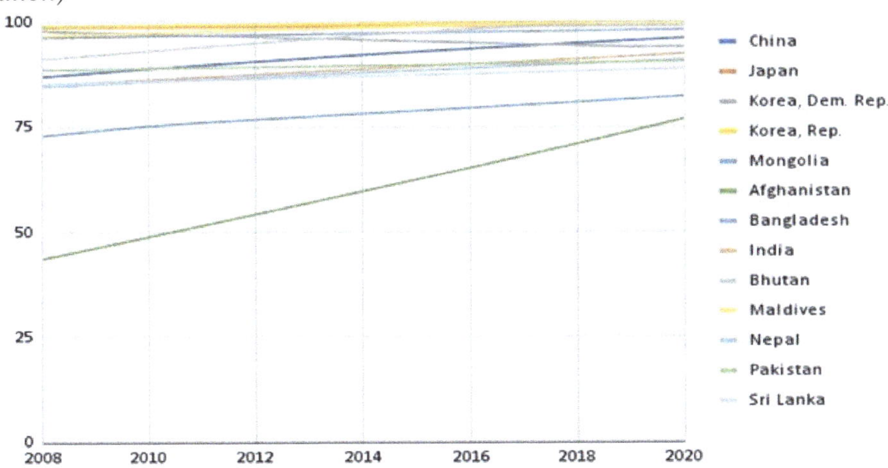

The *ADW* of upper middle-income nations such as China and the Maldives has seen a growth over time. In China, the *ADW* was 86.85% in 2008. The number increased to 95.89% by the end of 2020. In the Maldives, the ADW was 96.62% in 2008, but by the end of 2020, it increased to 99.54%. By the end of 2020, Mongolia's *ADW*, which was 72.87% in 2008, had dramatically increased to 82.12% in 2020. Bangladesh's *ADW* was 96.22% in 2008. *ADW* in Bangladesh had increased to 97.94% in 2020. Additionally, by the end of 2020, India's *ADW* increased from 84.91% in 2008 to 92.15% in 2020. Similarly, the ADW in Bhutan, Sri Lanka, and

Nepal were, in 2008, 90.97%, 85.15% and 84.46%, respectively, and increased to 98.98%, 88.69% and 90.76% in 2020. It suggests a twofold tendency over the years, as evidenced by the graph of low-income nations such as Afghanistan and the Democratic People's Republic of Korea. The proportion of people using at least basic drinking water services in Afghanistan was 43.31% in 2008. Substantially, it increased to 76.72% in Afghanistan by the end of 2020.

Trend in Population with Access to Clean Fuels and Technology for Cooking

The term population with access to clean fuels and technology for cooking (*ACF*) helps to enhance environmental quality and maintain environmental sustainability. Japan and the Republic of Korea have seen stagnant growth in the share of *ACF* over time (Figure 11). Japan and the Republic of Korea, being the developed nations, had the *ACF* as 100% from 2008 to 2020. In China, the *ACF* was 53.3% in 2008. The number increased to 81.4% by the end of 2020. In the Maldives, the ACF was 88.6% in 2008, but by the end of 2020, the ACF in the Maldives increased to 99.4%.

Mongolia's *ACF* was 31.2% in 2008, while it had increased to 51.4% in 2020. Bangladesh's *ACF* was 11% in 2008. *ACF* in Bangladesh increased to 25% in 2020. Additionally, by the end of 2020, India's *ACF* increased from 32% in 2008 to 67.9% in 2020. The *ACF* in Pakistan was 32.8% in 2008. It increased to 49% by the end of 2020. The proportion of *ACF* in Bhutan, Sri Lanka, and Nepal was 57.8%, 20.8% and 18.4%, respectively, in 2008. The proportion of the *ACF* in Afghanistan was 16.7% in 2008. Substantially, it increased to 33.2% by the end of 2020. The proportion of the *ACF* in the Democratic People's Republic of Korea increased from 4.7% in 2008 to 11.8% in 2020.

Figure 11. Population with access to clean fuels and technology for cooking (WHO, 2024)

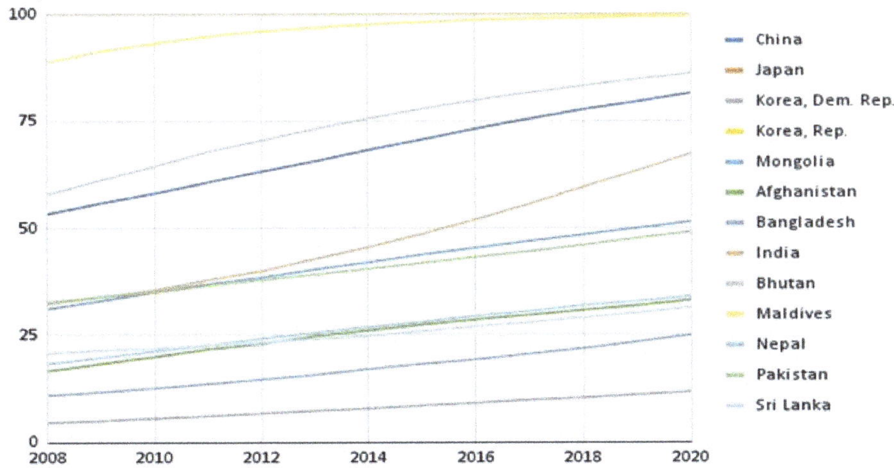

Trend in People Using at Least Basic Sanitation Services (share of population)

Sanitation is a vital component of human development. This variable considers the proportion of the population that makes use of at least the most fundamental sanitation services, as well as enhanced sanitation facilities that are private and are not shared among other households.

Figure 12. People using at least basic sanitation services (% of population) (WHO/ UNICEF 2023)

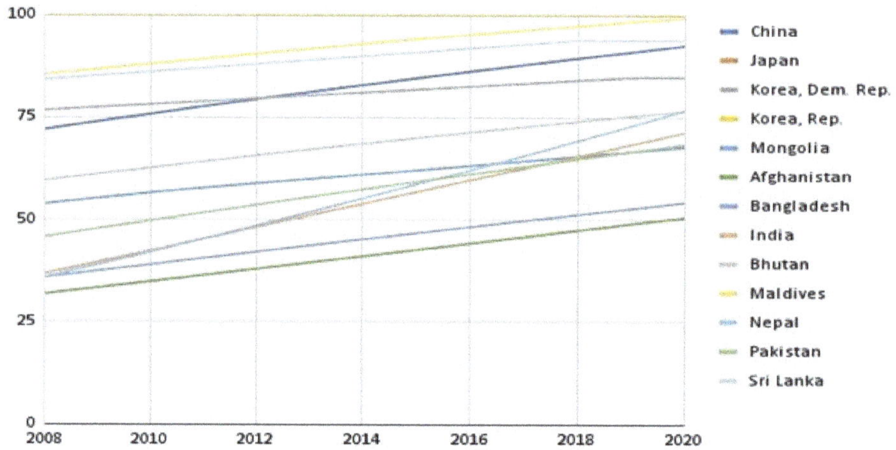

Japan and the Republic of Korea have seen growth in the proportion of people using at least basic sanitation services (*BSS*) over time (Figure 12). Japan had 99.97% as its proportion of *BSS* in 2008. By the end of 2020, it had slightly decreased to 99.92%. Additionally, the Republic of Korea's proportion of *BSS* was 99.99% in 2008. By the end of 2020, it had slightly dropped to 99.93%. Japan and South Korea have invested heavily in sanitation services and have achieved nearly universal access. In China, the proportion of *BSS* was 71.93% in 2008. The number increased to 92.37% by the end of 2020. In the Maldives, the proportion of BSS was 85.33% in 2008, but by the end of 2020, the proportion of BSS in the Maldives increased to 99.15%.

By the end of 2020, Mongolia's proportion of people using at least basic sanitation services, which was 53.77% in 2008, had increased to 67.74% in 2020. Bangladesh's proportion of *BSS* was 35.89% in 2008. The proportion of *BSS* in Bangladesh had increased to 54.16% in 2020. By the end of 2020, India's proportion of *BSS* rose from 36.80% in 2008 to 71.26% in 2020. The proportion of *BSS* in Pakistan was 45.75% in 2008. The proportion of *BSS* in Pakistan increased to 68.39% by the end of 2020. The proportion of *BSS* in Bhutan, Sri Lanka, and Nepal was 59.48%, 84.06% and 35.90%, respectively, in 2008. These nations have made significant progress in improving sanitation facilities in urban areas, but due to rural-urban disparities, rural areas still face challenges. It is reported that the proportion of BSS has risen over the years, as evidenced by the graph of low-income nations such as Afghanistan and the Democratic People's Republic of Korea. The proportion of *BSS* in Afghanistan was 31.87% in 2008. Substantially, it increased to 50.49% by the end of 2020. The proportion of *BSS* in the Democratic People's Republic of Korea increased from 76.61% in 2008 to 84.66% in 2020.

Trend in Access to Electricity

The term access to electricity (*ATE*) includes a broader range of activities than simply the supply of electricity to a household. In addition to this, it specifies that homes must consume a particular minimum quantity of power.

Figure 13. Trend in access to electricity (IEA, IRENA, UNSD, World Bank, WHO, 2023)

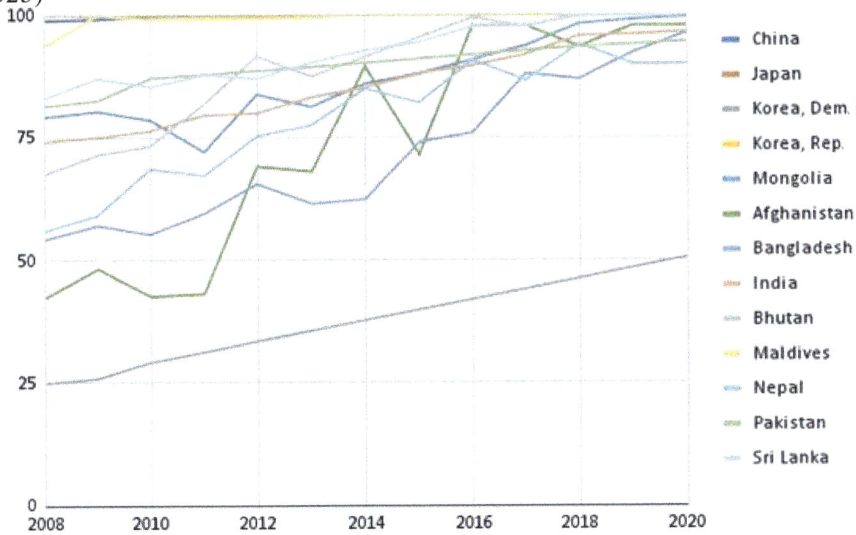

Access to electricity (*ATE*) varies among various South and East Asian nations (Figure 13). Japan's share of people with *ATE* was 100% which remained the same during the decade. Additionally, the Republic of Korea's share of people with ATE was 100% in 2008, which remained the same during the decade. This signifies that Japan and the Republic of Korea have universal *ATE* with 100% coverage. In China, the share of people with *ATE* was 98.79% in 2008. The share increased to 100% by the end of 2020. In the Maldives, the share of people with ATE was 93.55% in 2008, but by the end of 2020, the share of people with ATE in the Maldives increased to 100%. This signifies that China and the Maldives have made significant progress in providing access to electricity for their populations. China and the Maldives have achieved nearly universal access to electricity with 100% coverage (Figure 13).

By the end of 2020, Mongolia's share of people with *ATE* had increased dramatically from 79.10% in 2008 to 99.50%. Bangladesh's share of people with *ATE* was 54.26% in 2008. The share of people with *ATE* in Bangladesh had increased to 96.20% in 2020. By the end of 2020, India's share of people with *ATE* increased from 74.11% in 2008 to 96.50% in 2020. The share of people with *ATE* in Pakistan was 81.35% in 2008. The share of people with *ATE* in Pakistan increased to 94.48% by the end of 2020. The share of people with *ATE* in Bhutan, Sri Lanka, and Nepal was 67.55%, 82.86% and 55.95%, respectively, in 2008. Further, it increased to 100%, 99.97% and 89.90%, respectively, in these countries in 2020. Therefore, lower-middle-income nations are making efforts to increase the share of the population with *ATE*.

The share of the population with *ATE* in Afghanistan was 42.40% in 2008. Substantially, it increased to 97.70% by the end of 2020. On the contrary, the share of people with *ATE* in the Democratic People's Republic of Korea rose from 25% in 2008 to 50.52% in 2020. These nations face challenges in providing access to electricity to their population due to various reasons such as political instability, infrastructural limitations, and reliance on traditional fuels for energy generation.

4.2. Discussion on Empirical Results

Random effect model is adopted to determine the effect of *ACF, ADW, ATE, COE, BMW*, BSS, *CFC, EF, REC, REF, REG,* and *EGR* on *BC* (Table 2). There exists a negative impact of *EF* on BC. An increase in per capita annual ecological footprints highlights that individuals are consuming a greater number of resources and producing a larger quantity of waste than the ecosystem can sustainably support. An increase in consumption and the development of excessive waste can result in environmental deterioration. An ecological deficit occurs when the utilisation of resources and production of waste by a population exceeds the capacity of ecosystems to regenerate resources and absorb waste, as measured by the ecological footprint and biocapacity, respectively. South and East Asian nations experience a combination of dense population and fast economic growth, resulting in significant ecological footprints that surpass the region's biocapacity.

Table 2. Results for random effect estimation method with dependent variable BC

Dependent Variable: BC [Method: Panel EGLS (Cross-section random effects)]				
Name of the variables	**Estimated Coefficient**	**Standard Error**	**t-Stat**	**Probability value**
COE	-0.743355	0.018394	-40.41184	0.0000
EF	-0.695382	0.025746	104.6898	0.0000
CFC	0.410452	0.019408	21.14809	0.0000
REC	-0.009440	0.001726	5.469449	0.0000
REF	-0.029922	0.005575	-5.367151	0.0000
EGR	-0.874227	0.044566	-19.61638	0.0000

continued on following page

Table 2. Continued

Dependent Variable: BC [Method: Panel EGLS (Cross-section random effects)]				
Name of the variables	**Estimated Coefficient**	**Standard Error**	**t-Stat**	**Probability value**
REG	-0.035559	0.001295	-27.46295	0.0000
BMW	0.170822	0.034616	4.934796	0.0000
ACF	-0.045933	0.001431	-32.10611	0.0000
ATE	0.007724	0.001799	4.293846	0.0000
ADW	0.005550	0.004941	1.123317	0.2632
BSS	0.003249	0.002458	1.321913	0.1883
Constant coefficient	-0.053730	0.485989	-0.110558	0.9121

Weighted Statistics
R-squared: 0.846877 F-statistic 33.18419
Adjusted R-squared: 0.821357 Prob (F-statistic) 0.000000
Source: Author's Estimation.

There exists a negative relationship between *BC* and *COE*. Therefore, it creates a large impact on the *COE* per person. Additionally, high dependence on fossil fuels deteriorates the natural ecosystem and ultimately results in the decline of *BC* per capita. Also, a positive relationship between *BC* and *CFC* is observed. South and East Asian nations depend heavily on fossil fuels for generating energy. Therefore, they effectively maintain their bio-capacity with the help of other sectors such as agriculture and forestry. This reduces the environmental consequences caused by CO_2 emissions from fuel burning. A negative relationship between *BC* and *REC* can be seen. Renewable energy initiatives, particularly bioenergy and hydropower, require land and water resources for their establishment, which exerts stress on natural resources and ecosystems. Hence, this reduces the amount of bio-capacity per person. Also, it is observed that *REF* negatively impacts *BC*. Although renewable energy sources are more sustainable and produce fewer carbon emissions, their installation and maintenance still require natural resources like water, metals, and other materials. The shift to renewable energy sources replaces the traditional land-use patterns, such as agriculture and forestry, which have a positive impact on the biocapacity of the region. Hence, this shift reduces the amount of usable arable land and resources, which diminishes the biocapacity per person.

Additionally, a negative relationship is observed between *EGR* and *BC*. This is because an ample amount of land is required to install renewable energy sources. However, in highly populated areas of South and East Asia, the land dedicated to renewable energy infrastructure impacts natural ecosystems and agricultural land, resulting in a decrease in the available biocapacity per capita. Also, a negative impact of REG on BC is noticed. This is because the desired amount of efficiency is not achieved by renewable energy projects in the selected South and East Asian countries. Such a situation occurs due to poor planning, incorrect placement, or a lack of appropriate technology and maintenance. Moreover, there exists a positive impact of *BMW* on *BC*. Biofuels such as wood, charcoal, and crop residues, as well as renewable municipal waste such as organic waste, are usually obtained from sustainable sources. These materials have the potential to replenish themselves comparatively faster, which helps in increasing the bio capacity per person. Therefore, the dependence on fossil fuels can be reduced by including solid biofuels and renewable municipal waste in the nation's energy mix. This change would help protect natural ecosystems and reduce the ecological footprint due to fossil fuels, and sustain bio-capacity.

A negative relationship is observed between *BC* and *ACF*. Accessibility of cleaner fuels and technology for cooking increases the energy consumption and improves the living standard of the people. Therefore, the demand for these resources increases as more people shift to cleaner fuels for cooking. So, this reduces the bio capacity per person, and it may be due to the use of clean fuels for cooking, which reduces the amount of waste and carbon emissions. Further, the study indicates a positive association between *BC* and *ATE*. Since access to electricity is vital for economies to function more efficiently, as it forms the basis for every sector in the economy. The demand in any sector boosts the demand in the energy sector, and to meet this demand, fossil fuels are extensively used, and they form an important part of the energy mix of South and East Asian nations. So, there is a need to bring diversity in the energy mix using the renewable energy resources, and this will result in increased bio-capacity per person, having a negligible impact on the environment.

Also, the study highlights a positive association between *BC* and *ADW*. Basic drinking water facilities lead to increased public health, improved water resource management, and a better understanding of water conservation methods. It enhances the sustainable use of resources and conserves the environment. Therefore, public health derived from the accessibility of basic drinking water services positively affects the biocapacity per person of the selected regions. Also, there exists a positive relation between *BC* and *BSS*. Providing access to basic sanitation services enhances healthier lifestyles, more sustainable resource management, and high-quality water and land. All these factors are responsible for the expansion of bio capacity per capita. Sanitation services can contribute to increasing the biocapacity of the area by supporting sustainable practices to create a healthier environment.

5. CONCLUSION AND POLICY IMPLICATIONS

The most effective way to live within the Earth's biocapacity is the promotion of a circular economy. The adoption of a circular economy reduces the ecological stress and ensures long-term sustainable development (Lima et al., 2021). This study found that ecological footprint and carbon emissions have negative impacts on bio-capacity, which may be due to unsustainable consumption of fossil fuels that degrade the natural environment. Similarly, renewable energy consumption and generation may result in unsustainable land use change or biomass use, thereby impacting bio-capacity in South and East Asian economies. Use of solid biofuels as a traditional practice may cause air pollution, but it may reflect low ecological strains, thus having a positive impact on bio-capacity.

This study suggests the following policy guidelines: There is a need to focus on sustainable energy transitions by improving grid efficiency and supporting decentralized renewable systems to improve bi-capacity. Government policies should focus on decarbonisation and emission control by implementing suitable environmental regulations, providing subsidies for green technologies, and energy efficiency standards. Circular economy is helpful to increase the zero emissions (Khalifa et al., 2022). It signifies zero carbon emissions from the system (Garg et al., 2025). Policy makers should focus on promoting balanced biomass utilization through campaigns and training programs. Policy makers should also focus on modernizing municipal waste systems using circular economic models. The government must invest in promoting public awareness and education through campaigns on sustainable consumption and waste reduction.

6. NOVELTY AND INNOVATION

This chapter makes a worthy contribution to theoretical literature for several reasons. It explores the contribution of the circular economy to maintaining the sustainable use of resources for further sustainable development. It applies a trend analysis to explain the comparative performance of the undertaken indicators in selected countries. Random effect model is applied to examine the most crucial variables on bi-capacity. Finally, it suggests specific policy suggestions that can be beneficial for sustaining bi-capacity, promoting the sustainable use of resources, and enhancing sustainable development in selected countries.

7. LIMITATIONS AND SCOPE OF FURTHER RESEARCH

This chapter could not include many variables, such as population growth, urbanization, industrialization, foreign direct investment, and agricultural intensification, in its analysis of bio-capacity. Hence, further research can be conducted on the variables mentioned above to identify additional variables that could lead to increased biocapacity and sustainable development in Asian and other countries.

REFERENCES

Abad-Segura, E., Fuente, A. B. D. L., González-Zamar, M. D., & Belmonte-Ureña, L. J. (2020). Effects of circular economy policies on the environment and sustainable growth: Worldwide research. *Sustainability (Basel)*, *12*(14), 5792. DOI: 10.3390/su12145792

Adami, L., & Schiavon, M. (2021). From circular economy to circular ecology: A review on the solution of environmental problems through circular waste management approaches. *Sustainability (Basel)*, *13*(2), 925. DOI: 10.3390/su13020925

Al-Wahaibi, A., Osman, A. I., Al-Muhtaseb, A. A. H., Alqaisi, O., Baawain, M., Fawzy, S., & Rooney, D. W. (2020). Techno-economic evaluation of biogas production from food waste via anaerobic digestion. *Scientific Reports*, *10*(1), 15719. DOI: 10.1038/s41598-020-72897-5

Ashton, W. S., Fratini, C. F., Isenhour, C., & Krueger, R. (2022). Justice, equity and the circular economy: Introduction to the special double issue. *Local Environment*, *27*(10-11), 1173–1181. DOI: 10.1080/13549839.2022.2118247

Chen, C. C., & Pao, H. T. (2024). Cicular economy and ecological footprint: A disaggregated analysis for the EU. *Ecological Indicators*, *160*, 111809. DOI: 10.1016/j.ecolind.2024.111809

Chen, W. M., & Kim, H. (2019). Circular economy and energy transition: A nexus focusing on the non-energy use of fuels. *Energy & Environment*, *30*(4), 586–600. DOI: 10.1177/0958305X19845759

Dong, L., Liu, Z., & Bian, Y. (2021). Match circular economy and urban sustainability: Re-investigating circular economy under sustainable development goals (SDGs). *Circular Economy and Sustainability*, *1*(1), 243–256. DOI: 10.1007/s43615-021-00032-1

Elia, V., Gnoni, M. G., & Tornese, F. (2017). Measuring circular economy strategies through index methods: A critical analysis. *Journal of Cleaner Production*, *142*(1), 2741–2751. DOI: 10.1016/j.jclepro.2016.10.196

Ember - Yearly Electricity Data. (2023). Ember - European Electricity Review (2022);Energy Institute - Statistical Review of World Energy. (2023) – with major processing by Our World in Data. https://ember-energy.org/latest-insights/european-electricity-review-2022/

Ezeudu, O. B., & Ezeudu, T. S. (2019). Implementation of circular economy principles in industrial solid waste management: Case studies from a developing economy (Nigeria). *Recycling*, *4*(4), 42–57. DOI: 10.3390/recycling4040042

Feng, W., Mao, Y., & Chen, H. (2007). Study on development pattern of circular economy in chemical industry parks in China. *Modern Chemical Industry*, *27*(3), 7–17.

Fiksel, J., Sanjay, P., & Raman, K. (2021). Steps toward a resilient circular economy in India. *Clean Technologies and Environmental Policy*, *23*(1), 203–218. DOI: 10.1007/s10098-020-01982-0

Gallego-Schmid, A., Chen, H. M., Sharmina, M., & Mendoza, J. M. F. (2020). Links between circular economy and climate change mitigation in the built environment. *Journal of Cleaner Production*, *260*, 121115. DOI: 10.1016/j.jclepro.2020.121115

Garg, A., Raut, R. D., Kumar, M., Zhang, C., & Ghokhale, R. (2025). Does the circular economy transition aid to carbon neutrality? Examining net-zero policy and stakeholder impact from the environmental justice viewpoint. *Journal of Cleaner Production*, *491*, 144851. DOI: 10.1016/j.jclepro.2025.144851

Global Carbon Budget. (2023). Population based on various sources (2023) [Online]. OurWorldInData.org/co2-and-greenhouse-gas-emissions

IEA, IRENA, UNSD, World Bank, WHO. (2023). Tracking SDG 7: The Energy Progress Report. World Bank, Washington DC. https://trackingsdg7.esmap.org/time

IRENA. (2023). *Renewable Capacity Statistics 2023; & IRENA (2023), Renewable Energy Statistics 2023*. The International Renewable Energy Agency.

Ishaq, M., Ghouse, G., Fernandez-Gonzalez, R., Puime-Guillen, F., Tandir, N., & Santos de Oliveira, H. M. (2022). From fossil energy to renewable energy: Why is circular economy needed in the energy transition? *Frontiers in Environmental Science*, *10*, 941791. DOI: 10.3389/fenvs.2022.941791

Kalmykova, Y., Sadagopan, M., & Rosado, L. (2018). Circular economy–From review of theories and practices to development of implementation tools. *Resources, Conservation and Recycling*, *135*(1), 190–201. DOI: 10.1016/j.resconrec.2017.10.034

Khalifa, A. A., Ibrahim, A. J., Amhamed, A. I., & El-Naas, M. H. (2022). Accelerating the transition to a circular economy for net-zero emissions by 2050: A systematic review. *Sustainability (Basel)*, *14*(18), 11656. DOI: 10.3390/su141811656

Khan, S. A. R., Ponce, P., Thomas, G., Yu, Z., Al-Ahmadi, M. S., & Tanveer, M. (2021). Digital technologies, circular economy practices and environmental policies in the era of COVID-19. *Sustainability (Basel)*, *13*(22), 12790. DOI: 10.3390/su132212790

Kim, H. (2018). Economic and environmental implications of the recent energy transition on South Korea's electricity sector. *Energy & Environment*, *29*(5), 752–769. DOI: 10.1177/0958305X18759177

Laumann, F., & Tambo, T. (2018). Enterprise architecture for a facilitated transformation from a linear to a circular economy. *Sustainability (Basel)*, *10*(11), 3882. DOI: 10.3390/su10113882

Leontief, W. (1991). The economy as a circular flow. *Structural Change and Economic Dynamics*, *2*(1), 181–212. DOI: 10.1016/0954-349X(91)90012-H

Lima, P. A., Jesus, G. M., Ortiz, C. R., Frascareli, F. C., Souza, F. B., & Mariano, E. B. (2021). Sustainable development as freedom: Trends and opportunities for the circular economy in the human development literature. *Sustainability (Basel)*, *13*(23), 13407. DOI: 10.3390/su132313407

MacArthur, E. (2013). Towards the circular economy, economic and business rationale for an accelerated transition. Ellen MacArthur Foundation: Cowes, UK, 1. https://www.ellenmacarthurfoundation.org/towards-the-circular-economy-vol-1-an-economic-and-business-rationale-for-an

MacArthur, E., Zumwinkel, K., & Stuchtey, M. R. (2015). Growth within: a circular economy vision for a competitive Europe. *Ellen MacArthur Foundation*, 100. https://www.ellenmacarthurfoundation.org/growth-within-a-circular-economy-vision-for-a-competitive-europe

Macarthur, E. L. L. E. N., & Heading, H. E. A. D. I. N. G. (2019). How the circular economy tackles climate change. *Ellen MacArthur Found*, 1(1), 1-71. https://www.ellenmacarthurfoundation.org/completing-the-picture

Majeed, M. T., & Luni, T. (2020). Renewable energy, circular economy indicators and environmental quality: A global evidence of 131 countries with heterogeneous income groups. [PJCSS]. *Pakistan Journal of Commerce and Social Sciences*, *14*(4), 866–912. https://www.econstor.eu/handle/10419/228728

Mongo, M., Laforest, V., Belaïd, F., & Tanguy, A. (2021). Assessment of the impact of the circular economy on CO2 emissions in Europe. *Journal of Innovation Economics & Management*, I107-29. https://shs.cairn.info/revue-journal-of-innovation-economics-2022-3-page-15?lang=en

Mutezo, G., & Mulopo, J. (2021). A review of Africa's transition from fossil fuels to renewable energy using circular economy principles. *Renewable & Sustainable Energy Reviews*, *137*, 110609. DOI: 10.1016/j.rser.2020.110609

National Footprint and Biocapacity Accounts. (2023). *GDP, International Financial Statistics (IFS); Population*. U.N. Food and Agriculture Organization.

Nguyen-Phung, H. T., & Le, H. (2024). Elderlywell-being amidst energy poverty: Exploring the health, social, and economic impacts in Vietnam. *Energy Research & Social Science*, *118*, 103762. DOI: 10.1016/j.erss.2024.103762

Niwalkar, A., Indorkar, T., Gupta, A., Anshul, A., Bherwani, H., Biniwale, R., & Kumar, R. (2023). Circular economy based approach for green energy transitions and climate change benefits. *Proceedings of the Indian National Science Academy. Part A, Physical Sciences*, *89*(1), 37–50. DOI: 10.1007/s43538-022-00137-7

Okafor, C., Madu, C., Ajaero, C., Ibekwe, J., & Otunomo, F. (2021). Situating coupled circular economy and energy transition in an emerging economy. *AIMS Energy*, *9*(4), 651–675. DOI: 10.3934/energy.2021031

Purvis, B., Celebi, D., & Pansera, M. (2023). A framework for a responsible circular economy. *Journal of Cleaner Production*, *400*, 136679. DOI: 10.1016/j.jclepro.2023.136679

Rathore, P., & Sarmah, S. P. (2020). Economic, environmental and social optimization of solid waste management in the context of circular economy. *Computers & Industrial Engineering*, *145*, 10–22. DOI: 10.1016/j.cie.2020.106510

Rolewicz-Kalińska, A., Lelicińska-Serafin, K., & Manczarski, P. (2020). The circular economy and organic fraction of municipal solid waste recycling strategies. *Energies*, *13*(17), 43–66. DOI: 10.3390/en13174366

Schröder, P. (2020). Promoting a just transition to an inclusive circular economy (pp. p-33). Royal Institute of International Affairs. https:/Promoting a just transition to an inclusive circular economy

Schroeder, P., Anggraeni, K., & Weber, U. (2019). The relevance of circular economy practices to the sustainable development goals. *Journal of Industrial Ecology*, *23*(1), 77–95. DOI: 10.1111/jiec.12732

Schumann, F. R. (2020). Circular economy principles and small island tourism Guam's initiatives to transform from linear tourism to circular tourism. *Journal of Global Tourism Research*, *5*(1), 13–20. DOI: 10.37020/jgtr.5.1_13

Sharma, H. B., Vanapalli, K. R., Samal, B., Cheela, V. S., Dubey, B. K., & Bhattacharya, J. (2021). Circular economy approach in solid waste management system to achieve UN-SDGs: Solutions for post-COVID recovery. *The Science of the Total Environment*, *800*, 149605. DOI: 10.1016/j.scitotenv.2021.149605

Shukla, P. R., Skeg, J., Buendia, E. C., Masson-Delmotte, V., Pörtner, H. O., Roberts, D. C., . . . Malley, J. (2019). Climate Change and Land: an IPCC special report on climate change, desertification, land degradation, sustainable land management, food security and greenhouse gas fluxes in terrestrial ecosystems. https://www.ipcc.ch/srccl/

Stahel, W. R. (1982). The product life factor. an inquiry into the nature of sustainable societies: the role of the private sector (Series: 1982 Mitchell Prize study), NARC, 74-96. https://www.quebeccirculaire.org/data/sources/users/4/32217.pdf

Suárez-Eiroa, B., Fernández, E., & Méndez, G. (2021). Integration of the circular economy paradigm under the just and safe operating space narrative: Twelve operational principles based on circularity, sustainability and resilience. *Journal of Cleaner Production*, *322*(1), 12–33. DOI: 10.1016/j.jclepro.2021.129071

Sun, L., Li, Z., Fujii, M., Hijioka, Y., & Fujita, T. (2018). Carbon footprint assessment for the waste management sector: A comparative analysis of China and Japan. *Frontiers in Energy*, *12*(3), 400–410. DOI: 10.1007/s11708-018-0565-z

Tiwari, S., Mohammed, K. S., Mentel, G., Majewski, S., & Shahzadi, I. (2023). Role of circular economy, energy transition, environmental policy stringency and supply chain pressure on CO2 emissions in emerging economies. *Geoscience Frontiers*, *15*(3), 1–14. DOI: 10.1016/j.gsf.2023.101682

Tsironis, G., Daglis, T., & Tsagarakis, K. P. (2024). The circular economy through the prism of machine learning and the YouTube video media platform. *Journal of Environmental Management*, *368*, 121977. DOI: 10.1016/j.jenvman.2024.121977

Tunn, V. S., Bocken, N. M., van den Hende, E. A., & Schoormans, J. P. (2019). Business models for sustainable consumption in the circular economy: An expert study. *Journal of Cleaner Production*, *212*(1), 324–333. DOI: 10.1016/j.jclepro.2018.11.290

Wastling, T., Charnley, F., & Moreno, M. (2018). Design for circular behaviour: Considering users in a circular economy. *Sustainability (Basel)*, *10*(6), 1743. DOI: 10.3390/su10061743

WHO. (2024). *Proportion of population with primary reliance on clean fuels and technologies for cooking (%)*. [Online]. https://www.who.int/data/gho/data/indicators/indicator-details/GHO/gho-phe-primary-reliance-on-clean-fuels-and-technologies-proportion WHO/UNICEF (2023). [Online]. washdata.org.

WHO/UNICEF (2023). Joint Monitoring Programme (JMP) for Water Supply, Sanitation and Hygiene. washdata.org.

Yang, M., Chen, L., Wang, J., Msigwa, G., Osman, A. I., Fawzy, S., Rooney, D. W., & Yap, P. S. (2023). Circular economy strategies for combating climate change and other environmental issues. *Environmental Chemistry Letters*, *21*(1), 55–80. DOI: 10.1007/s10311-022-01499-6

Chapter 2
Sustainable Circular Economy Through Artificial Intelligence and the Circular Age

P. V. Sanesh
https://orcid.org/0000-0001-9100-1794
Department of Management Studies, CMS Business School, Jain University, Gandhinagar, India

M. Vijay Anand
https://orcid.org/0000-0003-1727-7930
Department of Mechanical Engineering, Erode Sengunthar Engineering College, Perundurai, India

Malathi Narra
https://orcid.org/0000-0002-6076-1464
Department of Civil Engineering Department, Velagapudi Ramakrishna Siddhartha Engineering College, Vijayawada, India

Anishkumar Karia
Department of MBA, PCET's S.B. Patil Institute of Management, Pune, India

W. Sudhakar
https://orcid.org/0009-0000-0343-4451
SaiSriram Engineering College, India

A. Rajalakshmi
https://orcid.org/0009-0009-5179-4844
Department of English, Kongu Engineering College, Erode, India

ABSTRACT

In this book chapter the intersection of artificial intelligence (AI) and circular economy is invented, which focuses on durable business models. As the global economy turns to a circular to reduce environmental influence, AI emerges as a major technique that facilitates this transition. The chapter is investigated how AI enables resource efficiency, waste reduction and closed-loop systems in industries. The main subjects

DOI: 10.4018/979-8-3373-9923-2.ch002

include AI-powered forecast maintenance, smart resource allocation and advanced recycling processes. Case Studies Circular Explains the successful integration of AI in professional models, highlighting benefits such as cost savings, enhanced production life cycle management and improved environmental metrics. The chapter ends with the insights of the future AI application, challenges and circular businesses.

INTRODUCTION

In recent years, the concept of a circular economy has gained significant traction as a durable alternative to the traditional linear model of production and consumption. In the principles of waste reducing, reusing materials and recycling resources, the purpose of the original, circular economy is to create a closed-loop system where products and materials maintain their value for as long as possible. The shift of this example is crucial in eliminating global challenges such as lack of resource, environmental degeneration and weather change. The center of this change is the integration of artificial intelligence (AI), which is a fast -growing technique with deeper effects for professional models in the circular economy. The ability to analyze a large amount of AI, the ability and predict the results makes it a powerful tool to make circular goals come true. By providing AI's benefit, businesses can achieve greater efficiency in the use of materials, increase product design for recyclability, and optimize logistics to reduce waste (Awan & Sroufe, 2022).

AI circular promises on various aspects of the economy. A significant area is forecast maintenance, where AI algorithms analyze data from the sensors embedded in machinery, forecast for maintenance requirements. This active approach not only reduces the downtime and operational costs, but also expands the lifetime of the equipment, which adjusts with the principle of production of the circular economy. Moreover, the AI facilitates smart resources allocation by pting the product schedule based on real-time demand and supply data. This capacity reduces excessive production and further inventory, thus reducing waste during the supply chain. In addition, AI-propelled analytics can identify opportunities for recycling and recycling, enabling businesses to maximize value from ED products and waste currents (Lahti et al., 2018).

Many leading companies have effectively accepted AI to run circular business models. For example, in the automotive industry, AI -powered simulations help form vehicles that are easy to disassemble and recycled. Companies like Tesla and BMW use AI to pt over battery recycling processes, effectively receiving precious content such as lithium and cobalt. In the fashion industry, A.I. Algorithms analyze customer preferences and product data to predict demand, reducing textile waste from soldiers. Innovations like Editas and H&M explore AI-powered solutions for durable fabrics recycling, transforming old garments into new materials for future products(Tunn et al., 2019).

Despite its changing probability, integrating AI into circular professional models pose a number of challenges. One of the major concerns is the quality and accessor of the access to the ACCIs, as the AI algorithms require strong datasets to accurately predict and deliver insights. Ensuring data privacy and safety is another crucial consideration, especially when sharing information on a supply chain or with a third-party recycle. Moreover, the clear cost of the implementation of AI technologies can prevent some businesses, especially small and medium sized enterprises (SMEs) from adopting circular methods. Need collaborative efforts of policies, industry stakeholders and technical providers to address these obstacles. To develop Scalable AI solutions that are accessible and affordable for all businesses (Witjes & Lozano, 2016).

Looking forward, AI's future in the circular economy is suitable with innovation and growth opportunities. Emerging technologies such as machine learning and computer vision are willing to further enhance recycling processes and improve material exploration. By investing in AI research and development, businesses can unle Lock new income trends by innovative product designs and services that organize with circular principles. Moreover, the evolution of the circular economy will lead to the demand for AI-powered solutions that support sustainable practices in various industries. From agriculture to electronics recycling, provides the use of AI resource to reduce environmental influence, and to make value from waste(L-ewandowski, 2016).

Therefore, the AI circular represents a transformative force to shape sustainable professional models in the economy. By using AI capabilities, businesses can achieve more efficiency, profitability and environmental stewards. However, unified efforts are needed to eliminate technical, financial and regulatory challenges to realize these benefits. As businesses and policies collaborate to advance AI-based innovations, the vision of a circular economy powered by intelligent technologies can be achieved, where economic prosperity coordinates with environmental stability (Comin et al., 2020).

Circular economy represents a shift away from the traditional linear model of production and consumption, which aims to reduce waste and maximize resource efficiency. The main principles include the composition of products for durability and repair, promoting reuse use and recycling of materials, and the use of the source of the product in the production life cycle. By closing the loop on the content and energy pest flow, businesses can reduce environmental influence and increase economic elasticity. At its origin, the circular economy emphasizes many principles: promoting products for longevity, re -use and repair, optimizing recycling materials and resource efficiency. These principles aim to create a closed-loop system where resources are consistently used, reducing the need for virgin materials and producing waste (Pieroni et al., 2019).

Durable professional models arranged with the principles of the circular economy are crucial to reduce environmental influence, increase elasticity, and meet the expectations of the stakeholder. By adopting practices of resources efficiency and waste reduction, businesses can reduce operational costs, improve efficiency and separate themselves in the market. Moreover, sustainable practices make confidence in positioning companies as consumers, investors and regulatory organizations, responsible corporate citizens. Sustainable professional models include challenges such as initial investment costs, regulatory complications and organizational shifts. Collaboration in fields and value chains is required to eliminate systemic barriers to effectively measure and adopt circular methods (Geissdoerfer et al., 2018)

The future of the circular economy hinges on technological advancements and evolving consumer preferences towards sustainability. Innovations in AI, IoT, and material sciences will play a pivotal role in optimizing resource use and enabling closed-loop systems. Businesses that embrace sustainable practices not only mitigate environmental risks but also seize opportunities for innovation and long-term growth in a resource-constrained world(Ferasso et al., 2020). Embracing circular economy principles through sustainable business models is essential for achieving environmental sustainability while fostering economic prosperity. By redesigning processes and products to prioritize resource efficiency and waste reduction, businesses can create value, enhance competitiveness, and contribute to a more sustainable future.

Background

The circular economy represents a shift from the traditional linear model of 'take-make-dispose' to a regenerative system aimed at maximizing resource efficiency and minimizing waste. This model promotes the reuse, repair, refurbishment, and recycling of products and materials, creating a closed-loop system that extends the lifecycle of resources. As environmental concerns and resource scarcity intensify, the circular economy has gained traction as a viable solution for sustainable development.

Artificial Intelligence (AI) plays a crucial role in advancing the circular economy. AI technologies, such as machine learning, predictive analytics, and IoT, enable more efficient resource management, optimize supply chains, and enhance recycling processes. For instance, AI-powered systems can predict maintenance needs to extend product life, improve the accuracy of material sorting in recycling facilities, and optimize production processes to reduce waste. By integrating AI with circular economy principles, businesses can innovate sustainable business models that not only mitigate environmental impact but also drive economic growth and resilience.

Scope

The integration of artificial intelligence (AI) in the circular economy opens numerous opportunities for the development of sustainable professional models in various industries. In smart manufacturing, AI excellent production processes for reducing waste and energy consumption. By providing the benefit of machine learning algorithms, manufacturers can identify disqualification, predict maintenance requirements and streamline operations, which can lead to more resource-efficient production methods. In the maintenance of the forecast, the AI algorithms analyzes the forecast data before sensors and machinery failure. This active approach not only expands the lifetime of products and machinery, but also reduces downtime and maintenance costs, contributing to the management of a more durable life cycle. AI also increases recycling and waste management. Advanced AI-powered systems improve the rattling and processing of recyclable materials, ensuring high accuracy and efficiency. AI -equipped robots can accurately identify and separate materials, increase the quality of recycled products, and reduce contamination rate.

Objectives

The purpose of this chapter is to explore the integration of artificial intelligence (AI) in sustainable professional models in terms of circular economy. He wants to explain that AI technologies can facilitate circular transition by optimizing the use of resources, increasing production life cycle management and reducing waste in industries. This chapter will investigate key AI applications such as forecast maintenance, smart resource allocation and advanced recycling processes, providing insights about their benefits and challenges. By publishing cases studies and real-world examples, the aim is to show the practical implementation of the AI-powered strategy that supports environmental stability and economic efficiency in the structure of the circular economy.

ROLE OF AI IN THE CIRCULAR ECONOMY

Artificial intelligence (AI) plays a transformative role in advancing the principles of circular economy by optimizing the resource efficiency, increasing durability and reducing waste in different fields. This section provides an overview of AI techniques and invents their applications to achieve these objectives(Ostermann et al., 2021).

Figure 1. Role of Artificial Intelligence (AI) in the circular economy

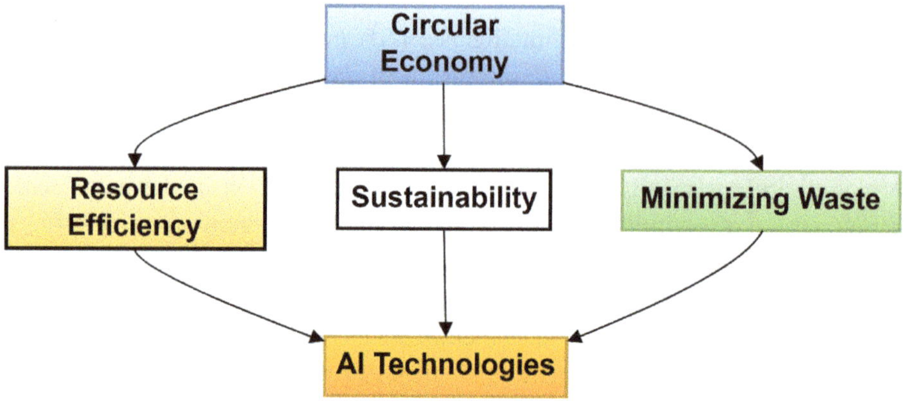

Figure 1 presents a flowchart showcasing the role of Artificial Intelligence (AI) in the Circular Economy, highlighting its role in optimizing resource efficiency.

Artificial intelligence (AI) is more and more referred to as a transformative power in different fields, including the possibility of revolutionizing the concept of a circular economy. The purpose of the circular economy is to reduce economic development from resource consumption by promoting recycling, recycling and promoting products and content regeneration. AI's capabilities can significantly increase and accelerate the transition to the circular economy by the use of OPTIM, improving waste management and promoting innovation in the industry.

Optimizing Resource Use: AI circular can play a key role in optimizing the use of resources in the structure of the economy. Through advanced data analytics and forecast modeling, AI systems can analyze the complex patterns of resource consumption, production and supply chain. This enables businesses to identify the inaccuracy and opportunities of the resource recovery and re -use. For example, AI algorithms can pt Optimize Inventory Management, predict demand more accurately and reduce further production, generating waste.

Improving Waste Management: Effective waste management is essential for the success of the circular economy. AI -powered technologies, such as smart rattling systems, can increase recycling processes by automating the rattling of recyclable materials based on their composition and characteristics. Machine learning algorithms can continuously learn from data to improve rattling accuracy, there is an increase in the quality and quantity of materials that can be recycled.

Enabling Product Lifecycle Management: From AI design to disposal, facilitates better tracking and management of products during their life cycle. This capability is crucial for applying circular professional models such as product-a-a-service

(PAAS) and re-manufacturing. By integrating IoT (Internet of Things) devices with AI analytics, companies can monitor the use of product consumption, predict maintenance requirements, and facilitate the return of products for innovation or recycling at the end of their lives.

Fostering Innovation and Design: AI-powered insights can stimulate innovation in production design and production processes that organize with circular principles. Products for durability, repair and recyclability are more possible with AI-generated insights of customer behavior and environmental effects. AI -powered generative design OPTIM can create ptimise designs that reduce the use of materials when maximizing operations, contributing to durable production methods.

Despite its possibility, integrating AI into a circular economy presents challenges. It is important to consider the privacy concerns related to data storage and sharing to ensure transparency and trust in stakeholders. Moreover, the clear cost of AI implementation and the need for skilled employees in AI technologies, especially for small businesses, generate obstacles. Looking forward, progresses in AI techniques such as persuasive AI and federated learning promise to eliminate these challenges. XAI AI can increase the transparency of decision -making processes, while federated learning allows multiple entities to cooperate with AI models without sharing sensitive data. This development circular can promote the widespread adoption of AI in the economy, enabling more incorporated and sustainable practices in industries.

The AI resource uses the powerful tool to move the circular economy by optimizing the use of the resource, improving waste management, promoting innovation in product design, and enabling the life cycle management. While challenges exist, ongoing technological advances and collaborative efforts can eliminate these obstacles, unlading the full probability of AI creating a more durable and elastic economy. AI includes many technologies that enable machines to imitate human intelligence, learn from data, and make decisions based on algorithms. Key AI techniques include machine learning (ML), Natural Language Processing (NLP), Computer Vision and Robotics. These tools are adept at analyzing large datasets, identifying patterns and complex processes, making them invaluable to enhance efficiency and durability in the circular economy.(De Angelis, 2018).

AI Applications in Resource Efficiency

The AI-powered forecasting system expects failure of devices before analyzing real-time data of the sensor and IoT devices. By accurately predicting maintenance requirements, businesses can reduce downtime, extend the life expectancy of machinery, and reduce resource consumption associated with premature changes. AI algorithms, resource allocation by analyzing demand forecasts in real time, supply chain mobility and production schedule. This capacity helps businesses to reduce more production, reduce inventory waste, and the consumption of Energy and content in production and distribution processes.

A.I. Circular design principles support by facilitating the design of products that are easy to improve, disassemble and recycled. Designed by AI simulation ensures that the products are durable, resource-efficient and environmentally friendly from beginners. AI -powered robotics and computer vision techniques increase the efficiency and accuracy of the rattling and recycling processes of waste. These systems can identify a variety of materials and sort, such as plastic, metals and paper, recycling rates and re -recovery of valuable resources from waste currents.

Real-World Examples

Companies like Tesla, Google and IBM have successfully used AI techniques to advance the principles of the circular economy. Tesla electric vehicle uses AI to predict battery forecasts, while Google and Foundation Food Supply to Optimizing and reduce waste. IBM and plastic bank have created a recycling ecosystem in developing countries promoting environmental stability and economic empowerment(Ostermann et al., 2021).

Integrating AI in a circular economy represents challenges such as high initial costs, concerns of data privacy and skilled workforce requirements. Cooperation and standardization are needed to ensure interoperability. The future of AI in the circular economy is based on the adoption of innovation and advanced technologies. AI-powered Optimization, robotics and decentralized systems can transform resource management and contribute to the circular economy. As businesses accept AI -based solutions, they can accelerate the transition to a more efficient, elastic and durable global economy.

AI AND WASTE REDUCTION

Artificial Intelligence (AI) has emerged as a powerful tool in addressing waste reduction and optimizing waste management processes across various industries. This section explores AI-driven strategies for waste minimization and their applications in waste management systems(Tan & Abd Rahim, 2024). Figure 2 illustrates AI-driven strategies for waste reduction and waste minimization.

Figure 2. AI driven waste reduction

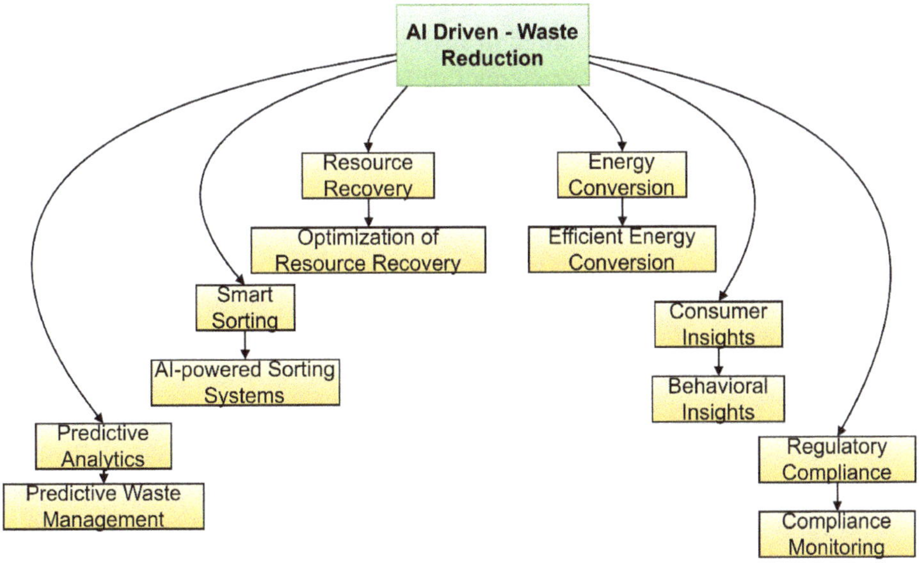

AI-driven Strategies for Waste Minimization

Artificial intelligence (AI) is becoming a sport-conscience in waste management strategy, providing innovative solutions to produce waste, improve recycling rates, and promote sustainable practices in industries. By using advanced data ticks, machine learning algorithms and Automation, AI can grow decisions and transform waste management into more efficient and environmentally friendly efforts (Huang & Fan, 1993).

- **Forecasts:** AI uses forecast analysts to predict patterns of waste generation based on historical scenic data, seasonal variations, and customer behavior. By analyzing these factors, businesses can expect a peak waste period and adjust the product, inventory and logistics accordingly. This active approach reduces excessive production and reduces the amount of goods sold that ends as a waste.
- Increase the efficiency of recycling processes by automating AI techniques, including machine learning and computer vision, automation, and identifying recyclable materials, including Recycling Processes: Machine Learning and Computer Vision. Advanced sensors and robotic systems can categorize and separate different types of waste such as plastic, metals and paper, where

there is an increase in recycling rates and reinvesting valuable resources from waste currents.

- **Circular design and production life cycle management:** AI supports the principles of the circular economy that is easy to disassemble and recycled, simplifying the design of the products. Designed by AI-based simulation ensures optimization that products are durable, resource-efficient and environmentally friendly during their life cycle. This approach reduces waste pay generation and promotes re -use of content in new products or applications.
- **Optimization of Resource Recovery:** In industries such as production and construction, the resource re-recovery by identifying the opportunities for AI materials and by-products, best of recovery. The AI algorithms analyzes product data to identify re -installed or recyclable waste currents within the production cycle. This circular approach reduces the extraction of raw material, reduces waste disposal costs, and increases overall resource efficiency.
- **Energy Recovery and Conversion:** AI facilitates efficient Energy Recovery procurement through sophisticated modeling techniques. Machine learning algorithms the combustion process in waste-to-energy facilities, improving the output of Energy to reduce emissions. Moreover, AI-powered forecasting systems emerge the reliability and lifetime of Energy regeneration devices, reducing downtime and operational costs.
- **Consumer Behavior Insights:** AI analyzes consumer behavior patterns to promote waste reduction and promote durable consumption habits. By analyzing the data of IoT devices, social media platforms and transaction records, AI produces insights of consumer preferences, production trends and disposal behavior. Businesses can use this information to create longevity products, promote alternatives to environmental friends, and to implement effective recycling education campaigns.
- **Regulatory Compliance and Reporting:** AI facilitates regulatory compliance with data collection, analysis and reporting processes. AI -powered systems monitor environmental rules, trac the waste disposal methods and comply with compliance standards. This reduces administrative burdens on businesses and government agencies while promoting transparency and responsibility.

Waste Management

Effective waste management is essential for achieving sustainable development goals and minimizing environmental impact. AI enhances waste management practices through several key applications(Fang et al., 2023):

AI-powered sensors and IOT devices enable smart waste collection systems that optimize routes and schedules based on real-time data, reduce fuel consumption and improve operational efficiency. A.I. Algorithms analyze the data of landfill sites reduce methane emissions, and prefer waste diversion strategies. AI tools also facilitate regulatory compliance by monitoring and analyzing data to enable waste disposal, recycling rate and environmental influence metrics, streaming adherence processes and tabulating their progress towards durability targets.

AI's future promises for more innovation and durability in waste reduction and management. Deep Wanda will enable the progress in AI techniques, including education and decentralized systems, globally rattling more accurate waste rattles, improved resource recovery and enhance enhanced environmental scenery(Zhao et al., 2020). Therefore, AI-powered strategy plays a crucial role in achieving waste reduction goals and improving waste management methods. OPTIM can pt the use of resources and contribute to the use of resources, producing waste, providing garbage by providing the benefits of smart waste collection systems and advanced recycling technologies, businesses and municipalities. As AI continues to grow, its requests in waste management will potentially expand, providing new opportunities to reduce innovation and environmental influence in the coming years.

AI and Waste Reduction: Procedure

Integrating Artificial Intelligence (AI) into waste reduction strategies involves a systematic approach that spans several stages, from data collection and analysis to implementation and continuous optimization(Harikaran et al., 2023; Janardhana et al., 2023; Koshariya et al., 2023; Maguluri et al., 2023).

- Data Collection and Analysis: The first step to using AI to reduce waste is a comprehensive data collection. Sensors and IoT devices have been arranged to collect real-time data on the use of waste, produce waste in various stages of production and consumption, material flow and resource use. This data contains information about the types of waste produced and the dose, machinery status and functionality of recycling processes. AI algorithms then analyze this data to identify the opportunities to reduce patterns, inaccuracies and waste.

- Predictive Maintenance and Optimization: Once data is collected and analyzed, AI-propelled forecast maintenance can be applied. Machine learning models predict the failure and maintenance requirements of the equipment based on historical accuracy data and real-time monitoring. Before the potential issues lead to disruption or inappropriate, businesses may reduce the waste associated with unplanned downtime and failure of devices. This active approach ensures that the machinery works on the best efficiency, reducing the deterioration of the resource.
- Smart Manufacturing and Process Optimization: AI Excellent production processes by analyzing product data to identify waste reduced areas. This includes the use of content OPTIM, reducing ENERGY minimum consumption and improvement of product timetable. For example, AI algorithms may indicate adjustments to product parameters to reduce scrap rate or recommend more efficient material handling practices. By constantly purifying these processes, manufacturers can achieve a significant reduction in waste production.
- Enhanced Recycling and Sorting: In recycling facilities, AI-powered robots and systems increase the accuracy and efficiency of rattling material. Computer Vision and Machine Learning Algorithms enable these systems to identify and separate different types of materials from high precision, reduce contamination rate and improve the quality of recycled products. It can be routing of AI recyclable materials, ensuring that they process in a very efficient and durable way.
- Supply Chain Management: AI improves supply chain management by providing accurate demand forecasts and inventory. By predicting future demand, businesses can avoid excessive production and reduce excessive inventory that often leads to waste. AI also best does logistics and transport routes, reduces fuel consumption and reduces emissions associated with moving goods through a supply chain.
- Circular Economy Platforms: AI Circular runs the development of economy platforms that facilitate the distribution, leasing and resale of products. These platforms use AI algorithms to match users with products available, and enhance their life cycle. By promoting reuse of products, this platform reduces the need for a new product and reduces waste.
- Continuous Monitoring and Improvement: The final step involves constant monitoring and improvement. AI systems provide continuous insights to produce waste and use of resources, enable businesses to constantly improve data -based decisions and reduce their waste. This repetitive process ensures that the waste reduction efforts remain effective and adaptive to the changing conditions.

ENHANCING SUPPLY CHAIN TRANSPARENCY

In today's globalization economy, it is important to increase the supply chain transparency for businesses to reduce the risks for businesses, ensure compliance with the rules, and to meet the customer's demand for moral and sustainable practices. This department explores how artificial intelligence (AI) solutions, Supply chain operations while promoting transparency and trackability(Mohanty et al., 2023).

AI Solutions for Supply Chain Optimization

Artificial intelligence (AI) is revolutionizing supply chain management by providing advanced analytics, in insights and efficiency of prediction, response and elasticity. In today's dynamic and interconnected business environment, AI - powered solutions are increasingly necessary to reduce risks, and meet customer's expectations (Verma et al., 2024).

Figure 3. AI solutions for supply chain optimization

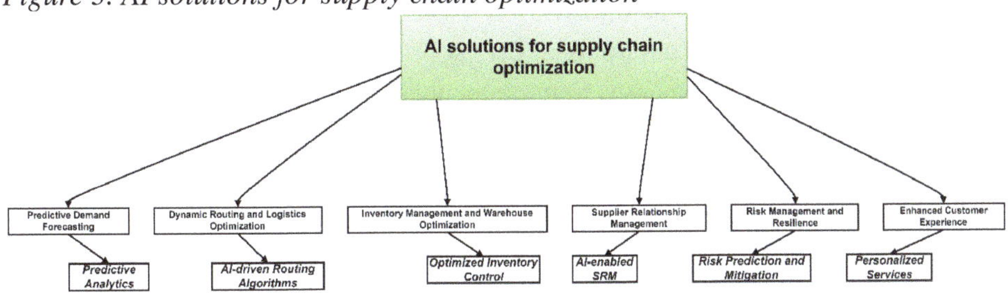

Figure 3 presents a flowchart showcasing AI solutions for supply chain optimization, including predictive demand forecasting, dynamic routing, inventory management, supplier relationship management, risk management, and enhanced customer experience.

Predictive Demand Forecasting: AI is best in prediction analyzes, enabling more accurate demand based on historical hypocrisy data, market trends and external factors. Machine learning algorithms can analyze large datasets in real-time, identifying patterns and correlations that will ignore traditional methods. This capability allows businesses to pt the inventory levels, reduce stockouts, and reduce more inventory, there is an overall supply chain efficiency and response.

Dynamic Routing and Logistics Optimization: In view of factors such as traffic patterns, weather conditions and delivery deadline, AI-powered algorithms dynamically logistics and transport routes. These solutions improve delivery time, reduce transportation costs, and increase fleet management efficiency. For example,

AI -powered forecast main maintenance models may expect the failure of the Delo devices, reducing disruptions to the supply chain.

Inventory Management and Warehouse Optimization: Inventory management enhances AI stock level, storage locations and replenishing schedules. Through real-time data analysis and predictive insights, AI systems can prevent excessive and stockouts, ensuring excessive inventory turnover and cost efficiency. In addition, AI-powered warehouse management systems (WMS) improve packing, packing and s ing rutting processes, reducing operational disqualification and increasing the accuracy of order fulfillment.

Supplier Relationship Management: AI supplier exhibits smart supplier relationship management (SRM) by analyzing supplier exhibition, market trends and geographical political risks. Predictable analyzes help to identify potential disruptions to businesses and actively manage supplier relationships to ensure continuity and quality. AI -powered tools also help negotiate contracts, and maintain transparency in the supply chain network.

Risk Management and Resilience: AI actively increases the supply chain elasticity by identifying and reducing risks. Machine learning models analyze historical hypocritical data and real-time information to predict potential disruptions such as natural disasters, geographical political events or supplier bankruptcy. The ability of this forecast enables businesses to implement contingent plans, diversify supply sources, and maintain operational continuity even in unstable environments.

Enhanced Customer Experience: AI-Powered Supply Chain Solutions Improves Customer's Experience By Enabling Rapid Order Processing, accurate delivery estimates and personal service. Predictable analyzes expect customer preferences and behaviors, allowing businesses to have an inventory level and fulfillment strategy accordingly. AI-powered chatbots and virtual assistants increase communication and response, providing real-time updates and support to customers.

Transparency and Traceability Benefits

- **Improved Product Traceability:** AI enables traceability from end to end of products by capturing and analyzing data at each stage of the supply chain. Blockchain technology associated with AI guarantees the tamper-proof record of production, production processes and distribution channels. This transparency creates confidence among consumers and stakeholders by providing visibility to the integrity and durability of the product.
- **Compliance and Risk Management:** AI-powered compliance management systems monitor regulatory requirements and industry standards in global supply chains. By automating compliance verification and ITS, businesses

reduce the risk of non-compliance penalties and maintain moral practices throughout their operation.

- **Enhanced Supplier Collaboration:** AI promotes collaboration and transparency with suppliers through data-based insights and performance analysts. AI-powered supplier relationship management platforms facilitate real-time communication, contract management and exhibition evaluations, enable businesses to make aware decisions and promote long-term partnership based on transparency and mutual trust.

Despite the advantages, integration of AI for supply chain transparency, challenges such as data privacy, inter-efficiency issues between various AI systems, and the need for skilled talent capable of managing AI-based technologies. To eliminate these challenges, collaboration between technical providers, industry stakeholders and regulatory organizations is required to establish standards and best efforts for AI implementation in supply chain management (Dhanya et al., 2023; Mohanty et al., 2023). The future of AI has been adopted by constantly innovation and advanced techniques to increase supply chain transparency, which promotes real-time data visibility, predictive analysis, and blockchain-enabled traceability. As businesses prefer more and more durability and moral sourcing, driving in transparency, elasticity and efficiency on the global supply chain will play an important role.

In conclusion, AI provides significant opportunities for businesses to pt to ZE to supply chain operations when increasing solutions, transparency and traceability. By providing predictive analyzes, real-time monitoring and blockchain technology, companies can improve decisions, reduce risks, and meet customer expectations developing for moral and durable supply chain methods. As AI continues to grow, its role in promoting supply chain transparency will become increasingly inevitable in gaining long -term business success and global supply chain elasticity.

CIRCULAR DESIGN AND AI

In recent years, the concept of circular design reduces environmental influence and is famous as an important strategy for creating products that promote durable consumption. This section searches the intersection of circular design principles with innovative capabilities of artificial intelligence (AI) tools to drive sustainable product development(Hussain et al., 2023; Ingle et al., 2023; Vijaya Lakshmi et al., 2024). Figure 4 shows the concept of circular design as a crucial strategy.

Figure 4. Concept of circular design as a crucial strategy

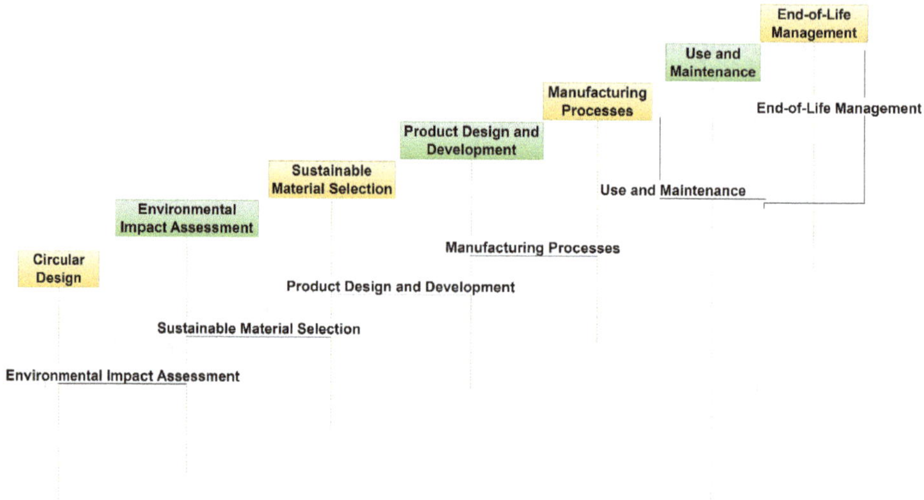

Innovations in Circular Product Design

Circular design focuses on creating products that are regenerative by design, aiming to eliminate waste and maximize the lifespan of materials through strategies such as:

Circular design focuses on simpler disassemble and component separation, expands product longevity and reduces virgin content. It prefers renewable, biodegradable or recycled materials, increasing durability and recyclability. Modular design allows a simple component replacement, expands the product lifetime and reduces resource consumption. This strategy supports customization and scalability, convenient to change customer preferences and technological advances. Innovations in the physical expression enables the development of bio-based polymer and durable fabrics.

AI Tools for Sustainable Product Development

AI technologies offer transformative capabilities that complement circular design principles, enhancing the efficiency and effectiveness of sustainable product development processes(Myilsamy Sureshkumar, 2018):

Circular design focuses on simpler disassemble and component separation, expands product longevity and reduces virgin content. It prefers renewable, biodegradable or recycled materials, increasing durability and recyclability. Modular design allows a simple component replacement, expands the product lifetime and reduces resource consumption. This strategy supports customization and scalability, convenient to change customer preferences and technological advances. Innovations in the physical expression enables the development of bio-based polymer and durable fabrics.

Despite the advantages, adoption of AI tools in circular designs challenges such as data privacy, technical complexity and need for intercourse cooperation between designers, engineers and durability specialists. To overcome these challenges, AI requires investment in literacy, cross-sector partnership and regulatory framework that promotes the use of moral AIs in production development. Circular design and the future of AI promise for more innovation and durability in the development of production. Progress in AI technologies, including machine learning and Augmented Reality, will empower designers to create products that are not only functional and aesthetically enjoyable, but also environmentally responsible and socially beneficial. Therefore, the integration of AI tools with circular design principles presents a transformative approach to sustainable production development. By providing AI-powered generating design, life cycle assessment and benefits of predicted analyzes, businesses can accelerate transitions to the circular economy, generate waste, protect resources, and meet the customer's demand for moral produced goods. As companies continue to accept AI -operated innovations, they play a major role in shaping the more durable future where the planetary borders are designed for development while valuing the society.

In recent years, the concept of circular design reduces environmental influence and is famous as an important strategy for creating products that promote durable consumption. This approach perfectly adjusts with the innovative capabilities of artificial intelligence (AI), providing a transformative probability in the field of sustainable production development. This section discovers the intersection of circular design principles with AI tools, highlighting how they can cooperate with durability. Circular design is based on the principles of a circular economy, which is intended to use resources for as long as possible, the maximum value from them when in use, and receives and regenerates the products and materials at the end of their service life. This is intense contrasting with the traditional linear economy.

The Role of AI in Circular Design

AI can significantly enhance the implementation of circular design principles through its capabilities in data analysis, predictive modeling, and automation(Dhanya et al., 2023; Hussain et al., 2023; Ingle et al., 2023).

AI algorithms can improve the life expectancy of the product by predicting failure and enabling timely maintenance. They can also increase resource efficiency by optimizing production processes to reduce waste and energy consumption. AI can predict a more accurate prediction of textile production, supply chain, and demand. It can also accurately identify the content in recycling facilities and also facilitate recycling by rubbing the SORT. AI tools can help designers in making products that are easy to disassemble, promoting effective recycling. AI can promote the use of existing resources and reuse and reuse through the powering platform by powering platforms, by the use of existing resources. These include the use of machine learning to predict the component life and guide the production process again.

AI has been successfully integrated into circular design principles by Adidas, Google and renewable companies. Adidas uses AI at its speed factory to produce reduced shoes in the material waste, while the Google project uses ARA AI to design modular components for easy replacement. The renewable sort uses AI to enhance the rattling and recycling processes. While consolidation is still in its early stages, it is likely to innovate in physical expression and to help governments monitor and enforce the rules of the circular economy. Future progresses may include a wide AI platform of production life cycle. The harmony between circular design and AI has immense promise for sustainable production development. By benefiting the capabilities of AI, businesses can promote production longevity, resource efficiency, recyclability and reuse and reuse. This intersection opens not only environmental stability, but also new economic opportunities, pave the way for a more durable future.

CHALLENGES / COMPLEXITIES AND OPPORTUNITIES

As Artificial Intelligence (AI) continues to proliferate across industries, addressing data privacy and security concerns, along with navigating regulatory considerations, are paramount for ensuring responsible and effective AI integration(Barros et al., 2021; Comin et al., 2020).

Addressing Data Privacy and Security

The AI systems depend on sensitive data for algorithm training and decisions. To protect this, strong data protection steps such as encryption and anonymity are applied. Transparency and liability are encouraged by the structure of user information and liability. Moral affairs are included in AI development and deployment strategy to support user trust, reduce social risks, and promote responsible innovation in AI techniques.

Regulatory Considerations in AI Integration

Regulatory frameworks play a crucial role in governing AI integration to protect consumer rights, ensure fairness, and mitigate potential risks(Huang & Fan, 1993; Tan & Abd Rahim, 2024):

Data Protection Regulations, such as GDPR and CCPA, command bodies to protect data privacy and consent to the process. The algorithmic responsibility initiative aims to consider partiality and discrimination in AI systems, requiring ITS dets and transparency. Sector-specific rules, such as healthcare, money and automotive, ensure safety, reliability and moral standards in AI application. Regulatory organizations collaborate with industry designers to develop standards, certificates and guides for AI-powered technologies, prioritizing consumer safety and public confidence.

Challenges: Multinational institutions face challenges in compliance with various and developing regulatory requirements in various jurisdiction, which requires extensive strategy and regulatory intelligence. Another challenge is to balance the flow of global data with local data sovereignty laws. Deep is the need for agile regulatory approaches to promote innovation and reduce risks, as AI technologies will advance existing frameworks, such as Deep Wanda education and autonomous systems.

Opportunities: Regulatory framework enhances consumer trust by promoting data privacy and security standards, increasing the brand's reputation and competitive gains. They encourage the cooperation between industry, academia and government stakeholders to develop responsible AI standards. This framework also ranks organizations as global leaders in AI Ethics, runs sustainable innovation, and reduces the risks associated with AI deployment.

Thus, with data privacy and safety concerns, with navigating regulatory considerations, responsible AI integration is important. By implementing strong data protection measures, promoting transparency and responsibility and complying with developed regulatory frameworks, organizations can reduce the risks, increase consumer trusts and invest in ethical AI innovation opportunities. Accepting global norms and collaborating with the stakeholders of the field will pave the way to the future where AI technologies contribute a positive contribution to society when supporting moral principles and regulatory compliance.

FUTURE TRENDS IN AI AND THE CIRCULAR ECONOMY

The intersection of Artificial Intelligence (AI) and the circular economy represents a transformative force in shaping sustainable practices across industries. This section explores emerging technologies, innovations, and predictions for AI's impact on advancing circular economy principles. The figure 5 depicts the upcoming trends in AI and the circular economy(Lahti et al., 2018).

Figure 5. Future trends in AI and the circular economy

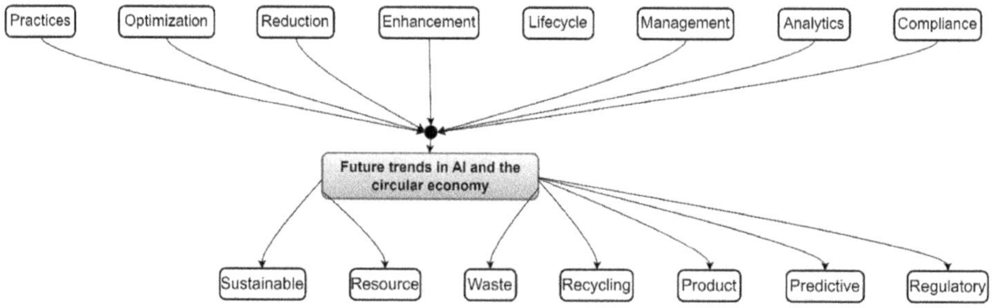

Emerging Technologies and Innovations

- **AI-driven Recycling and Waste Sorting:** Optimize recycling processes by automating advanced AI techniques, including machine learning and computer vision. AI -powered robotic systems can identify and distinguish various materials, such as plastic, metals and paper, precision, increase recycling rate and reduce contamination in waste currents.
- **Predictive Analytics for Resource Management:** AI -operated forecasts, supply chain disturbances and availability of resources. By analyzing the data of various sources, including IoT sensors and history, AI models allocate Resource Allocation, Product Template and Inventory Management optimizes, Reduces waste and increase resource efficiency.
- **Circular Design and Product Lifecycle Management:** Circular design and production generating design algorithms explore innovative product arrangements that maximize material efficiency, durability and recyclability. AI simulations, evaluating environmental effects during the life cycle of production, guide designers to make durable design decisions.

Predictions for AI's Impact on Circular Practices

- **Enhanced Supply Chain Transparency:** Increases transparency in the supply chain by providing real-time visibility to AI production origin, production processes and distribution channels. Blockchain technology associated with AI guarantees the Temper-proof record of product Provence and Sustainability credentials promoting confidence in consumers and stakeholders.

- **Closed-Loop Systems and Resource Optimization:** AI-system Close-Loop Systems Promotes Resource optimization by the convenience of reuse, reuse and recycling products and materials. Smart sensors and AI algorithms monitor the use of wealth, enabling businesses to increase production lifetime, produce waste, and regain valuable resources from the final products of life.
- **Regenerative Agriculture and Sustainable Practices:** AI applications in agriculture, such as precision farming and crop management, increase durability by to making inputs such as water and pesticides, and promoting the health of the soil by the use of resources. AI-powered analytics predicts crop yields, reduces climate risks, and supports regenerative methods that restore ecosystems and biochemical.

Therefore, the integration of AI in the circular economy represents the pattern of durable and resurgent methods. Using recycling, supply chain transparency and AI-based innovations in durable agriculture, organizations can accelerate the transition from a circular economy to the Model Dell that protects resources, reduces waste and promotes environmental surplus. As stakeholders have collaborated to cope with challenges and achieve opportunities presented by AI, they pave the way to the future where technical global durability goals and serves as a catalyst to assure prosperity for the upcoming pay -generations.

CONCLUSION

The integration of artificial intelligence (AI) in the circular economy presents a profound opportunity to redefine sustainable practices in the industry. Throughout this chapter, we have discovered the transformative possibility of recycling, supply chain transparency, production life cycle management and AI-powered innovations in durable agriculture. AI technologies enable business efficiency, reduce waste and advanced data analytics, forecast modeling and enhancing environmental stabs through Automation. AI-propelled recycling processes that improve the Sort rating accuracy and recycling rate for predictive analyzes that the resource management and supply chain operations, the possibility of enhancing the principles of the circular economy.

Moreover, AI promotes transparency and liability by providing real-time visibility to the original and durability of the product, there, creating confidence among consumers and stakeholders. AI-powered design and manufacturing promotes circular by promoting innovations, reusing products, re-production and recycling, expanding their life cycle and reducing environmental influence. Despite this progress, challenges such as data privacy concerns, regulatory complications and moral consideration must be carefully explored. Addressing these challenges requires collaborative efforts between industry leaders, policy makers and technical innovation to establish standards, policies and best practices promoting AI deployment in the circular economy.

Looking forward, the future of AI in the circular economy promises for constant innovation and durability. As organizations accept AI techniques to operate circular methods, they contribute to the more elastic and resource-efficient economy that meets the needs of current and future pay generations. After all, using the power of AI to integrate the principles of circular economy into daily business operations, we can move to a sustainable future where economic growth organizes with environmental defense and social well-being. Together, we can take advantage of AI's capabilities to achieve global durability goals and to create permanent positive effects on our planet.

REFERENCES

Awan, U., & Sroufe, R. (2022). Sustainability in the circular economy: Insights and dynamics of designing circular business models. *Applied Sciences (Basel, Switzerland)*, *12*(3), 1521. DOI: 10.3390/app12031521

Barros, M. V., Salvador, R., do Prado, G. F., de Francisco, A. C., & Piekarski, C. M. (2021). Circular economy as a driver to sustainable businesses. *Cleaner Environmental Systems*, *2*, 100006. DOI: 10.1016/j.cesys.2020.100006

Comin, L. C., Aguiar, C. C., Sehnem, S., Yusliza, M.-Y., Cazella, C. F., & Julkovski, D. J. (2020). Sustainable business models: A literature review. *Benchmarking*, *27*(7), 2028–2047. DOI: 10.1108/BIJ-12-2018-0384

De Angelis, R. (2018). *Business models in the circular economy: Concepts, examples and theory*. Springer. DOI: 10.1007/978-3-319-75127-6

Dhanya, D., Kumar, S. S., Thilagavathy, A., Prasad, D., & Boopathi, S. (2023). Data Analytics and Artificial Intelligence in the Circular Economy: Case Studies. In *Intelligent Engineering Applications and Applied Sciences for Sustainability* (pp. 40–58). IGI Global.

Fang, B., Yu, J., Chen, Z., Osman, A. I., Farghali, M., Ihara, I., Hamza, E. H., Rooney, D. W., & Yap, P.-S. (2023). Artificial intelligence for waste management in smart cities: A review. *Environmental Chemistry Letters*, *21*(4), 1959–1989. DOI: 10.1007/s10311-023-01604-3

Ferasso, M., Beliaeva, T., Kraus, S., Clauss, T., & Ribeiro-Soriano, D. (2020). Circular economy business models: The state of research and avenues ahead. *Business Strategy and the Environment*, *29*(8), 3006–3024. DOI: 10.1002/bse.2554

Geissdoerfer, M., Morioka, S. N., de Carvalho, M. M., & Evans, S. (2018). Business models and supply chains for the circular economy. *Journal of Cleaner Production*, *190*, 712–721. DOI: 10.1016/j.jclepro.2018.04.159

Harikaran, M., Boopathi, S., Gokulakannan, S., & Poonguzhali, M. (2023). Study on the Source of E-Waste Management and Disposal Methods. In *Sustainable Approaches and Strategies for E-Waste Management and Utilization* (pp. 39–60). IGI Global. DOI: 10.4018/978-1-6684-7573-7.ch003

Huang, Y., & Fan, L. (1993). Artificial intelligence for waste minimization in the process industry. *Computers in Industry*, *22*(2), 117–128. DOI: 10.1016/0166-3615(93)90059-A

Hussain, Z., Babe, M., Saravanan, S., Srimathy, G., Roopa, H., & Boopathi, S. (2023). Optimizing Biomass-to-Biofuel Conversion: IoT and AI Integration for Enhanced Efficiency and Sustainability. In *Circular Economy Implementation for Sustainability in the Built Environment* (pp. 191–214). IGI Global.

Ingle, R. B., Swathi, S., Mahendran, G., Senthil, T., Muralidharan, N., & Boopathi, S. (2023). Sustainability and Optimization of Green and Lean Manufacturing Processes Using Machine Learning Techniques. In *Circular Economy Implementation for Sustainability in the Built Environment* (pp. 261–285). IGI Global. DOI: 10.4018/978-1-6684-8238-4.ch012

Janardhana, K., Singh, V., Singh, S. N., Babu, T. R., Bano, S., & Boopathi, S. (2023). Utilization Process for Electronic Waste in Eco-Friendly Concrete: Experimental Study. In *Sustainable Approaches and Strategies for E-Waste Management and Utilization* (pp. 204–223). IGI Global.

Koshariya, A. K., Khatoon, S., Marathe, A. M., Suba, G. M., Baral, D., & Boopathi, S. (2023). Agricultural Waste Management Systems Using Artificial Intelligence Techniques. In *AI-Enabled Social Robotics in Human Care Services* (pp. 236–258). IGI Global. DOI: 10.4018/978-1-6684-8171-4.ch009

Lahti, T., Wincent, J., & Parida, V. (2018). A definition and theoretical review of the circular economy, value creation, and sustainable business models: Where are we now and where should research move in the future? *Sustainability (Basel)*, *10*(8), 2799. DOI: 10.3390/su10082799

Lewandowski, M. (2016). Designing the business models for circular economy—Towards the conceptual framework. *Sustainability (Basel)*, *8*(1), 43. DOI: 10.3390/su8010043

Maguluri, L. P., Ananth, J., Hariram, S., Geetha, C., Bhaskar, A., & Boopathi, S. (2023). Smart Vehicle-Emissions Monitoring System Using Internet of Things (IoT). In *Handbook of Research on Safe Disposal Methods of Municipal Solid Wastes for a Sustainable Environment* (pp. 191–211). IGI Global.

Mohanty, A., Venkateswaran, N., Ranjit, P., Tripathi, M. A., & Boopathi, S. (2023). Innovative Strategy for Profitable Automobile Industries: Working Capital Management. In *Handbook of Research on Designing Sustainable Supply Chains to Achieve a Circular Economy* (pp. 412–428). IGI Global.

MYILSAMY SURESHKUMAR, V. R. P., S. BOOPATHI, M. SABAREESH. (2018). The improving Wear Resistance Properties of Molybdenum Alloy Under Cryogenic Treatment. *International Journal of Mechanical and Production Engineering Research and Development*, *8*(7), 724–728.

Ostermann, C. M., Nascimento, L. da S., Steinbruch, F. K., & Callegaro-de-Menezes, D. (2021). Drivers to implement the circular economy in born-sustainable business models: A case study in the fashion industry. *Revista de Gestão, 28*(3), 223–240. DOI: 10.1108/REGE-03-2020-0017

Pieroni, M. P., McAloone, T. C., & Pigosso, D. C. (2019). Business model innovation for circular economy and sustainability: A review of approaches. *Journal of Cleaner Production, 215*, 198–216. DOI: 10.1016/j.jclepro.2019.01.036

Tan, W. Y., & Abd Rahim, M. H. I. (2024). Potential of Implementing Artificial Intelligence (AI) for Reducing Waste at Construction Site. *Research in Management of Technology and Business, 5*(1), 1559–1575.

Tunn, V. S., Bocken, N. M., van den Hende, E. A., & Schoormans, J. P. (2019). Business models for sustainable consumption in the circular economy: An expert study. *Journal of Cleaner Production, 212*, 324–333. DOI: 10.1016/j.jclepro.2018.11.290

Verma, R., Christiana, M. B. V., Maheswari, M., Srinivasan, V., Patro, P., Dari, S. S., & Boopathi, S. (2024). Intelligent Physarum Solver for Profit Maximization in Oligopolistic Supply Chain Networks. In *AI and Machine Learning Impacts in Intelligent Supply Chain* (pp. 156–179). IGI Global. DOI: 10.4018/979-8-3693-1347-3.ch011

Vijaya Lakshmi, V., Mishra, M., Kushwah, J. S., Shajahan, U. S., Mohanasundari, M., & Boopathi, S. (2024). Circular Economy Digital Practices for Ethical Dimensions and Policies for Digital Waste Management. In *Harnessing High-Performance Computing and AI for Environmental Sustainability* (pp. 166–193). IGI Global., DOI: 10.4018/979-8-3693-1794-5.ch008

Witjes, S., & Lozano, R. (2016). Towards a more Circular Economy: Proposing a framework linking sustainable public procurement and sustainable business models. *Resources, Conservation and Recycling, 112*, 37–44. DOI: 10.1016/j.resconrec.2016.04.015

Zhao, L., Dai, T., Qiao, Z., Sun, P., Hao, J., & Yang, Y. (2020). Application of artificial intelligence to wastewater treatment: A bibliometric analysis and systematic review of technology, economy, management, and wastewater reuse. *Process Safety and Environmental Protection, 133*, 169–182. DOI: 10.1016/j.psep.2019.11.014

Chapter 3
Circular Economy and Food Sovereignty Management in the Food Sector:
A Socioeconomic Approach to Sustainability

María E. Raygoza-L.
https://orcid.org/0009-0000-5969-6602
Universidad Politécnica de Baja California, Mexico

Gabriel Trujillo-Hernández
https://orcid.org/0000-0003-1556-387X
Universidad Politécnica de Baja California, Mexico

Diego Bonilla-G.
https://orcid.org/0000-0003-1131-2635
Universidad Autónoma de Baja California, Mexico

Fabian N. Murrieta-Rico
https://orcid.org/0000-0001-9829-3013
Universidad Politécnica de Baja California, Mexico

ABSTRACT

This chapter explores the importance of resource management, circular economy, and food sovereignty as strategies for transforming the global agri-food system. Food production contributes approximately one-third of global greenhouse gas emissions, estimated at 17.318 billion metric tons of CO_2 equivalent per year 57% of which

DOI: 10.4018/979-8-3373-9923-2.ch003

originates from animal-based foods, 29% from plant-based products, and 14% from other uses. In response to the dominant linear model characterized by waste, corporate concentration, and ecological degradation a regenerative approach is proposed, based on resource reuse and agroecological diversification. Through an integrated analysis, the chapter addresses the environmental impacts of food waste and the potential of circular technologies, artificial intelligence, and renewable energy to build more resilient food systems. It concludes with key recommendations for stakeholders aimed at consolidating a circular and sovereign food economy.

INTRODUCTION

Food production accounts for approximately one-third of global greenhouse gas (GHG) emissions, estimated at 17.318 billion metric tons of CO_2 equivalent per year. Of this total, 57% are attributed to animal-based foods, 29% to plant-based products, and the remaining 14% to other uses, such as rubber and cotton cultivation (Agencia SINC, 2021). A particularly alarming component of this dynamic is food waste, which alone generates around 9.3 gigatons of CO_2 equivalent annually nearly half of the total emissions from the food system. Between 2010 and 2019, agriculture, forestry, and land use contributed between 13% and 21% of global GHG emissions, with nitrous oxide and methane being the primary contributors, accounting for more than half of these emissions, Food and Agriculture Organization of the United Nations (FAO) This scenario underscores the urgent need to transform the global food system towards more sustainable models (FAO, 2020).

Against this backdrop, circular economy and food sovereignty have emerged as strategic pillars for enabling systemic transformation of the agri-food sector. According from United Nations in contrast to the traditional linear model characterized by resource extraction, intensive production, and massive disposal and in the face of challenges such as climate change, population growth, and biodiversity loss, both approaches offer integrative alternatives geared toward social well-being, ecological resilience, and economic empowerment of communities. It is projected that the global population will reach 9.7 billion by 2050, significantly increasing pressure on food systems and natural resources (United Nations, 2022). This demographic trend demands a rethinking of production models to ensure universal access to nutritious food without compromising the planet's ecological base. Simultaneously, climate change has introduced adverse conditions for agriculture, including droughts, floods, loss of fertile soils, and declining yields in essential crops, exacerbating food insecurity in vulnerable regions, particularly in the Global South (IPCC, 2019).

The application of circular economy principles to the food sector presents an integrated strategy for redesigning production, distribution, and consumption systems. Its main goal is to close production cycles through sustainable practices such as composting, reuse of organic waste, agroecology, and regenerative agriculture. These actions help to reduce waste, regenerate soils, valorize by-products, incorporate clean energy, and build more sustainable food systems (Ellen MacArthur Foundation, 2019). Unlike the linear model, which views waste as the end of the process, the circular model redefines waste as a resource. While the linear approach depletes ecosystems and externalizes social and environmental costs, the circular approach seeks to regenerate natural resources, redistribute benefits, and redesign production processes to be more equitable, efficient, and inclusive.

This transition transcends technological domains, requiring profound cultural, institutional, and economic transformations. The benefits of a circular economy in the food domain are manifested across three main dimensions. Environmentally, it reduces GHG emissions, improves soil health, decreases water and air pollution, and promotes biodiversity. Economically, it fosters green job creation, reduces long-term costs, improves resource-use efficiency, and opens opportunities in emerging sectors such as biotechnology and bioindustries.

Socially, it empowers local communities, strengthens territorial economies, promotes intergenerational equity, and enhances food security. Moreover, food sovereignty and circular economy together offer a viable and necessary roadmap for addressing the ecological, social, and economic challenges of the 21st century. The concentration of power in large agri-food corporations has increasingly constrained the autonomy of small-scale producers and restricted equitable access to healthy, nutritious, and culturally appropriate food. This logic of accumulation reproduces asymmetrical power relations, undermining community food sovereignty and deepening dependency on external inputs and markets (Patel, 2009). A critical factor is the heavy reliance on globalized supply chains designed around economies of scale and logistical optimization. This model has proven particularly fragile in the face of disruptions caused by armed conflicts, pandemics, energy crises, market volatility, and natural disasters. The centralization of agri-food systems has revealed its inability to respond resiliently to crisis scenarios, further exacerbating food insecurity, economic inequality, and territorial exclusion.

BACKGROUND

The Relationship Between Food Sovereignty, Food Security, and Self-Sufficiency

The linear model of food production based on the logic of "extract, produce, consume, and dispose" remains the dominant paradigm globally. While this approach enabled a rapid expansion of productive capacity throughout the 20th century, its collateral impacts on the environment, public health, and social equity have been extensively documented. This industrialized system disregards the regeneration of the resources it consumes, resulting in high levels of waste and pollution across the entire agri-food chain (FAO, 2021). It is estimated that approximately one-third of all food produced globally is either lost or wasted each year. This not only translates into a significant economic loss but also reflects an inefficient use of critical resources such as water, soil, energy, and human labor (United Nations Environment Programme, 2020). Such structural inefficiencies reveal the fragility of the global food system, especially in the context of climate crises, water scarcity, and growing food demand. Intensive food production is heavily reliant on agrochemicals, synthetic fertilizers, and fossil fuels, increasing its ecological footprint and making it particularly vulnerable to energy and environmental crises.

The expansion of industrial agriculture has been associated with massive deforestation, soil erosion, biodiversity loss, aquifer depletion, and widespread contamination of water bodies and the atmosphere (Altieri & Nicholls, 2017). In light of these structural limitations, there is an urgent need to transition towards agri-food models grounded in circular economy principles and aligned with the objectives of food sovereignty. This transition entails prioritizing the relocalization of production, strengthening short supply chains, promoting technological sustainability, decentralizing decision-making capacities, and encouraging active community participation. These models not only aim to reduce the environmental impact of the food system but also to enhance its long-term resilience, equity, and self-sufficiency (González de Molina & Toledo, 2014). To better understand the environmental burden of current dietary patterns and the potential for emissions reduction through sustainable choices, it is essential to compare the average greenhouse gas emissions associated with different food categories. Table 1 provides a detailed breakdown of CO_2-equivalent emissions per kilogram of food product, highlighting the stark contrast between animal-based and plant-based items in terms of their climate impact.

Table 1. Average greenhouse gas emissions by type of food (kg CO_2e per kg of product)

Food Group	Food Item	Emissions (kg CO_2e/kg)	Notes
Animal-based products	Cheese	26.9	High emissions due to milk production and methane from cattle
	Fish (wild-caught)	23.9	Industrial fishing emits heavily due to fuel-intensive operations
	Lamb	24	High methane from rumination and low feed conversion efficiency
	Beef	60	Highest emissions due to methane and land use
	Pork	13.6	Lower than beef but requires intensive feed and inputs
	Poultry	12.3	Requires less land but emits more than plant-based alternatives
	Eggs	4.7	More efficient than meat, still animal-derived
	Cow's milk	3.2	Includes emissions from livestock and processing
Legumes and plant-based proteins	Tofu	3.2	Low impact; alternative plant-based protein source
	Legumes (lentils, beans)	2	Efficient in both emissions and water use
Cereals and derivatives	Rice	4	High methane emissions from flooded paddy fields
	Wheat (bread, pasta)	1.6	Low emission levels
	Maize	1.7	Common staple with moderate impact
Fruits and vegetables	Fruits (average)	0.9	Very low impact; among the most sustainable crops
	Vegetables (average)	0.7	One of the most sustainable food groups in terms of emissions
Other crops	Potatoes	0.5	High productivity with low environmental impact
	Nuts and seeds	0.4–2.4	Variable impact: almonds require significant water resources

Source: Own development

Animal-based foods, particularly beef and lamb, exhibit the highest CO_2-equivalent emissions per kilogram of product. This is primarily due to enteric fermentation (methane emissions from digestion), the intensive use of resources such as water, land, and forage, and the inefficient conversion of plant-based inputs into animal protein (Poore & Nemecek, 2018). In contrast, plant-based products, including legumes and cereal derivatives, have significantly lower GHG impacts. Their cultivation requires less energy, land, and water, and they are not typically associated with substantial direct emissions of methane or nitrous oxide. This makes them key components of sustainable diets with a lower environmental footprint (FAO, 2021). One notable exception is rice, which is among the leading agricultural sources of methane emissions worldwide. As a staple for over half of the global population, rice cultivation accounts for approximately 30% of methane emissions and 11% of nitrous oxide emissions in the agricultural sector (IPCC, 2019; FAO, 2021). These emissions are largely due to traditional flood irrigation systems, which create anaerobic soil conditions that favor methane production by microorganisms. Nevertheless, various practices can substantially mitigate this impact. For instance, Alternate Wetting and Drying (AWD) irrigation management can reduce emissions by up to 50% without compromising crop yields (Richards & Sander, 2014). Additionally, the adoption of improved rice varieties adapted to low-water or non-flooded conditions has proven to be an effective technological strategy for reducing the sector's environmental impact. To better understand the environmental footprint of different food sources, the following table presents average GHG emissions by type of food, measured in kilograms of CO_2 equivalent per kilogram of product. This comparative overview underscores the significant disparities between animal-based and plant-based food products, highlighting the environmental advantages of diversified, low-emission diets as part of a broader transition toward circular and sovereign food systems (González de Molina & Toledo, 2014).

Food Security, Food Sovereignty, and the Circular Economy

Food security focuses on ensuring physical, economic, and social access to sufficient, safe, and nutritious food. This perspective promoted by institutions such as the FAO follows a logic of coverage and availability at national or international levels. However, it often depoliticizes the food issue, overlooking power relations, production models, and the associated environmental impacts. In contrast, food sovereignty a concept advanced by the La Vía Campesina movement introduces a political, cultural, and ecological dimension. It defends the right of peoples to define their own systems of food production, distribution, and consumption, prioritizing sustainability, social justice, and self-determination (La Vía Campesina, 2019). This approach promotes self-sufficiency and agrarian justice as essential pillars in addressing current systemic crises. The integration of circular economy principles into these approaches contributes to the development of regenerative, decentralized, and resilient food systems capable of responding to global challenges with context-sensitive solutions. According to FAO data, more than 70% of the world's food is produced by small-scale farmers who, paradoxically, are among the most marginalized within the dominant agro-industrial model (FAO, 2014). Reversing this exclusion and strengthening the role of rural communities is crucial for the sustainability of the system.

The convergence between the circular economy and food sovereignty allows for the design of sustainable agri-food models that prioritize the well-being of people and ecosystems. This articulation promotes the use of local resources, waste reduction, biodiversity conservation, and the communal reappropriation of production systems. Practices such as agroecology, permaculture, composting, crop rotation, and the use of biofertilizers contribute to soil regeneration, climate resilience, and reduced dependence on external inputs (Altieri & Nicholls, 2017). Moreover, these practices help recover ancestral knowledge while integrating technological innovations adapted to local contexts, thus strengthening community capacities in territorial management and reducing ecological footprints. From an economic and social standpoint, this integration revitalizes rural economies, fosters decent employment, and stimulates the development of short supply chains. Initiatives such as urban gardens, seed banks, cooperative stores, and local markets contribute to reterritorializing food systems, reconnecting consumers with producers, and promoting a fairer distribution of added value (González de Molina & Toledo, 2014).

Sustainable Food Production: A Foundation for a Resilient System

Sustainable food production is a strategic and urgent pillar for ensuring global food security, mitigating the impacts of climate change, and preserving the ecosystems essential to life on Earth. Far from being an optional privilege or a niche trend, it has become a structural necessity in response to the ongoing degradation of natural resources, biodiversity loss, soil deterioration, and the climatic stress already affecting agricultural systems in various regions worldwide (FAO, 2022). Agriculture and biodiversity are both close and bidirectional. On the one hand, the expansion of intensive agriculture has been one of the main drivers of deforestation, soil and water pollution, genetic erosion, and habitat destruction. According to the IPBES (2019), the intensive use of agrochemicals, crop homogenization, and landscape fragmentation have significantly contributed to the collapse of insect populations, pollinators, and microorganisms essential to soil fertility. On the other hand, sustainable production models seek to reverse these trends by integrating ecological processes into agricultural practices. This includes the conservation of biological corridors, preservation of native seed banks, promotion of polycultures, and implementation of regenerative practices that restore natural cycles and enhance the ecological resilience of agroecosystems (Gliessman, 2016).

Sustainable food production is defined as the ability to meet current food needs without compromising the capacity of future generations, while integrating economic, social, and environmental objectives into a coherent operational framework. This vision is structured around three core principles:

- **Efficiency in the use of natural resources**: This involves optimizing the use of water, soil, energy, nutrients, and biodiversity, minimizing waste and environmental impact. It is supported by practices such as precision agriculture, crop rotation, moisture conservation, and regenerative farming techniques (Rockström et al., 2017).
- **Equity and social justice for rural communities**: Food sustainability cannot be achieved without ensuring fair labor conditions, equitable access to productive resources, and active participation of small-scale producers, women, and Indigenous peoples. This principle also encompasses secure land tenure, financial inclusion, and the democratization of access to technology and markets (HLPE, 2013).
- **Environmental sustainability**: Agriculture must avoid ecosystem degradation, reduce greenhouse gas emissions, protect natural habitats, and promote the restoration of degraded landscapes. Achieving this requires closing nutrient and energy cycles, utilizing local inputs, conserving functional biodiversity, and tailoring practices to ecological contexts (Raygoza-L, et all

These three principles converge in the concept of regenerative agri-food systems, which aim not only to be sustainable but also restorative of ecological balance, resilient to systemic crises, and transformation of production, distribution, and consumption relations. The current model of agricultural production is highly dependent on fossil fuels from the manufacturing of fertilizers and pesticides to the transport and refrigeration of food. This dependency increases vulnerability to energy fluctuations, hidden environmental costs, and greenhouse gas emissions. In contrast, sustainable production advocates a transition toward post-fossil systems by integrating renewable energy sources, clean technologies, and bio-inputs, while fostering resilience through the relocalization and decentralization of production (Schneider et al., 2011). The circular economy emerges as a transformative strategy for agri-food systems, offering a regenerative, inclusive, and sustainable model that breaks away from the linear logic of "extract, produce, consume, and discard." Instead, it promotes reuse, repair, recycling, and resource valorization, with the objective of closing production loops, minimizing waste, and reducing pressure on natural ecosystems (Ellen MacArthur Foundation, 2019). When contextualized within rural and peasant territories, the circular economy takes on a critical socio-political dimension: it becomes a tool for empowering small producers by strengthening their productive autonomy, diversifying income streams, and enhancing economic, social, and ecological resilience in the face of contemporary systemic crises. Sustainable production refers to the capacity to meet current food needs without compromising the ability of future generations, integrating economic, social, and environmental goals within a unified operational framework. This is guided by three fundamental principles:

- **Efficiency in the use of natural resources**: This involves optimizing the use of water, soil, energy, nutrients, and biodiversity, minimizing waste, and reducing environmental impact. Achievements in this area include precision technologies, crop rotation, moisture conservation, and regenerative agriculture practices (Rockström et al., 2017).
- **Equity and social justice for rural communities**: Food sustainability cannot be achieved without ensuring fair labor conditions, equitable access to productive resources, and active participation of smallholders, women, and Indigenous peoples. This also entails land tenure security, financial inclusion, and democratized access to technology and markets (HLPE, 2013).
- **Environmental sustainability**: Agriculture must avoid environmental degradation, reduce greenhouse gas emissions, protect natural ecosystems, and promote the restoration of degraded landscapes. This requires closing nutrient and energy loops, using local inputs, conserving functional biodiversity, and adapting practices to the ecological context.

These three pillars converge in the concept of regenerative agri-food systems, which aim not only for sustainability but also for ecological restoration, crisis resilience, and the transformation of production, distribution, and consumption relationships. The current agricultural model is highly dependent on fossil fuels from the production of fertilizers and pesticides to the transportation and refrigeration of food. This reliance makes it vulnerable to energy fluctuations, hidden environmental costs, and greenhouse gas emissions. In contrast, sustainable production advocates for a transition toward post-fossil systems, integrating renewable energy, clean technologies, and bio-inputs, while promoting resilience through the relocalization and decentralization of production (Schneider et al., 2011). The circular economy emerges as a transformative strategy for agri-food systems by proposing a regenerative, inclusive, and sustainable model that breaks with the linear logic of "extract, produce, consume, and dispose." Instead, it encourages reuse, repair, recycling, and resource valorization, aiming to close production cycles, minimize waste, and reduce pressure on natural ecosystems (Ellen MacArthur Foundation, 2019). When contextualized in rural and peasant territories, the circular economy takes on a crucial sociopolitical dimension: it becomes a tool for empowering small-scale producers by enabling them to strengthen their productive autonomy, diversify income sources, and increase their economic, social, and ecological resilience in the face of systemic crises.

Strategies for Productive Autonomy

One of the foundational pillars of circular transition in rural areas is productive autonomy, understood as the capacity of farming families to produce, transform, and market their own inputs and goods without structural dependence on industrial supply chains, intermediaries, or extractive technologies.

Among the most relevant strategies to strengthen this autonomy are:

- **Local production of natural inputs**: This includes the development of biofertilizers, compost, organic pesticides, efficient microorganisms, and native seeds adapted to the agroecological conditions of the territory.
- **Small-scale agro-industrial processing**: The artisanal production of value-added goods such as jams, whole-grain flours, cheeses, essential oils, fermented beverages, and natural cosmetics enables communities to retain control over local economic flows.
- **Reuse of agricultural and household waste**: The implementation of biodigesters for biogas generation, organic composting, greywater recovery for irrigation, and biomass-based energy production exemplifies circular approaches to waste.
- **Design of integrated ecological farms**: These are holistically planned systems where crops, animals, water, energy, and waste interact through closed cycles that enhance energy efficiency and soil fertility mimicking the functioning of natural ecosystems (Mollison, 1990).

These practices help reduce costs, improve self-sufficiency, and reintegrate value into local systems rather than extracting it, thus fostering a regenerative economy grounded in environmental stewardship and productive dignity. The circular economy finds a natural synergy with solidarity economy frameworks, as both promote an alternative vision of development based on reciprocity, equity, and collective benefit. Cooperative models, in particular empower small-scale producers to jointly address production, commercialization, and investment challenges while preserving their autonomy and strengthening community cohesion (Coraggio, 2011).

Key advantages of cooperative organization in rural contexts include:

- **Shared use of machinery, knowledge, and technologies**, leading to reduced individual costs and enhanced collective innovation.

- **Joint access to fairer and more direct markets**, such as agroecological fairs, digital sales platforms, local public procurement systems, and urban–rural solidarity trade networks.
- **Management of community savings and investment funds**, enabling producers to capitalize themselves without commercial debt and fostering endogenous reinvestment.
- **Democratic participation in productive and commercial decisions**, ensuring that environmental and social criteria are present at every stage of the economic process.

Solidarity economy networks also promote **short supply chains**, encourage knowledge exchange, and connect conscious producers and consumers. These connections reduce the ecological footprint of transportation and packaging, while reinforcing **local control over food systems**.

Environmental, Social, and Economic Benefits of Circular Agri-Food Systems

The implementation of circular economy principles by small rural producers yields positive impacts across multiple dimensions. To comprehensively assess the transformative potential of circular economy strategies in agri-food systems, it is crucial to analyze their multifaceted benefits across environmental, social, and economic dimensions. Table 2 presents a synthesized overview of these benefits, demonstrating how circular practices can reduce ecological footprints, strengthen local economies, promote community resilience, and enhance food sovereignty. These dimensions reinforce the relevance of circular approaches as strategic levers for sustainable and inclusive rural development. This approach not only transforms production methods but also redefines the relationships between communities, the environment, and the broader economic system. Its benefits can be grouped into three main domains:

Table 2. Environmental, social, and economic benefits of the circular economy in agri-food systems

Dimension	Benefit	Description
Environmental	Waste reduction	Comprehensive utilization of by-products, on-farm composting, and recycling.
	Soil health improvement	Regenerative practices that enhance organic matter and soil biodiversity.
	Water savings and reuse	Implementation of efficient irrigation, rainwater harvesting, and treated greywater systems.
	Reduction of GHG emissions	Use of renewable energy, bio-inputs, and fewer synthetic inputs.
	Biodiversity conservation	Crop diversification, native seed preservation, and ecological restoration.
Social	Recovery of traditional knowledge	Integration of ancestral knowledge into agroecological land management.
	Strengthening of community bonds	Collaborative models for production, processing, and commercialization.
	Improved access to nutritious and culturally appropriate food	Local food circuits and recovery of discarded foods to enhance nutritional access.
	Recognition of rural women's roles	Active participation of women in key economic and community processes.
	Territorial empowerment	Promotion of food sovereignty and community engagement in productive decision-making.
Economic	Income diversification	Use of by-products, environmental services, and diversified production.
	Reduction in production costs	Replacement of external inputs with locally available natural resources.
	Financial stability	Access to niche markets and community-based solidarity funds.
	Creation of rural green jobs	Employment in recycling, artisanal agro-industry, clean energy, and ecosystem services.
	Reduced dependency on global markets	Strengthening of local economies through productive relocalization.

Source: Own development

THE CIRCULAR ECONOMY IN THE FOOD SECTOR: TOWARD TERRITORIAL SOVEREIGNTY AND REGENERATIVE SYSTEMS

When implemented with a territorial perspective, the circular economy in the food sector represents a comprehensive strategy to redefine both food distribution and waste management two key links in the agri-food chain where the linear model has produced systemic inefficiencies, social exclusion, and environmental degradation.

This systemic transformation enables the construction of fairer, more resilient, and regenerative food circuits, with concrete impacts on food sovereignty, community empowerment, and climate change mitigation. One of the most significant pillars of this transformation is the consolidation of short supply chains a strategy that promotes the local distribution of food, reduces intermediaries, improves product traceability, and strengthens the relationship between producers and consumers (Raygoza-Limón et al., 2025).

These circuits include agroecological fairs, farmers' markets, solidarity baskets, and digital platforms that directly link production and processing units with nearby communities. Proximity-based economies not only reduce emissions from food transport, but also foster fairer and more transparent trade, where producers receive a more equitable income and consumers gain access to fresh, sustainable, and culturally meaningful foods (FAO, 2019).

Beyond economic and environmental impacts, localized food systems reinforce territorial identity and shorten the time between harvest and consumption, improving the nutritional and sensory quality of food. This model also revalues local culinary knowledge and reactivates the deep connections between food, culture, and territory. In parallel, the management and valorization of organic waste has become one of the most innovative axes of circularity in agriculture. Confronted with a linear model that produces more than 931 million tons of food waste annually (United Nations Environment Programme, 2021), the transformation of organic waste into energy, agricultural inputs, or new products emerges as a strategic pathway for establishing regenerative agri-food chains. These technological solutions when embedded within community-based strategies and supported by active public policy contribute to closing production cycles, reducing waste, improving energy efficiency, and strengthening local economies. Together, they represent a concrete step toward territorial food sovereignty, rooted in environmental stewardship, intelligent resource use, and the recognition of rural actors as key agents of sustainable development.

DIGITAL TECHNOLOGIES AND AGRI-FOOD INNOVATION: ENABLING SMART AND RESILIENT CIRCULAR SYSTEMS

In addition to agroecological strategies, digital technologies are profoundly transforming how agricultural production is planned, monitored, and managed. The advent of Agriculture 4.0 has introduced a suite of tools including Internet of Things (IoT) sensors, drones, satellite imagery, Geographic Information Systems (GIS), artificial intelligence (AI) platforms, and blockchain-based solutions that enhance traceability and sustainability across the agri-food value chain (Wolfert et al., 2017). These technologies enable real-time, data-driven decision-making, thereby optimizing the use of water, fertilizers, and energy. They also improve logistical efficiency and significantly reduce waste. Precision agriculture, for example, allows for the identification of specific areas within a field that require differentiated input levels, avoiding overapplication and minimizing environmental impact. This results not only in lower operational costs but also in a reduced ecological footprint for agricultural practices. Moreover, digital traceability systems provide end-to-end visibility throughout the life cycle of food products from seed to consumer enhancing transparency, mitigating food fraud, and strengthening consumer trust in local and sustainable supply chains. In rural areas, such technologies further facilitate financial inclusion and improve access to differentiated markets through digital platforms and cooperative models (Kamilaris et al., 2017). Together, the integration of regenerative and digital technologies reinforces circularity within the agri-food sector. It fosters the emergence of decentralized, efficient, and resilient food systems that are better equipped to respond to the multifaceted challenges posed by climate change, public health crises, and global economic instability in the 21st century.

Within the framework of the circular economy, the sustainable transformation and distribution of food represents both a challenge and an opportunity. Unlike the linear model of "produce–consume discard," the circular economy proposes closing the food life cycle by minimizing waste, maximizing ecological and social value, and reducing the environmental footprint of the agri-food system. Sustainable food processing is based on technological and organizational strategies aimed at reducing environmental impact and improving efficiency:

- **Use of clean technologies and energy efficiency**: This includes the adoption of low-consumption cooking systems, heat recovery technologies, intelligent automation, and the use of renewable energy sources such as solar, biomass, or wind power.
- **Water recirculation and waste reduction**: The use of closed-loop water reuse systems and reductions in water consumption within the industry.
- **By-product valorization**: Transformation of peels, seeds, pulps, bones, and bagasse into products such as flours, cosmetics, snacks, fertilizers, or biocomposites.
- **Sustainability certifications**: Implementation of standards for fair trade, clean production, organic or regenerative practices to access responsible markets.

Circularity also promotes a **territorial approach** to input sourcing:

- **Locally sourced ingredients**: Use of local and seasonal food products to reduce emissions from transportation and to strengthen the local economy.

- **Food recovery**: Utilization of products discarded from formal markets for aesthetic or logistical reasons (e.g., fruits, vegetables, surpluses), which are transformed into preserves, sauces, juices, flours, or dehydrated goods.
- **Partnerships with food banks and community kitchens**: Collaboration with social actors to facilitate food access for vulnerable sectors and reduce food waste.

Proximity economy, strategies, and distribution logistics in circular commercialization circuits

Circular models prioritize decentralized, low-carbon distribution systems:

- **Direct sales** at local fairs, community hubs, or agroecological markets.
- **Digital platforms** that connect producers directly with consumers (agroecological e-commerce).
- **Community-Supported Agriculture (CSA)** systems, where consumers invest upfront in the production process.
- **Collaborative logistics**, including partnerships between processors and cooperatives for shared transportation.
- **Local currencies and bartering** as tools of solidarity-based economies in rural and peri-urban areas.

To fully realize the potential of circular food systems, it is essential to adopt a set of complementary innovation strategies that go beyond production and distribution. These strategies serve as catalysts for systemic change by enhancing material efficiency, fostering technological integration, and promoting a culture of sustainability across all stakeholders. The following key areas represent critical enablers for the consolidation of circular practices in agri-food value chains: Circular packaging design:

- **Use of compostable,** returnable, or recyclable materials based on plant fibers, cellulose, or starch.
- **Sustainable digitalization**: Deployment of IoT sensors, blockchain technologies, and traceability platforms to improve operational efficiency and transparency.
- **Circular education and culture**: Training of workers, producers, and consumers in sustainable practices and food co-responsibility.
- **Industrial symbiosis**: Cross-use of waste between local industries (e.g., agricultural residues used as substrates for mushroom cultivation or biomass energy).

- **Public policies and green incentives**: Government support through subsidies, soft loans, technical assistance, and tax incentives for producers and cooperatives that adopt circular models.

Logistics and Distribution: Critical Links in the Circular Agri-Food Chain

Logistics and distribution constitute critical links within the agri-food system. Beyond their role in economic efficiency, they directly influence GHG emissions, food loss during transportation, and the intensive use of polluting materials, particularly in packaging and product preservation. In the current linear model, these processes are characterized by long, fragmented supply chains that are heavily dependent on fossil fuels and offer limited socio-environmental traceability (FAO, 2022; Ellen MacArthur Foundation, 2019). In response to these challenges, the circular economy proposes a comprehensive redesign of the logistics system: shortening distances, minimizing waste, promoting the use of clean energy, and fostering more equitable, transparent, and localized commercial relationships.

Reducing the Impact of Food Transport and Sustainable Supply Chains

Transport accounts for approximately 5% to 10% of the total carbon footprint of food products, and this figure can exceed 20% for perishable goods or those imported by air (FAO, 2022). To mitigate this impact, a range of circular strategies are being implemented across the sector:

- **Route optimization through artificial intelligence**: Platforms such as Route4Me use algorithms to optimize delivery routes, achieving up to a 30% reduction in emissions by enhancing transportation efficiency.
- **Fleet electrification and sustainable transport**: Cities like Amsterdam, Paris, and Bogotá have adopted electric vehicles, cargo tricycles, and biofuels derived from organic waste to support urban food distribution.
- **Collaborative logistics**: Rural enterprises and cooperatives coordinate shared transportation systems, reducing redundant travel, particularly in geographically dispersed regions.
- **Promotion of local consumption**: Local markets and community-supported agriculture (CSA) programs can reduce transportation-related emissions by up to 70% compared to air-imported fruits and vegetables (EIT Food, 2023).

A circular supply chain not only optimizes the physical flow of goods but also ensures a more equitable distribution of value, supports fair labor practices, and guarantees social and environmental traceability across all stages. Key strategies include:

- **Resource use efficiency**: Companies such as Imperfect Foods market cosmetically flawed but otherwise edible products, thereby diverting millions of kilograms of food waste annually from landfills.
- **Digital traceability and blockchain integration**: These technologies facilitate real-time tracking of product origins and conditions, enabling audits and bolstering consumer confidence in sustainable value chains.
- **Solidarity-based contracts and fair-trade models**: These arrangements establish direct links between producers and consumers, eliminating exploitative intermediaries and upholding labor and cultural rights.
- **Certification of circular practices**: Low-impact and regenerative production seals such as *Cradle to Cradle* enhance the market value of sustainably produced goods.

More than 60% of all plastic packaging originates from the food sector, yet less than 15% is effectively recycled (Ellen MacArthur Foundation, 2021). The circular economy advocates replacing such packaging with low-impact materials intentionally designed to be part of a closed-loop system. Innovative solutions in circular packaging are central to reducing the environmental footprint of food systems. These approaches aim to eliminate unnecessary packaging, promote material recovery, and inform consumer choices through transparency. Notable developments include:

- **Agricultural-based bioplastics**: Companies such as *Notpla* and *TIPA* manufacture packaging from materials like seaweed cellulose, potato starch, and banana peels. These alternatives decompose naturally without leaving behind microplastics, offering an effective response to plastic pollution.
- **Returnable packaging systems**: Initiatives like *Loop* promote reusable containers by offering economic incentives to consumers who participate in closed-loop packaging schemes, thereby extending the life cycle of materials and reducing waste.
- **Bulk sales and reduction of over-packaging**: Bulk purchasing models allow consumers to bring their own containers, minimizing the need for single-use wrapping and lowering both material consumption and emissions related to packaging production and disposal.
- **Environmental labeling**: The European *Eco-Score* informs consumers about the environmental impact of food products and their packaging. By offering a

standardized metric, this tool encourages more informed and environmentally responsible purchasing decisions.

These strategies are not only technological innovations but also cultural shifts that foster consumer awareness, producer responsibility, and systemic change. Their integration into broader circular economy frameworks highlights the potential for packaging reform to drive sustainability across the agri-food chain.

Environmental and Economic Impact of Food Waste

Food waste stands as one of the most striking symptoms of the failure of the linear agri-food model. Under the prevailing "produce–consume–discard" logic, vast quantities of food are lost or discarded at every stage of the value chain, leading to structural inefficiencies, significant economic costs, and a profound environmental footprint.

According to the UNEP Food Waste Index Report (2021), over 931 million tonnes of food were wasted in 2022, representing nearly one-third of global food production. This loss encompasses not only the final food products but also the embedded water, soil, energy, and labor required for their production and distribution. The climate impact of food waste is also substantial: if food waste were a country, it would rank as the third-largest emitter of greenhouse gases globally only behind China and the United States (FAO, 2020).

In response, the circular economy proposes a systemic transformation of the food system. Rather than treating surplus food as waste, it encourages valorization, nutrient recovery, and the promotion of a regenerative culture based on shared responsibility. Effective strategies to address food waste include:

- **Food rescue initiatives** that transform rejected products into new consumables.
- **Redistribution of surplus** through food banks, community kitchens, and grassroots markets.
- **Food education and conscious consumption**, which help reduce waste at the household and retail levels.
- **Innovations in smart packaging and digital platforms** that extend shelf life and improve inventory management across the supply chain.

Food loss and waste represent one of the most critical global challenges in the agri-food system. According to the *UNEP Food Waste Index* (2021), approximately 931 million tonnes of food were wasted in 2019 alone, accounting for 17% of the total food available to consumers. However, this waste is unevenly distributed across different sectors, as shown in the following Figure 1:

Figure 1. Food waste distribution by sector

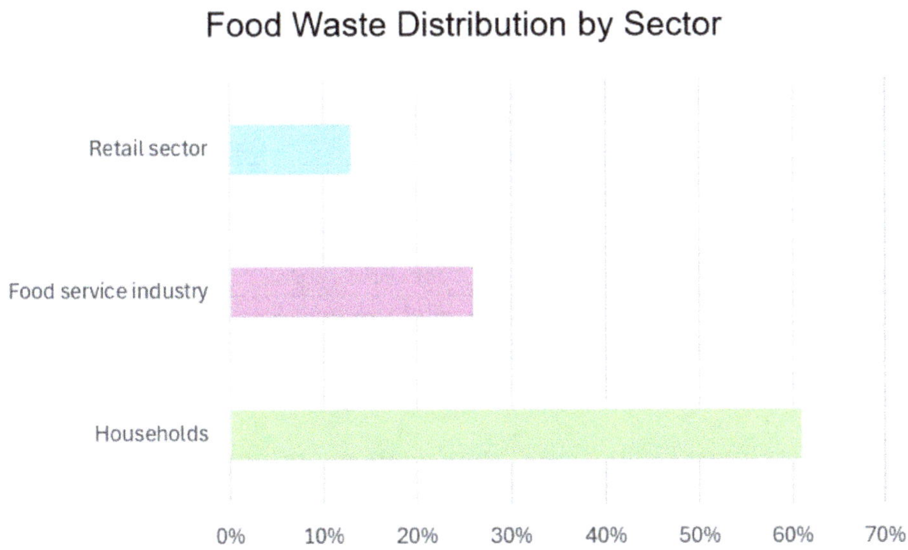

The Food and Agriculture Organization of the United Nations estimates that one-third of all food produced globally is never consumed, representing a loss of approximately 1.3 billion tons per year. This occurs in a context where more than 828 million people suffer from hunger, and 2.3 billion experience moderate or severe food insecurity (FAO, 2022). Table3 below presents these global indicators.

Table 3. Key indicators on food waste and food insecurity

Indicator	Estimated Value
Food wasted	931 million tonnes
Share of total food wasted	17%
Food lost annually	1.3 billion tonnes
People suffering from hunger	828 million
People with moderate or severe food insecurity	2.3 billion
Global economic cost of food waste	Over USD 1 trillion per year

Source: Author's own elaboration based on data from FAO and UNEP.

Food waste not only entails the loss of the final product, but also of all the resources and processes involved in its production: water, land, energy, human labor, transportation, and storage. This phenomenon generates a large-scale cumulative ecological burden, as detailed in Table 4.

Table 4. Environmental consequences of food waste

Environmental Impact	Description
Greenhouse Gas Emissions	Food waste generates 8%–10% of global GHG emissions. If it were a country, it would be the third largest emitter after China and the United States.
Water Overuse	Producing uneaten food consumes approximately 250 km^3 of freshwater per year equivalent to the annual flow of major global rivers.
Soil Degradation & Biodiversity Loss	Unnecessary production leads to deforestation, fertilizer overuse, habitat loss, and pollinator decline.
Energy Waste	All energy used in planting, harvesting, processing, packaging, and transportation is lost along with wasted food.

Source: Author's own elaboration

Economic and Social Dimensions of Food Waste and the Transition to Circular Agri-food Systems

From an economic standpoint, food waste represents an annual loss exceeding one trillion USD, not including indirect costs related to public health, environmental degradation, or the lost opportunities for local producers. Moreover, it perpetuates the inefficiencies of the linear model, where overproduction, visual standardization, and the intentional destruction of surpluses are incentivized to maintain competitiveness in markets dominated by large corporations.

In contrast to this unsustainable model, **circular economy principles** and **food sovereignty** call for a structural transformation of the system, guided by the following pillars:

- **Redesigning value chains** to prevent losses at the source.
- **Redistributing surplus food** through food banks, community kitchens, and solidarity networks.
- **Promoting territorial supply systems**, which have a lower ecological footprint and foster social equity.
- **Encouraging responsible consumption and food education** as tools for cultural change.

The structural reduction of food waste does not rely solely on technological solutions. It requires political decisions, cultural transformations, and active community participation that reframe food as a common good, not as a disposable commodity. The transition toward sustainable agri-food systems cannot be achieved solely through production or institutional policies. Consumption understood as both a daily practice and a political act plays a transformative role, directly affecting the sustainability of the system. In this context, sustainable consumption, community organization, and food sovereignty emerge as foundational pillars of a circular economy based on social justice, ecological efficiency, and territorial resilience (FAO, 2021; United Nations Environment Programme, 2020). Sustainable consumption entails redefining decisions regarding purchasing, eating, and food distribution, not only for individual reasons, but as part of a collective process aimed at reducing waste, supporting local production, and promoting regenerative systems.

A key strategy in this framework involves diets based on local biodiversity, which celebrate native species, traditional foods, and cultural practices of specific territories. These diets provide essential nutrients while also encouraging ecological conservation and reinforcing food sovereignty. Models such as the Mesoamerican milpa system which integrates maize, beans, squash, and chili stand as living examples of agroecological, culturally relevant, and sustainable food systems (Toledo & Barrera-Bassols, 2008). In parallel, the recovery of food surpluses and the role of food banks serve as circular mechanisms to reduce waste and combat food insecurity. According to FAO (2022), recovering just 25% of wasted food could feed 870 million people, equivalent to the number of individuals suffering from hunger globally. These initiatives also foster solidarity networks, generate local employment, and, in some cases, transform surpluses into processed goods like preserves or flours, adding value to the territorial economy. However, such change will not be possible without a deep commitment to education for conscious consumption. From homes, schools, and media platforms, society must promote an understanding of the environmental and social impacts of our food choices. School garden programs, ecolabel campaigns, ecological footprint calculators, and digital platforms that connect consumers with producers are vital tools to empower citizens as agents of change (UNESCO, 2021).

At the same time, organized community movements play a central role in building a circular and just food system. Responsible consumption cooperatives, for example, reconfigure the relationship between production and consumption through solidarity, fair trade, and horizontal governance. These organizations eliminate speculative intermediaries, strengthen local economies, and educate members on environmental and social co-responsibility practices. Urban agriculture and community gardens are additional expressions of food sovereignty within cities. Beyond food production, they function as spaces for environmental regeneration, social cohesion, and popular education. Through composting, rainwater harvesting, and sustainable technologies such as hydroponics or vertical farming, these spaces close material cycles, reduce waste, and reinforce neighborhood self-reliance. Eventually, transforming the agri-food system demands a critical, organized, and active citizenry, capable of reimagining food as a common good rather than a disposable commodity. Integrating sustainable consumption with collective action allows society to advance toward a circular economy model that is not only materially efficient, but also just democratic, and culturally vibrant.

Integration of Renewable Energy and Energy Efficiency in Food Production and Processing

The transition toward sustainable and regenerative agri-food systems requires not only ecological practices and territorial governance but also the integration of clean energy sources that reduce the sector's environmental footprint. Given the high dependence of food production and processing on fossil fuels ranging from irrigation and machinery to refrigeration and transport the adoption of renewable energy and energy efficiency technologies has become a strategic imperative. These innovations contribute not only to reducing greenhouse gas emissions, but also to enhancing the autonomy, resilience, and productivity of rural territories. Circular economy principles reinforce this transition by promoting decentralized, low-impact energy solutions that close material and energy loops while empowering small-scale producers.

Solar Energy in Agriculture

Solar energy has become one of the most accessible, modular, and scalable sources for the agricultural sector. Its implementation includes:

- **Solar-powered irrigation systems**, replacing diesel engines in regions such as Mexico's Bajío or Colombia's Valle del Cauca, significantly reducing both costs and emissions.
- **Solar dryers**, used to preserve fruits, grains, and spices without electricity, as seen in Indigenous communities in Guatemala for coffee and cacao processing.
- **Passive solar greenhouses**, which allow thermal control without fossil fuels essential in cold climate zones.

Various international cooperation programs have developed autonomous rural solar kits with batteries and sensors, designed for small-scale farmers without access to the electrical grid (Deutsche Gesellschaft für Internationale Zusammenarbeit, 2019).

Biogas in Agro-Industry

Anaerobic digestion technology enables the conversion of organic waste such as manure, crop residues, and food waste into biogas and natural fertilizer. This not only provides renewable local energy but also reduces methane emissions and replaces highly polluting synthetic fertilizers. A notable example is Nestlé's plant in Lagos de Moreno, Mexico, which transforms 8,000 tons of organic waste per year into energy, illustrating the potential of this technology for rural energy self-sufficiency and climate resilience (European Biogas Association, 2023). Another emerging field is the **production of bioplastics** from agricultural waste, allowing the replacement of conventional plastics with biodegradable materials derived from sugarcane bagasse, corn starch, or potato peels. Startups such as *AgriLoop* (Spain) are spearheading this transition, producing compostable packaging and utensils, fostering green innovation and generating sustainable jobs in biomass-rich areas (European Bioplastics, 2022).

Decentralized Biogas Systems

Biogas is also produced and utilized on a small scale.

AI and Smart Waste Management

Artificial intelligence is revolutionizing waste management through predictive, automated, and connected tools. Systems like *Winnow* have reduced food waste in industrial kitchens by up to 50% using machine learning algorithms.

Energy Efficiency Across the Food System

Energy efficiency is essential for optimizing resource use and lowering operational costs throughout the food supply chain. To advance towards a truly sustainable food system, it is necessary to integrate renewable energy sources, energy-efficient technologies, and smart digital tools to optimize processes at every stage of the value chain.

The following table summarizes key strategies and technological solutions applied to the agri-food sector under a circular economy framework. They are grouped into three main dimensions:

1. **Renewable energy sources** tailored to rural and agro-industrial contexts,
2. **Energy efficiency technologies** for food production, preservation, and distribution,
3. **Applications of AI and big data** to optimize logistics, reduce emissions, and enhance digital inclusion among small-scale producers.

The transition toward a sustainable agri-food system requires the integration of renewable energy sources, energy-efficient technologies, and smart digital tools. This comprehensive approach not only reduces the sector's environmental footprint, but also enhances energy autonomy, operational efficiency, and the inclusion of small-scale producers. In rural and agro-industrial contexts, such innovations are instrumental in optimizing irrigation, food processing, distribution logistics, and cold chain infrastructure, while also promoting resilience and reducing greenhouse gas emissions. Table 5 summarizes key applications across three interconnected categories: (1) renewable energy sources adapted to agricultural settings; (2) energy efficiency technologies in food preservation, lighting, and transport; and (3) artificial intelligence and big data tools applied to logistics and smallholder support. Each row links specific innovations with their anticipated impacts, demonstrating the transformative potential of circular strategies in the agri-food sector (Raygoza-L. *et al.*, 2025).

Table 5. Renewable energy, energy efficiency, and smart technologies in the agri-food system

Subcategory	Applications / Technologies / Examples	Benefits / Expected Outcomes
Solar	Irrigation pumping systems, solar dryers, passive greenhouse climate control	Reduced operational costs and fossil fuel dependence; enhanced energy autonomy
Biogas	Thermal and electric energy generation in agro-industries and family farms	Waste utilization, methane reduction, production of organic fertilizers
Wind	Water pumping in arid regions, hybrid microturbines, refrigeration in artisanal fisheries	Off-grid solutions, use of natural resources, reduced diesel consumption
Refrigeration	Direct solar cooling, solar-powered cold storage, CO_2 absorption-based systems	Lower energy use, improved food preservation, access in remote areas
Lighting	Agricultural LED lighting, natural light tunnels, automated switching systems	Cost reduction, environmental improvement, increased operational efficiency
Distribution logistics	Electric vehicles, solar battery systems, cold-chain delivery bicycles	Lower carbon footprint, efficient delivery systems, reduced urban congestion

continued on following page

Table 5. Continued

Subcategory	Applications / Technologies / Examples	Benefits / Expected Outcomes
Route optimization	EVOLVE Logística (Mexico): AI-driven shorter routes and reduced fuel consumption	22% fewer kilometers traveled and 18% fuel savings
Delivery time reduction	AlimenCoop (Spain): dynamic order clustering	40% reduction in delivery time; improved logistics efficiency
Support for small producers	Agros (Colombia), Chiapas (Mexico): AI-based apps for optimized rural delivery routes	Up to 25% energy savings; enhanced digital inclusion for isolated communities

Source: Author's own elaboration

SUCCESS STORIES, CHALLENGES, AND ROADMAP FOR A CIRCULAR AND SOVEREIGN FOOD SYSTEM

The application of circular economy principles and food sovereignty is already a tangible reality across multiple regions worldwide. Various experiences demonstrate that it is possible to build sustainable, regenerative, and culturally relevant agri-food models by recovering traditional practices, fostering technological innovation, and strengthening local economies. The following table 6 summarizes selected international success stories that may serve as references for the adaptation and scaling of transformative territorial policies:

Table 6. International cases of circular economy and food sovereignty

Region	Success Story	Description
Latin America	Agroforestry in the Amazon	Integration of trees and food crops to restore soils, promote biodiversity, and improve local incomes.
	Regenerative agriculture in the Andes	Systems that combine ancestral techniques with modern practices to capture carbon and strengthen community-based food production.
	Peasant cooperatives and local markets	Networks of fair trade and agroecology that empower smallholders and promote short supply chains.
Europe	EU Bioeconomy Strategy	A political framework driving circular economy, agricultural sustainability, and bioproduct innovation since 2012.
	Organic production and quality certifications	Systems ensuring traceability and high added value through recognized sustainable practices.
	Advanced composting and recycling	Technologies for organic waste treatment converting it into fertilizers or energy (Germany, Netherlands).

continued on following page

Table 6. Continued

Region	Success Story	Description
Africa & Asia	Agroecology and climate resilience	Community initiatives recovering native seeds and promoting regenerative practices in response to climate change (Ethiopia, Senegal).
	Circular rice production in Asia	Alternate wetting, biofertilizers, and waste reuse to reduce methane emissions (India, Philippines).
	Rural food sovereignty initiatives	Projects aimed at strengthening food self-sufficiency and the right to shape food systems (Nepal, Kenya).

Source: Author's own elaboration

These experiences will be analyzed in detail in the following sections, with a focus on circular technologies, community-based strategies, and replicable public policies.

Among the main obstacles are limited access to financing for small and medium-sized producers, difficulties in acquiring clean technologies (such as bio-inputs, composting systems, and solar irrigation), and the lack of appropriate infrastructure for local food processing. Moreover, products derived from circular systems often lack recognized certifications or access to competitive marketing channels, limiting their reach in the marketplace (FAO, 2022; United Nations Environment Programme, 2021).

The loss of traditional knowledge and the cultural marginalization of agroecological practices hinder the continuity of resilient agricultural systems. Resistance within conventional agri-industrial models persists, reinforced by regulations designed around linear chains. Additionally, the unequal distribution of technological benefits often favors urban areas or capital-rich producers, exacerbating access inequalities (Altieri & Nicholls, 2020).

Despite these barriers, the transition to a circular model offers vast opportunities to transform the food system:

- **New sustainable business models**, such as direct marketing platforms, regenerative agro-consulting services, or local processing with added value.
- **Application of emerging technologies**, including AI, sensors, and drones that optimize water, fertilizer, and energy use.
- **Development of bio-inputs, biomaterials, and bioenergy** from organic waste, enabling closed-loop systems, income diversification, and carbon footprint reduction.

When implemented with an inclusive approach, these innovations can enhance productive autonomy, digital sovereignty, and local competitiveness.

FINAL RECOMMENDATIONS AND ROADMAP TOWARD A CIRCULAR AND SOVEREIGN FOOD SYSTEM

Building a fair, regenerative, and resilient food model requires a shared roadmap among governments, civil society, local communities, responsible businesses, and academia. The following strategic actions are proposed to support this transition.

Key Actions for Governments and Policymakers

- **Regulatory reforms aligned with the circular economy**, including clean production standards, sustainable certification systems, fiscal incentives, and penalties for food waste.
- **Comprehensive support for family and community farming**, including financing, technical training, and promotion of agroecological systems, milpas, polycultures, and native seed conservation. According to FAO (2019), family farming accounts for 70–80% of global food production.
- **Promotion of energy transition in agriculture**, through subsidies for solar panels, biodigesters, microturbines, and clean irrigation systems, thereby increasing rural energy autonomy.

Strategies for Civil Society and Rural Communities

- **Promotion of self-managed food systems**, such as seed banks, urban gardens, agroecological cooperatives, and local consumption networks.
- **Food and knowledge exchange networks**, via community platforms, farmers' markets, and partnerships with academic institutions.
- **Active participation in responsible consumption movements**, by choosing locally produced, pesticide-free, fair-trade, and low-impact food products.

These strategies not only strengthen food sovereignty and territorial circularity but also consolidate new regenerative economies oriented toward the common good.

Toward a Transformative and Inclusive Agenda

The transformation of the food system demands a clear and multisectoral roadmap that connects government leadership, community participation, civil society advocacy, and scientific-technological support. Advancing toward a fairer, regenerative, and resilient model implies designing integrative public policies, promoting social and technological innovation, and reinforcing territorial participation.

Two strategic axes are identified:

1. **The role of decision-makers**, who must implement regulatory frameworks grounded in circular economy principles, including production norms, fiscal mechanisms, and strong legal tools to prevent waste.
2. **The protagonism of rural and urban communities**, through grassroots food initiatives, seed preservation, local trade, and environmental stewardship.

Simultaneously, fostering circular consumption and community mobilization allows everyday decisions such as what to eat, where to buy, and how to support local production to become acts of resistance and regeneration.

Community food initiatives, responsible consumption cooperatives, and urban farming not only provide sustenance but regenerate ecosystems, build solidarity, and reframe food as a public good rather than a disposable commodity. The convergence between sustainable consumption, collective action, and circular economy offers realistic and necessary responses to today's global crises hunger, ecological collapse, and social inequality. Far from utopian, this vision is grounded in lived experiences and ready to scale.

CONCLUSION

The transformation of the global agri-food system represents one of the most urgent and complex challenges of the 21st century. The scientific and empirical evidence presented throughout this chapter underscores the unsustainability of food models grounded in a linear economy marked by waste, fossil fuel dependence, corporate concentration, and ecological degradation in the face of climate change, food insecurity, and deepening social inequality. In this context, the convergence of circular economy principles with food sovereignty emerges not only as a viable alternative but as a structural necessity to uphold the human right to food, restore ecosystems, and foster resilient territories. The circular economy, when applied to the food sector, offers systemic strategies to close production loops, reduce losses and waste, repurpose resources, integrate renewable energy, and promote low-impact, context-appropriate technologies. In parallel, food sovereignty provides the political, cultural, and ethical framework that enables communities to define their own food systems based on social justice, biocultural diversity, and territorial autonomy. Together, these frameworks support a transition toward regenerative agroecological models that nourish not only populations with nutritious food, but also revitalize identities, strengthen local economies, and enhance the resilience of rural and urban communities alike.

The documented benefits across environmental, social, and economic dimensions including reductions in greenhouse gas emissions, recovery of ancestral knowledge, creation of green jobs, technological inclusion, and the development of short supply chains demonstrate that this transformation is not utopian. Rather, it is technically feasible and socially desirable. However, its realization demands sustained collective effort, coherent public policies, appropriate incentives, access to circular technologies, decentralized infrastructure, education for conscious consumption, and, most critically, the political will to challenge entrenched power structures that dominate global food systems. This chapter has outlined a roadmap that involves all societal actors governments, producers, consumers, cooperatives, academia, and civil society in building a new food economy anchored in the common good, ecological regeneration, and equity. Overcoming extractive paradigms and rejecting the reduction of food to a mere commodity requires the imagination, design, and defense of a fundamentally different model one where food becomes a deeply political, relational, and ecological act. In this light, circular economy and food sovereignty are not isolated concepts but foundational pillars of a broader civilizational transformation that places life and sustainability at the center.

REFERENCES

Agencia, S. I. N. C. (2021). *El sistema alimentario mundial genera el 34% de las emisiones de gases de efecto invernadero*. https://www.agenciasinc.es

Altieri, M. A., & Nicholls, C. I. (2017). Agroecology: A brief account of its origins and currents of thought in Latin America. *Agroecology and Sustainable Food Systems, 41*(3–4), 231–237. DOI: 10.1080/21683565.2017.1287147

Altieri, M. A., & Nicholls, C. I. (2020). *Agroecología: Bases científicas para una agricultura sustentable*. CLACSO.

Coraggio, J. L. (2011). *Economía social y solidaria: El trabajo antes que el capital*. Ediciones Abya Yala.

Deutsche Gesellschaft für Internationale Zusammenarbeit. (2019). *Solar-powered irrigation systems: A farmer's guide*. https://www.giz.de/en/downloads/giz2019-en-solar-powered-irrigation.pdf

Ellen MacArthur Foundation. (2019). *Cities and circular economy for food*. https://ellenmacarthurfoundation.org/cities-and-circular-economy-for-food

Ellen MacArthur Foundation. (2019). *Completing the picture: How the circular economy tackles climate change*. https://ellenmacarthurfoundation.org/completing-the-picture-climate-change

Ellen MacArthur Foundation. (2021). *The new plastics economy global commitment*. https://ellenmacarthurfoundation.org

European Biogas Association. (2023). *Biogas: Fit for the future*. https://www.europeanbiogas.eu

European Bioplastics. (2022). *Bioplastics market data 2022*. https://www.european-bioplastics.org/market

FAO. (2014). *The state of food and agriculture: Innovation in family farming*. https://www.fao.org/3/i4040e/i4040e.pdf

FAO. (2019). *El estado de la agricultura y la alimentación en el mundo*. https://www.fao.org/3/ca6030es/ca6030es.pdf

FAO. (2020). *Emissions due to agriculture*. https://www.fao.org/3/ca1334en/ca1334en.pdf

FAO. (2021). *The state of food and agriculture 2021: Making agrifood systems more resilient to shocks and stresses*. https://www.fao.org/publications/sofa/2021

FAO. (2022). *Food systems and climate change*. https://www.fao.org/climate-change

FAO & IFOAM. (2020). *Bioinsumos: Herramientas clave para la sostenibilidad de la agricultura*. https://www.fao.org/3/ca6797es/ca6797es.pdf

Food, E. I. T. (2023). *The future of sustainable food systems in Europe*. https://www.eitfood.eu

Gliessman, S. R. (2016). *Agroecology: The ecology of sustainable food systems* (3rd ed.). CRC Press.

González de Molina, M., & Toledo, V. M. (2014). *The social metabolism: A socio-ecological theory of historical change*. Springer., DOI: 10.1007/978-3-319-06358-4

HLPE. (2013). *Investing in smallholder agriculture for food security*. High Level Panel of Experts on Food Security and Nutrition. https://www.fao.org/3/i2953e/i2953e.pdf

IPBES. (2019). *Global assessment report on biodiversity and ecosystem services*. https://ipbes.net/global-assessment

IPCC. (2019). *Climate change and land: An IPCC special report on climate change, desertification, land degradation, sustainable land management, food security, and greenhouse gas fluxes in terrestrial ecosystems*. https://www.ipcc.ch/srccl/

Kamilaris, A., Kartakoullis, A., & Prenafeta-Boldú, F. X. (2017). A review on the practice of big data analysis in agriculture. *Computers and Electronics in Agriculture*, *143*, 23–37. DOI: 10.1016/j.compag.2017.09.037

La Vía Campesina. (2019). *Declaration of the rights of peasants and other people working in rural areas*. https://viacampesina.org/en/declaration-of-the-rights-of-peasants/

Mollison, B. (1990). *Permaculture: A practical guide for a sustainable future*. Island Press.

Patel, R. (2009). Food sovereignty. *The Journal of Peasant Studies*, *36*(3), 663–706. DOI: 10.1080/03066150903143079

Poore, J., & Nemecek, T. (2018). Reducing food's environmental impacts through producers and consumers. *Science*, *360*(6392), 987–992. DOI: 10.1126/science.aaq0216 PMID: 29853680

Raygoza-L., M. E., Orduño-Osuna, J. H., Trujillo-Hernández, G., & Murrieta-Rico, F. N. (2025). AI in public administration: Transformative opportunities for climate resilience and sustainable development. *Revista de Ciencia, Innovación y Tecnología, 8*(2), Artículo e398. https://doi.org/DOI: 10.37636/recit.v8n2e398

Raygoza-Limón, M. E., Orduño-Osuna, J. H., Trujillo-Hernández, G., Bravo-Zanoguera, M. E., Amezquita Garcia, J. A., Ramírez-Hernández, L. R., Flores-Fuentes, W., Antúnez-García, J., & Murrieta-Rico, F. N. (2025). Supply chain management in renewable energy projects from a life cycle perspective: A review. *Applied Sciences (Basel, Switzerland), 15*(9), 5043. DOI: 10.3390/app15095043

Richards, M., & Sander, B. O. (2014). *Alternate wetting and drying in irrigated rice: Implementation guidance for policymakers and investors*. CGIAR Research Program on Climate Change, Agriculture and Food Security. https://cgspace.cgiar.org/handle/10568/35421

Rockström, J., Steffen, W., Noone, K., Persson, Å., Chapin, F. S.III, Lambin, E., Lenton, T. M., Scheffer, M., Folke, C., Schellnhuber, H. J., Nykvist, B., de Wit, C. A., Hughes, T., van der Leeuw, S., Rodhe, H., Sörlin, S., Snyder, P. K., Costanza, R., Svedin, U., & Foley, J. A. (2017). A safe operating space for humanity. *Nature, 461*(7263), 472–475. DOI: 10.1038/461472a PMID: 19779433

Schneider, M., & McMichael, P. (2011). Deepening, and repairing, the metabolic rift. *The Journal of Peasant Studies, 37*(3), 461–484. DOI: 10.1080/03066150.2010.494371 PMID: 20645448

Toledo, V. M., & Barrera-Bassols, N. (2008). *La memoria biocultural: La importancia ecológica de las sabidurías tradicionales*. Icaria Editorial.

UNESCO. (2021). *Education for sustainable development: A roadmap*. https://unesdoc.unesco.org/ark:/48223/pf0000374802

United Nations. (2022). *World population prospects 2022: Summary of results*. United Nations, Department of Economic and Social Affairs. https://www.un.org/development/desa/pd/content/world-population-prospects-20224

United Nations Environment Programme. (2020). *Preventing the next pandemic: Zoonotic diseases and how to break the chain of transmission*. https://www.unep.org/resources/report/preventing-future-zoonotic-disease-outbreaks

United Nations Environment Programme. (2021). *Food waste index report 2021*. https://www.unep.org/resources/report/unep-food-waste-index-report-2021

Wolfert, S., Ge, L., Verdouw, C., & Bogaardt, M.-J. (2017). Big data in smart farming – A review. *Agricultural Systems, 153*, 69–80. DOI: 10.1016/j.agsy.2017.01.023

KEY TERMS AND DEFINITIONS

Agri-food systems: Integrated networks that encompass the production, processing, distribution, consumption, and disposal of food. These systems involve ecological, economic, and social interactions across local and global scales.

Artificial Intelligence (AI): The simulation of human intelligence in machines: allowing them to perform tasks such as learning, reasoning, and decision-making. In agri-food systems, AI is used for precision agriculture, logistics optimization, and waste management.

Circular economy: An economic model that prioritizes the reuse, recycling, and regeneration of resources, aiming to close production loops and minimize waste. Applied to food systems, it promotes sustainable practices such as composting, local sourcing, and renewable energy integration.

Degradation: The process by which natural ecosystems lose their structure, function, or productivity due to human activity or environmental stressors. In food systems, degradation includes soil erosion, biodiversity loss, and water contamination caused by industrial agriculture.

Food sovereignty: The right of peoples and communities to define their own food systems, prioritizing culturally appropriate, ecologically sustainable, and locally controlled production and distribution. It opposes dependency on globalized supply chains.

Food waste: Edible food that is discarded, lost, or uneaten throughout the supply chain, from production to consumption. Food waste contributes significantly to greenhouse gas emissions and resource inefficiency.

Renewable energy: Energy derived from natural sources that are continuously replenished, such as solar, wind, hydro, and biogas. Its use in agri-food systems reduces fossil fuel dependency and carbon emissions.

Resource efficiency: The strategic use of natural resources to achieve maximum output with minimal environmental impact. In food systems, this involves optimizing inputs like water, soil, and energy while minimizing losses.

Sustainable consumption: The practice of choosing, using, and disposing of food and resources in ways that support environmental health, social equity, and economic viability. It includes reducing food waste and supporting local and ethical food sources.

Territorial resilience: The capacity of a specific region or community to adapt to and recover from environmental, economic, or social disruptions. In the context of food systems, it refers to local self-sufficiency, circular production models, and community empowerment.

Chapter 4
Economic and Sustainability Perspectives on Organic and Conventional Banana Farming

P. Naveen Kumar
https://orcid.org/0000-0003-3839-1329
Amrita School of Agricultural Sciences, Amrita Vishwa Vidyapeetham, Coimbatore, India

M. Yasodha
https://orcid.org/0000-0002-0933-2621
Amrita School of Agricultural Science, Amrita Vishwa Vidyapeetham, Coimbatore, India

Thomas Felix Kannan
https://orcid.org/0000-0002-9285-9765
ADRTC, Institute for Social and Economic Change, Bengaluru, India

ABSTRACT

India, with 60% of its population reliant on agriculture, faces challenges like soil degradation and excessive chemical use, threatening sustainability. Despite ranking second in global organic farmland and first in organic producers, India lacks comparative studies on the profitability of organic versus conventional farming. This study addresses this gap through a cost-and-return analysis of organic and conventional banana farming in Tamil Nadu. Using multistage sampling, 40 organic and 40 conventional farmers from Coimbatore were surveyed. Results show organic

DOI: 10.4018/979-8-3373-9923-2.ch004

farming has 13.56% higher production costs but earns higher net income (6,12,583/ha) and a better benefit-cost ratio (3.40) than conventional farming (4,65,081/ha; BCR 3.07). Although yields are slightly lower, organic farming offers benefits like soil health and premium pricing. Key adoption drivers include reduced chemical use and consumer demand, while barriers include high initial costs and certification challenges. Policy support, input subsidies, and market infrastructure are essential for broader adoption.

INTRODUCTION

Background of Indian Agriculture and Sustainability Concerns

India is an agrarian nation, with approximately 60 percent of its population directly or indirectly relying on agriculture. In ancient times, the practice of agriculture was regarded as a paramount service to society, being deeply intertwined with their traditions and culture (Pandey et al., 2019). Over the past 30 years, cropping intensity has risen from 118% to 135%. However, the expansion of agriculture has led to a rapid decline in arable land. One of the most significant challenges is the excessive use of chemical fertilizers, which gradually degrade soil quality (Gir & Pokhrel, 2022) and pose long-term environmental risks. Additionally, land degradation caused by human activities, such as mining, further disrupts the soil and surrounding areas, aggravating the issue. To overcome this issue, practice of organic farming is highly recommended. Organic farming (OF) promotes a significant increase in microbial activity, which can help offset any potential yield reductions when applying equal quantities of nutrients through organic methods (Tautges et al., 2016; Lori et al., 2017; Ricono et al., 2024). Organic farming has been shown to improve soil structure, water-holding capacity, and nutrient cycling, ultimately leading to higher and more consistent yields over the long term (Singh et al., 2023).

The Role of Organic Farming in Sustainable Agriculture

Organic farming plays a vital role in making agriculture more sustainable by balancing environmental health, economic profitability, and social well-being. It contributes to sustainability in several key ways, including improving soil health, promoting biodiversity, maintaining water quality, and helping combat climate change.

One of the biggest benefits of organic farming is its positive impact on soil health. By increasing organic matter, improving soil structure, and encouraging microbial activity, organic practices help maintain fertile and resilient soils. Techniques like crop rotation, using organic manure, and minimizing soil disturbance all contribute to healthier soils (Kareem et al., 2022; Wijesinghe et al., 2023). Organic farming also plays a crucial role in supporting biodiversity. It creates habitats for various species, including birds, beneficial insects, and soil organisms. This, in turn, helps with natural pest control and pollination, leading to a more balanced ecosystem (Kazi et al., 2014; Gamage et al., 2023).

Another important aspect is water quality. Since organic farming avoids synthetic fertilizers and pesticides, it significantly reduces the risk of water pollution. Cleaner water sources mean healthier aquatic ecosystems and less risk of issues like eutrophication, which can harm marine life (Kareem et al., 2022; Wijesinghe et al., 2023). When it comes to climate change, organic farming contributes through carbon sequestration and lower greenhouse gas emissions. Practices like using cover crops and organic soil amendments help trap carbon in the soil, making it a valuable tool in climate mitigation (Gamage et al., 2023).

On the economic front, organic farming can be financially beneficial for farmers. While organic yields may sometimes be slightly lower than conventional yields, farmers often earn more due to premium prices for organic products and lower input costs. Additionally, organic farming can boost rural economies by creating jobs and supporting local markets, thus adding value to agricultural products (Nastase, 2013; Rahmaniah et al., 2020).

Finally, the social benefits of organic farming are significant. Organic food is free from synthetic chemicals, making it a healthier and safer choice for consumers. Research also suggests that organic products often have higher nutritional content and fewer harmful residues (Kazi et al., 2014; Singh et al., 2023). Beyond food quality, organic farming fosters a stronger sense of community and environmental responsibility. It supports the well-being of farming communities by encouraging sustainable practices and a deeper connection to the land (Soni & Yadav, 2019; Rahmaniah et al., 2020). Overall, organic farming isn't just about growing food without chemicals it's focused on building a more sustainable and resilient agricultural system that benefits farmers, consumers, and the environment.

Global Position in Organic Farming: Trends and Statistics

The global organic farming area expanded by 2.5 million hectares in 2023, totalling nearly 99 million hectares. That same year, organic food sales reached approximately 136 billion euros. Currently, nearly 188 countries are engaged in organic farming activities. In 2023, organic agricultural land expanded across all regions except North America and Oceania (Figure 1). Latin America saw the highest absolute growth at 10.8%, followed by Europe at 4.1% and Africa at 24.4%. In contrast, organic farmland declined in North America by 7.7% and in Oceania by 0.02%.

Figure 1. Organic Agriculture land (OAL) around the world

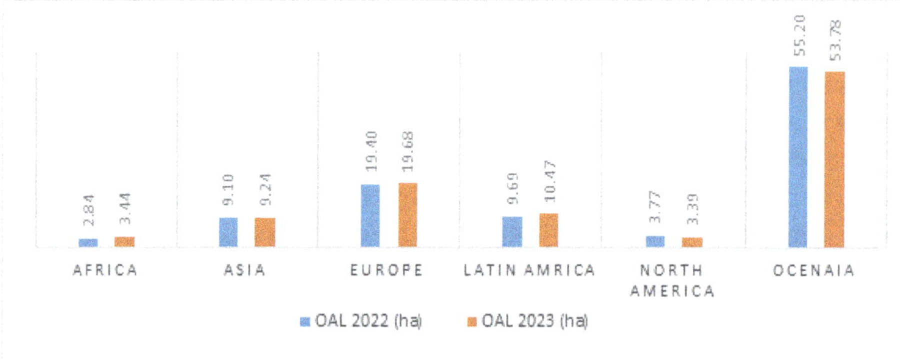

Source: FiBL,2025

Australia had the largest organic agricultural land, with an estimated 99% of it being extensive grazing areas. India ranked second, followed by Argentina in third place (Willer et al., 2025). India ranks second position in organic producers and exporter of organic products such as rice, cocoa, coffee, dry pulses, fruits, oilseeds, vegetables, sugar and organic cakes. Organic products are exported to countries including the USA, European Union, Canada, the United Kingdom, Sri Lanka, Switzerland, Vietnam, Australia, Thailand, New Zealand, Japan, and South Korea (APEDA, 2025).

In India, Maharashtra is the leading producer of organic products, followed by Madhya Pradesh, Rajasthan, Karnataka, and Gujarat. Among organic commodities, fiber crops account for the largest share, followed by oilseeds, sugar crops, cereals and millets, medicinal/herbal and aromatic plants, spices and condiments, fresh fruits and vegetables, pulses, and tea and coffee (APEDA, 2025). Sikkim, India's first fully organic state, has been recognized for its outstanding policies promoting sustainable food systems. The Food and Agriculture Organization (FAO) awarded Sikkim the prestigious Future Policy Award 2018, often referred to as the "Oscar for best policies." Sikkim emerged victorious from a pool of 51 nominees from 25 countries, earning this esteemed accolade for its pioneering efforts in agro-ecological practices (PIB, 2023).

According to the Tamil Nadu Policy Note (2024), Tamil Nadu ranks 14th in India for organic farming, with 31,629 hectares dedicated to organic practices. This land comprises 14,086 hectares of certified organic area and 17,543 hectares undergoing the certification process. In 2020-2021, the state held the 11th position in organic food production, yielding 24,826 tonnes, of which 4,223 tonnes were exported.

Figure 2. Area under organic farming in Tamil Nadu over five years

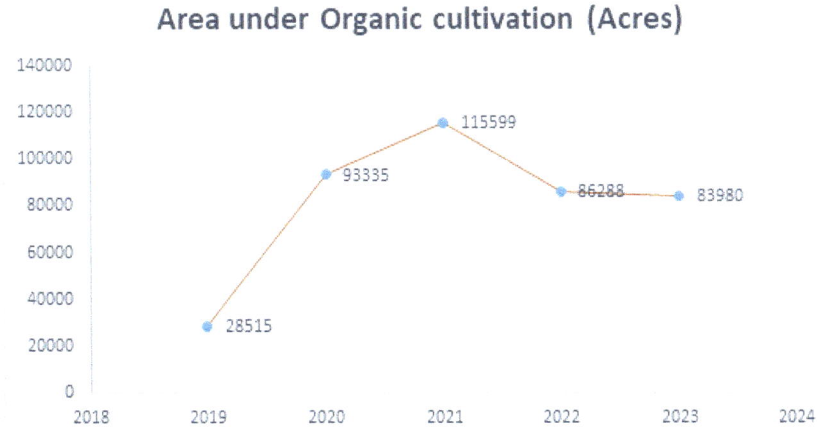

Figure 2 illustrates the area dedicated to organic farming in Tamil Nadu. A substantial expansion is evident between 2019 and 2021, with the land under organic cultivation increasing dramatically from 28,515 acres to 115,599 acres. However, this growth trend reversed after 2021, as the area began to contract, falling to 86,288 acres in 2022 and further to 83,980 acres in 2023 (Tamil Nadu Policy Note, 2024).

Rationale for Studying Organic vs. Conventional Banana Farming

The rising global demand for organic products is driven by consumer preferences for healthier and environmentally friendly products (Ribeiro et al., 2012; Castro et al., 2015). This demand can provide economic opportunities for farmers who adopt organic practices. Organic banana farming can be economically viable, especially when considering lower price volatility and the potential for higher market prices. However, the transition to organic farming can involve higher initial costs and technical challenges (Coulis et al., 2022). Existing literature provides a limited comparative analysis of organic and conventional farming, particularly in terms of cost of cultivation and profitability. Many studies fail to offer a detailed or in-depth examination of these critical aspects. While cost of cultivation is a key factor, previous research often lacks a comprehensive assessment of costs, returns, and overall profitability in organic farming (Majunatha & Puttaswamaiah, 2021). To bridge this gap, this study aims to conduct a thorough comparison of the costs and returns associated with both organic and conventional farming practices.

Objectives of the study:

- To estimate the costs and returns of organic banana farming vs Conventional farming,
- To explore the reason behind farmer's adoption and non-adoption of organic farming

REVIEW OF LITERATURE

The flowchart illustrates the structured progression of the literature review on organic farming. It begins with foundational concepts and evolves through thematic areas such as comparative studies, economic and social dimensions, environmental impacts, and concludes with post-harvest handling and consumer perspectives (Figure 3.).

Figure 3. Roadmap of the literature review

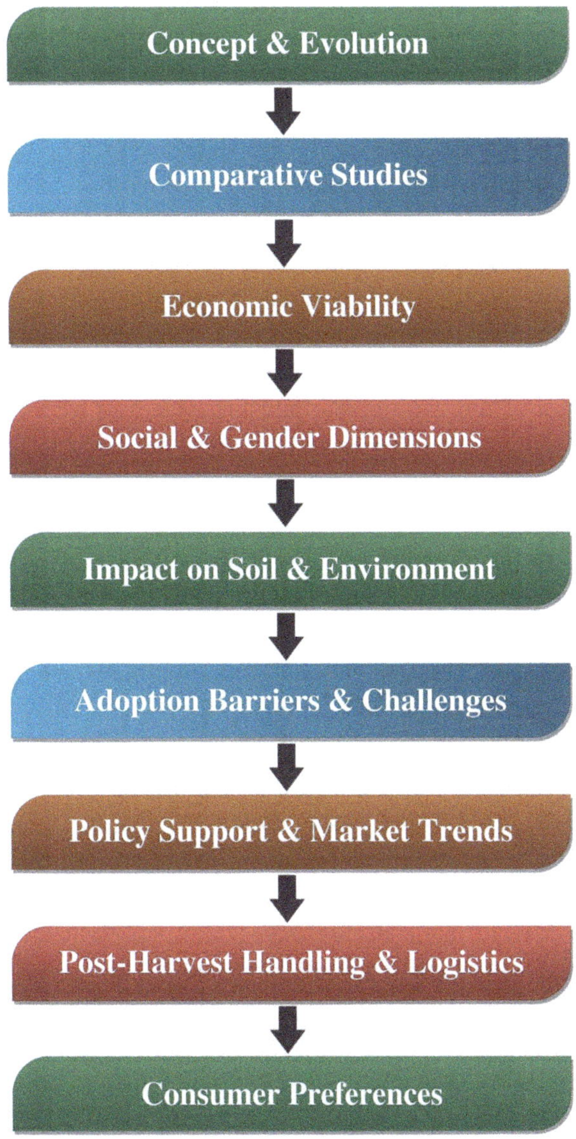

Concept and Evolution of Organic Farming

Organic farming is an agricultural system that prioritizes sustainability, environmental protection, and the conservation of soil and water resources. It avoids synthetic chemicals, genetically modified organisms (GMOs), instead relying on natural processes to maintain soil health and ecosystem balance (Mehla & Kumari, 2012; Kishore et al., 2023).

Historically, organic farming emerged from concerns about soil fertility, sustainable food production, and animal welfare. Before the widespread use of synthetic fertilizers, traditional farming practices such as crop rotation, composting, and manure application were commonly used to enhance soil fertility (Lampkin, 1990). Ancient civilizations, including those in Mesopotamia, India, and China, practiced sustainable agriculture by preserving soil health and biodiversity (King, 2004).

The foundations of modern organic farming were laid by Sir Albert Howard, often regarded as the father of organic agriculture. His work in India emphasized composting, green manuring, and soil fertility, which he documented in An Agricultural Testament (Howard & Moubray, 1940). His principles became the cornerstone of organic farming. Around the same period, J.I. Rodale played a crucial role in popularizing organic farming in the United States during the 1940s and 1950s. Through his publications, such as *Organic Gardening and Farming*, he advocated for soil health and organic food production, significantly influencing the growth of the organic movement (Rodale, 1945).

By the latter half of the 20th century, increasing concerns over chemical pesticide use and food safety led to the establishment of organic certification systems. Organizations such as the UK's Soil Association (established in 1946) and the USDA Organic Certification program (launched in 2002) introduced regulatory standards to ensure the integrity of organic farming practices (Guthman, 2000).

Behera et al. (2012) provide an extensive review of the history and techniques of organic farming, tracing its evolution from traditional agricultural methods to modern organic practices. Their work highlights the contributions of pioneers like Albert Howard and Rudolf Steiner, emphasizing key techniques such as soil health management, composting, crop rotation, and biological pest control. Organic farming not only enhances soil fertility but also contributes to climate change mitigation by reducing greenhouse gas emissions and promoting sustainable food production. Overall, the organic farming movement remains a vital strategy for ecological balance and long-term agricultural sustainability.

Table 1. Comparative studies on organic and conventional farming: Global and Indian perspectives

Aspect	Organic Farming	Conventional Farming	Global Perspective	Indian Perspective
Input Costs	Lower Input costs (Paneerselvam et al., 2010; Khunt et al., 2022; Reddy et al., 2022; Sahu et al., 2024)	Higher input costs (Aslam et al., 2020; Forster et al., 2013; Thakur et al., 2024)	Lower input costs due to reduced use of synthetic fertilizers and pesticides (Ponti et al., 2012)	Lower input costs without affecting net margins (Paneerselvam et al., 2010), reduced costs by 14-19% (Reddy et al., 2022)
Yield	Generally lower yields (80% of conventional) (Ponti et al., 2012)	Higher yields (Ponti et al., 2012; Aslam et al., 2020)	Organic yields are 80% of conventional yields on average (Ponti et al., 2012)	Lower yields for rice and wheat, but higher for intercropping (Paneerselvam et al., 2010), 25% lower yields (Khunt et al., 2022)
Profitability	Potentially higher due to lower costs and price premiums (Khunt et al., 2022; Reddy et al., 2022; Sahu et al., 2024)	Higher gross margins initially, but can be lower due to higher input costs (Forster et al., 2013)	Organic farming can be more profitable due to lower input costs and price premiums (Ponti et al., 2012)	Higher profitability due to lower costs and price premiums (Khunt et al., 2022; Reddy et al., 2022; Sahu et al., 2024)
Food Security	Can improve food security by reducing indebtedness (Paneerselvam et al., 2010)	Higher yields contribute to food security (Aslam et al., 2020)	Organic farming can contribute to food security by reducing input costs (Sahu et al., 2024)	Can improve food security for smallholders by reducing costs and maintaining yields (Paneerselvam et al., 2010)

Economic Feasibility

The study by Srogi et al. (2015) provides a comprehensive cost-benefit analysis comparing conventional and organic olive farming in the Mediterranean region. It highlights that while organic farming incurs higher initial costs due to certification and lower yields, it offers long-term economic and environmental benefits. The study underscores the premium prices and sustainability advantages of organic olives, making them a viable alternative. However, challenges such as pest management and labor intensity remain significant barriers. The research effectively balances economic and ecological perspectives, making it a valuable reference for policymakers and farmers. Overall, it presents a strong case for transitioning to organic practices despite short-term financial constraints. The study by Kuwornu, et al. (2018) provides a comprehensive cost-benefit analysis of conventional and integrated crop management (ICM) systems for vegetable production, highlighting the economic and environmental trade-offs. The findings suggest that ICM practices, while sometimes requiring higher initial investments, offer long-term benefits such as improved soil health, reduced pesticide use, and higher profitability. The research underscores the importance of adopting sustainable farming practices to enhance productivity and resilience. However, the study also identifies challenges in farmer adoption, including knowledge gaps and resource limitations. Overall, it offers valuable insights for policymakers and farmers aiming to balance economic and ecological sustainability in vegetable production.

Akram et al. (2019) evaluate the economic feasibility of organic farming in Pakistan, emphasizing its long-term profitability. The study highlights that lower input costs and premium prices contribute to financial sustainability. However, challenges such as certification expenses, limited market access, and low awareness hinder widespread adoption. The authors suggest that policy support and infrastructure development are essential for promoting organic agriculture. Overall, the paper provides valuable insights into the economic potential of organic farming in Pakistan. Raj (2019) examines the economic viability of organic farming in Himachal Pradesh through an empirical study. The research highlights that organic farming can be financially sustainable due to lower input costs and premium prices for organic produce. However, challenges such as lower initial yields, market access issues, and certification costs pose significant barriers to widespread adoption. The study emphasizes the role of government support and farmer awareness programs in promoting organic practices. Overall, the paper provides valuable insights into the economic potential and constraints of organic farming in hilly regions.

Souza et al. (2024) analyze the economic viability of traditional and organic yerba mate cultivation, focusing on sustainability and market potential. The study finds that while organic yerba mate farming incurs higher initial costs, it offers long-term financial and environmental benefits. Premium pricing and growing consumer demand enhance its profitability, but challenges such as certification expenses and lower initial yields persist. The authors emphasize the need for policy incentives and sustainable farming practices to support organic cultivation. Overall, the paper provides valuable insights into balancing economic feasibility with environmental responsibility in yerba mate production. Uma and Kumar (2025) explore the key issues, challenges, and opportunities in organic fruits production. The study highlights the benefits of organic farming, including sustainability and consumer demand, but also addresses constraints such as high costs and pest management. The authors emphasize the need for policy support and technological advancements to enhance organic fruit cultivation. Overall, the paper provides a well-rounded analysis of the organic fruit industry's future prospects.

Across these studies, a common theme emerges: organic and sustainable farming systems hold strong long-term economic and environmental potential, yet they face significant adoption barriers, particularly in terms of initial costs, certification challenges, and market access. To maximize the benefits of organic farming, targeted policy support, infrastructure development, and farmer education programs are essential.

Social and Gender Dimensions

Organic banana farming, while environmentally sustainable, also involves complex social dynamics, particularly regarding gender roles. Women play a vital role in cultivation and post-harvest activities but often face limited access to land, credit, and training, which restricts their ability to adopt organic practices. Although this review does not include gender-disaggregated data, literature suggests that inclusive extension services and community-based models can enhance women's participation and resilience in organic agriculture (Suresha et al., 2025). Addressing gender disparities is essential for both equity and the long-term sustainability of organic farming systems.

Environmental Sustainability

Organic farming offers several advantages over conventional agriculture, particularly in terms of soil health, biodiversity, and environmental sustainability. Studies have shown that organic practices, such as crop rotation, the use of animal manures, and biological pest control, contribute to improved soil health and increased biodiversity (Lynch et al., 2012; Arora et al., 2024). This is particularly important for banana cultivation, as healthy soil is crucial for the long-term productivity of plantations.

Soil health plays a critical role in sustainable farming, influencing crop yield, environmental sustainability, and food security. Biswas et al. (2014) review the role of organic farming in maintaining soil fertility and sustainability. The authors demonstrate that organic practices enhance soil fertility by increasing soil organic matter and microbial activity, while reducing chemical inputs and improving soil structure. Similarly, Tahat et al. (2020) emphasize the importance of soil biodiversity, organic matter, and nutrient balance in enhancing soil resilience. They highlight sustainable practices such as crop rotation, organic amendments, and reduced tillage, which contribute to long-term agricultural productivity while addressing challenges like soil degradation and climate change. Reeve et al. (2016) further explore the relationship between organic farming, soil health, and food quality, drawing from a broad range of studies. They emphasize that composting, cover cropping, and reduced chemical inputs contribute to healthier soils and more nutritious crops. However, the authors acknowledge that factors such as soil type, climate, and management strategies significantly influence the overall outcomes. Their research underscores the importance of considering long-term environmental and nutritional benefits rather than focusing solely on yield.

Tiwari (2021) conducts a comparative analysis of organic farming practices, examining their effects on soil health, crop yield, and environmental sustainability. The study confirms that organic methods enhance soil fertility and reduce environmental impact, though yield variations depend on factors like soil type and management approaches. Similarly, Wang et al. (2025) investigate the effects of reducing nitrogen fertilizer usage while incorporating organic substitutions in tea plantations. The findings suggest that integrating organic amendments with reduced nitrogen inputs significantly enhances soil health by improving microbial activity, nutrient availability, and soil structure. This approach not only boosts tea yield but also enhances tea quality by increasing beneficial compounds such as polyphenols and amino acids. The study highlights the dual benefits of reducing environmental pollution from excessive nitrogen use while promoting sustainable tea production. Lorenz and Lal (2016) provide a broader environmental perspective on organic agriculture. Their research highlights key benefits, including improved soil health, biodiversity conservation, and carbon sequestration, while also reducing chemical inputs and pollution. However, they also address challenges such as lower yields and the need for more land to produce the same output as conventional farming. The study emphasizes the necessity of improving organic farming efficiency to maximize environmental benefits while maintaining food security.

Organic farming is often viewed as a climate-friendly alternative to conventional agriculture due to its reduced reliance on non-renewable energy and its positive effects on soil and water quality. However, life cycle assessments (LCAs) reveal that organic systems may produce higher greenhouse gas (GHG) emissions per unit of output due to lower yields (Clark, 2020). This paradox highlights the need for innovation within organic agriculture, including the adoption of site-specific assessment tools and emerging technologies to improve efficiency and reduce emissions. Addressing climate change should be central to the organic movement's values, and integrating scientific insights into policy and practice is essential for enhancing its environmental performance.

Figure 4. Bibliometric analysis of organic farming and sustainability

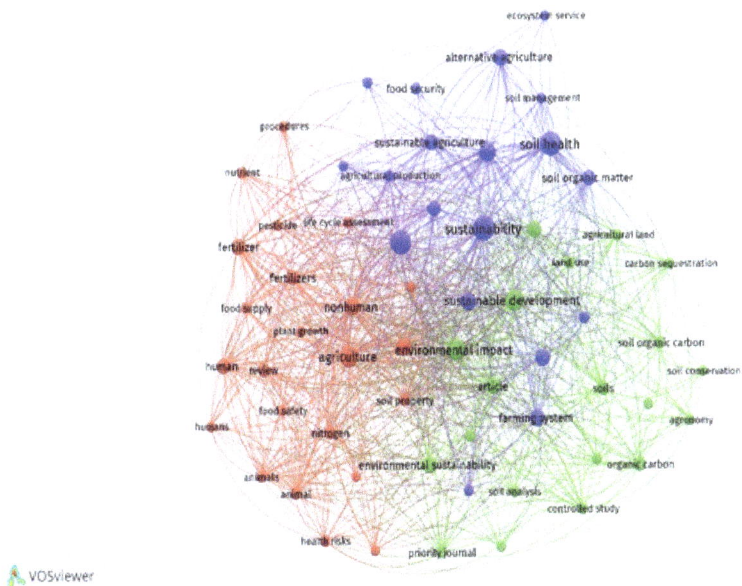

Bibliometric analysis of keyword co-occurrence (Network Visualization) is given in Figure 4 for "Organic farming" and "Sustainability," generated using VOSviewer software. The data were collected from the Scopus database, covering the period from 1999 to 2025. The analysis identifies three keyword clusters: Cluster 1 (23 items) in red, Cluster 2 (20 items) in blue, and Cluster 3 (19 items) in green. The most frequently used keywords by authors include organic farming, sustainability, environmental impact, sustainable agriculture, soil organic carbon, soil organic matter, and soil health.

Adoption Barriers and Challenges in Organic Farming

The transition to organic farming has been extensively studied over the years, with various researchers identifying barriers that hinder its widespread adoption. This review presents a chronological analysis of key studies that have explored these challenges (Figure 5.), providing insights into how perceptions and constraints have evolved over time.

Although organic farming is widely promoted for its environmental and health benefits, farmers often encounter substantial challenges in its adoption and implementation. Smallholder farmers in Punjab, for instance, reported difficulties in accessing certified organic inputs and maintaining post-harvest hygiene due to inadequate infrastructure and training (Singh et al., 2023). Additionally, the transition to organic practices involves navigating complex certification procedures, which are often time-consuming and costly. Mariappan et al. (2025) further highlight that farmers face initial yield reductions, labour-intensive practices, and limited market access. The reliance on indigenous inputs such as cow dung and urine, while ecologically sound, can be impractical for farmers without livestock. These real-life experiences underscore the need for targeted policy support, farmer training, and inclusive market systems to make organic farming economically viable and socially equitable.

One of the earliest studies on barriers to organic farming was conducted by Fisher (1989), who analyzed the challenges faced by farmers in Canterbury, New Zealand. His research identified financial risks, lack of knowledge, and uncertainty about market returns as primary concerns preventing conventional farmers from adopting organic methods. Building on this, Schneeberger et al. (2002) examined barriers to organic farming adoption among cash-crop producers in Austria. Their study found that skepticism about the economic viability of organic farming, difficulties in transitioning from conventional methods, and concerns about lower yields were significant deterrents. They emphasized that while organic farming had potential, many farmers remained hesitant due to uncertainty in profitability and market stability.

Risks, Uncertainties, and Pest Management Challenges in Organic Farming

Organic farming, while environmentally beneficial, presents significant challenges for farmers, including high production costs, lower initial yields, and complex certification processes (Gignarta et al., 2024). Pest and disease management is particularly difficult due to the prohibition of synthetic pesticides. Farmers must rely on biological alternatives that require technical expertise and often show inconsistent results. Diseases like crown rot, anthracnose, and cigar-end rot—caused by Colletotrichum musae and Fusarium spp.—can lead to substantial post-harvest losses (Singh & Singh, 2022). Moreover, biological control methods are limited by environmental variability and pathogen resistance (Tjamos et al., 1992).

A study in Kerala highlighted the severity of Fusarium wilt in banana, with incidence reaching 43.65% and severity up to 49.57% in key cultivars (Lishma et al., 2024). An integrated management strategy using Pseudomonas fluorescens, Trichoderma viride, and tebuconazole proved effective under field conditions. However, such approaches are difficult to adopt in organic systems due to restrictions on chemical inputs and the need for consistent biocontrol efficacy. These challenges underscore the importance of realistic and inclusive policies that address technical and financial barriers, ensuring that smallholder farmers can transition to organic farming with adequate support.

Barriers in Iran and Developing Countries (2010s–2020s)

Soltani et al. (2014) further contributed to the discourse by exploring the factors influencing organic agriculture adoption in Iran. They identified high certification costs, inadequate government support, and limited consumer awareness as major obstacles. The study also highlighted that while environmental benefits were recognized, economic concerns often outweighed them, making the transition difficult for farmers. As interest in organic farming grew in developing nations, Dixit et al. (2024) analyzed barriers using a grey-DEMATEL and ISM approach. Their research provided a structured framework for understanding how various constraints—such as inadequate infrastructure, policy gaps, and resistance to change—interact and reinforce one another. They emphasized the need for integrated solutions that address multiple challenges simultaneously.

Recent Perspectives on Economic Sustainability and Systemic Challenges (2023–2025)

Bottazzi et al. (2023) introduced a broader framework that looked beyond motivations and examined systemic barriers to organic farming adoption in northern Senegal. Their study revealed that land tenure issues, institutional inefficiencies, and a lack of technical support played crucial roles in discouraging farmers from transitioning. They argue that addressing these systemic barriers requires a holistic approach that considers socio-economic and policy-related factors. Luczka et al. (2024) investigated the opportunities and barriers faced by conventional farmers in Europe when considering organic farming. Their research underscored the importance of financial incentives, access to training programs, and improved market conditions in encouraging farmers to make the switch. Eti (2025) provided one of the most recent perspectives, examining the effects of economic sustainability perceptions on organic farming implementation. The study highlighted that while some farmers viewed organic farming as a long-term investment, short-term financial challenges, including high input costs and limited access to premium markets, continued to act as major determinants.

Luczka and Kalinowski (2020) explore the barriers hindering the growth of organic farming in Poland, offering insights into both economic and structural challenges. Their study identifies key obstacles such as high production costs, insufficient government support, and limited market access, which discourage farmers from transitioning to organic methods. The authors also highlight the role of consumer awareness and demand, emphasizing that a lack of strong market incentives further complicates the expansion of organic agriculture. Additionally, they discuss the difficulties in obtaining organic certification and the technical knowledge gap among farmers.

Policy Support and Market Trends in Organic Agriculture

Stolze and Lampkin (2009) emphasize that organic agriculture provides public goods like environmental sustainability and biodiversity, justifying policy support through subsidies, certification, and market incentives. However, they also highlight challenges such as policy inconsistencies and limited funding. Nandwani and Nwosisi (2016) note the global rise of organic farming, driven by consumer demand for healthier, eco-friendly food. They underline benefits like improved soil fertility and reduced chemical use, while acknowledging barriers such as higher costs, lower yields, and complex certification. Reganold and Wachter (2016) compare organic and conventional systems, finding ecological advantages in organic farming but also noting its lower productivity and higher labor needs. They call for innovation and policy support to enhance organic farming's scalability.

Figure 5. Organic farming challenges

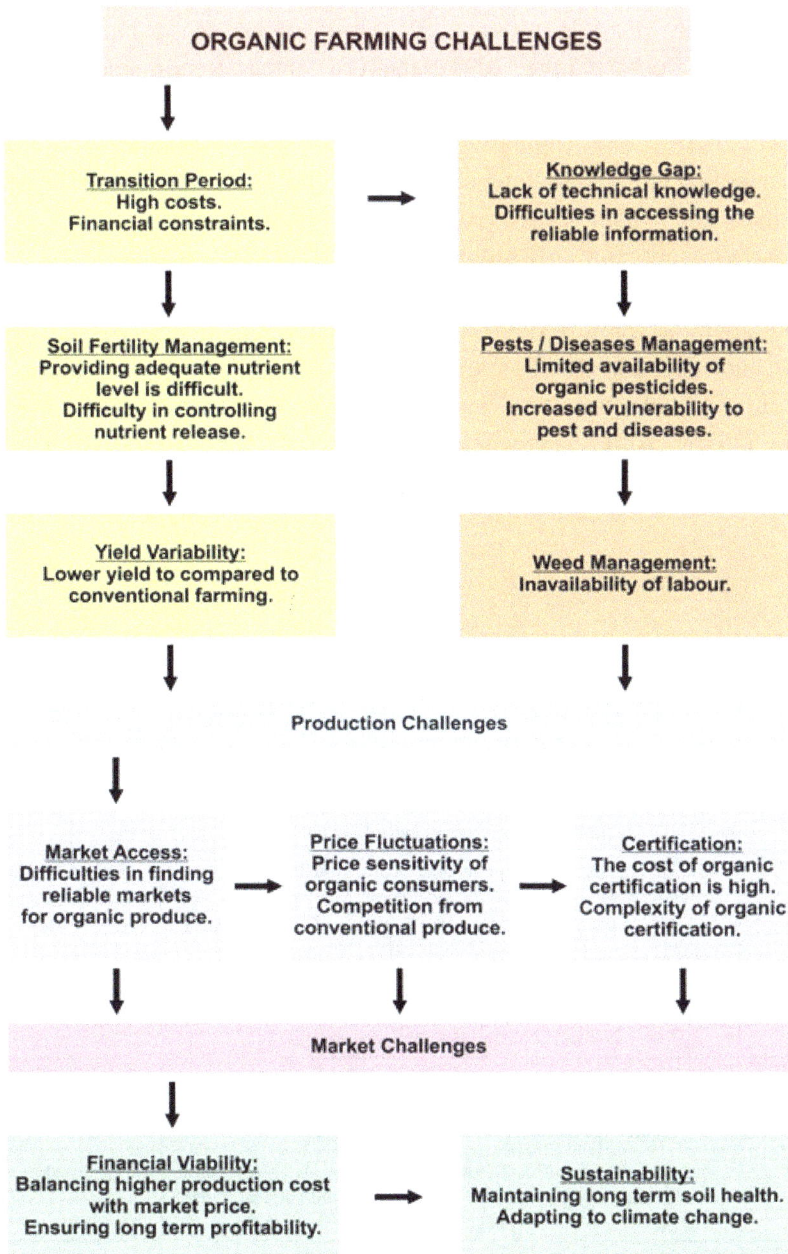

Willer et al. (2021) document global growth in certified organic land and consumer demand, attributing progress to supportive policies and market dynamics, though challenges like certification costs and regional disparities persist. National approaches vary: Australia promotes R&D and market access but must improve stakeholder readiness (Clune, 2021); the U.S. integrates organic farming into mainstream agriculture via crop insurance and conservation programs (Dimitri & Effland, 2020); China emphasizes biodiversity and rural development through long-term policy initiatives (Yang et al., 2024); and Turkey faces issues in nutrient management and market access, requiring targeted policy reforms.

In conclusion, organic agriculture holds significant potential for promoting sustainability, biodiversity, and soil health, but its widespread adoption faces challenges such as higher costs, lower yields, and policy gaps. Effective policy frameworks, research, and education are essential to address these barriers and integrate organic farming into global agricultural systems. By learning from diverse national approaches, policymakers can create more cohesive strategies to support the growth and scalability of organic agriculture.

Table 2. Market trends in organic agriculture

Aspect	Details	References
Production Practices	Organic farming relies on crop rotation, animal manures, crop residues, green manures, and biological pest control. The use of green and animal manures is common, while practices like organic mulch/compost have declined.	Mpanga et al., 2021; Litterick and Watson, 2016
Product Categories	Major organic products include fresh fruits and vegetables, cereals, coffee, tea, cocoa, spices, herbs, oilseeds, pulses, milk products, honey, meat, and edible nuts.	Mitra, 2008
Market Growth	The organic market is experiencing steady growth, with a 30% annual increase. The number of certified organic farms, land area, and sales in the USA increased by 5%, 6%, and 12% respectively from 2008 to 2019.	Goncharova et al., 2020; Mpanga et al., 2021
Consumer Demand	There is a growing consumer demand for organic products due to increased awareness of health and environmental issues. This demand is predominantly in urban areas.	Simonne et al., 2016; Sondhi and Vani, 2007
Challenges	Key challenges include complex regulations, high production costs, and issues with pest control. Farmers also face difficulties in predicting market trends and securing price premiums.	Simonne et al., 2016; Lemke et al., 2024
Regional Trends	There has been significant growth in organic production in Least Developed Countries (LDCs), supported by international trade negotiations.	Zbikowska, 2020
Future Directions	The potential for expansion in organic farming includes increased adoption of regenerative agricultural practices and addressing primary challenges through farm-level research and policy reviews.	Simonne et al., 2016; Lemke et al., 2024

The current market trends in organic agriculture are driven by increasing consumer demand, environmental awareness, and the economic viability of organic products.

Consumer preferences, such as environmental awareness and diversity of products, play a significant role in shaping market trends. The economic implications of market trends in organic agriculture are closely tied to the regulatory environment, environmental impact, and the potential consumption of organic food products per capita.

Post-Harvest Handling, Logistics, and Marketing Channels

Effective post-harvest handling is vital for maintaining banana quality, minimizing losses, and ensuring food safety. Bananas are highly perishable and prone to mechanical injury, moisture loss, and microbial decay. The process begins with harvesting at the mature-green stage, followed by careful de-handing, washing to remove latex and contaminants, and grading by size and appearance (Esguerra & Rolle, 2018). Organic and conventional systems differ significantly: organic bananas use natural coatings like cassava starch, chitosan, or whey protein to reduce transpiration and delay ripening, while conventional systems rely on synthetic waxes, fungicides, and ethylene for ripening (Ruiz Medina & Ruales, 2024). Organic cleaning agents include food-grade vinegar or hydrogen peroxide, and packaging is typically biodegradable, unlike the plastic-based materials used in conventional systems (Singh et al., 2023; Indian Council of Agricultural Research, 2013).

Figure 6. Flow chart of sample design

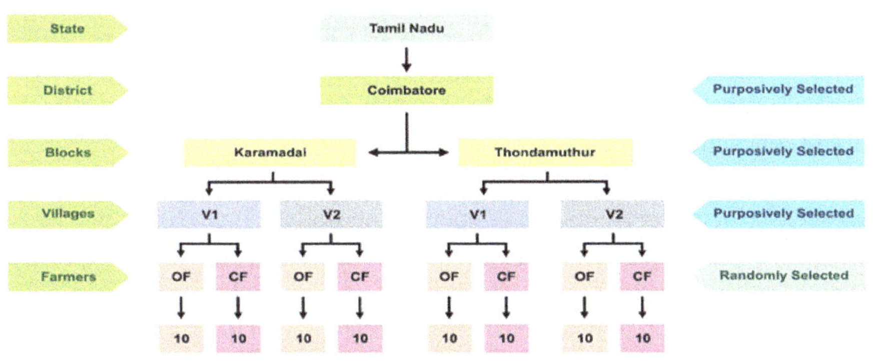

Transport and marketing further distinguish the two systems. Conventional bananas are shipped in fungicide-treated containers to control crown rot and anthracnose, while organic bananas require sanitized, chemical-free containers and strict traceability (University of California, n.d.). Refrigerated transport at 13–15 °C and 85–95 % RH helps reduce physiological and microbial damage, with innovations like insulated containers cutting losses by up to 4 % (Indian Council of Agricultural Research, 2013). Organic bananas are marketed through certified retailers and niche export channels, often earning a 25–40 % premium, while conventional bananas dominate bulk and wholesale markets. Traceability and eco-friendly logistics are central to organic marketing, enhancing certification integrity and consumer trust (Aditi & Singh, 2022).

Consumer Preferences for Organic Bananas

Consumers increasingly prefer organic bananas due to their perceived health benefits, environmental sustainability, and absence of synthetic chemicals. This preference is particularly strong among health-conscious and urban consumers who associate organic bananas with safer food choices and ethical farming practices. Singh et al. (2023) emphasize that post-harvest handling practices—such as the use of biodegradable packaging, natural cleaning agents, and traceability systems—not only preserve the quality of organic bananas but also reinforce consumer trust in organic certification. Moreover, value-added products like dried organic banana snacks and organic banana-based spreads cater to evolving consumer demands for convenience and premium quality, further enhancing market appeal.

Methodology:

This study employed a multi-stage sampling strategy to ensure the selection of representative farmers. First, Coimbatore district, a leading region for organic farming in Tamil Nadu which is actively promoted by the Tamil Nadu Organic Certification Department, were purposively selected due to its significant banana production and adoption of organic practices. Second, two blocks within Coimbatore known for banana cultivation will be purposively chosen based on the prevalence of both organic and conventional banana farms. Within each block, two villages was selected. Finally, 40 organic and 40 conventional banana farmers were selected from these villages, ensuring a representative sample for the study (Figure 6).

The Primary data was collected through structured interviews using a pre-tested questionnaire. The questionnaire covered various aspects, including farm characteristics (land size, irrigation sources, and banana variety), input usage (seeds, fertilizers, pesticides, and labor), cultivation costs (land preparation, planting, maintenance, and harvesting), and yield (number of bunches and banana weight). Additionally, it explored farmers' perceptions and motivations for adopting or not adopting organic practices. Specific questions assessed the cost differences between organic and conventional inputs (such as biofertilizers and compost), labor requirements for different farming methods, and market access for organic bananas.

Tool of Analysis

Gross Margin analysis was calculated to assess the financial viability of organic and conventional banana farming. Gross Margin analysis gives an estimate of the difference between the gross returns (GR) and variable costs VC (GR- VC). GR was estimated based on yield and market prices. Net profit, gross margin, and benefit-cost ratio were used to compare the profitability of the two farming systems (Majunatha & Puttaswamaiah, 2021). Qualitative data on farmers' perceptions, and reasons for adoption/non-adoption will be analyzed using thematic analysis to identify key themes and patterns.

RESULTS AND DISCUSSION

Cost of Cultivation for Organic Banana and Conventional Banana Farming

Cost of Cultivation was analysed between organic and conventional banana farming is presented in Table 3. Banana is a water- and labor-intensive crop (Rattanapan & Ounsaneha, 2021; Toyosumi et al., 2021). The total cost of cultivation for Organic Banana Farming (OBF) per hectare is approximately 2,55,417, whereas Conventional Banana Farming (CBF) costs around 2,24,919. This indicates that OBF incurs 13.56% higher costs than CBF.

Table 3. Cost of cultivation for organic banana and conventional banana farming

Particulars	Organic Banana (/Ha/ Annum.)	Conventional (/Ha/ Annum.)	Mean
Value of Land Preparation	12597 (4.93)	11362 (5.05)	1235
Value of Manure	41685 (16.32)	39400 (17.52)	2285
Cost of Suckers	18350 (7.18)	16445 (7.31)	1905
Value of Fertilizer (or) Organic Fertilizer	41380 (16.20)	40627 (18.06)	753
Value of Plant Protection Chemicals / Organic pest control	28750 (11.26)	13015 (5.79)	15735
Irrigation Charge	15485 (6.06)	13550 (6.02)	1935
Value of Supporting Sticks	29640 (11.60)	24700 (10.98)	4940
Human Labour	52650 (20.61)	50400 (22.41)	2250

continued on following page

Table 3. Continued

Particulars	Organic Banana (/Ha/ Annum.)	Conventional (/Ha/ Annum.)	Mean
Machine Labour	14880 (5.83)	15420 (6.86)	-540
Cost of Cultivation	255417 (100)	224919 (100)	30493
Yield (kg/Ha)	24800	27600	-2800
Price Per Kg	35	25	10
Gross Income	868000	690000	178000
Net Income	612583	465081	147502
Benefit cost ratio	3.40	3.07	0.33

Source: Field Survey, (2023-2024). Note: figure in brackets indicates percentage

These findings align with the study by Coulis et al. (2022) in Martinique, which reported that production costs for organic systems were about 37% higher than conventional systems. Human labour accounts for a significant portion of the total cultivation cost, representing 20.61% in OBF and 22.41% in CBF. The second highest expense is fertilizers, with organic fertilizers contributing 16.20% of the total cost, while inorganic fertilizers make up 18.06%. This suggests that although organic fertilizers require a higher financial investment, their relative share in total costs is slightly lower than inorganic fertilizers. The difference in cultivation costs between OBF and CBF is 30,493/ha per annum.

Conventional banana farming yields 27,600 kg/ha, which is higher than the 24,800 kg/ha produced in organic farming (Jimenez et al., 2007; Aslam et al., 2020). This difference highlights the effectiveness of chemical fertilizers and pest control in enhancing productivity. Despite producing a lower yield, OBF sells at a significantly higher price (35/kg vs. 25/kg for CBF), reflecting the premium consumers place on organic produce. Consequently, organic farming achieves a higher gross income of 8,68,000/ha, compared to 6,90,000/ha in conventional farming, even with reduced production levels. These findings align with Lin et al. 2008 who reported that organic bananas in the United States have a significant price premium, estimated at 13 cents per pound, which translates to a 20% premium over conventional banana.

Figure 7. Reasons for adoption of organic farming by the farmers

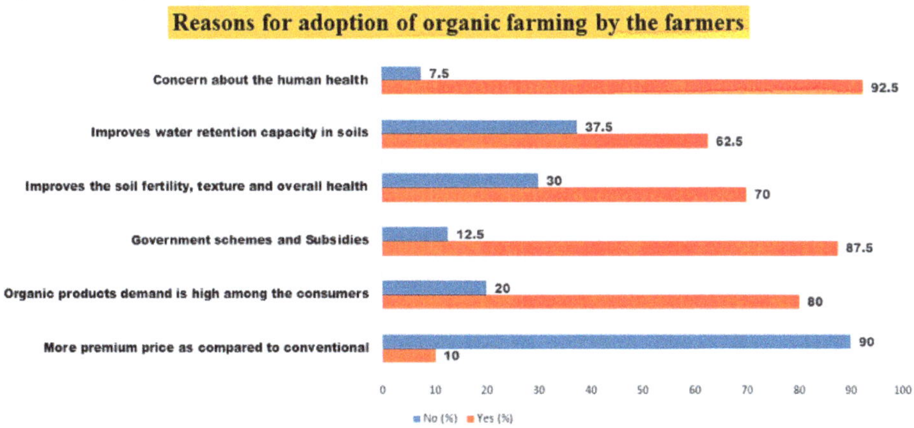

Figure 8. Reasons for non-adoption of organic farming by the farmers

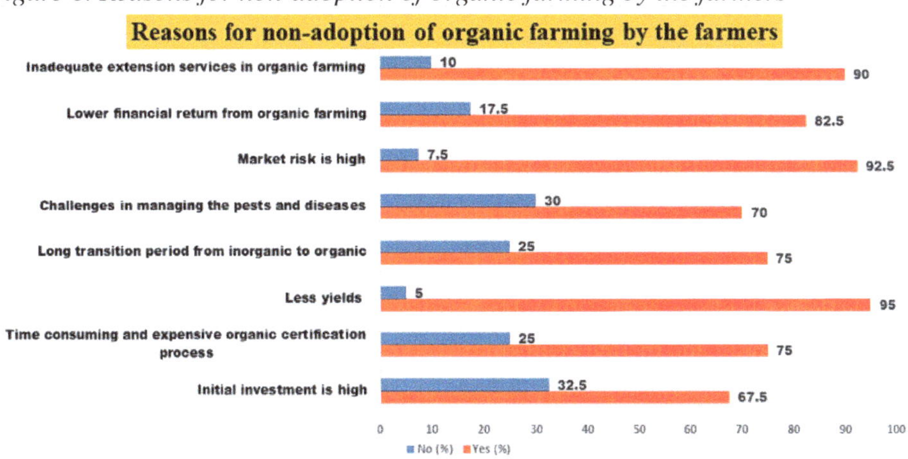

REASONS FOR ADOPTIONS OF ORGANIC FARMING BY FARMERS

Figure 7, Illustrates that a majority of 92% of organic farmers adopted organic farming due to concerns about human health. Similarly, Singh et al. (2023) found that nearly 95% of farmers in India told that organic farming adoption for its positive impact on human health. Additionally, 90% of farmers perceived that organic produce fetches a higher premium price than conventional produce due to strong consumer demand. Government support also played a significant role, with 87.5% of farmers adopting organic farming due to the availability of organic schemes and subsidies. During the survey, one of the organic banana farmers expressed, "Even if the yield was a little less in the first year, now it's stable, and my soil gives good produce without much expense." The results are consistent with Ume and Bahta (2024) who observed that in Nigeria, providing premiums for organic products and informal certification effectively encouraged farmers to expand their organic farming practices.

Similarly, Yang et al. (2024), conducted a study in China, extensive government policies and subsidies have significantly boosted organic agriculture, particularly in poorer regions, by converting ecological advantages into economic benefits. Moreover, approximately 70% and 60% of farmers believed that organic farming improves soil fertility, texture, and water retention capacity, contributing to long-term agricultural sustainability (Jeyaseeli et al., 2021; Gopinath et al., 2023).

REASONS FOR NON-ADOPTION OF ORGANIC FARMING BY THE FARMERS

Reasons for non-adoption of organic farming by farmers are explained in Figure 8. The primary reason quoted by the farmer for non-adoption of organic farming is a less yields. This is because farmers often perceive organic farming as yielding less compared to conventional methods, especially during the transition period (Panneerselvam et al., 2012; Home et al., 2019). The second reason was the market risk is high and difficulty of finding a market for organic produce. Farmers feel that the demand for organic products is limited, making challenging to find consistent and reliable market. These results align with the study of Azam & Ponnam (2024); Azam et al. (2019). Additionally, 90% of farmers stated the reason for non-adopting is inadequate extension service in organic farming. Research by Dube et al. (2025) and Bottazzi et al. (2023) also confirmed the same results that inadequate extension services are a major barrier for adoption of organic farming. The non-adopter revealed that lower financial return from organic farming and it takes longer transition period from conventional to organic. This longer transition period, combined with lower initial returns, discourages farmers from making the shift. Furthermore, seventy-five percent of farmers highlighted the time consuming and expensive organic certification process as the reason for non-adopting organic farming. Studies by Sing (2023), Agarwal et al. (2023), Eti (2025) also revealed the same results is that the certification process is described as tedious, difficult to understand, and costly, which deters many farmers from pursuing organic certification. Lastly, farmers reported that challenges in managing the pests and diseases and initial investment for organic farming is high (Singh et al., 2023) is the reasons for non-adoption. During the survey, one of the conventional banana farmer expressed "Without chemicals, it's hard to control pests and fungal diseases like sigatoka or crown rot. Many times, crops get damaged." Organic farming often demands more intensive pest and disease management strategies compared to conventional farming due to the limited use of synthetic pesticides and fertilizers, which can lead to higher incidences of pests and diseases (Brevault and Bouyer, 2014).

CONCLUSION

Organic farming represents a sustainable alternative to conventional agriculture, offering significant environmental, economic, and social benefits. Despite challenges such as higher initial costs, lower yields, and certification barriers, its long-term advantages in soil health, biodiversity, and premium market prices make it a viable option. Policy support, improved market access, and farmer education are crucial to overcoming adoption barriers. By addressing these challenges, organic farming can contribute to global food security, environmental sustainability, and improved farmer livelihoods. Embracing organic practices is essential for building a resilient and sustainable agricultural future. The study highlights the economic and environmental implications of organic and conventional banana farming in Coimbatore, Tamil Nadu. Organic banana farming incurs higher production costs (approximately 13.56% more than conventional farming), primarily due to increased expenditures on organic fertilizers, pest management, and labour. However, it provides substantial benefits, including premium market prices, improved soil health, and environmental sustainability. Despite slightly lower yields (organic: 24,800 kg/ha vs. conventional: 27,600 kg/ha), organic banana farming generates a significantly higher net income (6,12,583/ha) than conventional farming (4,65,081/ha), resulting in a better benefit-cost ratio (3.40 vs. 3.07). This suggests that organic farming can be a profitable alternative if farmers can effectively manage costs and access premium markets.

The key reasons for adopting organic farming include soil health improvement, reduced chemical dependency, and growing consumer demand for organic produce. However, barriers such as high initial costs, certification challenges, and market accessibility remain critical concerns for non-adopting farmers. Addressing these issues through better policy support, subsidies for organic inputs, and stronger market linkages can encourage more farmers to transition to organic cultivation. Overall, organic banana farming presents a viable and sustainable agricultural model that balances economic viability with ecological conservation. However, widespread adoption requires targeted interventions to make the transition smoother and more rewarding for farmers. The study suggests that the government should provide subsidies for organic inputs such as bio-fertilizers and compost to lower production costs. Additionally, establishing minimum support prices (MSP) and dedicated organic markets can help ensure stable income for organic farmers.

REFERENCES

Aditi, & Singh, R. (2022). Eco-friendly post-harvest technologies of banana: A review. The Pharma Innovation Journal, 11(7), 4375–4381.

Agarwal, S., Agarwal, A., Sharma, G. L., Kothari, H., & Maloo, S. R. (2023, August). Organic Farming Issues and Challenges: Application of ICT. In *International conference on WorldS4* (pp. 189-204). Singapore: Springer Nature Singapore.

Agricultural and Processed Food Products Export Development Authority (APEDA). (2025). *Organic products in India*. https://www.apeda.gov.in/OrganicProducts

Agricultural and Processed Food Products Export Development Authority (APEDA). (2023–2024). *Organic products in India.* https://apeda.gov.in/apedawebsite/organic/Organic_Products.htm

Akram, M. W., Akram, N., Hongshu, W., & Mehmood, A. (2019). An assessment of economic viability of organic farming in Pakistan. *Custos E Agronegocio Line*, *15*(1), 141–169.

Arora, M., Gupta, S., & Mittal, A. (2024). Qualitative Insights Into Harvesting Sustainability: The Role of Organic Agriculture in Advancing Sustainable Development Goals. In *The Emerald Handbook of Tourism Economics and Sustainable Development* (pp. 41-62). Emerald Publishing Limited.

Aslam, W., Shahzad Noor, R., Ullah, S., & Chen, H. (2020). Comparative economic analysis of crop yield under organic and conventional farming systems in Punjab, Pakistan. *Asian Journal of Agriculture and Biology*, *8*(2), 113–118. DOI: 10.35495/ajab.2020.02.093

Azam, M. S., & Ponnam, A. (2024). Disparity in Agri-Marketing Challenges in India: Organic vs. Conventional Food Producers. *Journal of International Food & Agribusiness Marketing*, *36*(5), 870–898. DOI: 10.1080/08974438.2023.2228783

Azam, M. S., Shaheen, M., & Narbariya, S. (2019). Marketing challenges and organic farming in India—Does farm size matter? *International Journal of Nonprofit and Voluntary Sector Marketing*, *24*(4), e1654. DOI: 10.1002/nvsm.1654

Behera, K. K., Alam, A., Vats, S., Sharma, H. P., & Sharma, V. (2012). Organic farming history and techniques. *Agroecology and strategies for climate change*, (pp.287-328).

Biswas, S., Ali, M. N., Goswami, R., & Chakraborty, S. (2014). Soil health sustainability and organic farming: A review. *Journal of Food Agriculture and Environment*, *12*(3-4), 237–243.

Bottazzi, P., Seck, S. M., Niang, M., & Moser, S. (2023). Beyond motivations: A framework unraveling the systemic barriers to organic farming adoption in northern Senegal. *Journal of Rural Studies*, *104*, 103158. DOI: 10.1016/j.jrurstud.2023.103158

Brévault, T., & Bouyer, J. (2014). From integrated to system-wide pest management: Challenges for sustainable agriculture. *Outlooks on Pest Management*, *25*(3), 212–213. DOI: 10.1564/v25_jun_05

Castro, L. M., Calvas, B., & Knoke, T. (2015). Ecuadorian banana farms should consider organic banana with low price risks in their land-use portfolios. *PLoS One*, *10*(3), e0120384. DOI: 10.1371/journal.pone.0120384

Clark, S. (2020). Organic farming and climate change: The need for innovation. *Sustainability (Basel)*, *12*(17), 7012. DOI: 10.3390/su12177012

Clune, T. (2021). Conceptualising policy for sustainable agriculture development. *Australian Journal of Public Administration*, *80*(3), 493–509. DOI: 10.1111/1467-8500.12436

Coulis, M., Sauvadet, M., Falk, A., Prochasson, A., Tsoukas, L., Gervais, L., & Guillermet, C. (2022, August). Multidisciplinary assessment of two organic banana production systems in Martinique. In *XXXI International Horticultural Congress (IHC2022): XII International Symposium on Banana: Celebrating Banana Organic 1367* (pp. 35-46).

De Ponti, T., Rijk, B., & Van Ittersum, M. K. (2012). The crop yield gap between organic and conventional agriculture. *Agricultural Systems*, *108*, 1–9. DOI: 10.1016/j.agsy.2011.12.004

Dimitri, C., & Effland, A. (2020). From farming to food systems: The evolution of US agricultural production and policy into the 21st century. *Renewable Agriculture and Food Systems*, *35*(4), 391–406. DOI: 10.1017/S1742170518000522

Dixit, A., Suvadarshini, P., & Pagare, D. V. (2024). Analysis of barriers to organic farming adoption in developing countries: A grey-DEMATEL and ISM approach. *Journal of Agribusiness in Developing and Emerging Economies*, *14*(3), 470–495. DOI: 10.1108/JADEE-06-2022-0111

Dube, P. I., Olorunfemi, O. D., & Nyawo, P. H. (2025). Perception and Utilisation of Organic Farming Practices among Smallholder Farmers: Evidence from a Micro-Level Survey in Ehlanzeni District South Africa. *South African Journal of Agricultural Extension, 53*(1), 169–192. DOI: 10.17159/2413-3221/2025/v53n1a18444

Esguerra, E. B., & Rolle, R. (2018). Post-harvest management of banana for quality and safety assurance: Guidance for horticultural supply chain stakeholders. Food and Agriculture Organization of the United Nations.

Eti, H. S. (2025). The Effects of Perceptions of Economic Sustainability and Barriers on Organic Farming Implementation. *Sustainability (Basel), 17*(2), 786. DOI: 10.3390/su17020786

Fisher, P. (1989). Barriers to the adoption of organic farming in Canterbury (*Doctoral dissertation, Lincoln College, University of Canterbury*).

Forster, D., Andres, C., Verma, R., Zundel, C., Messmer, M. M., & Mäder, P. (2013). Yield and economic performance of organic and conventional cotton-based farming systems–results from a field trial in India. *PLoS One, 8*(12), e81039. DOI: 10.1371/journal.pone.0081039

Gamage, A., Gangahagedara, R., Gamage, J., Jayasinghe, N., Kodikara, N., Suraweera, P., & Merah, O. (2023). Role of organic farming for achieving sustainability in agriculture. *Farming System, 1*(1), 100005. DOI: 10.1016/j.farsys.2023.100005

Gignarta, T. S., Borojo, D. G., & Guan, Z. (2024). The impacts of economic policy uncertainties on agriculture export. *Cogent Economics & Finance, 12*(1), 2382359. DOI: 10.1080/23322039.2024.2382359

Goncharova, Y. K., Kharitonov, E. M., Ochkas, N. A., Gapishko, N. I., & Neschadim, H. H. (2020). Features of rice (Oryza sativa L.) varieties for organic farming in connection with marker assisted breeding. *Selskokhozyaistvennaya Biologiya, 55*(5), 847–860. DOI: 10.15389/agrobiology.2020.5.847eng

Gopinath, K. A., Venkatesh, G., Manjunath, M., Jayalakshmi, M., Prasad, T. V., Rajkumar, B., & Singh, V. K. (2023). Impact of organic and integrated production systems on yield and seed quality of rainfed crops and on soil properties. *Frontiers in Nutrition, 10*, 1127970. DOI: 10.3389/fnut.2023.1127970

Guthman, J. H. (2000). *Agrarian dreams? The paradox of organic farming in California*. University of California.

Home, R., Indermuehle, A., Tschanz, A., Ries, E., & Stolze, M. (2019). Factors in the decision by Swiss farmers to convert to organic farming. *Renewable Agriculture and Food Systems, 34*(6), 571–581. DOI: 10.1017/S1742170518000121

Howard, A., & Moubray, J. (1940). The book of the quarter: 1 an agricultural testament. *African Affairs, 39*(CLVII), 367–375. DOI: 10.1093/oxfordjournals.afraf.a101058

Indian Council of Agricultural Research. (2013). Post-harvest management and value-addition. In DARE/ICAR Annual Report 2012–13 (pp. 68–73). ICAR.

Jeyaseeli, P., Jeyamangalam, F., Selvaraj, S., & Vella, D. S. (2021). Investigation of physico-chemical, physical properties and moisture content studies of soil using organic amendment. *Agricultural Technology (Thailand), 17*(3), 855–870.

Jimenez, M., Van der Veken, L., Neirynck, H., Rodríguez, H., Ruiz, O., & Swennen, R. (2007). Organic banana production in Ecuador: Its implications on black Sigatoka development and plant–soil nutritional status. *Renewable Agriculture and Food Systems, 22*(4), 297–306. DOI: 10.1017/S1742170507001895

Kareem, A., Farooqi, Z. U. R., Kalsom, A., Mohy-Ud-Din, W., Hussain, M. M., Raza, M., & Khursheed, M. M. (2022). Organic farming for sustainable soil use, management, food production and climate change mitigation. *Sustainable agriculture: technical progressions and transitions*, 39-59.

Khunt, R. S., Makadia, J. J., & Varasani, J. V. (2022). Review on prospects and constraints of organic production in India: A new paradigm in agricultural production. *Indian Journal of Economics and Development, 18*(4), 958–964.

King, F. H. (2004). Farmers of forty centuries: Organic farming in China, Korea, and Japan. *Courier Corporation*.

Kishore, A. R., Niveditha, K., Uriti, A., Anilkumar, C., Sarabu, A., & Prasanna, K. V. L. (2023, December). An in-depth Analysis of the Elements Shaping Organic Farmers: A Systematic Review. In *2023 International Conference on Energy, Materials and Communication Engineering (ICEMCE)* (pp. 1-5). IEEE. DOI: 10.1109/ICEMCE57940.2023.10434263

Kuwornu, J. K., Oduro, E., Amegashie, D. P., Fening, K. O., Yangyouru, M., MacCarthy, D. S., & Datta, A. (2018). Cost-benefit analysis of conventional and integrated crop management for vegetable production. *International Journal of Vegetable Science, 24*(6), 597–611. DOI: 10.1080/19315260.2018.1457585

Lampkin, N. (1990). *Organic Farming Farming Press Books and Videos*. Ipswitch.

Lemke, S., Smith, N., Thiim, C., & Stump, K. (2024). Drivers and barriers to adoption of regenerative agriculture: Cases studies on lessons learned from organic. *International Journal of Agricultural Sustainability, 22*(1), 2324216. DOI: 10.1080/14735903.2024.2324216

Lin, B. H., Smith, T. A., & Huang, C. L. (2008). Organic premiums of US fresh produce. *Renewable Agriculture and Food Systems*, *23*(3), 208–216. DOI: 10.1017/S1742170508002238

Lishma, N. P., Cherian, K. A., Louis, V., Sureshkumar, R., Kumar, P. N., Chandran, D., Pran, M., & Sharma, R. (2024). Integrated management of Fusarium wilt disease of banana in Kerala, India. *Vegetos*, *37*(1), 117–124. DOI: 10.1007/s42535-023-00576-7

Litterick, A. M., & Watson, C. A. (2016). *Organic Farming. Encylopedia of Applied Plant Sciences* (Vol. 3). Elsevier., DOI: 10.1016/B978-0-12-394807-6.00004-6

Lorenz, K., & Lal, R. (2016). Environmental impact of organic agriculture. *Advances in Agronomy*, *139*, 99–152. DOI: 10.1016/bs.agron.2016.05.003

Lori, M., Symnaczik, S., Mäder, P., De Deyn, G., & Gattinger, A. (2017). Organic farming enhances soil microbial abundance and activity—A meta-analysis and meta-regression. *PLoS One*, *12*(7), e0180442. DOI: 10.1371/journal.pone.0180442

Luczka, W., Smoluk-Sikorska, J., & Wojciechowska-Solis, J. (2024). Opportunities and Barriers to the Development of Organic Farming from the Perspective of Conventional Farms. *European Research Studies*, *27*(2), 607–619. DOI: 10.35808/ersj/3862

Lynch, D. H., Halberg, N., & Bhatta, G. D. (2012). Environmental impacts of organic agriculture in temperate regions. *CABI Reviews*, 1-17.

Mariappan, S., Arumugam, S., Ponnusamy, J., Natesan, R., & Kumar, S. S. (2025). Next-generation natural farming practices for crop improvement. In *Next-Generation Strategies for Crop Improvement* (pp. 307–354). Springer., DOI: 10.1007/978-981-95-0309-4_11

Mitra, S. K. (2008). Organic tropical and subtropical fruit production in India-prospects and challenges. In *IV International Symposium on Tropical and Subtropical Fruits 975* (pp. 303-307).

Mpanga, I. K., Tronstad, R., Guo, J., LeBauer, D. S., & Idowu, O. J. (2021). On-farm land management strategies and production challenges in United States organic agricultural systems. *Current Research in Environmental Sustainability*, *3*, 100097. DOI: 10.1016/j.crsust.2021.100097

Nandwani, D., & Nwosisi, S. (2016). Global trends in organic agriculture. *Organic farming for sustainable agriculture*, 1-35.

Nastase, M. (2013). Issues Regarding the Certification of Organic Vegetables in Romania. *Quality - Access to Success*, •••, 118–123.

Pandey, P. R., Gupta, J. K., Narvariya, R. K., Meena, S. C., & Narwariya, D. (2019). Constraints faced by farmers in adoption of integrated farming system in Vindhyan Plateau of Madhya Pradesh. *Plant Archives*, *19*(2), 512–514.

Panneerselvam, P., Halberg, N., Vaarst, M., & Hermansen, J. E. (2012). Indian farmers' experience with and perceptions of organic farming. *Renewable Agriculture and Food Systems*, *27*(2), 157–169. DOI: 10.1017/S1742170511000238

PIB. (2023). Research unit, Press Information Bureau, Ministry of Information and Broad, Government of India. https://static.pib.gov.in/WriteReadData/specificdocs/documents/2023/may/doc2023517199601.pdf

Rahmaniah, H., Darma, R., Asrul, L., & Taufik, D. K. (2020, October). The potential of organic agriculture, soil structure and farmers income for inclusive agriculture sustainability: A review. []). IOP Publishing.]. *IOP Conference Series. Earth and Environmental Science*, *575*(1), 012099. DOI: 10.1088/1755-1315/575/1/012099

Raj, T. (2019). Economic viability of organic farming in Himachal Pradesh: An empirical verification. *Indian Journal of Hill Farming*, *32*(1).

Rattanapan, C., & Ounsaneha, W. (2021). Water footprint assessment of Thai banana production. *International Journal of Environmental Science and Development*, Vol.12 (5), PP.151-156.

Reddy, A. A., Melts, I., Mohan, G., Rani, C. R., Pawar, V., Singh, V., Choubey, M., Vashishtha, T., Suresh, A., & Bhattarai, M. (2022). Economic impact of organic agriculture: Evidence from a Pan-India survey. *Sustainability (Basel)*, *14*(22), 15057. DOI: 10.3390/su142215057

Reeve, J. R., Hoagland, L. A., Villalba, J. J., Carr, P. M., Atucha, A., Cambardella, C., & Delate, K. (2016). Organic farming, soil health, and food quality: Considering possible links. *Advances in Agronomy*, *137*, 319–367. DOI: 10.1016/bs.agron.2015.12.003

Reganold, J. P., & Wachter, J. M. (2016). Organic agriculture in the twenty-first century. *Nature Plants*, *2*(2), 1–8. DOI: 10.1038/nplants.2015.221

Ribeiro, L. R., Oliveira, L. M. D., Silva, S. D. O., & Borges, A. L. (2012). Physical and chemical characterization of bananas produced in conventional and organic cultivation systems. *Revista Brasileira de Fruticultura*, *34*, 774–782. DOI: 10.1590/S0100-29452012000300017

Ricono, C., Mony, C., Alignier, A., Aviron, S., Bertrand, C., Precigout, P. A., & Vandenkoornhuyse, P. (2024). Effect of organic farming on root microbiota, seed production and pathogen resistance in winter wheat fields. *Plants, People, Planet.*

Rodale, J. I. (1945). Farming & gardening with composts. *Pay. dirt.*, 242.

Ruiz Medina, M. D., & Ruales, J. (2024). Post-harvest alternatives in banana cultivation. *Agronomy (Basel)*, *14*(9), 2109. DOI: 10.3390/agronomy14092109

Sahu, R. S., & Tiwari, M. (2024). Ensuring sustainable livelihoods and inclusive growth of Indian smallholder farmers through organic farming: A systematic literature review. *Socio-Ecological Practice Research*, *6*(3), 1–15. DOI: 10.1007/s42532-024-00190-0

Schneeberger, W., Darnhofer, I., & Eder, M. (2002). Barriers to the adoption of organic farming by cash-crop producers in Austria. *American Journal of Alternative Agriculture*, *17*(1), 24–31. DOI: 10.1079/AJAA20017

Simonne, A., Ozores-Hampton, M., Treadwell, D., & House, L. (2016). Organic and conventional produce in the US: Examining safety and quality, economic values, and consumer attitudes. *Horticulturae*, *2*(2), 5. DOI: 10.3390/horticulturae2020005

Singh, A., & Singh, R. (2022). Eco-friendly post-harvest technologies of banana: A review. The Pharma Innovation Journal, 11(7), 4375–4381. https://www.thepharmajournal.com/archives/2022/vol11issue7S/PartAI/SP-11-7-225-884

Singh, R., Solanki, C., & Bala, M. (2023). Post-harvest handling and value-addition of organic produce. *International Journal of Advanced Biochemistry Research*, *7*(2), 184–188. DOI: 10.33545/26174693.2023.v7.i2Sc.206

Soltani, S., Azadi, H., Mahmoudi, H., & Witlox, F. (2014). Organic agriculture in Iran: Farmers' barriers to and factors influencing adoption. *Renewable Agriculture and Food Systems*, *29*(2), 126–134. DOI: 10.1017/S1742170513000069

Sondhi, N., & Vani, V. (2007). An empirical analysis of the organic retail market in the NCR. *Global Business Review*, *8*(2), 283–302. DOI: 10.1177/097215090700800207

Soni, R., & Yadav, S. K. (2019). Prospects of organic farming as financial sustainable strategy in modern agriculture. *Soil fertility management for sustainable development*, 251-265.

Souza, A., Junior, C. K., Zarpellon, F. R., & da Veiga, C. P. (2024). Sustainable production and consumption: Assessing the economic viability of traditional and organic yerba mate cultivation. *Humanities & Social Sciences Communications*, *11*(1), 1–16. DOI: 10.1057/s41599-024-04014-0

Stolze, M., & Lampkin, N. (2009). Policy for organic farming: Rationale and concepts. *Food Policy, 34*(3), 237–244. DOI: 10.1016/j.foodpol.2009.03.005

Suresha, K. M., Joshi, H. G., & Joisa, J. (2025). Agri social entrepreneurship and rural transformation in Karnataka, India. *Discover Sustainability, 6*(1), 994. Advance online publication. DOI: 10.1007/s43621-025-01886-3

Tahat, M., M., M. Alananbeh, K., A. Othman, Y., & I. Leskovar, D. (. (2020). Soil health and sustainable agriculture. *Sustainability, 12*(12), 4859. DOI: 10.3390/su12124859

Tamil Nadu Policy Note. (2024). Agriculture Farmers welfare Department. Available at https://tnhorticulture.tn.gov.in/site_assets/site-pdfs/policy_note/AG-FW-Policy-Note-English-(2024-25).pdf. Accessed on 01.03.2025

Tautges, N. E., Sullivan, T. S., Reardon, C. L., & Burke, I. C. (2016). Soil microbial diversity and activity linked to crop yield and quality in a dryland organic wheat production system. *Applied Soil Ecology, 108*, 258–268. DOI: 10.1016/j.apsoil.2016.09.003

Thakur, N., Sharma, R., Roy, P., Kumar, S., Kumar, K., & Roy, T. N. (2024). Elucidating economic sustainability of organic vis-a-vis conventional vegetable production in North Western Himalayas. *Current Science (00113891)*, 127(10).

Tiwari, A. K. (2021). Comparative analysis of organic farming practices: Impacts on soil health, crop yield, and environmental sustainability. *Plant Science Archives, 1*(04).

Tjamos, E. C., Papavizas, G. C., & Cook, R. J. (1992). *Biological control of plant diseases: Progress and challenges for the future*. Springer., DOI: 10.1007/978-1-4757-9468-7

Toyosumi, I. D. S., Silva, T. S. M. D., Melo, D. M., Azevedo Neto, A. D. D., Soares, T. M., & Coelho Filho, M. A. (2021). Optimization of banana plantlets acclimatization by hydroponic cultivation. *Scientia Agrícola, 78*(suppl 1), e20200165. DOI: 10.1590/1678-992x-2020-0165

Uma, S., & Kumar, P. S. (2025). Organic Production of Fruits: Issues, Challenges, and Opportunities. *Advances in Agri-Food Systems, I*, 141–177. DOI: 10.1007/978-981-96-0759-4_9

Ume, C., & Bahta, Y. T. (2024). Policy support strategies for organic farming extensification in Nigeria. *Organic Agriculture, 14*(3), 1–22. DOI: 10.1007/s13165-024-00467-4

University of California Vegetable Research and Information Center. (n.d.). Organic farming practices: Postharvest handling. University of California. Retrieved from http://postharvest.ucdavis.edu

Vinay Mehla, V. M., & Saroj Kumari, S. K. (2012). Organic farming for health and sustainability. *Annals of Agri Bio Research*, *17*(2), 120–124.

Wang, B., Wang, S., Li, G., Fu, L., Chen, H., Yin, M., & Chen, J. (2025). Reducing nitrogen fertilizer usage coupled with organic substitution improves soil quality and boosts tea yield and quality in tea plantations. *Journal of the Science of Food and Agriculture*, *105*(2), 1228–1238. DOI: 10.1002/jsfa.13913

Wijesinghe, J., Botheju, S. M., Nallaperuma, B., & Kanuwana, N. (2023). Organic farming: the influence on soil health. *One Health: Human, Animal, and Environment Triad*, 185-197.

Willer, H., Trávníček, J., Meier, C., & Schlatter, B. (2021). The world of organic agriculture 2021-statistics and emerging trends.

Willer, H. J. T., & Schlatter, B. (Eds.). (2025). *The World of Organic Agriculture. Statistics and Emerging Trends 2025. Research Institute of Organic Agriculture FiBL*. Frick, and IFOAM – Organics International.

Yang, Y., Huang, S., & Wang, C. (2024). Public policies in support of organic agriculture in China. In *Organic Agriculture and Biodiversity in China* (pp. 65–81). Academic Press. DOI: 10.1016/B978-0-323-90602-9.00007-1

Chapter 5 Towards a Sustainable Zero-Waste Bioeconomy: The Time Travel of Organic Waste

Rania Indu
JIS University, India

Koly De
JIS University, India

Debosmita Das
University of Hyderabad, India

Dibyarupa Pal
https://orcid.org/0000-0002-8564-1485
JIS University, India

ABSTRACT

Global challenges like generation of biomass waste has raised serious concern to waste management processes. Not only the waste needs to be managed judiciously but ensuing circular bioeconomy is a possible strategy for addressing these universal problems. It emphasizes nature driven processes that reutilizes existing reserve into useful materials. Whereas sustainability instigate reduce and recycle of waste to reduce carbon footprint and enhance self-reliant economy. Efficient waste conversion methods transform biodegradable carbonaceous wastes into clean energy using thermochemical processes. Anaerobic digestion, composting, biochar processes convert organic waste into value added product like biofuel, biofertilizers. Sustainable management practices, like spent mushroom waste or nature based

DOI: 10.4018/979-8-3373-9923-2.ch005

solution can guarantee sustainability while valorizing wealth from waste. Biomass waste can be minimized through technological innovations to ensure sustainability and zero waste through circular economy models..

INTRODUCTION

Worldwide, waste management is the most pressing environmental problems possessing a significant challenge to public health, environmental stability and natural resource conservation. Several tonnes of urban and rural waste are generated each day and dumped openly, burned or goes into landfill site. Large-scale waste disposal goes into landfills which are designated sites of controlled disposal involving dumping, compaction and slope-loading of waste. Segregated waste undergoes advanced and controlled thermal treatment strategies like pyrolysis, gasification and incineration, which converts the garbage into ash within very less time. In the process, these options generate hazardous ash containing dioxins, heavy metals and other precarious materials, posing further disposal challenges. On the contrary, waste recycling and valorization are increasingly prioritized in solid waste management, aligning with circular economy by promoting resource recovery and generating useful products (Awasthi et al., 2021; Ghosh et al., 2023; Nordahl et al., 2023; Sarkar et al., 2022; Pajura, 2024).

Technological advancement in economy and globalization is associated with improvement in longevity, social status, economic resilience and a stronger commitment to sustainability. Embracing industry-driven economic model resulted in critical urban waste-cluster worldwide. At the same time, this urbanization necessitates a rapid socio-economic transformation, extensive expansion in the infrastructure to accommodate the growing population, and a significant amount of waste generation (Hamdan et al., 2025). Waste generation, including the production of various waste types such as municipal solid waste (MSW), industrial waste, food and hazardous materials, has become a serious global environmental concern. MSW generation is predicted to increase from 2.1 billion tonnes in 2023 to 3.8 billion tonnes by 2050 (UNEP, 2024). Rapid urbanization and economic advancement resulted in a substantial increase in waste generation in India with approxiamtely 160,038.9 tonnes of solid waste per day, with an average inclusion of 0.74 kg per person each day (Almansour & Akrami, 2024).

To improve ecosystem sustainability and to implement national bioeconomy perspectives, there is absolute need in policymaking and execution on a global scale to necessitate the development of assessment tools and indicators for waste categorization and reduction. From the humble beginnings as documented in the 2012 US Bioeconomy Blueprint, the focus has shifted towards 'zero waste', integrating bioeconomy concepts across other multidisciplinary areas. EU Bioeconomy Strategy revisions for 2023 focussed on use of waste biomass and its valorization to high-value products like bioenergy or compost production. The policy also encourages cutting-edge biorefineries that can utilize organic waste dumped in landfills and close the nutrient loops by producing beneficial resources, reduce Greenhouse gas emissions and generate revenues (Gardossi et al., 2023; Sinkko et al., 2023; Kumar et al., 2025). For instance, in Shangai, China, implementation of zero-waste tactics are cantered on legislation that encourages the development of environmentally friendly supply chains, initiatives to raise communities consciousness through education and promotion, and through zero-waste awareness campaigns (Chu et al., 2023). In Malaysian, 32% of waste generated comes from food sector which can be prevented or avoided. Their policy focusses on reduced food waste by fostering behavioural change and perception of the customer, by strategic planning, implementation and making the society aware of negative impacts on the environment (Baba-Nalikant et al., 2023).

Though percolation of 'zero waste' concept into each and every strata of a community is a challenging task, but it is crucial for the maintenance of a healthy planet and survival of mankind.

TYPES OF WASTE RESOURCES THAT REACHES LANDFILL

Various types of waste are generated across different sectors, each requiring specific handling and disposal methods. Therefore, proper classification and waste management are essential to ensure public health, environmental sustainability and resource conservation. The primary waste categories include:

1. ***Municipal Solid Waste (MSW)***: MSW, commonly referred to as trash or garbage, includes everyday items discarded by households, institutions, and commercial establishments. This comprises food scraps, paper products, packaging materials, plastics, glass, metals, and textiles. Effective management of MSW involves collection, transportation, recycling, composting, and landfilling.
2. ***Plastic waste***: Plastic is one of the most important inorganic solid waste generated in daily life. Plastic waste has become a significant environmental challenge due to its widespread use and improper disposal. Wildlife and ecosystems are adversely affected by the accumulation of plastic debris in natural habitats. Furthermore, degradation of plastics into microplastics and infiltration in food chains, pose potential health risks to humans. Comprehensive strategies, including reducing plastic production, promoting recycling and developing

biodegradable alternatives should be implemented to mitigate pollution and safeguard environmental and human health (Kibria et al., 2023).

3. ***Hazardous Waste***: This section encompasses materials that can cause substantial or potential harms to public health or the environment owing to their toxic, corrosive, ignitable, or reactive properties. Examples include certain chemicals, batteries, pesticides and medical waste. Therefore, it is essential to properly handle, treat and dispose to mitigate the risks associated with these hazardous wastes.
4. ***Industrial Non-Hazardous Waste*:** This category includes materials generated from industrial activities that are not classified as hazardous but still require proper management to ensure safety for the environment and public health. Examples are scrap metals, plastics, wood and packaging materials from manufacturing processes.
5. ***Agricultural and Animal Waste***: This category includes residuals from farming activities, such as crop residues, stubbles, manure and other organic materials. Improper management can lead to environmental issues like water, air and soil pollution.
6. ***Biomedical Waste***: Biomedical wastes include materials generated from healthcare facilities, such as hospitals, clinics, laboratories and biomedical research activities. Items like used needles, syringes, bandages and other contaminated materials fall under this category. This type of waste can be infectious and toxic. Therefore, proper management of discarding biomedical wastes is of utmost importance to avert environmental contamination and ensure the safety of the healthcare personnel and the public. With the advancement in medical facilities and the growing population, India has experienced a significant surge in the amount of biomedical waste production. As per the Union Ministry of Environment and Forests, India generates approximately 4,05,702 kg of biomedical waste per day. Proper segregation, treatment, and disposal are vital to prevent the spread of infections and protect public health (Dhole et al., 2024).
7. ***Construction and Demolition debris*:** The waste debris originate from activities including building, renovating, repairing and demolishing structures such as houses, roads, bridges, dams and others. It consists of materials like wood, gypsum, steel, masonry, concrete, plaster, asphalt and metal, sometimes containing hazardous substances like asbestos and lead. Estimates suggest that waste debris contributes approximately 15–20% of municipal solid waste (iCED, 2025).
8. ***Radioactive Waste*:** Radioactive wastes are hazardous wastes derived from nuclear power generation, nuclear medicine and other applications involving radioactive materials. These wastes pose significant health risks due to their radioactivity. Specialized handling, careful management and disposal is essential to protect human health and the environment.

9. ***Electronic Waste* (E-Waste):** E-waste originates from out-of-life electrical and electronic devices such as mobile phones, televisions, computers, and home appliances. Some of these items often contain hazardous materials like quicksilver, lead, mercury, brominated flame retardants and cadmium, necessitating proper recycling and disposal methods to avert environmental contamination.
10. ***Liquid Waste*:** All liquid waste materials, such as domestic sewage, domestic holding tank waste, commercial wastewater (restaurant grease traps, portable toilets, and commercial holding tanks), industrial effluents, and stormwater runoff, are included in this category. These wastes often contain toxic materials and pathogens that can affect the environment, pollute water bodies and jeopardize the aquatic ecosystems. Therefore, proper treatment and disposal should be ensured to prevent water pollution and protect aquatic lives.
11. ***Mining and Extraction Waste*:** These wastes are generated during the extraction of minerals and other geological materials. Hazardous wastes from mining may contain toxic metals and harmful substances, posing risks to the environment, and endangering human health and natural habitats. Improper disposal of these wastes can lead to soil and water contamination. Hence it is essential to implement stringent management policies to monitor proper treatment and disposal of these wastes (Cobîrzan et al., 2022).
12. ***Food waste*:** Food waste (FW) is one of the most prevalent forms of biowaste today, generated at every stage of the food supply chain right from production to consumption. During manufacturing and processing, FW arises from trimming, peeling, spillage, and quality rejections, while improper handling and storage lead to spoilage due to temperature fluctuations or pest infestations. In distribution and retail, edible food is often discarded due to aesthetic standards, overstocking, or short shelf life. Finally, at the consumer level, FW results from over-purchasing, poor meal planning, and confusion over expiration labels. Globally, an estimated 1.3 billion tons of food is wasted annually, contributing to greenhouse gas emissions, resource depletion, and economic losses. Addressing FW requires improved storage technologies, supply chain optimization, policy interventions and consumer awareness campaigns to promote sustainable consumption and waste reduction. These inefficiencies highlight the need for better food waste management and valorization strategies to reduce economic and environmental impacts (Song et al., 2021; Sarker et al., 2024).

CHALLENGES TO MANAGE WASTE RESOURCES

Technological constraints: The scarcity of modern facilities for sorting, recycling, and composting constitutes a vital infrastructure and technology hurdle to waste management. The efficient separation of complex waste items, like different plastics or e-waste, is still a laborious and dangerous operation unless modern material recovery facilities (MRFs) are furnished with optical sorters, magnets, and air classifiers. Dearth of accessible and well-managed composting facility diverts a substantial part of organic waste, towards landfills, where it decomposes anaerobically and releases methane, a greenhouse gas (Raźniewska, 2022).

Lack of Behavioural change and community participation: Behavioural change of the society is vital in transforming "take-make-dispose" archetype to 'take-make-reuse' model. This circular approach prioritizes reuse and recycling which forms the basis of zero-waste creation. The community residents can be alerted and engaged from waste collection to waste segregation, composting and the ill-effects of open dumping and burning. School children should learn waste management benefits and made knowledgeable to foster long-term behavioural change. Households should be encouraged to establish shared composting sites for larger volumes of organic waste to make fertilizer which would rather reduce pressure on landfills. Non-biodegradable waste like plastics, metals and glass could be sent to nearby urban recycling centres. This way rural communities can play a crucial role in sustainable waste management (SWM). Even social media can dismember attitudes and behaviours as they have special special ability to bring people together, dispense knowledge quickly, and form virtual communities (Achuthan and Khobragade, 2025).

Environmental policy and Governance: Waste resource management relies on a strong policy and governance framework, but insufficient enforcement and integrated planning on implementation like recycling targets are inconsistent between different sectors. Weak enforcement, leads to non-compliance by industries and the public, making illegal dumping a practice. The resilience exhibited by concerned enterprises originates through crisis perception, non-willingness to adaptation, and swift changes towards development of recycled products. Even lack of proper co-ordination between urban planners, environmentalists, and economic enlargement agencies leads to detached policies and unused waste resources. Noteworthy is that, a major chunk of waste collection, sorting and distribution occurs by informal sectors like waste recyclers, scrap pickers and dealers who have rudimentary knowledge of waste-incurred pollution or waste valorization (Kala and Bolia, 2024). Another constraint is the disparity in behaviour and consciousness among urban and rural settings towards environmental policy. Urban population faces more stringent measures in curtailing pollution, ecological rights, and investment in green infrastructure compared to rural areas. This inconsistency not only highlights environmental inequalities but creates gaps in implementation of thorough policies. This gap in the policy needs to be fulfilled at fundamental levels so that percolation of 'zero waste' can be utilized and instigated by different strata (Gardossi et al., 2023; Luo et al., 2025).

Waste volume and complexity: The mounting bulk waste and complexity adDs to an emerging constraint which can be addressed through advanced technologies. The amount and category of waste sent to landfill represents unique challenges and thus, treatment and disposal strategies should be tailor-made to minimize environmental impact, promote resource recovery, and defend community health (Nmere et al., 2020; Mishra et al., 2024; Al-Romeedy et al., 2025).

LIFE CYCLE ASSESSMENT (LCA) METRICS

LCA metrics provides information on environmental impact of a product's journey from generation to utilization and conversion to waste, till it's death. The procedure incorporates recycling, composting, and reusing can be used to measure the reduction of emitted pollutant greenhouse gases, fossil fuel generation, resource depletion and others.

Assessment of carbon footprint: The dumping grounds release large amounts of greenhouse gases, mainly carbon dioxide (CO_2) and methane (CH_4), which contribute to global warming. Landfills receiving huge quantity of organic waste undergo anaerobic digestion which release landfill gases. Carbon flux can be measured by quantitative and qualitative methods through soil sampling, biomass assessments and Remote sensing technologies. For quantitative measurement of carbon flux, the cumulative amount of carbon produced and sequestered per capita is calculated from each eligible source. Various LCA tools and databases can leverage the assessment process. Carbon neutrality can be obtained by practices like sustainable farming and forestry which add up carbon credits. Carbon credits serve as a vital tool in global climate mitigation efforts by creating economic incentives for Greenhouse gas emission reductions. In recycling systems, these credits quantify and monetize the environmental benefits achieved through waste recovery and valorization. When recyclable organic waste from landfills is reprocessed into new products, they consume less energy than manufacturing from virgin materials, resulting in reduced carbon emissions. This closed-loop approach transforms waste management practices into sustainable forms while supporting circular economy principles (Yaashikaa et al., 2022; Cao et al., 2023).

Assessment of Economic viability: Cost-benefit analyses compare carbon credit revenues against implementation costs, along with community resident's income surveys to evaluate livelihood improvements. Ecological benefits are measured through biodiversity audits, water quality testing, and monitoring of agrochemical use reduction. Long-term sustainability requires evaluating permanence through reforestation survival rates and leakage prevention by comparing project zones with control areas. This initiatives ensures carbon credit programs enhance environmental, economic and social sustainability in agriculture and forestry systems (Kamyab et al., 2024).

SMART WASTE TRACKING TECHNOLOGIES AND DIGITAL INNOVATIONS

Efficient waste management can only proceed with advanced technologies augmented with Artificial Intelligence (AI) platforms like sensor based waste collection and sorting, application of robots, waste disposal choices and data analytics platforms like block chain technology to track waste movement.

Sensor-based bin monitoring: Sensor-based bin monitor filled trash bins in real-time by embedding ultrasonic or infrared sensors within public and commercial containers. This data is sent to a central cloud platform for analysis so that on-demand service, deployment of vehicles and informing waste operators can be operated on requirement basis (John et al., 2022).

Waste Sorting Robots: Technological advancements include robotic arms that can use hyperspectral imaging and sophisticated cameras to distinguish and categorize different kinds of waste materials.

Pay-As-You-Throw: This platform introduces monetary incentive to reduce trash; to discourage excessive waste generation. Incentive-based recycling initiative foster responsible waste disposal habits to promote circular economy and sustainability. Thus awareness campaigns and education programs of the community residents can propagate the process (Zhou et al., 2021).

Blockchain technology: A waste management technology by embedding digital ledger to track waste through the entire lifecycle; from disposal through transportation and recycling into new products. The process generates transparency and accountability across complex supply chains to combat illegal dumping and ensuring that environmental commitments are met.

Thus to minimize waste and maximize disposal in intelligent manner, right from the point of generation to collection, transportation, and final processing, these solutions offer data-driven visibility beyond conventional approaches. Figure 1 highlights the different strata of travel of waste from accumulation to disposal and the final culmination.

Figure 1. The different strata of travel of waste and their destiny

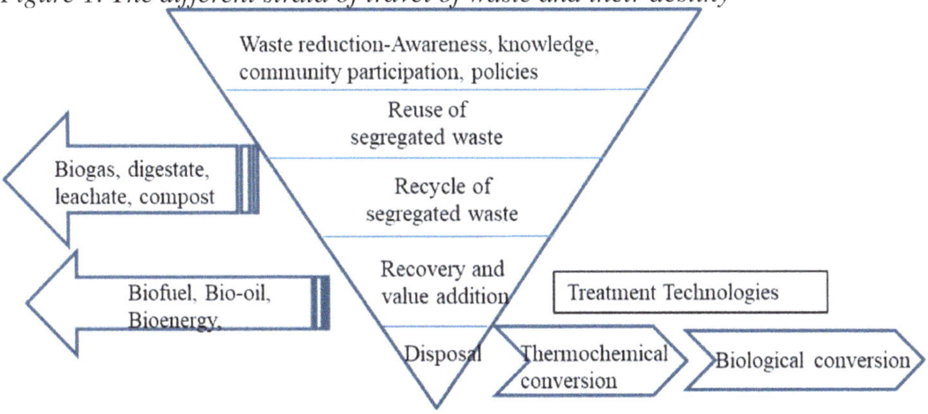

CASE STUDIES IMPLICATING ZERO-WASTE BIOECONOMY

China has achieved the 'zero waste city'' category by implementing and maintaining systematic planning, focusing on goals and addressing problems, deepening reforms and working in integrated manner where the government and the community people worked cooperatively. For example, The Ministry of Agriculture and Rural Affairs categorically supported pilot programmes based on resource utilization from livestock and poultry and agricultural by-products. The Ministry of Urban-Rural Development emphasized on classification of organic and non-biodegradable waste whereas, the Ministry of Commerce commenced model program based on recycling renewable resources. These endeavour based on integrated approach from all sectors of governance emphasizes a successful 'zero waste' concept model nurturing excellent economic development (Qi et al., 2024).

The Kamikatsu Town of Japan, has been pioneer on 'Zero Waste' by implementing rigorous practise of waste separation at source whereby the citizens actively participated. The Ministry of Environment initiated to shut down technically challenged industries promoting emission of gaseous pollutants. The media persuavely promoted recycling avenues and generating revenues without challenging the environmental health. Thus vigorous recycling reduced the landfill dumping and waste accumulation. The people were encouraged for financial subsidies for buying items like electric composters, to compost organic waste in the household. A "Kuru-kuru" shop was time-honoured to display recycled items and only the rural people were allowed to dump waste, but others can take it for free (Shenyoputro and Jones, 2023).

Different Processes to Harness Organic Waste

Biogas

Biogas is a renewable energy source produced through the anaerobic digestion (AD) of organic waste fraction, including food waste, agricultural residues and animal manure. It primarily composed of 50–75% methane (CH_4), 25–50% carbon dioxide (CO_2) with trace amounts (1–2%) of hydrogen sulfide (H_2S), hydrogen (H_2) and ammonia (NH_3) (Atelge et al., 2020). Landfills emit significant quantities of LFG, particularly methane, a potent greenhouse gas (GHG) with a calorific value of 26.882 MJ/m^3 (37.50 MJ/kg) and a density of 0.717 kg/m^3. For instance, in Chandigarh, 175 tons per day (TPD) of organic waste yielded 0.34 Gg/year of methane, producing 0.27–0.77 MW of electricity (Mor et al., 2024). Biogas can be valorized or upgraded in multiple ways: (1) direct combustion for heat/electricity generation, (2) upgrading to biomethane ($\geq$95% CH_4) for injection into natural gas grids or use as vehicle fuel, and (3) conversion into biohydrogen or syngas for industrial applications. Additionally, the by-product of AD, digestate, serves as a nutrient-rich biofertilizer, closing the nutrient loop in agriculture. Biogas valorization not only reduces greenhouse gas emissions from decomposing waste but also displaces fossil fuels, supporting circular economy goals. To refine biogas, CO_2 is removed via various physiochemical methods, or diverted to obtain high-purity biomethane (97% CH_4) applying adsorption and membrane permeation techniques (Bernardo et al., 2021; Marconi and Rosa, 2023). But challenges like high upfront infrastructure costs, need for efficient feedstock sorting, are de-accelerating its adoption globally. These approaches not only support cleaner energy production but also promote waste valorization, contributing to a more sustainable energy ecosystem.

Upgraded LFG (biomethane) can displace fossil fuels, mitigate climate impact and generate revenue for landfill operators (Ardolino et al., 2021). In India, 3,184 dumpsites could potentially produce 5,167–14,355 MW of power, translating to billions in annual revenue (Gross et al., 2021). These findings underscore the need for integrated waste management to harness waste-derived energy efficiently (Basso et al., 2021).

Digestate

Digestate, the nutrient-rich residual material remaining after anaerobic digestion (AD), represents a valuable by-product of biogas production. This complex organic material contains significant quantities of undigested lignocellulosic components along with essential macro and micronutrients that can be recovered and utilized. The composition of digestate directly correlates with the original feedstock characteristics, for instance, feedstocks with high cellulose and low lignin content may permit additional anaerobic processing to extract more biogas, while excess carbon content often indicates recalcitrant feedstock and suboptimal AD performance, suggesting the need for improved pre-treatment methods (Song et al., 2021). Zhao et al., 2018 found digestate from a mixture of maize silage (40%), grass silage (30%) and animal dung (30%) contained 35.8% cellulose, 3.95% hemicellulose and 24.9% lignin, while Cao et al., 2019 reported different compositions from food waste (85%) and yard trimmings (14%) feedstocks. The practical applications of digestate are equally important, with the solid fraction serving effectively as organic compost, soil amendment or animal bedding, and the liquid fraction functioning as nutrient-rich fertilizer or raw material for bio-based products. These diverse applications not only contribute to environmental sustainability through waste valorization but also create economic opportunities, enhancing the overall viability of AD operations while delivering multiple ecological benefits.

Digestate can be valorized into low-cost organic fertilizer and bioplastic production. Recycled digestate serve as fertilizer and thus avoids methane emissions from landfill, reduce greenhouse gas emissions and lowers the carbon footprint when compared to synthetic fertilizer. Rich in organic matter, digestate enhances soil health, improves water retention and microbial activity to promote sustainable agriculture. By maximizing digestate utilization, industries and farmers can achieve both economic gains and environmental sustainability, making it a key component of modern waste-to-resource strategies and support a circular economy (Lee et al., 2021; Selvaraj et al., 2022).

Landfill Leachate

Leachate form the landfill, is a liquid by-product formed when water percolates through organic waste, undergoing physiochemical and biological transformations. It is generated through three primary mechanisms: (1) the integral moisture content of landfill waste, (2) water infiltration from precipitation and (3) biochemical degradation of organic waste components. This complex effluent contains high concentrations of organic matter, inorganic compounds, nitrogen, phosphorus and potentially toxic substances. Despite its hazardous nature, leachate can be transformed into valuable energy and biofuel resources through proper treatment. One sustainable management approach involves leachate recirculation within landfills, which serves multiple purposes: it recovers essential nutrients, maintains optimal moisture levels to enhance waste decomposition and minimizes groundwater contamination risks. The increased moisture content promotes the activity of anaerobic bacteria, accelerating waste breakdown and subsequently boosting methane (CH_4) production rates. Recent studies suggest that amending leachate with additives such as coffee grounds or exogenous aerobic bacterial consortia can further optimize CH_4 generation, offering a promising strategy to improve both waste treatment efficiency and biogas recovery. These value-added applications not only mitigate environmental pollution but also contribute to renewable energy production, demonstrating the potential of leachate management in advancing circular economy principles within waste treatment systems (Lindamulla et al., 2022; Li et al., 2024).

High concentrations of nitrogen and phosphorus in leachate can be extracted and repurposed as liquid fertilizers, reducing dependency on synthetic alternatives, lowering agricultural costs and carbon emissions. Leachate can be processed in anaerobic digesters to produce biogas, which can be used for electricity generation or as a renewable fuel, creating revenue streams for waste facilities (Gao et al., 2021). Proper leachate treatment prevents methane, a potent Green House Gas from escaping into the atmosphere, mitigating climate impact. Treating leachate, minimizes the risk of toxic contamination in nearby groundwater water sources, preserving ecosystems and public health. Recovering nutrients and energy from leachate aligns with circular economy principles, reducing waste and promoting sustainability (Ibro et al., 2024).

Sustainable Approaches of Treating Organic Waste

Agricultural waste is a major contributor to global solid waste, leading to environmental pollution, greenhouse gas emissions, and public health risks when improperly managed. Transitioning to a circular bioeconomy by converting agro-waste into energy can help achieve Sustainable Development Goals (SDGs), particularly SDG 7 (Affordable and Clean Energy) and SDG 12 (Responsible Consumption and Production) (Rani et al., 2023).

Agricultural waste conversion to Spent Mushroom Substrate (SMS)

India generates 998 million tonnes (MT) of agro-waste rice straw, wheat husks, corn cobs, sugarcane waste) annually, primarily from rice-wheat cropping systems. They posess a significant disposal challenge in rural areas. Common edible mushrooms (*Agaricus, Pleurotus, Volvariella, Calocybe, Lentinula edodes*) thrive on these substrates when cultivated. Post cultivation, spent mushroom substrate (SMS) is generated which can be effectively repurposed into a by-product of mushroom that retains valuable nutrients and organic matter. This process not only reduces waste but also creates a sustainable resource for soil enrichment, livestock feed and bioenergy. It is estimated that by the year 2026, global mushroom production would reach to 20.84 million tonnes, which on the other hand significantly increase SMS waste. Approximately, 1 kg of mushrooms produces ~5 kg of SMS waste (Mamimin et al.,

2021; Shirur et al., 2021). Adopting valorization and integrated farming systems can turn waste into wealth while mitigating environmental harm. This aligns with India's sustainable agriculture goals and global circular bioeconomy trends.

Mushroom cultivation relies on lignocellulosic materials to break down polymers by their enzymes into simpler substrates as they grow and mature. The conversion begins by using agricultural waste as a primary substrate for growing mushrooms. Lignocellulosic materials like straw and sawdust are sterilized, inoculated with mushroom spawn (e.g., oyster or button mushrooms), and allowed to colonize. After harvesting the mushrooms, the remaining SMS is rich in partially decomposed organic matter, enzymes, bioactive substances and beneficial microbes. Unlike raw agricultural waste, the SMS has better water retention and a balanced carbon-to-nitrogen ratio, making it an excellent soil conditioner and compost additive. Farmers can apply it directly to fields to enhance soil fertility, reducing dependency on chemical fertilizers (Martín et al. 2023; Sarkar et al., 2024). Additionally, SMS can be further processed into animal feed supplements, particularly for ruminants, due to its residual fungal proteins and fibre content. It is also explored for its potential in biogas production through anaerobic digestion, offering a circular economy approach.

The growing accumulation of organic waste has drawn the scientific community to explore bioeconomy opportunities from this discard. A circular economy approach is being adopted to transform this waste into various value-added products. For instance, by converting agricultural waste into SMS, rural communities can achieve zero-waste farming, where every by-product is utilized efficiently. This method supports sustainable agriculture, reduces open burning of crop residues, and enhances economy. Governments and NGOs can promote this practice by providing training on SMS applications, ensuring long-term environmental and economic benefits for farmers.

Composting

Composting is an eco-friendly and effective method for managing organic waste into nutrient-rich soil amendments while promoting sustainability. It is a dynamic biological process of transforming biodegradable materials, by the sequential dominance of different microbial communities, like actinomycetes and fungi. Initially, easily degradable organic compounds are rapidly metabolized, while more complex or recalcitrant materials persist longer in the process. The process converts all forms of biodegradable organic waste, into valuable products. Composting not only diverts waste from landfills but also enhances soil health, reduces greenhouse gas emissions and promotes circular economy, making it a cornerstone of sustainable waste management strategies Additionally, composting reduces the need for chemical fertilizers, supporting sustainable agriculture (Meena et al., 2021; Mamo et al., 2021; Nordahl et al., 2023; Pajura, 2024).

Vermicompost is another option of organic fertilizer produced through the non-thermophilic biodegradation of organic waste by earthworms and microorganisms (Hajam et al., 2023). Further adoption of vermi-composting can contribute significantly to sustainable farming, waste minimization, and climate-smart agriculture. This system achieves true loop closure by returning essential nutrients like nitrogen, phosphorus and potassium back to the soil, reflecting natural biogeochemical cycles.

Biochemical and Thermochemical Waste Conversion Technologies

Biochemical

Anaerobic digestion (AD) operates through microbial decomposition of organic wastes in oxygen-free environments, yielding two primary outputs: (1) digestate (a nutrient-rich soil amendment) and (2) biogas (a methane-CO_2 mixture). The reaction process occurs through fermentation targeting the lignocellulosic biomass to produce bio-alcohols (ethanol), organic acids (lactic acid), or biohydrogen utilizing specialized microbes like *Clostridium* spp. Pre-treatment procedures are required for recalcitrant lignocellulosic biomasses like rich in lignin components. Physiochemical processes like mechanical grinding, steam explosion or enzymatic pre-treatment are needed to break down refractory organic matter. Anaerobic digestion produces biogas (a renewable energy source) and nutrient-rich digestate, which can be used as biofertilizer, by breaking down organic waste without oxygen. The aerobic breakdown of organic waste by microbes produces humus rich compost that improves soil fertility and structure (Kumar et al., 2024).

Thermochemical

Thermochemical conversion technologies offer a sustainable solution for managing rural and agricultural waste by transforming organic and non-recyclable materials into energy, fuels and valuable by-products. Processes like incineration, gasification, pyrolysis, and hydrothermal carbonization (HTC) use heat and chemical reactions to break down waste under oxygen-controlled environments, minimizing harmful emissions while maximizing resource recovery (Begum et al., 2024).

Incineration: Direct burning of waste at high temperatures (800–1,200°C) generates heat for electricity or district heating. Modern systems incorporate air pollution control (scrubbers, filters) to reduce emissions. While suitable for high-calorific waste (wood, crop residues), it is less ideal for wet or low-energy materials.

Gasification: A partial oxidation process (700–1,500°C) converts carbon-rich waste (rice husks, coconut shells, plastics) into syngas ($CO + H_2$), a fuel for engines, turbines, or chemical synthesis. Gasification is more efficient than combustion, with lower emissions, and can handle diverse feedstocks, making it viable for rural decentralized energy systems.

Pyrolysis: Pyrolysis heats organic material in a low-oxygen environment to create biochar, a stable, carbon-rich substance that improves soil quality, carbon sequestration and water retention. In the present context, there is a heightened focus on thermochemical and biochemical conversion processes aimed at enhancing the transformation of biomass into electricity, heat and biofuels. Heating waste in the absence of oxygen (300–800°C) produces bio-oil, syngas and biochar. Slow pyrolysis favors biochar (used as soil amendment), while fast pyrolysis maximizes liquid fuel production.

Hydrothermal Carbonization

Hydrothermal carbonization (HTC) is a thermochemical process of treating wet organic biomass in subcritical water under relatively mild conditions, typically at temperatures ranging from 180-250 °C and between 10-50 bar pressures. Under these conditions, water acts both as a reactant and as a solvent/reaction medium, facilitating the degradation of biomass through heterogeneous chemical reactions. Key mechanisms involved in HTC include dehydration, hydrolysis, aromatization and polymerization, which collectively transform the biomass into carbon-rich solid products. The output is referred as hydrochar (a coal-like solid fuel) which is nutrient-rich carbonized product suitable for fertilizer applications. HTC is energy-efficient process for high-moisture waste and need no pre-drying step. By adopting these technologies, zero-waste ecosystems achieve, turning waste into wealth while mitigating environmental degradation. Different processing pathways for bioenergy generation are highlighted in Table 1.

Table 1. Different bioenergy production pathways

Pathways	Process	Output	Advantages	References
Anaerobic Digestion	Microbes break down waste in absence of O	Biogas (CH_4 + CO_2)	Produces biogas and nutrient-rich digestate	Mamimin et al., 2021
Gasification	Partial combustion at high temperature	Syngas (CO + H_2)	High energy efficiency, low emissions	Yang et al., 2024
Pyrolysis	Thermal decomposition	biochar Bio-oil, syngas	Carbon sequestration via biochar	Parthasarathy et al., 2023
Incineration	Thermal decomposition	Ash and Flue gas	Volume Reduction	Jiang et al., 2022
HCT	wet biomass treated at 180-250 °C and 10-50 bar pressure	hydrochara and CO_2	Alternative to fossil fuels	Ischia and Fiori, 2021

Emerging Technologies Towards Zero-Waste Bioeconomy

Adoption of Precision agriculture

Precision agriculture harness data-driven approaches to revolutionize farm management by optimizing crop production and simultaneously minimizing environmental impact. By integrating real-time field monitoring systems with advanced sensor and analytics, these solutions enable precise management of soil conditions, water usage and crop health. Precision agricultural technologies leverage Artificial Intelligence (AI) to optimize irrigation, fertilizer applications, pest control, to ensure maximum resource efficiency.to revolutionize farm management. The technology integrates IoT sensors, satellite imagery and machine learning algorithms to significantly reduce carbon footprint of farming operations by preventing over-application of inputs and minimizing waste runoff. These technologies optimize crop health monitoring, yield prediction, fertilizer and pesticide application, pest/weed detection, addressing key limitations of conventional farming methods. AI processes satellite imagery, drone data and IoT sensor inputs optimizing light, temperature, humidity and soil nutrients to evaluate crop vigor, stress factors and disease susceptibility (Ghosh et al., 2024; Borah et al., 2025). Machine Learning (ML) models detect early signs of abiotic/biotic stress, enabling timely interventions. Deep Learning (DL) and Convolutional Neural Networks (CNN) identify pest-infested plants from image data, allowing targeted treatment before disease spreads. AI-driven systems reduce overuse of pesticides, lowering costs and environmental impact. Nevertheless, AI also analyzes soil and weather data to optimize irrigation, fertilizer application time and harvesting schedules, minimizing waste while maximizing yields. Predictive algorithms forecast crop performance under varying conditions, aiding strategic planning of farm management by integrating autonomous machinery like smart sprayers, robotic harvesters for precision execution (Ghosh et al., 2024; Borah et al., 2025). Agriculture accounts for approximately 25% of global greenhouse gas (GHG) emissions, primarily through three key sources: enteric fermentation in cattle producing methane, flooded rice paddies emitting methane and synthetic fertilizer use releasing nitrous oxide (Green et al., 2022; Thamarai et al., 2024; Borah et al., 2025).

Modern precision agriculture leverages cutting-edge technologies to optimize farming practices while promoting sustainability. Remote sensing platforms and drones provide high-resolution, real-time imagery that enables meticulous monitoring of crop health, soil variability, and pest infestations at scale. This aerial intelligence integrates seamlessly with ground-level IoT sensors that continuously track microclimate conditions, soil moisture and nutrient levels, creating a comprehensive data ecosystem (Getahun et al., 2024). The insights derived feed into GPS-guided machinery and Variable Rate Technology (VRT) systems, which precisely tailored planting patterns and input applications like delivering water, fertilizers and pesticides only where and when needed. This targeted approach achieves dual benefits like boosting operational efficiency by reducing input waste by 20-50% while simultaneously minimizing environmental harm through decreased chemical runoff and lower greenhouse gas emissions. By combining these technologies, precision agriculture establishes a closed-loop system where data-driven decisions enhance both productivity and ecological balance, conserving water resources, improving soil health and creating more sustainable farming systems for future generations. Emerging technologies, particularly blockchain, are revolutionizing waste management by introducing transparency, traceability and efficiency into traditionally fragmented systems. For rural communities struggling with inadequate waste infrastructure, blockchain combined with IoT, smart contracts, and big data analytics can optimize waste collection, recycling, and resource recovery while ensuring accountability at every stage (Zhang, 2019).

Derivation of Nutraceuticals from organic waste

The valorization of organic waste extends beyond biofuel into high-value functional compounds like proteins, fibers, antioxidants for various multidimensional purposes encompassing nutraceuticals, pharmaceuticals, food additives and biodegradable materials. Modern extraction techniques are employed which score over traditional extraction methods in term of efficiency, scalability and sustainability. For instance, Solvent extraction is a widely used method for isolating bioactive compounds, oils, antioxidants and other high-value substances from agro-waste (Chang, 2020). This technique involves using selective solvents based on the polarity and solubility of the target compounds for extraction purposes. Diverse lignocellulosic biomass types, like food waste, fruit peels, seed husks and crop residues, undergo extraction utilizing polar (water, ethanol and methanol) and non-polar solvents (hexane, petroleum ether, and chloroform). Phenolic compounds, flavonoids, polysaccharides, lipids, essential oils and waxes are the extracted valuable products of solvent extraction. For example, citrus peels can provide essential oils and pectin, grape pomace can supply polyphenols and anthocyanins, and rice bran can yield nutrient-rich oils. Recent advancements have introduced greener solvents, including supercritical fluids (e.g., CO_2) and ionic liquids, which minimize environmental impact and enhance extraction yields. Supercritical CO_2 extraction, for instance, operates at high pressures and low temperatures, preserving heat-sensitive compounds while eliminating organic solvent residues (Coelho et al., 2018). Microwave assisted extraction (MAE) uses microwave energy to disrupt plant cell walls, enhancing solvent penetration, while Ultrasound-Assisted Extraction (UAE) employs ultrasonic waves to generate cavitation, facilitating the release of intracellular compounds (Gupta et al., 2024; Buvaneshwaran et al., 2023). Different extraction techniques for organic waste valorization are exhibited in Table 2.

Table 2. Different extraction techniques for organic waste

Method	Mechanism	Advantages	Limitations	Applications
Solvent Extraction	Uses organic solvents (hexane, ethanol)	High yield, cost-effective	Toxic residues, environmental hazards	Phenolics, oils, pigments
Enzymatic Extraction	Enzymes (cellulase, pectinase) break bonds	Eco-friendly, selective, mild conditions	High enzyme cost, slow kinetics	Proteins, polysaccharides, flavors
Supercritical Fluid Extraction (SFE)	CO_2 at high pressure/ temperature	Solvent-free, high purity, tuneable selectivity	High capital cost, scalability challenges	Essential oils
Ultrasound-Assisted Extraction (UAE)	Cavitation disrupts cell walls	Faster, lower energy, higher yield	Limited to small-scale applications	Polyphenols, flavonoids, pectin
Microwave-Assisted Extraction (MAE)	Dielectric heating enhances solubility	Rapid, energy-efficient, scalable	Risk of thermal degradation	Alkaloids, terpenes, essential oils

Artificial intelligence (AI) for sustainable waste management

The crises of mounting waste and declining natural resources, demands a shift towards more sustainable waste management approaches. This transition is guided by waste sources systematically redirecting generated waste towards reuse, recycling and material recovery following the "zero waste" philosophy. However, effectively tracking waste sources and monitoring their origins presents significant challenges. Multiple complexities like the fragmentation of materials as products degrade into smaller components; regulatory frameworks that assign waste accountability to manufacturers; and the complication of abandoned waste through illegal dumping or littering are the growing challenges (Taylor et al., 2020). These real life factors demonstrate that current waste tracking systems often lack practical, scalable solutions capable to address real-world complexities. As a result, more robust, viable and adaptable mechanisms are needed to ensure accurate waste monitoring, enforce accountability and support circular economy objectives. Emerging technologies, particularly blockchain, are playing a transformative role in addressing critical waste management challenges, especially concerning problematic waste streams like plastic waste. Blockchain technology, with its integration of smart contracts, distributed ledgers, IoT, and big data analytics, enables the development of transparent and efficient smart waste management systems. For instance, when a farmer disposes of plastic waste, it is scanned via IoT-enabled bins and data logged on blockchain for verification (Saberi et al., 2019). Unlike traditional approaches, blockchain ensures data integrity by creating immutable, tamper-proof records of every stage in the waste management process i.e from collection and sorting to recycling and final disposal. This transparency not only enhances accountability among stakeholders but also facilitates better monitoring and optimization of waste streams. When combined with IoT-enabled smart bins and AI-driven analytics, blockchain can improve operational efficiency by optimizing collection routes and reducing unnecessary costs. Furthermore, blockchain opens doors to innovative business models, such as waste-to-resource marketplaces and plastic credit systems, which incentivize recycling and promote a circular economy. For example, automated payments token are rewarded to users for proper depositing plastic bottles. Plastic pollution has escalated to global crisis due to unchecked production, consumption and disposal making it the most persistent ecological and public health nuisance. Plastic waste now infiltrates every corner of the planet from the deepest ocean trenches to remote terrestrial ecosystems with devastating consequences. Blockchain technology addresses key drawbacks of conventional waste management systems, including inefficiencies, lack of traceability and low recycling rates. While challenges like scalability, transparency and energy consumption remain, the integration of blockchain with other digital technologies holds immense potential to revolutionize waste management, turning environmental liabilities into sustainable opportunities and paving the way for a zero-waste future (Taylor et al., 2020; Baralla et al., 2023; Jiang et al., 2023).

Life cycle assessment (LCA) towards sustainable waste management

The growing volumes of municipal solid waste (MSW) worldwide have intensified the need for sustainable management strategies that prioritize waste reduction, resource recovery and environmental impact mitigation. LCA has emerged as an indispensable methodology for evaluating the environmental sustainability of waste management systems right from landfilling and incineration to recycling and composting. A critical decision-support tool, enabling policymakers and waste managers to quantify the environmental burdens of different MSW management options, providing a comprehensive framework to quantify impacts across the entire waste value chain from collection, segregation, transportation to treatment, recycling and final disposal. By analyzing key indicators such as global warming potential (GWP), resource depletion, energy consumption and pollution emissions, LCA enables policymakers and waste managers to compare the ecological footprints of different waste management strategies, including landfilling, incineration, composting and advanced recycling technologies. For instance, LCA studies consistently highlights the benefits of organic waste diversion from landfills (where anaerobic decomposition generates methane) toward composting or anaerobic digestion, which can reduce GHG emissions by up to 50% while producing valuable biogas and fertilizers (Zhang et al., 2021). Similarly, LCA reveals that material recovery and recycling particularly for plastics, metals and paper often outperform virgin material production in terms of energy savings and carbon mitigation, though outcomes depend on local infrastructure and waste purity. The sustainability of converting MSW into chemicals is comprehensively evaluated through LCA, which analyzes critical environmental impact categories including global warming potential (GWP), resource depletion and energy consumption (Torkayesh et al., 2022). Energy consumption varies substantially by technology, with thermochemical processes requiring high energy inputs but potentially achieving energy positivity through syngas or bio-oil recovery, while biochemical routes like anaerobic digestion have lower energy demands but narrower feedstock applicability. The overall sustainability of these systems hinges on optimizing process efficiency, integrating renewable energy, and implementing advanced sorting technologies to maximize resource recovery while minimizing environmental impacts across the entire value chain, from waste collection to final chemical production. LCA serves as an indispensable tool to quantify these complex interactions, identify improvement opportunities, and ensure that waste-to-chemicals conversion contributes meaningfully to circular economy objectives without unintended environmental consequences (Ischia and Fiori, 2021; Sikarwar et al., 2021).

EMERGING GREEN INNOVATIONS

Nature Based Solutions (NBSs) represent a sustainable and eco-friendly approach to treat wastewater and mimics natural wetland processes to effectively remove contaminants through a combination of physical, chemical and biological mechanisms. By utilizing solutions that are close to nature, like trees, microbial consortia, constructed wetlands, reed beds and others to treat contaminants like leachate waste. NBSs provide sustainable chances to reclaim valuable resources from the leachate waste which consist of mainly organic fraction and mineral components. Constructed wetlands (CWs) is another such example of NBSs which has emerged as an increasingly attractive nature based solutions for wastewater treatment, offering multiple advantages including minimal energy requirements, operational simplicity and enhanced aesthetic value compared to conventional treatment systems. Ayadi et al., 2025, removed ammonium compounds and certain pharmaceutical compounds from a vertical CWs planted with *Phragmites Australis.* CWs engineered systems are particularly advantageous due to their low energy requirements, minimal operational costs and ability to integrate impeccably into natural landscapes while providing additional ecological benefits such as biodiversity enhancement and habitat creation. Wetlands typically consist of shallow basins or channels filled with porous media like gravel, sand, or soil and planted with emergent vegetation that facilitates pollutant removal through substrate filtration, microbial degradation and plant uptake. The treatment efficiency of CWs can be significantly enhanced by incorporating materials such as biochar, which improves contaminant adsorption, supports microbial activity and promotes plant growth (Panghal et al., 2024; Ayadi et al., 2025; Deng and Chang, 2025). The integration of biochar as a multifunctional substrate in CWs significantly enhances system performance due to its exceptional physicochemical properties, including high porosity, extensive surface area and abundant functional groups. Biochar serves three critical functions in CW systems: (1) acting as an effective adsorbent for various micro pollutants like heavy metals, pharmaceuticals and personal care products; (2) providing an optimal growth medium for wetland vegetation by improving water retention and nutrient availability; and (3) creating favourable habitats for diverse microbial communities that drive essential biogeochemical processes including nitrification, denitrification and organic matter degradation (Feng et al., 2023). This synergistic combination of biochar-amended CWs represents a sustainable, cost-effective approach to wastewater treatment that simultaneously addresses water purification, carbon sequestration and ecological enhancement while maintaining low operational and maintenance requirements.

Bio solids and other wastewater by-products are generated from the leachate fraction which are rich in organic matter and nutrients; used as fertilizers, biofuel and soil enricher. Reducing reliance on non-renewable resources and promoting circular economy concepts are achieved through transforming these by-products into resources with added value. The implementation of NBSs will facilitate the recycling of the most valuable natural resources on Earth, thereby enhancing the preservation of ecosystem health and biodiversity. On this sustainable forefront to confront challenges of the huge waste load, active research is required to promote and augment NBSs for waste treatment of leachate and valorisation of by-products. The technology offers environmentally sensitive wastewater treatment alternatives contributing towards zero waste bioeconomy. Thus adopting and applying NBSs can aid in reducing carbon footprint on Earth (Hale et al., 2021). Table 3 highlights the difference in two models; linear and Circular.

Table 3. Difference in points between linear and zero-waste model

Category	Traditional Linear model	Circular Zero-waste model
Strategic Principle	Take-Make-Dispose	Make-Use-Recycle/Reuse
Origin of resource	New resource exploited	Waste resources are resued/recycyled
Journey of waste	Waste goes from Cradle to Grave	Waste goes from Cradle to Cradlee
Production criteria	Production is cheap and of composite material	Production is lengthy, non-toxic and recycled material
Envivronment sustaiinable	Pollutants produced during manufacturing process, high carbon footprint	Reduced Greenhouse gas emissions or low carbon footprint

FUTURE DIRECTION

The 'zero waste' movement is gathering momentum with tech-driven transformation and rise of new business models. Emphasis is being given to tackle waste where it originates. Proactive legislation, governance and participation of all sectors is necessary to indulge towards circular economy. Moving away from the linear "take-make-waste" paradigm and moving toward a circular one will reduce waste disposal and with improved recycling technologies will reduce the burden of waste accumulation.

CONCLUSION

The key insights of sustainable resource management emphasizes on embracing resilient and efficient practice for a more better and sustainable future. The accumulation of organic waste presents a significant concern in contemporary society, which can only be alleviated through the implementation of advanced technologies and the process of waste valorization. To fully harness the potential of waste biomass, it is imperative to develop enhanced and sustainable technologies that facilitate large-scale commercialization through further research and investigation. The utilization of renewable resources derived from waste biomass is imperative for mitigating greenhouse gas emissions and enhancing energy security. Together, these paradigms provide the foundation for transforming waste management from a linear disposal system to a sustainable, closed-loop resource management strategy which is based on zero waste bioeconomy. Policies and regulations play a crucial role in enabling this transition by setting frameworks for waste reduction, recycling and sustainable production.

REFERENCES

Achuthan, K., & Khobragade, S. (2025). Content dynamics and emotional engagement in online zero waste communities: A longitudinal study. *Cities (London, England)*, *165*, 106119. DOI: 10.1016/j.cities.2025.106119

Al-Romeedy, B. S., Emam, M. E., & Tyagi, P. K. (2025). Exploring Waste Reduction Potential in Rural Tourism: What Solutions Can Be Implemented? In *Solid Waste Management for Rural Regions* (pp. 193-214). IGI Global Scientific Publishing.

Almansour, M., & Akrami, M. (2024). Towards Zero Waste: An In-Depth Analysis of National Policies, Strategies, and Case Studies in Waste Minimisation. *Sustainability (Basel)*, *16*(22), 10105. DOI: 10.3390/su162210105

Ardolino, F., Cardamone, G. F., Parrillo, F., & Arena, U. (2021). Biogas-to-biomethane upgrading: A comparative review and assessment in a life cycle perspective. *Renewable & Sustainable Energy Reviews*, *139*, 110588. DOI: 10.1016/j.rser.2020.110588

Awasthi, A. K., Cheela, V. S., D'Adamo, I., Iacovidou, E., Islam, M. R., Johnson, M., & Li, J. (2021). Zero waste approach towards a sustainable waste management. *Resources. Environmental Sustainability*, *3*, 100014.

Ayadi, M., Fersi, C., Mahjoub, B., Ben Salah, I., & Touati, F. (2025). Vertical Constructed Wetlands Integrated with Biochar: A Green Nature-Based Solution for Wastewater Treatment. *Chemistry Africa*, *8*(2), 607–618. DOI: 10.1007/s42250-024-01149-0

Baba-Nalikant, M., Syed-Mohamad, S. M., Husin, M. H., Abdullah, N. A., Mohamad Saleh, M. S., & Abdul Rahim, A. (2023). A zero-waste campus framework: Perceptions and practices of university campus community in Malaysia. *Recycling*, *8*(1), 21. DOI: 10.3390/recycling8010021

Baralla, G., Pinna, A., Tonelli, R., & Marchesi, M. (2023). Waste management: A comprehensive state of the art about the rise of blockchain technology. *Computers in Industry*, *145*, 103812. DOI: 10.1016/j.compind.2022.103812

Basso, B., Jones, J. W., Antle, J., Martinez-Feria, R. A., & Verma, B. (2021). Enabling circularity in grain production systems with novel technologies and policy. *Agricultural Systems*, *193*, 103244. DOI: 10.1016/j.agsy.2021.103244

Begum, Y. A., Kumari, S., Jain, S. K., & Garg, M. C. (2024). A review on waste biomass-to-energy: Integrated thermochemical and biochemical conversion for resource recovery. *Environmental Science. Advances*, *3*(9), 1197–1216. DOI: 10.1039/D4VA00109E

Bernardo, M., Lapa, N., Fonseca, I., & Esteves, I. A. (2021). Biomass valorization to produce porous carbons: Applications in CO2 capture and biogas upgrading to biomethane—a mini-review. *Frontiers in Energy Research*, *9*, 625188. DOI: 10.3389/fenrg.2021.625188

Borah, S. K., Dutta, C., Pal, D., Sarkar, S., & Sethi, L. N. (2025). Harnessing Artificial Intelligence in Agriculture for a Sustainable Future. 1:95-120. ISBN: 978-93-5860-467-2

Borah, S. K., Pal, D., Sarkar, S., & Sethi, L. N. (2025). AI-Powered Drones for Sustainable Agriculture and Precision Farming. In Sadiq, S., Ahmad, M., Karunakaran, N., & Atapattu, A. (Eds.), *Advancing Global Food Security With Agriculture 4.0 and 5.0* (pp. 69–98). IGI Global Scientific Publishing. DOI: 10.4018/979-8-3693-9964-4.ch004

Buvaneshwaran, M., Radhakrishnan, M., & Natarajan, V. (2023). Influence of ultrasound-assisted extraction techniques on the valorization of agro-based industrial organic waste–A review. *Journal of Food Process Engineering*, *46*(6), e14012. DOI: 10.1111/jfpe.14012

Cao, L., Wang, J., Xiang, S., Huang, Z., Ruan, R., & Liu, Y. (2019). Nutrient removal from digested swine wastewater by combining ammonia stripping with struvite precipitation. *Environmental Science and Pollution Research International*, *26*(7), 6725–6734. DOI: 10.1007/s11356-019-04153-x PMID: 30632036

Cao, X., Williams, P. N., Zhan, Y., Coughlin, S. A., McGrath, J. W., Chin, J. P., & Xu, Y. (2023). Municipal solid waste compost: Global trends and biogeochemical cycling. *Soil & Environmental Health*, *1*(4), 100038. DOI: 10.1016/j.seh.2023.100038

Chang, S. H. (2020). Utilization of green organic solvents in solvent extraction and liquid membrane for sustainable wastewater treatment and resource recovery—A review. *Environmental Science and Pollution Research International*, *27*(26), 32371–32388. DOI: 10.1007/s11356-020-09639-7 PMID: 32533493

Chu, Z., Li, Q., Zhou, A., Zhang, W., Huang, W. C., & Wang, J. (2023). Strategy formulation path towards zero-waste of municipal solid waste: A case study from Shanghai. *Journal of Cleaner Production*, *418*, 138091. DOI: 10.1016/j.jclepro.2023.138091

Cobîrzan N, Muntean R, Thalmaier G, Felseghi RA. Recycling of Mining Waste in the Production of Masonry Units. *Materials (Basel)*. 2022;15(2):594. Published 2022 Jan 13.

Coelho, J. P., Filipe, R. M., Robalo, M. P., & Stateva, R. P. (2018). Recovering value from organic waste materials: Supercritical fluid extraction of oil from industrial grape seeds. *The Journal of Supercritical Fluids, 141*, 68–77. DOI: 10.1016/j.supflu.2017.12.008

Deng, S., & Chang, J. (2025). Application of biochar as an innovative substrate in constructed wetlands/biofilters for wastewater treatment: Performance and ecological benefits. In *Emerging Developments in Constructed Wetlands* (pp. 595–628). Elsevier. DOI: 10.1016/B978-0-443-14078-5.00025-8

Dhole KS, Bahadure S, Bandre GR, Noman O. Navigating Challenges in Biomedical Waste Management in India: A Narrative Review. *Cureus*. 2024;16(3):e55409. Published 2024 Mar 2. DOI: 10.7759/cureus.55409

Gao, M., Li, S., Zou, H., Wen, F., Cai, A., Zhu, R., Tian, W., Shi, D., Chai, H., & Gu, L. (2021). Aged landfill leachate enhances anaerobic digestion of waste activated sludge. *Journal of Environmental Management, 293*, 112853. DOI: 10.1016/j.jenvman.2021.112853 PMID: 34044237

Gardossi, L., Philp, J., Fava, F., Winickoff, D., D'Aprile, L., Dell'Anno, B., Marvik, O. J., & Lenzi, A. (2023). Bioeconomy national strategies in the G20 and OECD countries: Sharing experiences and comparing existing policies. *EFB Bioeconomy Journal, 3*, 100053. DOI: 10.1016/j.bioeco.2023.100053

Getahun, S., Kefale, H., & Gelaye, Y. (2024, October 9). Application of Precision Agriculture Technologies for Sustainable Crop Production and Environmental Sustainability: A Systematic Review. *TheScientificWorldJournal, 2024*(1), 2126734. DOI: 10.1155/2024/2126734 PMID: 39421732

Ghosh, A., Kumar, S., & Das, J. (2023). Impact of leachate and landfill gas on the ecosystem and health: Research trends and the way forward towards sustainability. *Journal of Environmental Management, 336*, 117708. DOI: 10.1016/j.jenvman.2023.117708 PMID: 36913859

Ghosh, D., Siddique Md, A., & Pal, D. (2024). *AI driven approach for Precision Agriculture in the Book 'AI in Agriculture for Sustainable and Economic Management.* Taylor and Francis.

Global Waste Management Outlook. 2024. UNEP - UN Environment Programme. https://www.unep.org/resources/global-waste-management-outlook-2024

Green, T., Gourdain, E., Hirschy, G., Sine, M., Geyer, M., Laun, N., & de Jong, J. R. (2022). Farming system perspective. In *Handbook digital farming: digital transformation for sustainable agriculture* (pp. 277–339). Springer Berlin Heidelberg. DOI: 10.1007/978-3-662-64378-5_5

Gross, T., Breitenmoser, L., Kumar, S., Ehrensperger, A., Wintgens, T., & Hugi, C. (2021). Anaerobic digestion of biowaste in Indian municipalities: Effects on energy, fertilizers, water and the local environment. *Resources, Conservation and Recycling*, *170*, 105569. DOI: 10.1016/j.resconrec.2021.105569

Gupta, Y., Barrett, B., & Vlachos, D. G. (2024). Understanding microwave-assisted extraction of phenolic compounds from diverse food waste feedstocks. *Chemical Engineering and Processing*, *203*, 109870. DOI: 10.1016/j.cep.2024.109870

Hajam, Y. A., Kumar, R., & Kumar, A. (2023). Environmental waste management strategies and vermi transformation for sustainable development. *Environmental Challenges*, *13*, 100747. DOI: 10.1016/j.envc.2023.100747

Hale, S. E., Folde, M. S., Melby, U. H., Sjødahl, E. U., Smebye, A. B., & Oen, A. M. (2021). From landfills to landscapes—Nature-based solutions for water management taking into account legacy contamination. *Integrated Environmental Assessment and Management*, *18*(1), 99–107. DOI: 10.1002/ieam.4467 PMID: 34019725

Hamdan, A., Panda, S., Jain, M. S., Raj, V., & Mathew, S. (2025). Assessing Municipal solid Waste in Indian Smart Cities: A Path towards Waste-to-Energy. *Heliyon*, *e42770*(February), e42770. DOI: 10.1016/j.heliyon.2025.e42770

Ibro, M. K., Ancha, V. R., Lemma, D. B., & Pohl, M. (2024). Enhancing Biodegradability of Coffee Husk and Water Hyacinth Using Food Waste: Synergistic and Kinetic Evaluation Under Co-digestion. *BioEnergy Research*, *17*(3), 1953–1970. DOI: 10.1007/s12155-024-10750-7

International Centre for Environment Audit and Sustainable Development (iCED), Jaipur, India, The Energy and Resources Institute (TERI), New Delhi. Municipal Solid Waste Management in India-A Compendium Report. International Centre for Environment Audit and Sustainable Development (iCED). Published 2022. Accessed March 27, 2025.

Ischia, G., & Fiori, L. (2021). Hydrothermal carbonization of organic waste and biomass: A review on process, reactor, and plant modeling. *Waste and Biomass Valorization*, *12*(6), 2797–2824. DOI: 10.1007/s12649-020-01255-3

Jiang, P., Zhang, L., You, S., Van Fan, Y., Tan, R. R., Klemeš, J. J., & You, F. (2023). Blockchain technology applications in waste management: Overview, challenges and opportunities. *Journal of Cleaner Production*, *421*, 138466. DOI: 10.1016/j.jclepro.2023.138466

Jiang, X., Zhao, Y., & Yan, J. (2022). Disposal technology and new progress for dioxins and heavy metals in fly ash from municipal solid waste incineration: A critical review. *Environmental Pollution*, *311*, 119878. DOI: 10.1016/j.envpol.2022.119878 PMID: 35944780

John, J., Varkey, M. S., Podder, R. S., Sensarma, N., Selvi, M., Santhosh Kumar, S. V. N., & Kannan, A. (2022). Smart prediction and monitoring of waste disposal system using IoT and cloud for IoT based smart cities. *Wireless Personal Communications*, *122*(1), 243–275. DOI: 10.1007/s11277-021-08897-z

Kala, K., & Bolia, N. B. (2024). Empowering the informal sector in urban waste management: Towards a comprehensive waste management policy for India. *Environmental Development*, *49*, 100968. DOI: 10.1016/j.envdev.2024.100968

Kamyab, H., SaberiKamarposhti, M., Hashim, H., & Yusuf, M. (2024). Carbon dynamics in agricultural greenhouse gas emissions and removals: A comprehensive review. *Carbon Letters*, *34*(1), 265–289. DOI: 10.1007/s42823-023-00647-4

Kibria, M. G., Masuk, N. I., Safayet, R., Nguyen, H. Q., & Mourshed, M. (2023). Plastic Waste: Challenges and Opportunities to Mitigate Pollution and Effective Management. *International Journal of Environmental Research*, *17*(1), 20. DOI: 10.1007/s41742-023-00507-z PMID: 36711426

Kumar, D. J. P., Mishra, R. K., Chinnam, S., Binnal, P., & Dwivedi, N. (2024). A comprehensive study on anaerobic digestion of organic solid waste: A review on configurations, operating parameters, techno-economic analysis and current trends. *Biotechnology Notes*, *5*, 33–49. DOI: 10.1016/j.biotno.2024.02.001 PMID: 39660169

Kumar, R., Gupta, G., Hussain, A., Rani, A., Thapliyal, A., Gunsola, D., & Mitra, D. (2025). Pioneering zero-waste technologies utilization and its framework on sustainable management: International, national and state level. *Discover Applied Sciences*, *7*(3), 224. DOI: 10.1007/s42452-025-06693-z

Lee, M. E., Steiman, M. W., & Angelo, S. K. S. (2021). Biogas digestate as a renewable fertilizer: Effects of digestate application on crop growth and nutrient composition. *Renewable Agriculture and Food Systems*, *36*(2), 173–181. DOI: 10.1017/S1742170520000186

Lindamulla, L., Nanayakkara, N., Othman, M., Jinadasa, S., Herath, G., & Jegatheesan, V. (2022). Municipal solid waste landfill leachate characteristics and their treatment options in tropical countries. *Current Pollution Reports*, *8*(3), 273–287. DOI: 10.1007/s40726-022-00222-x

Luo, J., Dang, R., Lan, P., Hu, Y., & Yang, B. (2025). Urban-rural disparities in low-carbon policy intensity and residents' willingness to pay in environmental sustainability. *Cities (London, England)*, *159*, 105795. DOI: 10.1016/j.cities.2025.105795

Mamimin, C., Chanthong, S., Leamdum, C., O-Thong, S., & Prasertsan, P. (2021). Improvement of empty palm fruit bunches biodegradability and biogas production by integrating the straw mushroom cultivation as a pretreatment in the solid-state anaerobic digestion. *Bioresource Technology*, *319*, 124227. DOI: 10.1016/j.biortech.2020.124227 PMID: 33049444

Mamo, M., Kassa, H., Ingale, L., & Dondeyne, S. (2021). Evaluation of compost quality from municipal solid waste integrated with organic additive in Mizan–Aman town, Southwest Ethiopia. *BMC Chemistry*, *15*(1), 1–11. DOI: 10.1186/s13065-021-00770-1 PMID: 34281617

Marconi, P., & Rosa, L. (2023). Role of biomethane to offset natural gas. *Renewable & Sustainable Energy Reviews*, *187*, 113697. DOI: 10.1016/j.rser.2023.113697

Martín, C., Zervakis, G. I., Xiong, S., Koutrotsios, G., & Strætkvern, K. O. (2023). Spent substrate from mushroom cultivation: Exploitation potential toward various applications and value-added products. *Bioengineered*, *14*(1), 2252138. DOI: 10.1080/21655979.2023.2252138 PMID: 37670430

Meena, A. L., Karwal, M., Dutta, D., & Mishra, R. P. (2021). Composting: phases and factors responsible for efficient and improved composting. *Agriculture and Food: e-Newsletter, 1*, 85-90.

Mishra, S., Chauhan, M. S., Sundaramurthy, S., Raj, V., Vishwakarma, A., & Niranjan, U. S. (2024). Waste to Wealth: A Philosophy of Zero Waste. In *From Waste to Wealth* (pp. 85–107). Springer Nature Singapore. DOI: 10.1007/978-981-99-7552-5_5

Nmere, O. N., Abugu, J. O., Alio, F. C., & Anetoh, J. C. (2020). Influence of public relations' media public enlightenment campaign and community participation strategies on waste management. *Problems and Perspectives in Management*, *18*(1), 82. DOI: 10.21511/ppm.18(1).2020.08

Nordahl, S. L., Preble, C. V., Kirchstetter, T. W., & Scown, C. D. (2023). Greenhouse gas and air pollutant emissions from composting. *Environmental Science & Technology*, *57*(6), 2235–2247. DOI: 10.1021/acs.est.2c05846 PMID: 36719708

Pajura, R. (2024). Composting municipal solid waste and animal manure in response to the current fertilizer crisis-a recent review. *The Science of the Total Environment, 912*, 169221. DOI: 10.1016/j.scitotenv.2023.169221 PMID: 38101643

Panghal, V., Singh, A., Arora, D., & Kumar, S. (2024). Biochar-modified constructed wetlands using Eclipta alba as a plant for sustainable rural wastewater treatment. *Environmental Science and Pollution Research International, 31*(11), 17299–17310. DOI: 10.1007/s11356-024-32144-0 PMID: 38340301

Parthasarathy, P., Zuhara, S., Al-Ansari, T., & McKay, G. (2023). A review on catalytic CO2 pyrolysis of organic wastes to high-value products. *Fuel, 335*, 127073. DOI: 10.1016/j.fuel.2022.127073

Qi, S., Chen, Y., Wang, X., Yang, Y., Teng, J., & Wang, Y. (2024). Exploration and practice of "zero-waste city" in China. *Circular Economy, 3*(1), 100079. DOI: 10.1016/j.cec.2024.100079

Rani, G. M., Pathania, D., Umapathi, R., Rustagi, S., Huh, Y. S., Gupta, V. K., & Chaudhary, V. (2023). Agro-waste to sustainable energy: A green strategy of converting agricultural waste to nano-enabled energy applications. *The Science of the Total Environment, 875*, 162667. DOI: 10.1016/j.scitotenv.2023.162667 PMID: 36894105

Raźniewska, M. (2022). Compostable packaging waste management—Main barriers, reasons, and the potential directions for development. *Sustainability (Basel), 14*(7), 3748. DOI: 10.3390/su14073748

Saberi, S., Kouhizadeh, M., Sarkis, J., & Shen, L. (2019). Blockchain technology and its relationships to sustainable supply chain management. *International Journal of Production Research, 57*(7), 2117–2135. DOI: 10.1080/00207543.2018.1533261

Sarkar, B., Debnath, A., Chiu, A. S., & Ahmed, W. (2022). Circular economy-driven two-stage supply chain management for nullifying waste. *Journal of Cleaner Production, 339*, 130513. DOI: 10.1016/j.jclepro.2022.130513

Sarkar, S., Bayen, S., Samanta, S., & Pal, D. (2024). Spent Mushroom Substrate-Prospects and Challenges of Agrowaste management into sustainable solutions: A Review. *International Journal of Agriculture Environment and Biotechnology, 17*(04), 731–741.

Selvaraj, P. S., Periasamy, K., Suganya, K., Ramadass, K., Muthusamy, S., Ramesh, P., & Palanisami, T. (2022). Novel resources recovery from anaerobic digestates: Current trends and future perspectives. *Critical Reviews in Environmental Science and Technology, 52*(11), 1915–1999. DOI: 10.1080/10643389.2020.1864957

Shenyoputro, K., & Jones, T. E. (2023). Reflections on a two-decade journey toward zero waste: A case study of Kamikatsu town, Japan. *Frontiers in Environmental Science*, *11*, 1171379. DOI: 10.3389/fenvs.2023.1171379

Shirur, M., Barh, A., & Annepu, S. K. (2021). Sustainable Production of Edible and Medicinal Mushrooms: Implications on Mushroom Consumption. In Hebsale Mallappa, V. K., & Shirur, M. (Eds.), *Climate Change and Resilient Food Systems* (pp. 315–346). Springer. DOI: 10.1007/978-981-33-4538-6_12

Sikarwar, V. S., Pohořelý, M., Meers, E., Skoblia, S., Moško, J., & Jeremiáš, M. (2021). Potential of coupling anaerobic digestion with thermochemical technologies for waste valorization. *Fuel*, *294*, 120533. DOI: 10.1016/j.fuel.2021.120533

Sinkko, T., Sanyé-Mengual, E., Corrado, S., Giuntoli, J., & Sala, S. (2023). The EU Bioeconomy Footprint: Using life cycle assessment to monitor environmental impacts of the EU Bioeconomy. *Sustainable Production and Consumption*, *37*, 169–179. DOI: 10.1016/j.spc.2023.02.015

Song, S., Lim, J. W., Lee, J. T., Cheong, J. C., Hoy, S. H., Hu, Q., & Tong, Y. W. (2021). Food-waste anaerobic digestate as a fertilizer: The agronomic properties of untreated digestate and biochar-filtered digestate residue. *Waste Management (New York, N.Y.)*, *136*, 143–152. DOI: 10.1016/j.wasman.2021.10.011 PMID: 34666296

Taylor, P., Steenmans, K., & Steenmans, I. (2020). Blockchain technology for sustainable waste management. *Frontiers in Political Science*, *2*, 590923. DOI: 10.3389/fpos.2020.590923

Thamarai, P., Deivayanai, V. C., Saravanan, A., Vickram, A. S., & Yaashikaa, P. R. (2024). Carbon mitigation in agriculture: Pioneering technologies for a sustainable food system. *Trends in Food Science & Technology*, *147*, 104477. DOI: 10.1016/j.tifs.2024.104477

Torkayesh, A. E., Rajaeifar, M. A., Rostom, M., Malmir, B., Yazdani, M., Suh, S., & Heidrich, O. (2022). Integrating life cycle assessment and multi criteria decision making for sustainable waste management: Key issues and recommendations for future studies. *Renewable & Sustainable Energy Reviews*, *168*, 112819. DOI: 10.1016/j.rser.2022.112819

Wastes | US EPA. US EPA. https://www.epa.gov/report-environment/wastes. Published July 8, 2024. Acessed on 28.03.2025.

Yaashikaa, P. R., Kumar, P. S., Nhung, T. C., Hemavathy, R. V., Jawahar, M. J., Neshaanthini, J. P., & Rangasamy, G. (2022). A review on landfill system for municipal solid wastes: Insight into leachate, gas emissions, environmental and economic analysis. *Chemosphere*, *309*, 136627. DOI: 10.1016/j.chemosphere.2022.136627 PMID: 36181852

Yang, Y., Zhou, T., Cheng, M., Xie, M., Shi, N., Liu, T., & Li, B. (2024). Recent advances in organic waste pyrolysis and gasification in a CO2 environment to value-added products. *Journal of Environmental Management*, *356*, 120666. DOI: 10.1016/j.jenvman.2024.120666 PMID: 38490005

Zhang, D. (2019). Application of blockchain technology in incentivizing efficient use of rural wastes: A case study on yitong system. *Energy Procedia*, *158*, 6707–6714. DOI: 10.1016/j.egypro.2019.01.018

Zhao, X., Becker, G. C., Faweya, N., Rodriguez Correa, C., Yang, S., Xie, X., & Kruse, A. (2018). Fertilizer and activated carbon production by hydrothermal carbonization of digestate. *Biomass Conversion and Biorefinery*, *8*(2), 423–436. DOI: 10.1007/s13399-017-0291-5

APPENDIX: GLOSSARY OF TERMINOLOGIES

AD Anaerobic Digestion
CNN Convolutional Neural Networks
DL Deep Learning
HTC Hydrothermal carbonization
LCA Life Cycle Assessment
MSW Municipal Solid Waste
ML Machine Learning
MT Million Tonnes
SMS Spent Mushroom Substrate

Chapter 6
Water Resource Sustainability and Environmental Degradation in G20 Countries

Ajay Kumar Singh
https://orcid.org/0000-0003-0429-0925
Department of Humanities and Social Sciences, Graphic Era University, Dehradun, India

S. Srinivasan
https://orcid.org/0009-0002-0179-9849
Department of Humanities and Social Sciences, Graphic Era University, Dehradun, India

Bhim Jyoti
V.C.S.G., UUHF, College of Forestry, Ranichauri, India

Manas Kumar Pedi
https://orcid.org/0000-0002-6890-7819
Department of Economics, KIIT University, Bhubaneswar, India

Sanjeev Kumar
https://orcid.org/0000-0002-2074-1071
Department of Economics, Hansraj College, University of Delhi, Delhi, India

DOI: 10.4018/979-8-3373-9923-2.ch006

ABSTRACT

This chapter develops an empirical model to assess the impact of social-economic development, environmental degradation, green and digital technologies on water productivity in G20 countries. Therefore, water productivity is treated as a dependent variable, and it is adopted as a representative variable for water resources sustainability (WRS). While sex ratio, education expenditure, population growth, population density, urbanization, industrialization, capita GDP, per capita CO2 emissions, environmental technologies, renewable energy consumption, inflation, technological advancement, trade openness, foreign direct investment, cereal yield, and DTs are used as independent variables. Country-wise panel data of explained and explanatory variables are compiled to estimate regression coefficients. Log-linear regression model is adopted to estimate the impact of aforesaid variables on WRS. The descriptive result shows a decreasing trend in WRS in G20 countries during 1990-2022. Thus, G20 countries should take effective policies to increase WRS to increase sustainable development.

1. INTRODUCTION

Water resources sustainability (WRS) is supportive to increase social and economic development, and sustainable development (Golubev, 1983; FAO, 2017; Egbo et al., 2022; Zlati et al., 2024). Water resources have positive and significant implications on industrial and agricultural sectors. For instance, freshwater is found positive to increase productivity of the industrial sector in China and Russia (Egbo et al., 2022). Water resources, thus, has multiple uses and it can be used by humanity to achieve different goals. For example, clean water can be consumed by people as per their requirements. While WRS is significant to reduce environmental degradation and enhance ecosystem services. Therefore, many sustainable development goals (SDGs) proposed by UNDP cannot be achieved without WRS (Compoli et al., 2024). While water resources are negatively impacted due to urbanization, industrialization and population growth (Zlati et al., 2024; Xian, 2025). High economic growth is increasing the enormous pressure on WRS. Agricultural water demand also increases due to increase in industrial structure and increasing demand of food products (Huang et al., 2021). Water resources are also negatively impacting due to increase in transport, energy industry and industrialization (Zlati et al., 2024). The agricultural sector is consuming 70% of the withdrawal volume of water (FAO,

2017; FAO & OECD. 2021; Ingrao et al., 2023). Thus, agriculture uses the largest quantity of global water (Chang et al., 2024).

As industrial and infrastructural development is not possible without water resources (Azam et al., 2024). Fish and livestock rearing sector cannot cultivate without water resources. Water resources are significant for recreation of different species on earth. However, overwhelming urbanization produces a negative impact on healthcare and water supply (Li & Zhang, 2025). Further, extensive infrastructural development (e.g., road and building construction) has negative consequences in water resources. Water productivity is decreasing due to water pollution and environmental degradation (Golubev, 1983). Climate change is creating issues to sustain water resources. Water bodies are drying due to climate change (Musah & Yakubu, 2023). Consequently, it is causing water scarcity (Aryal et al., 2024) and reducing water supplies (O'Connell, 2017; Wang, Rauf, et al., 2024). Around 20% of the world's population is facing trouble to acquire clean and safe water.

Agricultural intensification and industrialization are increasing water pollution. Chemical and fertilizer manufacturing industries are increasing water pollution in many countries. Thus, continuous water scarcity would be a challenge for global communities to address multiple issues like food insecurity, hunger, and nutritional insecurity (Booker & Trees, 2021). Moreover, water scarcity is creating a barrier and obstacle for sustainable development (Flint, 2004). Hence, it is imperative to adopt scientific mechanisms and technological application to increase WRS. WRS, thus, has become the most crucial agenda for developing the path of sustainable development.

Past studies have identified the various issues which increase the attention of national and international policy makers to implement policies towards WRS. For this, existing researchers and international development organizations have provided different theories on WRS including various problems in price estimation of water in different sectors. WRS is associated with several other activities which are essential to increase the livelihood security of humans. Moreover, management of water resources and its sustainability have emerged as a key and competing objective in economic theories (Braden & van Lerland, 1999). Economic theories have a great history to estimate the correct pricing of existing private and public goods. Economic theories are expected to provide insights into policies to promote sustainable use of water and to maintain WRS in global economies (Braden & van Lerland, 1999; Heintz, 2004). It would be useful to make effective and minimum utilization of water in economic activities.

All segments of society and community would have an accessibility of water according to their needs. Appropriate pricing of private and public goods would be useful to increase gain in economic efficiency (Rogers et al., 2002). A wide range of researchers and scientists have provided their own view on water pricing. Also, availability of natural resources depends on the nature and geographical location of a country. It is noticed that human and natural activities are responsible for water scarcity in most economies (Wang et al., 2024). Social development and economic development, globalization, population growth and urbanization are the key drivers to increase water scarcity in most economies (Cosgrove & Loucks, 2015). Thus, it is essential to regulate the policy to maintain the high population growth, urbanization and overwhelming industrialization to meet the basic criteria of WRS. Water sustainability is a scientific technique in which water must be available for current and future generation without reducing its efficiency and efficacy in all economic activities. Water sustainability also reduces negative implication of production related activities on water resources. However, the scientific research community and international development organizations could not provide and develop scientific, viable and universal definitions on WRS. Most economies of the world are giving significant effort to search for effective measures of WRS. It must reduce costs of water, protect and conserve available natural resources, and reduce negative environmental impact.

Sustainability in agriculture, fisheries, livestock, forestry and industries can be achieved through WRS. Sustainable means continuing something without lessening (Flint, 2004). Lant (2004) argued that sustainability is a vague and debated term among the international research community. Water resources would be sustainable if the total quantity of water entering, leaving and being stored in the system. Water sustainability involves a sequence of various actions with inaccessible strategies. Sustainability builds the bridge between development related activities and environmental related concerns (Khan & Khan, 2012). WRS involves various activities like plans, quality and quality of water to improve life for all, and advocates consideration of spatial scales (Flint, 2004). Moreover, improving water productivity may be a favourable solution to increase water resource sustainability.

Previous researchers and international organizations have explored the impact of water resources and its productivity on social-economic development, human health, agricultural development, food security and other (For instance, Zlati et al., 2024; Biswas et al., 2022). Determinants of WRS are also clearly defined in the literature. However limited research could give attention to examine the water productivity influencing factors as giving more importance on environmental degradation. Moreover, existing literature seems unable to investigate the impact of environmental degradation on water productivity. High water productivity ensures that a country has better technologies and mechanisms to increase water efficiency and its multiple usages. Thus, this chapter have a crucial contribution in the conceptual and empirical literature as it proposed to answer the following research questions:

- What is the significance of WRS?

- What are the basic challenges for improving WRS in G20 countries?
- What may be the negative consequences of water scarcity in the global countries?
- Which SDGs are significantly linked with water productivity?
- What are the consequences of social-economic development, environmental degradation, and digitalization on water productivity?

This chapter is achieved following research objectives:

- To detect the determinants of WRS as per theoretical literature.
- To observe the implication of social-economic development, environmental degradation, and digitalization on water productivity in G20 countries through empirical investigations.
- To suggest policy implications to improve WRS and sustainable development.

This chapter provides the review of literature on WRS and valuation of water prices. It also applied a log-linear regression model to examine the impact of social-economic and environmental development, green and environmental and digitalization on water productivity in G20 countries. The current chapter is divided in 9 inclusive sections. The 1st section, provides the introduction on WRS and its prime determinants. It includes a concrete overview of sustainability and its crucial components. Thereupon, it provides the definition of WRS. Conceptual and empirical reviews are provided in the 2nd section. Critical discussion on findings of previous literature is also explained in this section. It produces the few key issues which are significantly associated with water resource sustainability and why global economies are needed to give significant focus towards WRS. The 3rd section emphasizes the economic theory of WRS. Nature of water and its scarcity is also given in this section. It also provides the importance of WRS in context of demand and supply of water. Efficiency and distributive justice of water for the public is explained. The 4th section, elaborates the research design, area of study, source of data, statistical and empirical investigation. The 5th section explains the results and discussion. Policy implications based on empirical findings and earlier studies are given in the 6th section. Innovation and novelty of the chapter is provided in the 7th section. The 8th section introduced the limitations and scope of further research. Last section (i.e., 9th) ends up with a summary and conclusion.

2. CONCEPTUAL AND EMPIRICAL REVIEW

2.1. WRS in the Global Countries

WRS has become a very crucial agenda in the world. Availability of water plays a significant role in maintaining socio-economic development in several ways (Egbo et al., 2022). Appropriate water availability is a catalyst which is useful to generate energy, public drinking water suppliers, irrigation and food production (i.e. agriculture, aquaculture and fishing, industries, etc.). Most economic activities depend upon water availability (e.g., agricultural and industrial activities). Food demand would increase at a high rate due to increasing population in near future. While food production can be improved with extension and intensification of the agricultural sector, subsequently the agriculture sector would require more water. While agriculture is a highly water intensive occupation in the world (Aryal et al., 2024). Agriculture sector will need more water for irrigation to sustain production of crops (Egbo et al., 2022). For instance, irrigated food production will double by 2025(FAO, 2017). Furthermore, commercialization of the agriculture sector provides the incentive to farmers to grow cash crops like sugarcane, groundnut. Commercialization of this sector would increase intensive use of water in the agriculture sector. Water bodies, thus, would be unable to meet the water requirement of the agriculture sector in future. The quantity of water in various sources like surface and ground is continuously decreasing. Due to this reason, the agricultural sector cannot meet the food requirement of a growing population in near future. Furthermore, water is a consumable commodity, thus it is an essential component to meet the nutritional requirements of people. Hence, it is essential to increase WRS in all economies. Accordingly, WRS is essential to generate energy, food production, and maintain sustainability of biodiversity and global changes (Tundisi, 2008).

2.2. WRS and Social-economic Developmental Activities

Water security is essential to increase social and economic development (Zlati et al., 2024). It is crucial to maintain human health, produce food production and manage the environment. Egbo et al. (2022) examined the impact of freshwater withdrawals and management on the agricultural and industrial sector in emerging countries. It is noted that freshwater withdrawal is found positive to increase crop and livestock index in Brazil. Subsequently, water is an important driver to increase economic growth (Goswami & Bisht, 2017). Zlati et al. (2024) examined the impact of water security on economic and social development in EU countries using structural equation modelling. Foreign direct investment, renewable energy consumption, foreign trade, trade openness, and financial development, etc. have a significant impact on WRS. Public investment in education and health sectors also have a significant impact on WRS. Employment opportunities are a crucial pillar to increase economic development which depend on water (WBG, 2025). While water demand may increase as economic development increases.

2.3. Water and Human Development

Water plays a significant role in increasing human development (Goswami & Bisht, 2017). Human development of an economy directly reflects adequate management of water resources. There are many economies such as the USA, Russia, Japan which have higher values of HDI and these economies have an adequate per capita water availability. Thus, it provides evidence that there is a significant and positive association of human development with per capita availability of water. In contrast, India, China, Bangladesh and Pakistan have a relatively poor position in human development (as per HDI report) due to low availability of water sources. Also, lack of water is a significant barrier to continue sustainable socio-economic development (Goswami & Bisht, 2017). Appropriate water supply enhances productivity in agriculture and its allied and energy sectors (WBG, 2025). Water resources work as an essential tool to reduce poverty (Egbo et al., 2022). Thus, appropriate water management is crucial to make the world free from poverty (WBG, 2025). These are essential to resolve barriers of sustainable development as reducing water scarcity (Katko & Hukka, 2015).

2.4. Demographic Change and Industrialization

Water availability is highly stressed at global level due to several reasons. These reasons have been identified in terms of high population growth, high urbanization and over industrialization world-wide (Schnoor, 2010; Flint, 2004; Arfanuzzaman & Rahman, 2017; Rios et al., 2018; Azam et al., 2024). Zlati et al. (2024) found a significant correlation between population density and pollution level which are also associated with water quality. Further, high population density and pollution increase the burden to increase water quality (Zlati et al., 2024). Moreover, industrialization is caused to reduce the water quality and increase water pollution (Azam et al., 2024). Ecological footprint increases due to industrialization (Li & Zhang, 2025). There are many reasons which increase the water demand due to population growth, urbanization and rising living standards. Therefore, it is estimated that the water crisis is increasing due to environmental, economic and social factors (Tundisi, 2008; Goswami & Bisht, 2017). Conversely, socio-economic development of people is being negatively influenced due to scarcity of water (Goswami & Bisht,

2017). Vallgårda (2018) found a positive association of the value of groundwater with population growth.

2.5. Water Resources and Ecosystem Re-creation

Moreover, water is an essential component of ecosystem services, which provide several goods and services to increase public health (WBG, 2025). Ecosystem is negatively influenced due to water pollution (Mehmood et al., 2023). If water is not sufficient then a country would be unable to do the cleaning of other ecosystem services which depend upon water. Provisioning services are water supply and energy sources, while regulating services are flood regulation services and cultural services, tourism and religious practices and education (Vallgårda, 2018). To maintain the WRS has emerged as a key concern for global economies in the era of changing socio-economic activities. Many economies are facing water scarcity due to changing socio-economic characteristics of humanity. Water shortage hampers the basic livelihoods of humanity (Lado, 1997).

2.6. Environmental Degradation and Climate change

Water productivity is associated with water scarcity. Water productivity can be improved by using its multiple uses in the production of goods and services. At present climate change has also brought several problems to maintain the WRS world-wide (Musah & Yakubu, 2023). Recently, climate change is observed in terms of high fluctuation in maximum and minimum temperature, changing rainfall patterns, drought and floods. Flood irrigation is a significant cause of water loss (Expósito & Cebollero, 2025). Variability in temperature is caused to reduce availability of groundwater. Melting of glaciers is also increasing due to increase in temperature. Occurrence of drought and change in rainfall pattern bring more water scarcity. Occurrence of drought would be caused to increase water demand in the agricultural sector (Chang et al., 2024). Further, hydrological cycles, quantity and quality of water is being adversely affected due to climate change (Goswami & Bisht, 2017; Vallgårda, 2018; Rios et al., 2018; Musah & Yakubu, 2023). Climate change has an adverse impact on the water cycle which further reduces groundwater and agricultural production (FAO, 2017).

Climate change has a direct and indirect impact on groundwater (Vallgårda, 2018; Ali et al., 2024). It may also cause increased contamination in water bodies like rivers, lakes and other. In drought prone areas ground water availability slightly declined. Thus, it negatively affected the agricultural production system and food production (Vallgårda, 2018). Largely agrarian countries in G20 groups would observe low agricultural productivity due to water scarcity. For instance, there is high variation in yield of a specific crop due to diversity in water availability across Indian states. Due to the above reason per capita food production and actual nutritional contents in the food products has declined. Furthermore, industrial growth is negatively impacted due to water scarcity in many countries. However, industrial and agricultural development are the cause and consequences of environmental degradation. As both sectors have a significant contributor of CO_2 and GHGs emissions. Further, these sectors would suffer more due to water scarcity in future. There are many areas like Africa and Asia where water scarcity has become a serious issue. Also, there is a severe water scarcity in Yemen and Jordan. Accordingly, these areas are facing an increase in the sustainable growth of the agricultural sector. Also, natural disasters (i.e., floods, drought, mudslides, overflows) are caused to change hydrological cycles of water bodies (Tundisi, 2008; Francis et al., 2015). Natural disasters are also increasing. Water contamination is increasing. Furthermore, it has a negative impact on biodiversity (Biswas et al., 2022). Hence, there is a need to increase WRS to maintain the agricultural productivity and production and industrial production in global economies.

2.7. WRS, Environmental Technologies and Digitalization

Use of green and environmental technologies are useful to increase the WRS. Green technologies are reducing water pollution and helping to increase WRS (Chopra et al., 2024). Water productivity is also improving using the digital technologies (DTs) and digitalization. DTs is helping to enhance water resilience and facilitating transparent water governance (Expósito & Cebollero, 2025). Digitalization is valuable to increase the sustainability of the system (Chopra et al., 2024). DTs are developing scientific processes and techniques to improve the water quality and its productivity. Expósito and Cebollero (2025) investigated the impact of digitalization on water management in Spain. However, Xian (2025) reported that fintech produces a positive and negative impact on environmental degradation in G20 countries. While irrigation technologies would be positive to reduce water scarcity (Booker & Trees, 2021; Ingrao et al., 2023). DTs are increasing water use efficiency in agricultural and industrial sectors. Chang et al. (2024) investigates the role of the digital economy for improving water efficiency in the agricultural sector of China. DTs can be effective to increase water efficiency, reduce wastage of water and increase water quality. DTs can be applied to save water in the agricultural sector. Many DTs like AI can be used to manage and monitor the water quality (WBG, 2025). Innovation would be positive to reduce water challenges in the world.

2.8. Water Resource Management (WRM) and Conservation

The preceding sections highlighted the importance of water resource sustainability and its influencing factors in numerous aspects. WRM and conservation would be a vital initiative to increase WRS in global countries. WRM would also increase the food production and meet the water requirements for other sectors (Aryal et al., 2024). WRM would be useful to increase efficient allocation of resources (Haq & Shafique, 2009). Water management includes the practices of rainwater harvesting and conservation (FAO, 2017; FAO & OECD. 2021). While poor WRM is caused to diminish water resources (Huang et al., 2021). Further, WRM and conservation would be supportive to increase sustainable development and SDGs in global countries. Appropriate water management techniques would be useful to achieve efficient and equitable economic growth (Goswami & Bisht, 2017). However, in most economies, water storage, treatment and distribution systems are very poor (Katko & Hukka, 2015). Hence, global countries should pursue an effective mechanism to increase water conservation to increase its sustainability.

3. VALUATION OF PRICE OF WATER AND ITS SUSTAINABILITY

There is much importance of economic theory in WRS. These theories are crucial to maintain the availability and productivity of available natural resources (Rogers et al., 2002). Water pricing policies play a vital role for sustainability of natural resources (Rogers et al., 2002). Furthermore, economic theories would be helpful to increase WRS in the global countries.

3.1. Nature of Water as a Giffen Goods

Giffen goods are essential to survive human livelihood. The demand of this type of goods increases when its price increases. Therefore, the elasticity of demand for Giffen goods is price inelastic. Therefore, water may be considered as Giffen goods, however there is no unanimity on the nature of water among the existing economists. A group of researchers claimed that water demand does not get any reflection due to increase its prices. Furthermore, water is an essential component of human livelihood and without its humanity cannot survive. Since, rising price of water would not affect its demand, thus water has a nature of Giffen goods. For more justification Diamond – Water Paradox can be given. If a person does not have water and diamond, he would wish to pay far more for the first one unit of water as compared to the first unit of diamond. Therefore, the marginal value curve for water will start out much higher than the marginal curve for diamonds. Total value for water is higher than diamonds in the market. If a consumer lost his water and all diamonds, then he would be willing to pay more for water saving as compared to saving the diamonds. Therefore, the consumer's surplus is much higher in the market for water than in the market for diamonds. Value of intermediate goods can be observed through the demand function of producers who provide the goods in the market. If water is a private commodity, then its value can be estimated using the consumer's demand function. As water is public goods and every person has an equal right to use it for their livelihoods. Thus, valuation of water pricing must be estimated through embedded travel cost or hedonic property value. Contingent valuation methods may be applied to estimate the water pricing.

3.2. Demand and Supply Function for WRS

Decreasing wastage of water will be helpful to reducing water scarcity and to increase the water consumption. On the demand side, the application of water efficient technology can be considered to reduce water consumption. Subsequently, it may be useful for water sustainability. Hence, effective supply-side to demand side management policy may be a viable option for increasing WRS. The water price estimation must include demand-side and supply-side functions (Wang et al., 2010). Demand curve identifies the maximum amount of water which a group of consumers willing to pay to acquire required water. Prices and quantities of other inputs may also be included in it. These inputs show the change in demand curve of water due to variation in these inputs. Similarly, producer's demand function can be formulated, thereafter it can be used for empirical and mathematical programming.

3.3. Water Supply and Demand Function through Empirical Model

Water demand function may be estimated through empirical models. Empirical model includes prices of water and other explanatory variables which have influence on water demand. This technique estimates the single-equation demand function and curve. This technique is beneficial to estimate water demand function in industries. However, the structure of water demand function varies across industries and depends upon production activities of industries. This approach accepts that productivity technology of industries can be estimated through cost function. For this, Cobb-Douglas production function may be considered to develop the cost function of water. Thereafter, it may be converted in demand function for water use in industries. Further, this approach accepts that industries choose factors of production to minimize their costs of production, which can be used to derive cost function with input function also. Furthermore, the translog cost function model may be considered to evaluate the cost and demand function of water. The model has several benefits like it avoids the presence of constant returns to scale and provides the strong separability of inputs. However, this model also comprises a single equation with the average cost of water as a proxy for price of water. When a direct demand schedule for water use is difficult due to unavailability of data, then the Alternative Cost approach is useful to formulate demand function. Earlier studies observed water demand is price inelastic (Höglund, 1999). Therefore, this technique is useful to derive demand function without actual estimation of demand curve.

3.4. Price Elasticity of Water and Missing Market Methods

Price elasticity of water is defined as variation in water demand due to variation in its price (Rogers et al., 2002). It is a ratio which measures the percentage change in water demand due to percentage change in its price. The method accepts that price elasticity of water is constant over a period of time. Missing market method is applicable in which the market fails to produce goods and services. Despite that, these goods and services are essential for human livelihood. Further, these have a high demand by the consumers in the market. A market can be formulated in a certain condition, while unaffordable conditions will be ineffective in the market. Therefore, there will be market failure in the short-term. The market may be in a position to search for the place of buyers and sellers in the long term. The above-mentioned issues will be applicable in case of public goods. Therefore, the nature of public goods and its ownership of all citizens of a country create the possibility of market failure. Public goods directly provide benefits to the consumer; thereby they can exist from the market. Market mechanisms in case of public goods, have a high possibility to meet the supply of goods and services. Although, the nature and characteristics of public goods are caused to increase market failure. For example, street lighting is available for all persons and its consumption does not diminish its quality. Non-diminishable are the public goods which cannot be diminished if another person is willing to use it. For this also, street lighting and public roads are good examples. These types of goods are also known as non-rivalry goods. As water is public goods (Lant, 2004), and every citizen of a country has a legal right to use it for various purposes. Also, earlier studies and international organizations have claimed that water can be considered as an economic good (Rogers et al., 2002). However, few economists concluded that water has a nature of private and public goods.

3.5. Efficiency and Distributive Justice (Accessibility, Availability and Affordability)

WRS is reflected with efficiency and distributive justice of available water in a region (Rogers et al., 2002). Public goods suppliers would not get any incentive to increase the supply as suppliers do not receive or do not generate substantial revenue to be engaged in production of public goods and services. Market is efficient to determine prices of goods and services based on their demand and supply. Demand depends upon consumer's ability to acquire water as per their needs. Also, consumers have an expectation to acquire high quality water with affordable and stable prices (Rogers et al., 2002). Supply is dependent upon the supplier's ability to supply the water with high prices. Suppliers are bound to cover all costs and they wish to receive stable revenue to maintain the supply (Rogers et al., 2002). If prices of goods and services are being adjusted as per the demand and supply by consumer and supplier respectively, then markets of such types of goods and services have a high tendency to fail. There are few external factors like property rights and legal contracts which do not cover the impacts of decision –maker's actions. Water does not have an open market where seller buyers do the selling and purchasing of water. Contingent valuation and CE are the non-market valuation techniques that can be used to estimate water price (Vallgårda, 2018). Contingent valuation methods estimate the economic value of non-market goods like water, for which many people are questioned about how much they would like to pay to use it.

4. RESEARCH METHODOLOGY

4.1. Study Area

The G20 countries have a greater share in world's GDP. The G20 countries are growing fast as compared to other countries. The G20 countries are using more water resources to attain high income growth. Many G20 countries are facing intensification of agricultural and industrial sectors. Moreover, the growth of the agricultural and industrial sectors is also dependent on water resources. Thus, the agricultural sector is facing risk due to water scarcity and water pollution (FAO, 2017; FAO & OECD. 2021). Hence, WRS is poorly maintained in many G20 countries. While WRS would be essential to increase sustainable development and SDGs in future (Compoli et al., 2024). Therefore, G20 countries are included as research areas in this chapter. Figure 1 explores the variation in total water productivity (*TWP*) as its mean value during 2016 -2022. Figure 2 provides the per capita contribution in CO_2 emissions in G20 countries.

4.2. Source of Data

The descriptive and empirical analysis of this chapter is based on secondary data. The required data is taken from the official website of world development indicators (The World Bank) and OECD. Further, the required data is also adopted from published research articles and government reports of G20 countries.

4.3. Rationality of Independent and Independent Variables

TWP and Environmental Degradation: Total water productivity (*TWP*) is used as a dependent variable in the investigation. While per capita emissions (*COEPC*) are included as a representative variable for environmental degradation. Thus, *TWP* and *COEPC* are applied as dependent and core independent variables, respectively in the model.

Public Investment in Education and Health Sectors: Education expenditure (*ASEE*) and health expenditure (*CHE*) are treated as mediator variables.

Agricultural and Allied Sector: Agricultural and livestock sectors cannot grow without water. Both are water intensive sectors (Ingrao et al., 2023). Hence, it is expected that water productivity may be negatively associated with arable land and livestock production. Thus, per person arable (*ALHPP*) and livestock production index *(LPI)* are included as independent variables (*IVs*) to examine their implications on *TWP*.

Figure 1. Variation in TWP across G20 countries

Figure 2. Per capita carbon dioxide (CO2) emissions across G20 countries in 2023

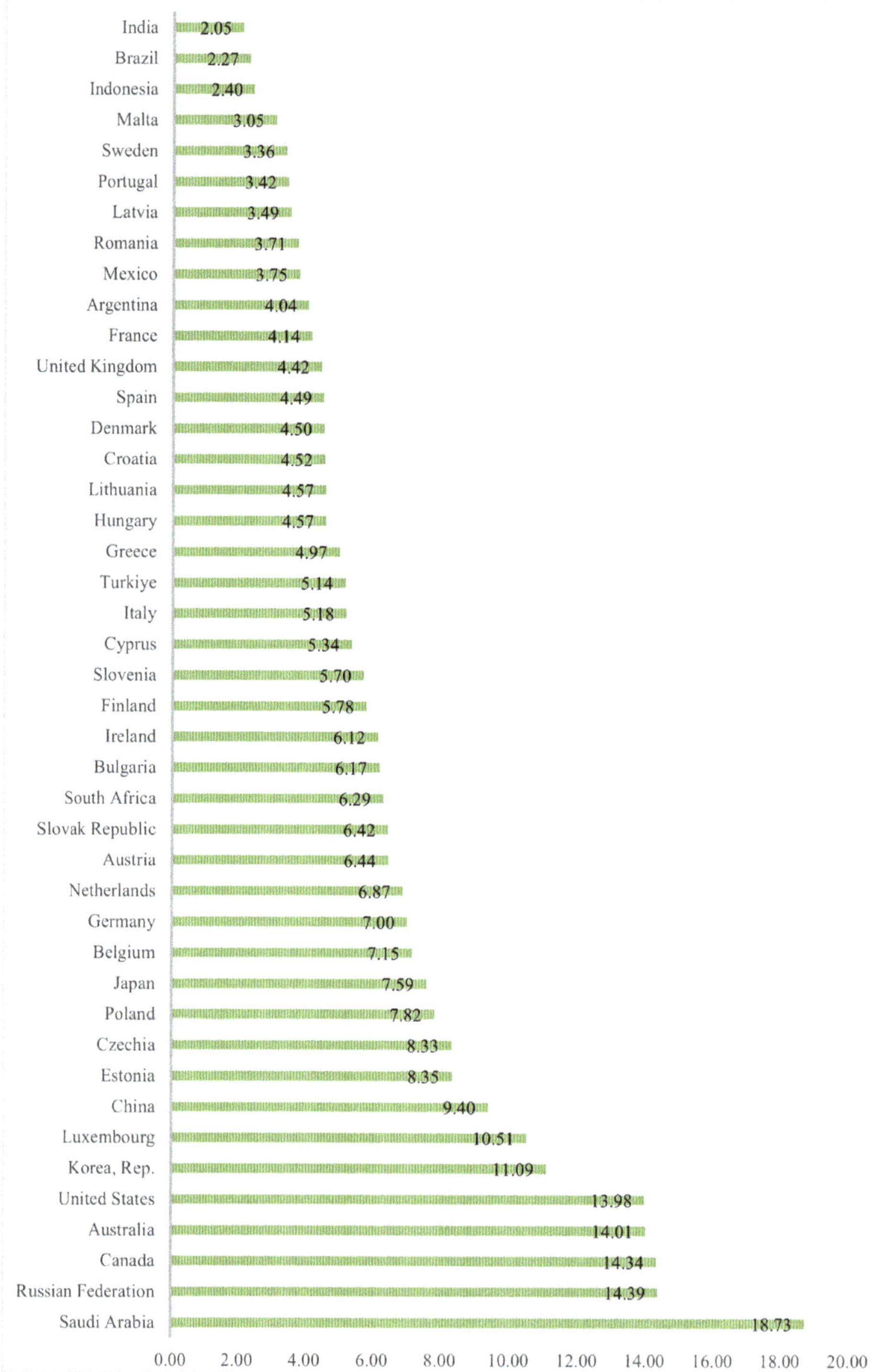

Table 1. Explanation of the variables

Indicator	Code	Unit	Variable's Category
Water productivity, total (constant 2015 US$ GDP per cubic meter of total freshwater withdrawal)	*TWP*	US$	Water resource
CO_2 emissions excluding LULUCF per capita (t CO_2e/capita)	*COEPC*	t CO2e/capita	Environmental degradation
Adjusted savings: education expenditure (% of GNI)	*ASEE*	%	Public investment in education and health sector
Current health expenditure (% of GDP)	*CHE*	%	
Arable land (hectares per person)	*ALHPP*	Ha./Person	Agricultural and allied sector
Livestock production index (2014-2016 = 100)	*LPI*	Number	
Scientific and technical journal articles	*STJA*	Number	Technological diffusion and infrastructural development
Gross capital formation (% of GDP)	*GCF*	%	
Employment in industry (% of total employment)	*EI*	%	Industrialization
Employment to population ratio, 15+, total (%)	*EPR*	%	Employment and economic development
Labor force participation rate, total (% of total population ages 15+)	*LFPR*	%	
Inflation GDP deflator (annual %)	*IGDPD*	%	
Final consumption expenditure (% of GDP)	*FCE*	%	
Energy use (kg of oil equivalent per capita)	*PCEU*	Kg./Capita	Energy sector
ICT goods exports (% of total goods exports)	*ICTGE*	%	Digital development
ICT goods imports (% total goods imports)	*ICTGI*	%	
Fixed telephone subscriptions (per 100 people)	*FTS*	Number	
Individuals using the Internet (% of population)	*IUI*	%	
Mobile cellular subscriptions (per 100 people)	*MCS*	Number	
Population growth (annual %)	*PG*	%	Demographic change
Urban population (% of total population)	*UP*	%	
Sex ratio at birth (male births per female births)	*SR*	Number	
Fertility rate, total (births per woman)	*FR*	Number	

Source: Finalized by authors as per the existing literature.

Technological Diffusion and Infrastructural Development: Technological development is caused to increase industrialization which has a negative implication on water productivity and quality. Infrastructural development has a negative impact on water productivity. Musah and Yakubu (2023) noted a negative relationship between technology and environmental sustainability in Ghana. Thus, gross capital formation (*GCF*) and scientific research articles (*STJA*) are used to capture the impact of infrastructural development and technological development, respectively on water productivity in this research.

Industrialization: Employment in industry (*EI*) is used to examine the impact of industrialization and technological change on *TWP*. This variable is applied to examine the impact of industrialization on water productivity in this study.

Employment and Economic Development: Employment opportunities have a crucial impact on water resources. Hence, employment to population ratio (*EPR*) and labor force participation rate (*LFPR*) are applied as *IVs* in the model. Inflation produces a negative impact on economic and social sectors. It is noticeable that inflation GDP deflator (*IGDPD*) is impactful on water productivity. Thereupon, final consumption expenditure (*FCE*) is also composed as *IV*.

Figure 3. Interlinkages of TWP with environmental degradation and other variables

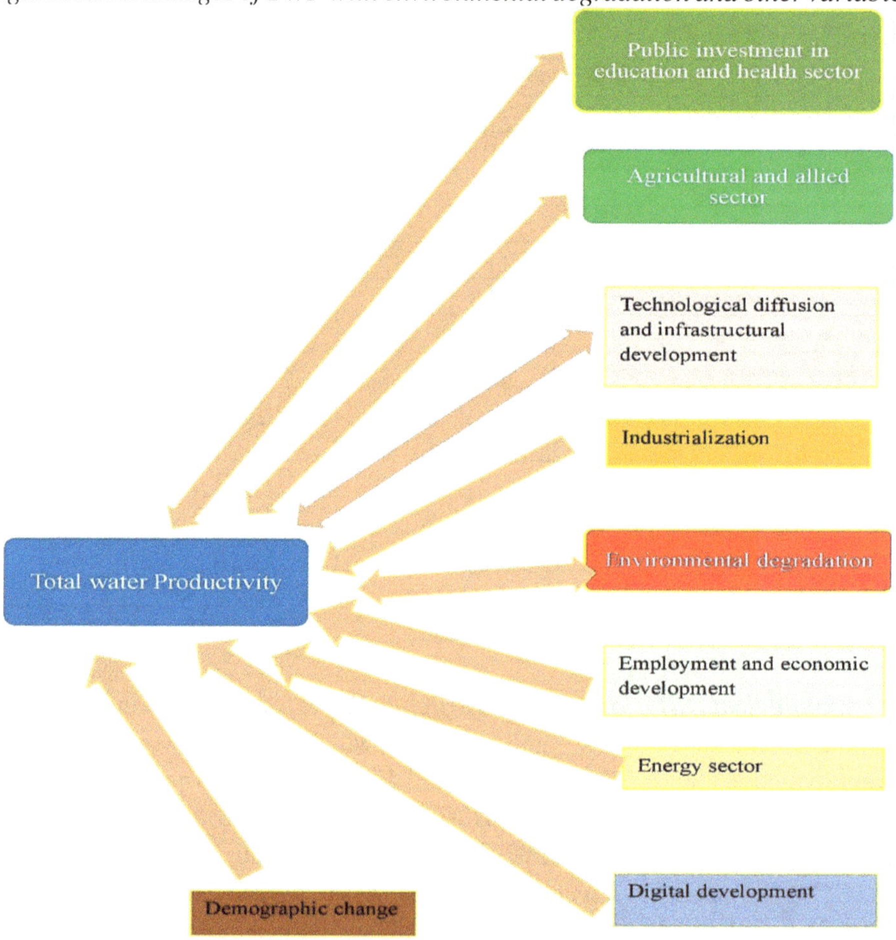

Energy Sector: Per capita energy use (*PCEU*) also has a crucial impact on water resources. Henc, *PCEU* is included as *IV*. Further, water resources are a prime driver to generate renewable energy. While renewable energy would be positive to increase WRS.

Digital Development: Nowadays, digitalization is playing a crucial role to increase the sustainability of resources. For instance, DTs can be effective to increase water use efficiency (Chang et al., 2024). Thus, digitalization developing indicators like ICT goods exports (*ICTGE*) and imports (*ICTGI*), fixed telephone subscriptions (*FTS*), individuals using the Internet (*IUI*), and mobile cellular subscriptions (*MCS*) have significant reflection on water productivity. Thus, these variables are used to examine the impact of digitalization on *TWP*.

Demographic Change: Population growth (*PG*), urban population (*UP*), sex ratio (*SR*), and fertility rate (FR) are included as explanatory variables to capture the impact of demographic characteristics on *TWP* in this chapter. These are used as core, mediator and control variables in the regression analysis (Table 1). Figure 3 explores the interlinkages of underlined variables with total water productivity.

4.4. Statistical and Empirical Analysis

This chapter compiles country-wise panel data of the stated dependent and independent variables during 2000 – 2022. Descriptive analysis is used to examine the variation in the variables across G20 countries. Spearman's rank correlation coefficient technique is used to examine the association among the variables. Existing scholars adopted various theories and empirical models to examine the impact of water security and sustainability on social and economic development. For instance, Zlati et al. (2024) applied structural equation models to assess the impact of water security on social and economic development in EU countries. Furthermore, most scholars also investigated the impact of social-economic development, industrial sector and tourism on water security. Extensive use of water is caused to increase depletion of natural resources. Hence, it is accountable for increasing environmental degradation. Log-linear regression model is formulated to examine the water productivity influencing factors. This chapter assumes that total water productivity (*TWP*) is a function of the mentioned variables in Table 1.

$$(TWP)_{ct} = \xi_0 + \xi_1 \, ln(COEPC)_{ct} + \xi_2 \, ln(ASEE)_{ct} + \xi_3 \, ln(CHE)_{ct} + \xi_4 \, ln(ALHPP)_{ct} + \xi_5 \, ln(LPI)_{ct} + \xi_6 \, ln(STJA)_{ct} + \xi_7 \, ln(EI)_{ct} + \xi_8 \, ln(EPR)_{ct} + \xi_9 \, ln(LFPR)_{ct} + \xi_{10} \, ln(PCEU)_{ct} + \xi_{11} \, ln(FCE)_{ct} + \xi_{12} \, ln(GCF)_{ct} + \xi_{13} \, ln(IGDPD)_{ct} + \xi_{14} \, ln(ICTGE)_{ct} + \xi_{15} \, ln(ICTGI)_{ct} + \xi_{16} \, ln(FTS)_{ct} + \xi_{17} \, ln(IUI)_{ct} + \xi_{18} \, ln(MCS)_{ct} + \xi_{19} \, ln(PG)_{ct} + \xi_{20} \, ln(UP)_{ct} + \xi_{21} \, ln(SR)_{ct} + \xi_{22} \, ln(FR)_{ct} + \phi_{ct} \qquad (1)$$

Here, ξ_0 is constant coefficient; ξ_1, ..., ξ_{22} are the elasticities of corresponding variables; *ln* is natural logarithm of related variables; *t* time; *c* is cross-sectional country; ϕ_{ct} is error-term in equation (1).

4.5. Final Estimation and Use of Statistical Software

The coefficients of variables are computed through *PCSE*s estimation. The SPSS statistical software is used for descriptive analysis of data. The empirical investigation is completed using STATA statistical software.

5. RESULTS AND DISCUSSION

5.1. Descriptive Results

The statistical measurement of the variables is presented in Table 2. It is a high variation in several variables like total water productivity (*TWP*), arable land (*AL-HPP*), technological change (*STJA*), final consumption expenditure (*FCE*), gross capital formation (*GCF*), inflation (*IGDPD*), ICT goods exports (*ICTGE*), ICT goods imports (*ICTGE*), population growth (PG), sex ratio (*SR*), and fertility rate (*FR*) in G20 countries. Accordingly, these variables have high leverage and are not normally distributed.

Table 2. Statistical measurement of the variables

Variable		*Mean*	*Std. Dev*	*Min*	*Max*	*Observations*	*Skewness*
WPT	Overall	98.4197	181.2596	1.2862	1478.65	*N*=989	
	Between		176.8260	2.5392	1103.20	*n* =43	4.8702
	Within		47.7896	383.8828	473.87	*T* =23	
COEPC	Overall	8.2735	4.6549	0.9387	26.0430	*N*=989	
	Between		4.5092	1.4269	19.4702	*n* =43	1.0453
	Within		1.3372	-0.0759	14.8463	*T* =23	
ASEE	Overall	4.5622	1.1801	1.5271	8.0700	*N*=989	
	Between		1.1007	1.7900	7.1862	*n* =43	0.2529
	Within		0.4561	3.0270	7.0953	*T* =23	
CHE	Overall	7.7740	2.5149	1.8530	18.8133	*N*=989	
	Between		2.3775	2.7136	15.6991	*n* =43	0.5278
	Within		0.8936	4.5649	11.0312	*T* =23	

Variable		*Mean*	*Std. Dev*	*Min*	*Max*	*Observations*	*Skewness*
ALHPP	Overall	0.3094	0.2856	0.0150	1.4188	*N*=989	1.7029
	Between		0.2862	0.0201	1.2508	*n* =43	
	Within		0.0389	0.0765	0.5126	*T* =23	
LPI	Overall	98.4466	16.2900	48.6600	189.9900	*N*=989	0.9996
	Between		8.0579	84.4696	127.4765	*n* =43	
	Within		14.2085	48.8736	186.7736	*T* =23	
STJA	Overall	42176.75	87797.03	45.34	898949.10	*N*=989	4.6286
	Between		80539.13	250.76	406662.30	*n* =43	
	Within		36962.22	253139.30	592525.00	*T* =23	
EI	Overall	25.2259	5.6083	9.1918	40.6374	*N*=989	0.3327
	Between		5.1191	14.2953	38.7637	*n* =43	
	Within		2.4150	18.0768	33.8558	*T* =23	
LFPR	Overall	59.1611	5.3255	46.2300	74.1900	*N*=989	-0.2262
	Between		5.0311	48.6848	70.4356	*n* =43	
	Within		1.9007	52.6851	69.1790	*T* =23	
EPR	Overall	54.4317	6.2779	36.7980	71.7710	*N*=989	-0.2468
	Between		5.8028	43.5736	67.2880	*n* =43	
	Within		2.5474	47.3909	65.5914	*T* =23	
PCEU	Overall	3427.35	1856.61	393.4471	9429.93	*N*=989	0.9010
	Between		1840.56	539.1867	7955.03	*n* =43	
	Within		367.13	822.7888	5377.52	*T* =23	
FCE	Overall	74.2537	8.7031	35.2378	93.8519	*N*=989	-1.2953
	Between		8.0898	51.2946	88.0657	*n* =43	
	Within		3.4287	54.9447	88.5914	*T* =23	
GCF	Overall	23.9005	5.7678	10.8539	53.7136	*N*=989	1.2438
	Between		4.7728	16.9319	42.2757	*n* =43	
	Within		3.3159	13.9027	50.5374	*T* =23	
IGDPD	Overall	4.7412	7.1310	0.0002	96.0362	*N*=989	5.4828
	Between		4.9976	0.9475	26.9111	*n* =43	
	Within		5.1411	21.1327	81.2458	*T* =23	
ICTGI	Overall	9.4461	5.0005	2.9700	42.3700	*N*=989	1.7927
	Between		4.1810	4.2139	22.3983	*n* =43	
	Within		2.8131	-1.7417	34.7883	*T* =23	

continued on following page

Table 2. Continued

Variable		*Mean*	*Std. Dev*	*Min*	*Max*	*Observations*	*Skewness*
ICTGE	Overall	7.5251	8.4979	0.0300	63.6400	*N*=989	
	Between		7.4994	0.1683	32.2048	*n* =43	2.2389
	Within		4.1505	-11.4597	38.9604	*T* =23	
FTS	Overall	34.1791	16.5453	1.4300	72.1000	*N*=989	
	Between		14.8232	2.6639	58.9957	*n* =43	-0.0312
	Within		7.6753	0.5225	65.0238	*T* =23	
MCS	Overall	102.09	35.6788	0.3376	208.09	*N*=989	
	Between		17.4434	48.8728	133.34	*n* =43	-0.7479
	Within		31.2326	-17.1132	188.74	*T* =23	
IUI	Overall	59.81	27.6764	0.5280	100.00	*N*=989	
	Between		17.3347	14.2477	85.70	*n* =43	-0.5868
	Within		21.7298	2.1490	109.33	*T* =23	
PG	Overall	0.8188	0.7628	0.0002	5.4115	*N*=989	
	Between		0.6284	0.1103	3.7442	*n* =43	2.4970
	Within		0.4426	-2.8507	3.9591	*T* =23	
UP	Overall	72.62	14.1279	27.6670	98.1530	*N*=989	
	Between		14.0821	31.4490	97.6776	*n* =43	-0.6201
	Within		2.3890	58.3117	85.9947	*T* =23	
SR	Overall	1.0588	0.0180	1.0380	1.1780	*N*=989	
	Between		0.0173	1.0389	1.1567	*n* =43	4.4576
	Within		0.0055	1.0061	1.0918	*T* =23	
FR	Overall	1.6842	0.4188	0.7780	4.2060	*N*=989	
	Between		0.3872	1.1339	2.9384	*n* =43	1.5824
	Within		0.1695	0.8858	2.9518	*T* =23	

Source: Author's estimation.

While some variables like education expenditure (*ASEE*), health expenditure (*CHE*), livestock production index (*LPI*), employment in industry (*EI*), labour force participation rate (*LFPR*), employment to population ratio (*EPR*), per capita energy use (*PCEU*), etc. have statistical value of skewness between + 1 to – 1. Thus, these variables are normally distributed. Moreover, it is perceived as a variation across overall, between and within the sample of individual variables. The association among the variables are observed through Spearman's rank correlation techniques (Table 3).

continued on following page

The estimates imply that environmental degradation (*COEPC*), education expenditure (*ASEE*), health expenditure (*CHE*), employment to population ratio (*EPR*), labour

Table 2. Continued

force participation rate (*LFPR*), per capita energy use (*PCEU*), inflation (*IGDPD*), fixed telephone subscriptions (*FTS*), individual using the internet (*IUI*) and mobile cellular subscriptions (*MCS*) are positively correlated with total water productivity (*TWP*). While *TWP* is negatively correlated with arable land (*ALHPP*), technological change (*STJA*), employment in industry (*EI*), final consumption expenditure (*FCE*), gross capital formation (*GCF*), sex ratio (*SR*) and fertility rate (*FR*).

Table 3. Correlation coefficients among the variables

Variable	*TWP*	*COEPC*	*ASEE*	*CHE*	*ALHPP*	*LPI*	*STJA*	*EI*	*EPR*	*LFPR*	*PCEU*	*FCE*
TWP	1	0.279**	0.198**	0.050	-0.149**	0.042	-0.103**	-0.379**	0.119**	0.057*	0.289**	-0.407**
COEPC	0.279**	1	0.211**	0.213**	0.275**	-0.007	0.194**	-0.060*	0.218**	0.160**	0.886**	-0.339**
ASEE	0.198**	0.211**	1	0.351**	0.039	0.084**	-0.255**	-0.244**	0.021	0.061*	0.348**	0.064*
CHE	0.050	0.213**	0.351**	1	0.116**	0.095**	0.317**	-0.237**	0.112**	0.141**	0.370**	0.333**
ALHPP	-0.149**	0.275**	0.039	0.116**	1	-0.05	-0.01	-0.008	0.111**	0.170**	0.276**	0.188**
LPI	0.042	-0.007	0.084**	0.095**	-0.050	1	0.016	0.184**	-0.03	-0.056*	0.029	0.051
STJA	-0.103**	0.194**	-0.255**	0.317**	-0.010	0.016	1	-0.061*	0.284**	0.264**	0.167**	-0.086**
EI	-0.379**	-0.060*	-0.244**	-0.237**	-0.008	0.184**	-0.061*	1	-0.198**	-0.268**	-0.145**	0.084**
EPR	0.119**	0.218**	0.021	0.112**	0.111**	-0.03	0.284**	-0.198**	1	0.908**	0.245**	-0.379**
LFPR	0.057*	0.160**	0.061*	0.141**	0.170**	-0.056*	0.264**	-0.268**	0.908**	1	0.177**	-0.263**
PCEU	0.289**	0.886**	0.348**	0.370**	0.276**	0.029	0.167**	-0.145**	0.245**	0.177**	1	-0.298**
FCE	-0.407**	-0.339**	0.064*	0.333**	0.188**	0.051	-0.086**	0.084**	-0.379**	-0.263**	-0.298**	1
GCF	-0.186**	-0.002	-0.376**	-0.418**	-0.100**	0.034	0.244**	0.299**	0.293**	0.167**	-0.064*	-0.478**
IGDPD	-0.131**	-0.132**	-0.093**	-0.233**	0.238**	-0.059*	-0.098**	0.018	-0.080**	-0.092**	-0.179**	0.002
ICTGE	0.008	0.034	-0.165**	-0.080**	-0.271**	0.024	0.207**	0.225**	0.251**	0.153**	-0.010	-0.210**
ICTGI	-0.076**	0.104**	-0.165**	-0.031	-0.082**	-0.011	0.317**	0.197**	0.377**	0.317**	0.032	-0.217**
FTS	0.265**	0.366**	0.167**	0.467**	-0.084**	0.036	0.046	-0.127**	0.092**	0.025	0.394**	0.064*
IUI	0.318**	0.257**	0.321**	0.524**	0.061*	0.277**	0.110**	-0.264**	0.258**	0.218**	0.396**	-0.114**
MCS	0.218**	0.125**	0.247**	0.247**	-0.038	0.321**	-0.030	-0.064*	0.013	-0.022	0.155**	-0.063*
PG	0.179**	0.182**	0.231**	-0.268**	0.008	-0.161**	-0.122**	-0.333**	-0.014	-0.035	0.120**	-0.282**
UP	0.284**	0.374**	0.430**	0.483**	0.165**	0.068*	0.005	-0.370**	0.111**	0.065*	0.481**	0.029
SR	-0.085**	-0.154**	-0.452**	-0.328**	-0.139**	-0.098**	0.336**	0.072*	0.227**	0.201**	-0.252**	-0.335**
FR	-0.114**	-0.016	0.176**	-0.215**	0.032	-0.342**	-0.015	-0.296**	0.028	0.046	-0.032	-0.137**

Table 3. Correlation coefficients among the variables Conti...

Variable	*GCF*	*IGDPD*	*ICTGE*	*ICTGI*	*FTS*	*IUI*	*MCS*	*PG*	*UP*	*SR*	*FR*
TWP	-0.186**	-0.131**	0.008	-0.076**	0.265**	0.318**	0.218**	0.179**	0.284**	-0.085**	-0.114**
COEPC	-0.002	-0.132**	0.034	0.104**	0.366**	0.257**	0.125**	0.182**	0.374**	-0.154**	-0.016
ASEE	-0.376**	-0.093**	-0.165**	-0.165**	0.167**	0.321**	0.247**	0.231**	0.430**	-0.452**	0.176**
CHE	-0.418**	-0.233**	-0.080**	-0.031	0.467**	0.524**	0.247**	-0.268**	0.483**	-0.328**	-0.215**
ALHPP	-0.100**	0.238**	-0.271**	-0.082**	-0.084**	0.061*	-0.038	0.008	0.165**	-0.139**	0.032
LPI	0.034	-0.059*	0.024	-0.011	0.036	0.277**	0.321**	-0.161**	0.068*	-0.098**	-0.342**
STJA	0.244**	-0.098**	0.207**	0.317**	0.046	0.110**	-0.03	-0.122**	0.005	0.336**	-0.015
EI	0.299**	0.018	0.225**	0.197**	-0.127**	-0.264**	-0.064*	-0.333**	-0.370**	0.072*	-0.296**
EPR	0.293**	-0.080**	0.251**	0.377**	0.092**	0.258**	0.013	-0.014	0.111**	0.227**	0.028
LFPR	0.167**	-0.092**	0.153**	0.317**	0.025	0.218**	-0.022	-0.035	0.065*	0.201**	0.046
PCEU	-0.064*	-0.179**	-0.01	0.032	0.394**	0.396**	0.155**	0.120**	0.481**	-0.252**	-0.032
FCE	-0.478**	0.002	-0.210**	-0.217**	0.064*	-0.114**	-0.063*	-0.282**	0.029	-0.335**	-0.137**
GCF	1	0.018	0.297**	0.276**	-0.224**	-0.169**	-0.138**	0.015	-0.375**	0.539**	0.016
IGDPD	0.018	1	-0.172**	-0.087**	-0.315**	-0.225**	-0.131**	0.157**	-0.008	-0.024	0.235**
ICTGE	0.297**	-0.172**	1	0.856**	0.186**	-0.047	-0.157**	-0.158**	0.055*	0.323**	-0.197**
ICTGI	0.276**	-0.087**	0.856**	1	0.053*	-0.115**	-0.208**	-0.129**	0.051	0.285**	0.003
FTS	-0.224**	-0.315**	0.186**	0.053*	1	0.216**	-0.013	-0.166**	0.406**	-0.124**	-0.401**
IUI	-0.169**	-0.225**	-0.047	-0.115**	0.216**	1	0.698**	-0.164**	0.453**	-0.244**	-0.312**
MCS	-0.138**	-0.131**	-0.157**	-0.208**	0.013	0.698**	1	-0.091**	0.236**	-0.217**	-0.239**
PG	0.015	0.157**	-0.158**	-0.129**	-0.166**	-0.164**	-0.091**	1	0.064*	-0.041	0.529**
UP	-0.375**	-0.008	0.055*	0.051	0.406**	0.453**	0.236**	0.064*	1	-0.412**	-0.084**
SR	0.539**	-0.024	0.323**	0.285**	-0.124**	-0.244**	-0.217**	-0.041	-0.412**	1	-0.073*
FR	0.016	0.235**	-0.197**	0.003	-0.401**	-0.312**	-0.239**	0.529**	-0.084**	-0.073*	1

Source: Author's estimation. **Note:** **. Correlation is significant at the 0.01 level (1-tailed). *. Correlation is significant at the 0.05 level (1-tailed).

5.2. Empirical Results

Environmental degradation is responsible for climate and global warming. Thus, environmental degradation has a negative impact on *TWP*. The negative coefficient of CO_2EPC with *TWP* infer that water productivity declines as environmental degradation increases (Table 4). *TWP* is expected to be diminished by 0.2837% as 1% increases in environmental degradation. Further, the results can be justified that per capita CO_2 emissions are accountable for climate change and environmental degradation (Ali et al., 2024; Xian, 2025). Hence, it is rational to accept that water productivity is negatively impacted due to increase in environmental degradation.

Education is helpful to increase the understanding of people towards the water crisis and its sustainability. People also become more sensitive to saving water as their education level increases. Thus, education and health expenditure showed a positive impact on *TWP*. The estimates clarified that *TWP* is projected to be increased by 0.5572% and 0.9589% due to 1% increases in education and health expenditure, respectively.

Agricultural and livestock production require extensive water resources to increase their growth. Both the sectors use extensive quantities of water. Thus, the arable land and livestock production index showed a negative impact on *TWP*. *TWP* is expected to decline by 0.0434% and 0.1943% due to 1% increase in arable land and livestock production, respectively. Thus, WRS is negatively hampering due to growth in the agricultural sector in G20 countries.

Extensive industrialization requires more water and other resources. Industrialization is increasing the GHGs and CO_2 emission in the environment. Industrialization, thus, is a driver to reduce environmental degradation and water resources. Further, technological change is an effective determinant of industrial development. Hence, it appears that industrialization and technological change have a negative impact on water resources. The coefficients of *EI* and *STJA* with *TWP* are noticed negative. The estimates specified that water productivity is expected to decrease by 0.1697% and 0.7799% due to 1% increase in employment in industry and technological change, respectively.

Labour force participation (*LFPR*) may increase due to high population growth. *LFPR* also increases pressure on water resources. Thus, water productivity is negatively impacted by *LFPR*. The result indicates that TWP is likely to be decreased by 3.0334% due to 1% increase in *LFPR*. While employment population ratio (*EPR*) is found positive to increase *TWP*. TWP is to be improved by 2.4521% as *EPR* increases by 1%.

Per capita energy use (*PCEU*) has a positive impact on *TWP*. It is suggested that energy use may be productive to reduce pressure on water resources. Hence, *TWP* is expected to improve by 0.4179% due to 1% increase in *PCEU*.

FCE increases as demand for goods and services increases. While demand for products can be increased as they increase their production. Further, production of these goods requires water and other resources. Demand poses a negative impact on environment and water resources (Wang, Rauf, et al., 2024). Hence, *FCE* has a negative impact on water resources. *TWP* is likely to be decreased by 2.9005% due to 1% increase in FCE. Accordingly, gross capital formation (*GCF*) showed a negative impact on *TWP*. *TWP* is likely to be decreased by 0.8454% due to 1% increase in *GCF*. While inflation also has a negative impact on *TWP*.

Table 4. Impact of explanatory variables on TWP

Number of obs.		**989**		*R-squared*	**0.6882**	
Number of groups		**43**		*Wald Chi²*	**69673.23**	
Obs. per group		**23**		*Prob > Chi²*	**0.000**	
***ln*(*WPT*)=[DV]**	*Reg. Coef.*	*Std. Err.*	*z*	*P>|z|*	**[95% Conf. Interval]**	
ln(*COEPC*)	**-0.2837**	**0.0722**	**-3.93**	**0.000**	**-0.4251**	**-0.1422**
ln(*ASEE*)	0.5572	0.1060	5.25	0.000	0.3494	0.7650
ln(*CHE*)	0.9589	0.0814	11.79	0.000	0.7995	1.1184
ln(*ALHPP*)	-0.0434	0.0258	-1.68	0.093	-0.0941	0.0072
ln(*LPI*)	-0.1943	0.0945	-2.06	0.040	-0.3795	-0.0090
ln(*STJA*)	-0.1697	0.0121	-13.98	0.000	-0.1934	-0.1459
ln(*EI*)	-0.7799	0.0729	-10.69	0.000	-0.9228	-0.6369
ln(*LFPR*)	-3.0334	0.3722	-8.15	0.000	-3.7629	-2.3038
ln(*EPR*)	2.4521	0.3557	6.89	0.000	1.7549	3.1493
ln(*PCEU*)	0.4179	0.1094	3.82	0.000	0.2035	0.6324
ln(*FCE*)	-2.9005	0.2193	-13.23	0.000	-3.3303	-2.4707
ln(*GCF*)	-0.8454	0.1166	-7.25	0.000	-1.0740	-0.6169
ln(*IGDPD*)	-0.0441	0.0257	-1.72	0.086	-0.0944	0.0062
ln(*ICTGI*)	0.0230	0.0555	0.41	0.678	-0.0857	0.1317
ln(*ICTGE*)	0.1368	0.0208	6.57	0.000	0.0959	0.1776
ln(*FTS*)	0.1840	0.0477	3.86	0.000	0.0905	0.2774
ln(*MCS*)	0.0455	0.0690	0.66	0.509	-0.0897	0.1808
ln(*IUI*)	0.3238	0.0659	4.91	0.000	0.1945	0.4530
ln(*PG*)	-0.0108	0.0263	-0.41	0.680	-0.0623	0.0406
ln(*UP*)	-0.3370	0.0801	-4.21	0.000	-0.4939	-0.1800
ln(*SR*)	-3.2946	1.2028	-2.74	0.006	-5.6520	-0.9372

Number of obs.		**989**		*R-squared*	**0.6882**	
Number of groups		**43**		*Wald Chi²*	**69673.23**	
Obs. per group		**23**		*Prob > Chi²*	**0.000**	
ln(WPT)=**[DV]**	*Reg. Coef.*	*Std. Err.*	*z*	*P>|z|*	**[95% Conf. Interval]**	
ln(COEPC)	**-0.2837**	**0.0722**	**-3.93**	**0.000**	**-0.4251**	**-0.1422**
ln(FR)	-0.6443	0.0881	-7.31	0.000	-0.8170	-0.4716
Con. Coef.	20.5708	2.0874	9.85	0.000	16.4795	24.6620

Source: Author's estimation.

Table 5. Rationality of regression coefficients

Log-linear Regression Model								
No. of lags	*Lag* **(1)**	*Lag* **(2)**	*Lag* **(3)**	*Lag* **(4)**	*Lag* **(5)**	*Lag* **(6)**	*Lag* **(7)**	*Lag* **(8)**
Lag (1)	1.0000							
Lag (2)	0.9909*	1.0000						
Lag (3)	0.9823*	0.9911*	1.0000					
Lag (4)	0.9770*	0.9824*	0.9913*	1.0000				
Lag (5)	0.9714*	0.9764*	0.9821*	0.9912*	1.0000			
Lag (6)	0.9662*	0.9707*	0.9757*	0.9815*	0.9910*	1.0000		
Lag (7)	0.9618*	0.9659*	0.9701*	0.9754*	0.9814*	0.9909*	1.0000	
Lag (8)	0.9567*	0.9611*	0.9648*	0.9698*	0.9753*	0.9813*	0.9908*	1.0000

Source: Estimated by Authors.

Digital technologies (DTs) are bringing several opportunities and alternatives to enhance the productivity and efficiency of resources. DTs also increase water resource management. Hence, DTs would be supportive to increase *TWP*. The coefficients of all indicators (i.e., *ICTGI, ICTGE, FTS, MCS, IUI*) with *TWP* are noticed positive. These are effective DTs to develop digitalization and digital infrastructure. Hence, DTs appear positive to increase *TWP*. Earlier studies also claimed that DTs and digitalization are helping to increase harvesting of water, and water efficiency, quality and monitoring (Booker & Trees, 2021; Ingrao et al., 2023; Expósito & Cebollero, 2025). DTs are increasing the appropriate water management (WBG, 2025).

Population growth (*PG*), urban population (*UP*) and fertility rate (*FR*) also enhance extensive pressure on ecosystem services. Hence, these variables impose a negative impact on *TWP*. 1% increase in population growth and urban population are caused to reduce *TWP* by 0.0108% and 0.3370%, respectively. *TWP* is predicted to decrease by 0.6443% as fertility rate increases by 1%. *TWP* also declined due to

continued on following page

Table 4. Continued

an increase in sex ratio. The rationality of regression coefficients is given in Table 5. The correlation coefficients of error-terms with their various lags are noticed statistically significant. Hence, the regression coefficients have rationality.

6. POLICY IMPLICATIONS

At present there is water scarcity due to multiple reasons including social and economic development, agricultural growth, industrialization, infrastructural development and urbanization in most developed and developing economies. If world economies wish to maintain water resources, then they should control growing population and over industrialization. Economists and researchers need to formulate an appropriate technique to evaluate the water pricing, thereby preventing water resources from keeping view of the importance of water resources in socio-economic developmental related activities. Water conservation technologies must be innovated by scientists. Use of green and environmental technologies would increase the water resource sustainability and reduce environmental degradation (Xian, 2025). Recycling and re-use of water may be useful to increase its sustainability in the long-run. Water use efficiency through adoption of DTs and innovation would avoid the water scarcity in the world. Improvement in irrigation efficiency is necessary to increase water productivity. Moreover, rainwater harvesting and conservation are also required to minimize water scarcity (FAO, 2017).

There must be appropriate evaluation of water prices at national to global level. There are several suggestions that can be given to increase the water quality and quantity. It is essential to set the water pricing based on the actual value of water. Policy maker's need to estimate the water pricing based on income-group of peoples, these peoples in the society can avail the drinking as per their requirement. It is needed to create a hydrological model, accompanied by an economic optimization model to measure the water quality and to increase water conservation in G20 countries. Agricultural and industrial sectors should apply water management practices to increase WRS. Sustainable practices in the agricultural and livestock sectors would be positive to increase WRS. Public investment in education and health sectors would be effective to increase WRS. The global countries should also pursue climate change preventive mechanisms to increase WRS. Renewable energy consumption must be initiated to improve water productivity and reduce water consumption (Li & Zhang, 2025). Appropriate water governance is necessary to reduce water scarcity.

7. INNOVATION AND NOVELTY OF THE CHAPTER

This chapter has innovation and significance in the existing theoretical and empirical literature in following aspects: The comprehensive literature review related to WRS and its determinants are highlighted in this study. The theoretical foundation of economic theories in the areas of valuation of water price is described. The empirical association of social-economic, environmental degradation, technological change, digital infrastructure, agricultural intensification, livestock production, inflation, consumption expenditure, gross capital formation and demographic change related variables with water productivity are detected in this research. Thereupon, the valuation of water resources management in WRS is explained as per the theoretical literature. The scope of further research in various dimensions is also provided in this research.

8. LIMITATIONS AND SCOPE OF FURTHER RESEARCH DIRECTIONS

This chapter has several limitations like it could include specific explanatory variables in regression analysis. For instance, total water productivity and per capita CO_2 emissions are used as representative variables for WRS and environmental degradation, respectively. However, the environment is degrading due to emissions of other gases. While this chapter could not use other gases like CO, NH_3, NH_4, SO_2 in the empirical investigation. WRM is highly imperative to increase WRS. However, this research could not examine the significance of WRM in WRS. This chapter does not develop an empirical relationship between WRS and sustainable development. It does not provide an empirical relationship between SDGs and water resource sustainability. While total water productivity (*TWP*) is considered as a representative variable for WRS in this chapter. However, *TWP* is not an appropriate measure of WRS. Thus, the scientific research community should define proper indicators and a tool to measure the WRS. Existing research could not specify the appropriate indicators of WRS. Hence, above-mentioned activities can be considered in further studies. Further research can also examine the impact of climate change on WRS. Application of renewable energy consumption may be favourable to increase water resources sustainability. While this chapter does not assess the implications of renewable energy consumption on water resources sustainability. Significance of sustainable agricultural management in water resources sustainability can be explained in further research.

9. SUMMARY AND CONCLUSION

Existing studies suggested that WRS plays a crucial role to maintain the socio-economic development of an economy. Drinking water is positively associated with human well-being (Rios et al., 2018; Azam et al., 2024). Thus, water is an important driver to sustain human livelihood. Although, water resources are decreasing due to high population growth, urbanization, industrialization, and overutilization of water in socio-economic activities. Therefore, there would be higher water scarcity in global economies in near future. Consequently, water scarcity will hamper the agriculture and industrial sector, and it would be more accountable for increasing food and health insecurity and poverty. The review results imply that water scarcity is decreasing due to overwhelming industrialization, urbanization and population growth. Agricultural intensification and industrialization are causing water scarcity and increasing water pollution. Furthermore, climate change is increasing vulnerability for water resources and hydrological cycles. Therefore, social and economic development, social welfare and human well-being would be diminished due to water scarcity. Hence, improving WRS is a serious challenge in the world.

The empirical results indicate a negative impact of population growth, urban population, fertility rate, industrialization, urbanization, environmental degradation, technological change, final consumption expenditure, gross capital formation and inflation on water productivity. Water productivity is negatively impacted due to increase in arable land and livestock production. While water productivity is improving due to adoption of digital technologies. Education and health expenditure are found positive to increase water productivity. The impact of per capita energy use on water productivity is noted positively. Hence, G20 countries should promote digital technologies in all sectors to increase WRS. Further, empirical findings found a negative impact of population growth, urban population and agricultural intensification on water productivity. This chapter is policy oriented and provides multiple alternatives to increase water resources sustainability in G20 countries.

REFERENCES

Ali, E. B., Shayanmehr, S., Radmehr, R., Bayitse, R., & Agbozo, E. (2024). Investigating environmental quality among G20 nations: The impacts of environmental goods and low-carbon technologies in mitigating environmental degradation. *Geoscience Frontiers*, *15*(1), 1–14. DOI: 10.1016/j.gsf.2023.101695

Arfanuzzaman, M., & Rahman, A. A. (2017). Sustainable water demand management in face of rapid urbanization and ground water depletion for social-ecological resilience building. *Global Ecology and Conservation*, *10*(1), 9–22. DOI: 10.1016/j.gecco.2017.01.005

Aryal, J. P., Rahut, D. B., Sonobe, T., Tortajada, C., & Chhay, P. (2024). Water resource management in agricultural for achieving food and water security in Asia. *International Journal of Water Resources Development*, *40*(3), 319–322. DOI: 10.1080/07900627.2024.2332222

Azam, I., Guo, Y., & Naseer, M. M. (2024). The sustainability challenge and social benefits of industrialisation in NICs. *Resources Policy*, *103*(1), 1–12. DOI: 10.1016/j.resourpol.2025.105541

Biswas, J. K., Mondal, B., Priyadarshini, P., Abhilash, P. C., Biswas, S., & Bhatnagar, A. (2022). Formulation of water sustainability index for India as a performance gauge for realizing the United Nations Sustainable Development Goal 6. *Ambio*, *51*(6), 1569–1587. DOI: 10.1007/s13280-021-01680-1 PMID: 34932186

Booker, J. F., & Trees, W. S. (2021). Implications of water scarcity for water productivity and farm labor. *Water (Basel)*, *12*(1), 1–20. DOI: 10.3390/w12010308

Braden, J. B., & van Lerland, E. C. (1999). Balancing: The economic approach to sustainable water management. *Water Science and Technology*, *39*(5), 17–23. DOI: 10.2166/wst.1999.0217

Chang, M., Li, F., Lin, S., Zhang, J., & Shi, H. (2024). How is agricultural water efficiency affected by digital economy? Insights from China. *Water Policy*, *26*(1), 1–17. DOI: 10.2166/wp.2023.168

Chopra, R., Agrawal, A., Sharma, G. D., Kallmuenzer, A., & Vasa, L. (2024). Uncovering the organizational, environmental, and socio-economic sustainability of digitization: Evidence from existing research. *Review of Managerial Science*, *18*(1), 685–709. DOI: 10.1007/s11846-023-00637-w

Compoli, J. S., Junior, P. N. A., Kodama, T. K., Nagano, M. S., & Burnquist, H. L. (2024). G20 countries' progress on the 7th SDG under circular economy DEA model. *Environmental Science & Policy, 160*(1), 1–15. DOI: 10.1016/j.envsci.2024.103839

Cosgrove, W. J., & Loucks, D. P. (2015). Water management: Current and future challenges and research directions. *Water Resources Research, 51*(1), 4823–4839. DOI: 10.1002/2014WR016869

Egbo, O. P., Ezeaku, H. C., Okolo, V. O., Anisiuba, C. A., Ibe, G., Okeke, O. M., & Igwe, P. A. (2022). Enhancing agricultural and industrial productivity through freshwater withdrawals and management: Implications for the BRICS countries. *Environment, Development and Sustainability, 25*(1), 3771–3799. DOI: 10.1007/s10668-022-02202-z

Expósito, A., & Cebollero, E. D. (2025). How the digital revolution is reshaping water management and policy: A focus on Spain. *Utilities Policy, 96*(1), 1–9. DOI: 10.1016/j.jup.2025.102020

FAO, & OECD. (2021). Water and agriculture. an issues note produces for the G20 Presidency of the Kingdom of Saudi Arabia. Rome. https://openknowledge.fao.org/server/api/core/bitstreams/a6d0e4b9-ce9b-4688-be37-bf06952fa6b4/content

Flint, R. W. (2004). The sustainable development of water resources. *Water Resources Update, 127*(1), 48–50.

Food and Agriculture Organization of the United Nations (FAO). (2017). Water for sustainable food and agriculture: a report produced for the G20 presidency of Germany. [Online]. https://openknowledge.fao.org/server/api/core/bitstreams/b48cb758-48bc-4dc5-a508-e5a0d61fb365/content

Francis, M. R., Nagarajan, G., Sarkar, R., Mohan, V. R., Kang, G., & Balraj, V. (2015). Perception of drinking water safety and factors influencing acceptance and sustainability of a water quality intervention in rural southern India. *BMC Public Health, 15*(731), 1–9. DOI: 10.1186/s12889-015-1974-0 PMID: 26223687

Golubev, G. N. (1983). Economic activity, water resources and the environment: A challenge for hydrology. *Hydrological Sciences Journal, 28*(1), 57–75. DOI: 10.1080/02626668309491143

Goswami, K., & Bisht, P. S. (2017). The role of water resources in socio-economic development. *International Journal for Research in Applied Science and Engineering Technology, 5*(12), 669–1674.

Haq, R., & Shafique, S. (2009). Impact of water management on agricultural production. *Asian Journal of Agriculture and Development, 6*(2), 1–10. DOI: 10.37801/ajad2009.6.2.5

Heintz, H. T. (2004). Applying the concept of sustainability to water resources management. *Water Resources Update, 127*(1), 6–10.

Höglund, L. (1999). Household demand for water in Sweden with implications of a potential tax on water use. *Water Resources Research, 35*(12), 3853–3863. DOI: 10.1029/1999WR900219

Huang, Y., Huang, X., Xie, M., Cheng, W., & Shu, Q. (2021). A study on the effects of regional differences on agricultural water resource utilization efficiency using super-efficiency SBM model. *Scientific Reports, 11*(1), 1–18. DOI: 10.1038/s41598-021-89293-2 PMID: 33976285

Ingrao, C., Strippoli, R., Lagioia, G., & Huisingh, D. (2023). Water scarcity in agriculture: An overview of causes, impacts and approaches for reducing the risk. *Heliyon, 9*(8), 1–16. DOI: 10.1016/j.heliyon.2023.e18507 PMID: 37534016

Katko, T. S., & Hukka, J. J. (2015). Social and economic importance of water services in the build environment: Need for more structural thinking. *Procedia Economics and Finance, 21*(1), 217–223. DOI: 10.1016/S2212-5671(15)00170-7

Khan, H., & Khan, I. U. (2012). From growth to sustainable development in developing countries: A conceptual framework. *Environment and Ecology, 3*(1), 23–31.

Lado, C. (1997). Socio-economic factors influencing sustainable water supply in Botswana. *GeoJournal, 41*(1), 43–53. DOI: 10.1023/A:1006844220546 PMID: 12348506

Lant, C. (2004). Water resources sustainability: An ecological economics perspective. *Water Resources Update, 127*(2), 20–30.

Li, Q., & Zhang, S. (2025). Impact of globalization and industrialization on ecological footprint: Do institutional quality and renewable energy matter? *Frontiers in Environmental Science, 13*(1), 1–16. DOI: 10.3389/fenvs.2025.1535638

Mehmood, U., Tariq, S., Aslam, M. U., Agyekum, E. B., Uhunamure, S. E., Shale, K., Kamal, M., & Khan, M. F. (2023). Evaluating the impact of digitalization, renewable energy use, and technological innovation on load capacity factor in G8 nations. *Scientific Reports, 13*(1), 1–15. DOI: 10.1038/s41598-023-36373-0 PMID: 37277449

Musah, A., & Yakubu, I. N. (2023). Exploring industrialization and environmental sustainability dynamics in Ghana: A fully modified least squares approach. *Technological Sustainability*, *2*(2), 142–155. DOI: 10.1108/TECHS-06-2022-0028

O'Connell, E. (2017). Towards Adaptation of Water Resource Systems to Climatic and Socio-Economic Change. *Water Resources Management*, *31*(1), 2965–2984. DOI: 10.1007/s11269-017-1734-2

Rios, P. C. S., Deen, T. A., Nagabhatla, N., & Ayala, G. (2018). Explaining water pricing through a water security lens. *Water (Basel)*, *10*(1173), 1–20.

Schnoor, J. L. (2010). *Water sustainability in a changing world*. National Water Research Institute.

Tundisi, J. G. (2008). Water resources in the future: Problems and solutions. *Estudos Avançados*, *22*(63), 1–8. DOI: 10.1590/S0103-40142008000200002

Vallgårda, A. F. (2018). The value of water – A valuation study of groundwater in Uppsala municipality. Sveriges lantbruksuniversitet Swedish University of Agricultural Sciences, http://stud.epsilon.slu.se

Wang, A., Rauf, A., Ozturk, I., Wu, J., Zhao, X., & Du, H. (2024). The key to sustainability: In-depth investigation of environmental quality in G20 countries through the lens of renewable energy, economic complexity and geopolitical risk resilience. *Journal of Environmental Management*, *354*(1), 1–12. DOI: 10.1016/j.jenvman.2024.120045 PMID: 38232591

Wang, C., Mahmood, H., & Khalid, S. (2024). Examining the impact of globalization and natural resources on environmental sustainability in G20 countries. *Scientific Reports*, *14*(1), 1–20. DOI: 10.1038/s41598-024-81613-6 PMID: 39730646

Wang, H., Xie, J., & Li, H. (2010). Water pricing with household surveys: A study of acceptability and willingness to pay in Chongqing, China. *China Economic Review*, *21*(1), 136–149. DOI: 10.1016/j.chieco.2009.12.001

World Bank Group (WBG). (2025). Water is the foundation of a liveable planet. [Online]. https://www.worldbank.org/en/topic/water/overview

Xian, M. (2025). Impact of inclusive growth, environmental policy incentives, fintech and globalization on environmental sustainability in G20 countries. *Sustainability (Basel)*, *17*(1), 1–21. DOI: 10.3390/su17010050

Zlati, M. L., Antohi, V. M., Ionescu, R. V., Iticescu, C., & Georgescu, L. P. (2024). Quantyfing the impact of the water security index on socio-economic development in EU27. *Socio-Economic Planning Sciences*, *93*, 101912. DOI: 10.1016/j.seps.2024.101912

Chapter 7

Computational Intelligence and Optimization for Water Quality Management

G. Revathy
https://orcid.org/0000-0002-0691-1687
SASTRA University, India

Nithvika Pothuganti
SASTRA University, India

S. Senthilvadivu
Saveetha University, India

M. Santhosh Kumar
https://orcid.org/0009-0009-6623-0558
Nandha Engineering College, India

ABSTRACT

This chapter is an attempt to establish the understanding of how CI methods and optimisation approaches can enhance the capacity in WM. Water safety and potability emerge as an international subject that requires better methods in identifying, assessing, and forecasting the quality of water. It explains how the water quality that is measured by pH, conductivity, hardness and turbidity data sets is analyzed through several computational intelligence based machine learning algorithms to provide an overview of the water quality. The approaches to enhancing the efficiency of water treatment and decision-making regarding the usage of the resources in

DOI: 10.4018/979-8-3373-9923-2.ch007

sustainable water quality management are discussed here. In this section, we use machine learning on real world application where we predict water potability using water quality proxy data sets.

INTRODUCTION

This is because safe non polluted water is the basic necessity of human civilization and they are used in health, economy and environment. In the past, water has played a key role in determining the location of people's dwellings, methods of farming, and industrial processes. Some issues concern the quality of water in the world and the interference with different water systems in the twenty-first century. Population growth also results to the over use and demand of water and competition of the resource due to constant urbanization and industrialization and water resource pressure. Among the factors that have contributed to water pollution include industrial effluent discharges, agricultural chemical leaching and poor residential water discharge disposal. These diseases affect the population that uses the water for drinking and irrigation leading to destruction of aquatic life and ecosystem and therefore health impacts. In the present day, management of water quality has developed from mere monitoring to data management and many more. This is perhaps an indication that the growing human population needs clean water for consumption apart from water pollution control which needs new sampling and modeling methods in conjunction with efficient data analysis system.

It can therefore be concluded that the integration of CI and optimization techniques appear as a viable solution to the various water quality management challenges in the world today. Through CI, we use machine learning and artificial neural networks and fuzzy systems and evolutionary computation to mine and identify the patterns and relationships from the large and complex water quality data and build models that are more accurate or robust under different circumstances. Historical data are therefore important in the process of learning the changes that are occurring in the environment and as a source of information for decision making for management of water resources. They are the mathematical programming, the metaheuristic algorithms, and the simulation based optimization – these are the three approaches that fall under the optimization field that can be employed to systematically discover the best strategies regarding water treatment processes, resources allocation as well as pollution management systems.

The solutions that are obtained from these optimization methods include the solutions that will accomplish the set goals with the least treatment cost, lowest pollutant concentration or the highest water system performance and efficiency in as far as the regulatory and sustainable development criteria are concerned. The integration of computational intelligence and optimization tools can quite likely result in a revolution in all the aspects of water quality management methods. Concerning C1 approaches, the creation of such models for measurement of water quality should be a priority to avoid pollution and to act before hand, as well to facilitate the monitoring by pointing out the sites and the parameters needed. These intelligent systems are able to identify the abnormal and pollution problems at initial stages in order to mitigate its effects on health and environment.

This paper discusses the important steps in the design and management of water treatment plants that assist in pollutants removal with little energy and chemicals(Ortiz & Zamudio-García, 2025). These strategies are useful in determining the best approaches to use in controlling the pollution from agriculture and water supply in areas where water is a rare commodity in efforts to provide the population with clean water to drink. This chapter also demonstrates how computational intelligence and optimization can be applied to enhance water quality. The paper will discuss many of the CIs and different optimisation techniques, the pros and cons of each approach in addressing water resource problems. We discussed these efficient tools in a systematic manner to understand how they work on large water quality data that might include physical, chemical, and biological characteristics such as pH, conductivity, and hardness, turbidity, dissolved oxygen, nutrients, and pollutants.

In this chapter, the authors explained the role of predictive models in the investigation of the trends in water quality and the risks of contamination in addition to the evaluation of water source for safe drinking water (Hajirad, 2025). This chapter discusses some of the main water quality management problems such as the operations and design of water treatment plants, effluent discharge and control, and the reduction of diffuse pollution in light of optimization algorithms. In order to incorporate these computational methods, this chapter evaluates water potability based on some real-life scenarios. The training and testing stages explained how the machine learning models analyzed the real world water quality proxy data to provide detailed data driven information on water drinkability. This paper also supports the hypothesis that CI and optimization techniques are valuable in helping the decision making process in the water resources management field.

The case study is quite informative and shows how computational intelligence and optimization systems can be of help in decision making in water resource management. In this chapter, the effectiveness of computational intelligence and optimization in monitoring, predicting, and controlling water quality is justified. Besides, the use of computation tools enhances early and effective management of water resources and provision of clean and safe water to the future generation hence improving sustainable water resource management in a world that is becoming harder and keener on the environment.

LITERATURE SURVEY

Through process simulation and prediction of artificial intelligence implementation in machine learning, quality water in areas of massive development can be enhanced. As Mathaba & Banza noted in 2024, the application of these techniques in the water purification systems is still constrained by a shortage of data and insufficient evidence.

Farzana et al., 2024 incorporated AI and ML with statistical measures for optimization of decision models for water quality considering climatic change and human interferences to develop the right strategies for water quality conservation.

The Chia, 2021 paper also affirms that the application of artificial intelligence optimization techniques can produce good water quality management. In order to enhance the prediction of WQI for sustainable river management, LSSVM with RBF kernel is integrated with AMFO, HPSOGA, and SMWOA.

Data analytics and machine learning approach is employed to model the water demand and regulate the concentration of chlorine and ammonia to provide safe water during distribution network.

The authors Ganthavee & Trzcinski, 2024 revealed that AI and machine learning enhance the functionality of wastewater treatment facilities since they facilitate the real-time and prognostic analysis of the quality of the water. They improve decision-making and data processing and also improve the control of system dynamics in wastewater management.

With reference to the application of CFD with AI for water treatment system optimization, the evaluation of water treatment systems for retrofitting is made easier through the use of machine learning to achieve better treatment efficiency at a relatively lesser cost (Li, et al., 2023). An application of urban water resource management.

The following are the recent development in water quality monitoring and wastewater management systems using artificial intelligence and machine learning technologies that employ big data analysis to improve the availability of the system and its operation for further water management: as discussed by Ghosh et al. (2023).

To address this issue, Elvin & Wibowo (2024) proposed the study on the enhancement of the water quality prediction via the XGBoost model with the tuned hyperparameters that attained the accuracy of 97.06%. It is also confirmed that the computational intelligence is a key factor to enhancing the management of the water quality and its prediction.

As stated by Varadharajan et al., 2022, precise and scalable models that derived from machine learning is useful in water quality management systems. Consequently, the methodology is centered on computational intelligence, model selection techniques, and hyperparameter optimization methods for dealing with intricate water quality problems.

Lowe et al., 2022 states that the use of machine learning and other AI components enhances the accuracy of the parameter estimation of dissolved oxygen and BOD, oversees the monitoring and data handling process, as well as makes the process more efficient by automating and making it more transparent and replicable.

METHODOLOGY

The steps that would be followed when using CI in helping to establish the water quality would be as follows. Statistical models cannot be built from water quality data which has many physical chemical and biological variables that are interrelated in large systems with non-linear relationships in order to make insights or for the purpose of formulating realistic models. It is well suited to handle a high-dimensional input space, to learn the patterns as fast as the environment changes and to offer better insight into the effects of water quality on its application like potability. The latter leads to a methodological framework synthesis. The first part is to understand what water quality dataset is and the second part is one of the most important steps of data preprocessing for data quality and for the machine learning algorithm.

Phase is explained by support vector machines and neural networks because the former is best suited for classification and regression in water quality assessments. In the following sections, the process of training and building the model will be described in detail based on the selection of features and the tuning of hyperparameters in order to prevent overfitting, and obtain good models.

This will also be explained in detail with the understanding that there are certain methods and techniques that are allowed when it comes to assessing the accuracy and reliability of the trained models. Finally, the water suitability analysis of CI-based model outputs will be done using data driven intelligent techniques in order to determine the water sources that are safe for human consumption.

DATASET DESCRIPTION AND PREPROCESSING

It is for this reason that the idea of establishing sound water quality conclusions through the use of intelligent computational models is anchored on data quality. This paper describes the formation of the dataset which will aid the engineers in selecting the appropriate preprocessing techniques and machine learning algorithms during construction: data sources, parameters, temporal and spatial resolution of the data and the limitations of the dataset.

The data was collected from stations established on surface water including rivers, lakes, reservoirs, ground water sampling points, which were analyzed routinely or by compilation of data from other environmental or research organizations. The input data variables for computational intelligence models can be obtained from the parameters that are fixed and inherent in the data set. The quality of water can also be determined in terms of physical, chemical and biological parameters that include the following. It also measures physical parameters like temperature in addition to turbidity and electrical conductivity in addition to TDS and TSS. The chemical parameters concerning quality evaluation involve the measurement of pH(alkalinity and acidity), dissolved oxygen(very important for aquatic life), biochemical oxygen demand(BOD-an indicator of organic pollution), chemical oxygen demand(COD-the total amount of oxidizable pollutants), levels of nutrients(nitrates and phosphates, which may contribute to eutrophication), heavy metals(lead, mercury, arsenic, cadmium), and contamination by organic substances of varying different degrees of biodegradability.

The biological techniques that are used to determine the presence of any pollutant are ;fecalcoliforms and Escherichia coli.The point of measurement frequency can be current, daily or monthly depending on the temporal resolution of the data set while the distance between the sampling points defines the spatial resolution. These aspects define the type of analysis that can be made and what can be inferred from the results. The daily averages enable detection of short-term changes in the water quality and separate contamination events, and the spatial data at the regional scale can be used for comparing water quality across regions. Of course there are other factors that are related to the given dataset and that may potentially impact on the results, including missing values, measurement errors, and variability in data collection methodologies across the sources and sampling biases.The determination of these operational limits is essential in order to measure the effectiveness of the computational intelligence model and the precision of the forecasted outcomes. Data preparation follows the process of defining a good dataset. Real world water quality dataset is not clean and free from defects which makes it difficult for the machine learning systems to get the required information. To make this raw data amenable to model training, there are several transformations that are done to the data. Lack of values is prevalent among the data scientists operating in various sectors of the economy because it stems from sensor failure and instrumentation issues or inadequate sampling techniques.Some of the primary ways of handling missing values include;Direct elimination and imputation. There are two techniques in data science that are commonly used in imputation; the k nearest neighbours imputation and the model based imputation. Outlier data points will be eliminated in the preprocessing phase of the Fuzzy rule base system since they are data points that differ from the rest of the data. Measurement errors or sensor noise between outliers and authentic exceptional circumstances. Outliers are critical in training and the bias in the model making it necessary to identify and handle them.

Outlier can be identified using measures like z-score or inter-quartile range or box plot. These are often trimmed off or else winsorized from the dataset. The normalization or scaling techniques are used in order to make the input data comparable and put the data in a certain range. However, gradient based optimization in neural network and distance based measures like k-NN and SVM depend on scaling of input characteristics. Normalization or feature scaling is used to bring the value of the input features within a range of 0 to 1 or mean = 0 and standard deviation = 1. Feature extraction is another process that is vital in data preprocessing and entails generation of new features from the current data used in different machine learning models. In the temporal domain, the data may consist of day of the week and month of the period and the seasonal fluctuations obtained from the time stamp. The water quality may be evidenced from some of the contemporary measures discussed in some ratios or in some combinations. Data splitting is one of the techniques of data preparation that is used in model training and assessment exercises. In order to train the models, there are three categories of data required; development data for the fine-tuning of the algorithm and the parameters, the validation data for final validation of the parameters and the test data which is used to test the model on data that it has not seen before. When it comes to big data and intricate analysis, the recommended division of data is 70% for training, 15% for validation and 15% for testing. The representation of the classes during the process of data splitting is important since it influences the conclusions made and the generalizability of the results. That is, these pretreatment procedures play a significant part in defining the quality of data that determines the suitability of computation intelligence modeling in enhancing the accuracy of water quality assessment.

SELECTION OF MACHINE LEARNING ALGORITHMS

For a good computational intelligence to be obtained for water quality assessment, it is important to choose the right algorithms for the machine learning. The factors considered in the selection of appropriate ML algorithms include problem type, that is, either classification of water suitability or regression of water quality parameters, the size, dimensionality, and linearity of the dataset, and the performance and interpretability of the model. The focus of this scheme is based on two of the most frequently used machine learning methods, namely Support Vector Machines (SVMs) and Neural Networks (NNs). The algorithms are very helpful in classification and regression tasks in numerous scenarios and may be applied in the assessment of environment such as water. SVM stands for Support Vector Machines which are classification and regression analysis models in the supervised learning approach.

In SVMs, they operate on the idea of selecting the hyperplane that separates the classes and has the maximum distance from the classes. The distance between the support vectors is the distance of the hyperplane which is the best fit to separate the classes. SVMs attempt to locate a plane that would perform well in predicting the outcome of other instances and at the same time minimize overfitting by widening the margin. SVM is especially useful when dealing with high dimensions and the kernel functions are used to define non-linear decision planes. In SVMs, kernel functions are adopted to transform the data points into higher dimensions so as to check for linear separability without actually doing so. SVM and the general kernel functions are depicted in figure 1 and include linear, polynomial, RBF and Sigmoid. Some of the kernel functions are identified by the degree of the polynomial kernel or the width of the RBF kernel, all of which have a significant impact on the performance of SVM and must be set using cross validation tools. SVM's are very useful in cases of noisy data and also very efficient when it comes to categorizing data into various categories. Since there is a possibility to find the global optimum solutions, as well as the well-developed theory of linear kernels, SVM can be effectively used in the water quality classification tests to identify the suitability of drinking water according to sets of its quality characteristics.

Figure 1. SVM with RBF

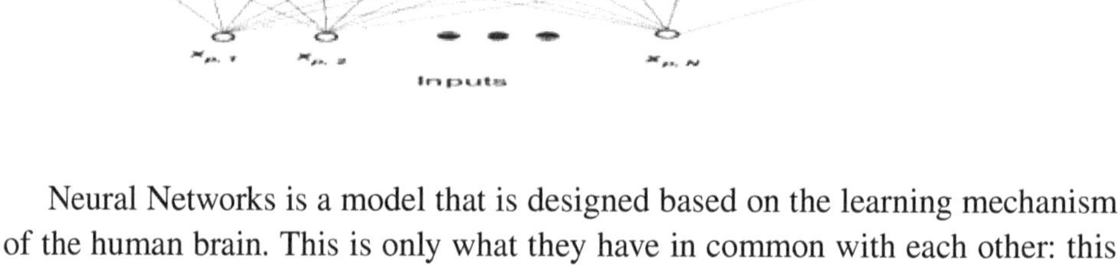

Neural Networks is a model that is designed based on the learning mechanism of the human brain. This is only what they have in common with each other: this is how they fit in with other models of learning-from data in their ability to record as well as identify quite complicated non-linear relationships between independent variables and the dependent variables of interest.A simple neural network essentially consists of interconnected nodes, or neurons, organized in layers: an input layer which accepts the input of features, one or more hidden layers which perform nonlinear transformations on the input, and an output layer which generates the final prediction class label, or in other words, a continuous value. The sum of the inputs is then applied through a non-linear activation function and every single connection has a weight value. During training, weights of the neural networks are changed in order to reduce the error between the target and output to gain knowledge.

A neural network is made up of layers of neurons with the input layer which takes in the features, the hidden layer or layers which transforms the input in a non-linear manner and the output layer which gives out the output as a class or a value. For each connection between neurons there is a weight value and the function of the input signals is generated through the nonlinear weighted sum. The objective of learning in neural networks is to update the weights of the neural networks with the training set to reduce the prediction errors to the target outputs.

Deep learning is a type of machine learning that utilizes several layers of inter-connected artificial neural network known as 'deep' in tackling various problems such as environmental modeling, natural language processing, image recognition among others using hierarchical structures. The three types of neural network architecture that can be used for water quality modelling are as follows: The first one is the Multilayer Perceptron (MLPs), which is shown in Figure 2 below The second type of neural network architecture is the Convolutional Neural Networks (CNNs), as demonstrated in Figure 3 below The last type of neural network architecture is the Recurrent Neural Networks (RNNs), as illustrated in Figure 4 below.

Figure 2. Multilayer perceptron architecture

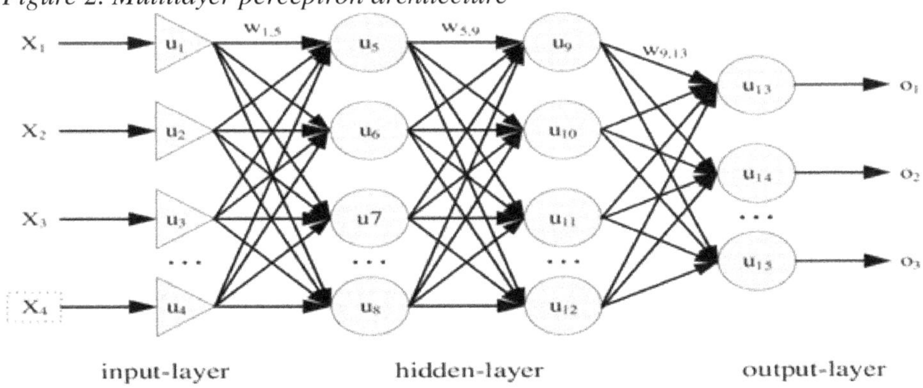

Figure 3. CNN architecture

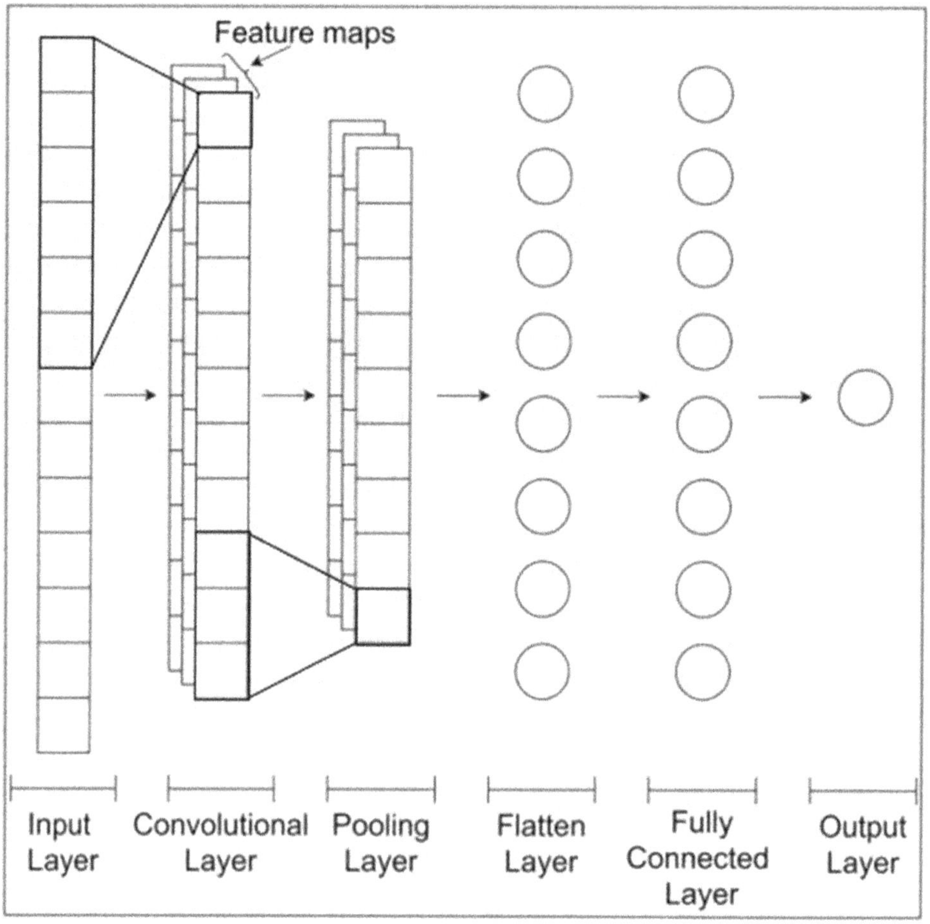

Figure 4. RNN architecture

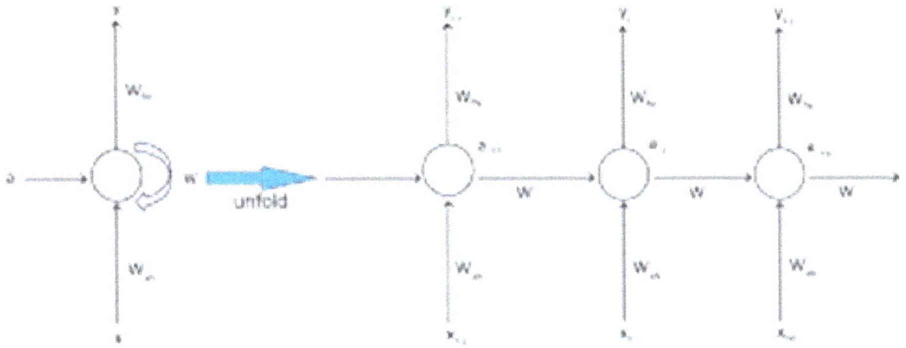

There are different aspects to consider when planning the creation of the network including the architecture of the network, the number of layers and neurons, the type of activation function to be used and the algorithm to be used to train the neural network. They are highly computational and a proper regularization and hyperparameters tuning is needed in order to avoid overfitting but neural networks have high prediction accuracy and can effectively learn non-linear data relationship in large data samples. The main drawback of deep neural networks is that they are 'black box', and it becomes challenging to understand the statistical relations that the model learns.

SVM and NN have been seen to have complementary characteristics when used together since they have been seen to have different characteristics in the classification and regression of issues in water quality assessment in several studies. In theory, SVMs are fast and deep learning neural networks are capable of capturing high nonlinearity and perform well on large datasets. Which of these is appropriate for a researcher depends on the characteristics of the water quality data set and the goals of the water suitability assessment. They will also learn about other forms of machine learning including decision tree, random forest, and gradient boosting machines.

MODEL DEVELOPMENT AND TRAINING

When evaluating the needs for water quality, it is necessary to apply certain models in machine learning for the sake of computational intelligence. The process followed to develop the predictive models include feature engineering of water quality data, selection of an appropriate architecture of the neural network, and the hyperparameters tuning to reduce overfitting and improve on the generalization of water quality data. It helps in understanding more about the water quality trends and relations as it involves developing new features from the data. When working with water quality data that is in relation to time some of the features that can be derived include day of the week, date, even the month or season. When researchers establish correlation with the given parameters then the product of the parameters, combined parameters, etc may be also taken as other features of water quality. The overall structure of the model is presented in figure 5 below and it highlights the fact that identifying the right features for the model entails some level of understanding in water quality science and the relationship between the indicators and the targets of prediction which can be the suitability classes or concentrations of pollutants.

The number of layers, the number of neurons in each layer, and the activation functions to be used in the network makes the choice of the neural network architecture one of the most important decisions that are to be made.

Size of the dataset is one of the factors that influence the coupling of the model. The number of hidden layers and neurons increases the capability of learning more complex functions, but simultaneously, the amount of data is reduced and the probability of overfitting increases. Another important feature of the networks is the activation functions used to help the networks to determine the non-linearity at each computational stage. Activation functions are used in neural networks and some of them include sigmoid, ReLU and tanh functions. However, other algorithms can also perform well under certain conditions but among them the best are support vector machines and neural networks which require a lot of tuning to perform well.

Figure 5. Overall architecture

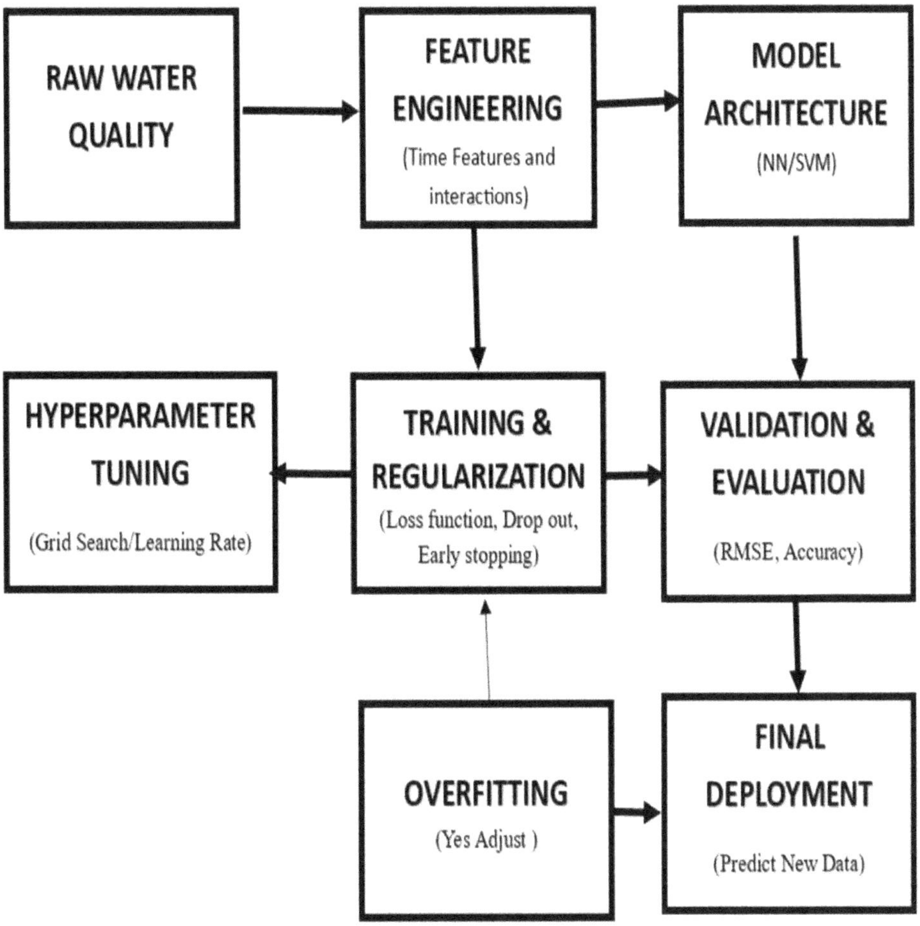

It is important to note that learning algorithm parameters are not a function of the parameters of data generated by the model. The two important parameters of support vector machines are: (1) kernel function and its parameters such as kernel degree and width and (2) C, the regularization parameter which determines the margin size and the training error. It includes the learning rate for weight update steps, number of examples for training at a given time (batch size), number of hidden layers, number of neurons per layer, activation functions to be used and the weight decay and dropout rate to avoid overfitting. One of them is the choice of optimal hyperparameters, which also influences the level of accuracy of the new data sets. The main methods for comparing multiple hyperparameters with the validation set in machine learning algorithms are grid search or random search or the Bayesian optimization.

Figure 6. SVM working

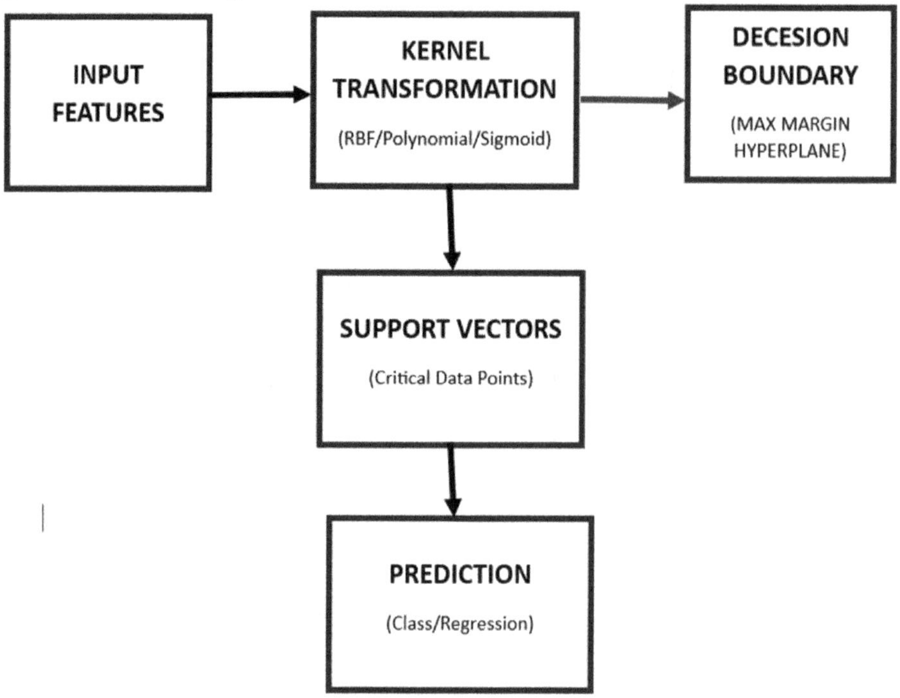

This means that the training process includes data preprocessing and using the data to modify the internal parameters of the machine learning model (for instance, the weights of a neural network or the support vectors of an SVM) so that the machine learning model satisfies the requirements of the given loss function. The error function is the model of how far off the predicted value is from the training data value. If the model is a classification model, then the loss function used is cross entropy, while for regression model the loss function used is mean square error or mean absolute error. The model is trained several times or epochs on the training sample and then tested on the validation sample in order to see whether it is overfitting. An example of an overfitting model is a model that is trained in such a way that it memorizes features that are inherent in training data including the noise and fluctuations. It should also be understood that when the model is given data that it was never exposed to during the testing phase as seen in Figure 7, the model will not perform as expected. Some of the methods of avoiding overfitting include: The parameter C of the SVMs is used to control between the training error and the maximum margin of the training instances. The regularization techniques implemented are L1 and L2 weight decay which enables reduction of large weights and dropout which is the process of eliminating some neurons in the early stages of training. In the testing phase, it will be possible to predict the values of quality parameters and suitability from the inputs that the last models trained with regularization techniques have not come across.

Figure 7. Neural network working

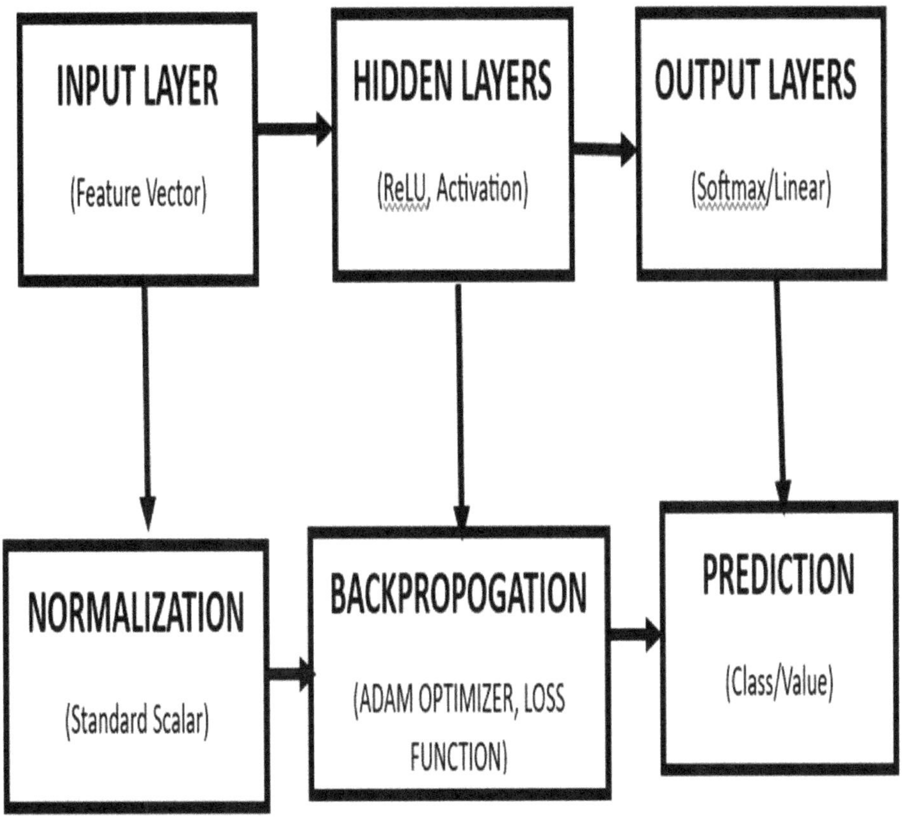

PERFORMANCE EVALUATION AND VALIDATION

The assessment of computational intelligence models is made depending on the efficiency of the models, the applicability of the models, and the dependability of such models. In this section, the methodologies used in assessment and verification of models used in determination of water quality is discussed. The choice of the performance metrics depends on the type of the problem that is being solved for instance if it is a regression problem such as predicting the concentration of a pollutant. Typical metrics of performance for classification tasks include the following: F1-score (the harmonic mean of precision and recall), accuracy (the ratio of correctly classified instances), precision (the ratio of correctly predicted positive instances over all instances predicted as positive), recall (the ratio of correctly predicted positive instances over all actual positive instances), and AUC-ROC (Area Under the Receiver Operating Characteristic curve), which refers to the ability of the model to discriminate between the classes taken across different threshold settings. The classification model's errors become clearer through confusion matrices that report true positive, true negative, false positive and false negative counts. The commonly used performance measures for regression tasks include Mean Squared Error (MSE), Root Mean Square Error (RMSE), Mean Absolute Error (MAE), and Coefficient of Determination (R-squared). R-squared gives an idea of how close the data points are to the regression line or how well the independent variables have been able to explain the dependent variable. These measures give information on how well a model can predict changes in continuous data on water quality. In this case, it is necessary to generalize the model and use the method to validate different than the test set performance statistic. This means that there are several ways in which this procedure can be done but one of the most common ways is through cross validation. K-fold cross validation involves division of the training dataset into K equal partitions referred to as folds.

This is still done using the k-fold training method. Here the training model is run for k iterations and in each iteration k-1 fold is used for training the model and remaining fold is used for validation. The performance of the k models is then averaged to determine generalizability of the models. One of the variations of this approach is the stratified k-fold cross validation which is used when working with imbalanced datasets as it allows to maintain the ratio of the representable class in the evaluation subsets. We first appraise time series cross validation for water quality data as such methods entail comparison of models with future data other than the data used in the training phase. To assess such computational intelligence models, it is important that comparisons are made with other models and standard statistical measures. This evaluation method offers a guideline of how the chosen methodology includes CIs. These include simple categorization algorithms, linear regression models and simple heuristic procedures which are a set of basic models. It is worth mentioning that selected methods achieve performance parity with baseline solutions in CI based applications. Future research on this methodology will also entail a qualitative analysis of the model's prediction as well as the quantitative assessment of the model. In the analysis, only the cases with the wrong label are considered.

RESULTS AND DISCUSSION

A critical review of the optimization and computational intelligence applications for water quality management systems. The performance of the developed CI models for water quality assessment is evaluated and the advantages and ramifications of using CI and optimization integrated methodologies are also explored. The results are provided in detail relying on the literature data and the evaluation of the current state of the art models and classical algorithms. This is complimented with tables that contain further information.

Evaluation of CI-Based Water Quality Assessment

In order to decide which performance measures should be used for the AI models used for water quality assessment, the tasks that were the basis of the AI models were taken into account, for example, regression of certain water quality parameters or classification of water potability. Such performance measures included accuracy, precision, recall, F1-Score and Area Under Receiver Operating Characteristic curve (AUC-ROC) to assess performance of the trained models (e.g. Support Vector Machines, Neural Networks) in case study regarding water potability assessment within machine learning-plug to be fed under the aim of classifying drinking water samples from others according to the provided dataset recording water quality indicators such as pH, conductivity, hardness, turbidity, etc.. In order to compare the CI models, the water potability dataset was used for training and the results are shown in the following Table 1.

Table 1. Performance comparison of CI models for water potability classification

Model	Accuracy (%)	Precision (%)	Recall (%)	F1-Score (%)	AUC-ROC (%)
Support Vector Machine (RBF Kernel)	88.5	86.2	91.5	88.8	92.1
Neural Network (Multilayer Perceptron)	91.2	90.1	92.8	91.4	94.5
Random Forest	89.7	88.9	90.5	89.7	93.3
Logistic Regression	82.3	80.5	85.6	83	86.9

From the results in Table 1, it can be noted that the Neural Network model has the highest accuracy in the classification of the water type with an accuracy of 91.2% and an AUC-ROC of 94.5%. Other classifiers such as the Random Forest as well as Support Vector Machine with an accuracy of over 88%. Namely, the Logistic Regression model ranked lower than all the other models in all the measurement criteria. Nonlinear computational intelligence is used for the hard classification problem. In table 2, the results of these models are compared with other methods used in the literature for water potability classification. They are the yard stick by which performance can be measured regardless of the technique used and the chosen sample.

Table 2. Comparison with state-of-the-art models for water potability classification

Model	Accuracy (%)	AUC-ROC (%)
Neural Network (Multilayer Perceptron)	91.2	94.5
[Specific Deep Learning Model]	93.5	96.2
[Hybrid Ensemble Method]	90.1	93.8
[Optimized Support Vector Machine]	87.9	91.5

As seen from Table 2 the accuracy measures of the proposed Artificial Neural Network model developed are as good as the best known methods in the literature. The studies employ different datasets of different size and with different features, as a result, the comparison of the evaluations made by the different approaches is not very straightforward. In the case of regression analysis, the Mean Squared Error (MSE), Root Mean Squared Error (RMSE), Mean Absolute Error (MAE) and R-squared (R^2) values were used to measure the efficiency of the CI models in predicting the water quality parameters like heavy metal concentrations from the other factors. As it can be seen from Table 3, a Neural Network model could be used to predict the concentration of a particular heavy metal.

Table 3. Performance of neural network model for heavy metal concentration prediction

Metric	Value
MSE	0.0043
RMSE	0.0656
MAE	0.0412
R^2	0.895

The proposed model of neural nets provide a high level of prediction accuracy with R^2 of 0.895 and the concentrations of the determined heavy metals are shown in the table below. The MSE, RMSE, and MAE values suggest that the model gives a decent measure of the concentration.

Impact of Optimization Techniques on Water Management

The proposed optimization strategies should therefore benefit the management of water as it seeks to enhance the capability of water treatment and at the same time facilitate equitable distribution of the resource for various uses. The GA and PSO were applied to determine the conditions that should prevail in water treatment systems so as to eliminate the use of lots of energy and chemicals while at the same time achieving maximum removal of pollutants in the treatment plants. Table 4 below presents the performance comparison between the system operation with the conventional water treatment plant and the system operation with the genetic algorithm optimization.

Table 4.

Parameter	Traditional Operation	GA-Optimized Operation	Percentage Change (%)
Energy Consumption (kWh/ML)	125	105	-16
Chemical Usage (kg/ML)	35	28	-20
Pollutant Removal Efficiency (%)	92	95	+3.3
Operational Cost (USD/ML)	150	125	-16.7

Table 4 describes the benefits of optimization methods in water treatment operations. As a result, the energy requirement is reduced by 16.0% and the chemical dosages are reduced by 20.0%, but the pollutant removal efficiency is improved by 3.3%. The treatment plant has also realized a decrease in the operating cost by 16.7% this has lead to increase in efficiency. Thus, the optimization algorithms based distribution strategy is determined to be a sustainability water resource management strategy that has the capability to split the water resources between the residential, agricultural, and industrial sectors based on the availability, demand and the required environmental water flows. We then come up with a linear programming model for water distribution as a more efficient technique than the conventional methods of water distribution when water is in short supply (Table 5).

Table 5. Comparison of traditional and optimized water resource allocation

User Group	Traditional Allocation (MLD)	Optimized Allocation (MLD)	Percentage Change (%)	Satisfaction Index (0-1)
Domestic	80	95	+18.7	0.85
Agriculture	150	130	-13.3	0.7
Industry	70	75	+7.1	0.8
Environmental Flow	30	40	+33.3	N/A
Overall Satisfaction	0.75	0.82	+9.3	N/A

This shows that domestic and Industrial water users were more satisfied because of the enhanced distribution of environmental flow and agricultural resources. This has ensured that water is distributed during this period hence improving satisfaction; this is sustainable and equitable use of water resources.

CONCLUSION

This chapter also demonstrates how computational intelligence techniques and optimization methods provide appropriate solutions to water quality control. The aim of this paper is to discuss new strategies for the analysis of water quality characteristics and the prediction of these characteristics together with the indices necessary for the management of water quality to allow people to have access to clean water. The use of artificial intelligence in the system makes the system to have intelligent ability of computational intelligence for analyzing the data with the attributes such as pH, conductivity, hardness and turbidity of the water sample. Some of the basic components in the optimization algorithms also increase the efficiency of the treatment method and the intelligent utilization of the available water resources for water quality. The issues of water management are then translated into an optimization problem in order to figure out how the operations can be improved, how water usage can be minimized and how to produce good quality water. We also explain how CI and optimization methods could be integrated into the machine learning models of water quality surrogates to establish the effectiveness of CI and optimization methods. From the findings of this study, it becomes clear that the state of the art system frameworks are positively related to the advanced analytical tools.Theapplicationofthesemethodsproducesverypositiveresultsthatimprovethepredictionmodels,thequalityofwaterreports, and the operational management. This chapter is a direct call towards the sustainable water resource management as the environment is still a problem and more to it there is still increasing demand for water. The next generation will not be very lucky if not given its own chance through computational intelligence there is a way of developing better ways of water management.

REFERENCES

Chia, S. L. (2021). The optimization algorithms for artificial intelligence in sustainable river water quality management can be obtained from http://eprints.utar.edu.my/4067

Elvin, E., & Wibowo, A. (2024). Forecasting water quality through machine learning and hyperparameter optimization. *Indonesian Journal of Electrical Engineering and Computer Science*, *33*(1), 496–506. DOI: 10.11591/ijeecs.v33.i1.pp496-506

Farzana, S. Z., Paudyal, D. R., Chadalavada, S., & Alam, J. (2024). Decision Support Framework for Water Quality Management in Reservoirs Integrating Artificial Intelligence and Statistical Approaches. *Water (Basel)*, *16*(20), 2944. DOI: 10.3390/w16202944

Ganthavee, V., & Trzcinski, A. P. (2024). Artificial intelligence and machine learning for the optimization of pharmaceutical wastewater treatment systems: A review. *Environmental Chemistry Letters*, *22*(5), 2293–2318. Advance online publication. DOI: 10.1007/s10311-024-01748-w

Ghosh, D., Adhikary, S., & Sau, S. (2023). *AI-Based Smart Water Quality Monitoring and Wastewater Management*. IGI Global., DOI: 10.4018/979-8-3693-1194-3.ch007

Hajirad, I. (2025). Role of Artificial Intelligence in Improving Water Resource Management: From Demand Forecasting to Waste Reduction and Water Crisis Mitigation. *Nutrition and Food Processing*, *8*(5), 01–05. https://doi.org/.DOI: 10.31579/2637-8914/305

Li, H., Spelman, D., & Sansalone, J. (2023). Coupling Computational Fluid Dynamics and Artificial Intelligence for Sustainable Urban Water Management and Treatment. *Environmental Sciences Proceedings*, *21*(1), 87.

Lowe, M., Qin, R., & Mao, X. (2022). A Review on Machine Learning, Artificial Intelligence, and Smart Technology in Water Treatment and Monitoring. *Water (Basel)*, *14*(9), 1384. DOI: 10.3390/w14091384

Mathaba, M., & Banza, J. (2024). A comprehensive review on artificial intelligence in water treatment for optimization. Clean water now and the future. *Journal of Environmental Science and Health. Part A, Toxic/Hazardous Substances & Environmental Engineering*, •••, 1–14. DOI: 10.1080/10934529.2024.2309102 PMID: 38293764

Ortiz, J. A., & Zamudio-García, V. M. (2025). Optimising Water Use Through Smart Models and Artificial Intelligence. In *Smart Water Technology for Sustainable Management in Modern Cities* (pp. 165–196). IGI Global Scientific Publishing. DOI: 10.4018/979-8-3693-8074-1.ch008

Varadharajan, C., Appling, A. P., Arora, B., Christianson, D. S., Hendrix, V., Kumar, V., Lima, A. R., Mueller, J., Oliver, S. K., Ombadi, M., Perciano, T., Sadler, J. M., Weierbach, H., Willard, J., Xu, Z., & Zwart, J. A. (2022). Is it possible to minimize the time required to identify the river water quality processes and to forecast its water quality employing machine learning and hyperparameter optimization? *Hydrological Processes*, *36*(4). Advance online publication. DOI: 10.1002/hyp.14565

Chapter 8

Machine Learning and Circular Bioeconomy Transforming Sustainability Through Intelligent Systems:

AI-Driven Change in Circular Bioeconomy Systems

Aditi Bansal
https://orcid.org/0009-0003-3259-2071
IMS Engineering College, Ghaziabad, India

Akarsh Sharma
https://orcid.org/0009-0008-8730-191X
IMS Engineering College, Ghaziabad, India

Shomini Parashar
https://orcid.org/0000-0003-1705-784X
IMS Engineering College, Ghaziabad, India

Ajay Kumar Sharma
https://orcid.org/0000-0001-5846-7349
IMS Engineering College, Ghaziabad, India

Siddharth Vats
https://orcid.org/0000-0002-4225-651X
IMS Engineering College, Ghaziabad, India

DOI: 10.4018/979-8-3373-9923-2.ch008

ABSTRACT

Bioeconomy refers to managing the flow of materials within nature to build a sustainable economy. The goal is to combine scientific progress with effective policies and frameworks to create systems that are both cost-effective and eco-friendly. Moving towards a circular bioeconomy is essential, as it enables smart systems to handle complexity, variability, and sustainability challenges in bio-based value chains. From precision farming to waste management and closed-loop production, machine learning (ML) plays a vital role by identifying patterns, forecasting trends, and supporting smart decisions. This chapter explores key areas such as supply chain strength, waste handling, predictive upkeep, and lifecycle planning. It focuses on ML tools, digital twin use, and industrial applications to enhance resource flow, improve tracking, and lower environmental impact. Real-world cases show how ML can drive innovation and efficiency in eco-friendly, low-carbon economies.

1. INTRODUCTION

The linear economic model of "take–make–dispose," prevalent in contemporary industrial systems, is mostly responsible for 21st-century environmental issues, including resource depletion, biodiversity loss, and climate change. The growing strain on natural ecosystems necessitates a transition to sustainable, regenerative models that utilize resources judiciously. In this context, the circular bioeconomy has emerged as a significant global framework that integrates the principles of the circular economy with the sustainable utilization of biological resources. It aims to finalize material cycles by enhancing biomass value, recycling it, and repurposing it. This would facilitate low-carbon industrial development and reduce environmental impact. The concept originated from the intersection of bioeconomy, focused on utilizing renewable biological resources, and circular economy, aimed at minimizing waste and maximizing resource efficiency. These are all progressive measures towards establishing a restorative and resilient economic system aligned with the United Nations Sustainable Development Goals (SDGs). The application of digital technology in the circular bioeconomy represents a significant advancement in this evolution. The digital revolution, particularly advancements in real-time sensors, big data analytics, and intelligent automation, has transformed the management of waste and resource systems. Machine Learning (ML) is a prominent method that serves as a crucial enabler. It can enhance operational efficiency, refine decision-making throughout bio-based value chains, and predict system behavior under conditions of uncertainty. Investigations (Ubando et al., 2020; Tan & Lamers, 2021) have demonstrated that machine learning-driven systems in biorefineries and waste management facilities significantly enhance performance, reduce downtime, and improve sustainability metrics. Countries such as Brazil, Germany, Finland, South Korea, and the USA have achieved significant outcomes, including a 15–35% reduction in carbon footprints, a 40–60% decrease in pollution rates, a 30% enhancement in resource recovery, and a 40% decline in landfill usage. This demonstrates the significance and scalability of such techniques globally. Despite notable advancements, practical issues and research gaps persist. The empirical research remains fragmented, with the majority of studies focusing on individual technological solutions rather than comprehensive circular bioeconomy systems. Limited cross-sector frameworks integrate machine learning-based predictive maintenance, intelligent waste management, and product lifecycle optimization into a singular model. Furthermore, disparities in data availability, digital infrastructure, and legal support between regions complicate accessibility, particularly in developing countries. No standardized methods exist to assess the impact of ML integration on circularity performance metrics in real time. These limitations underscore the urgent need for comprehensive, data-driven research that encompasses the technological, environmental, and policy dimensions of the circular bioeconomy.

This study seeks to address the research question: "How can machine learning-based smart waste management systems and predictive analytics enhance the operational efficiency, sustainability, and policy framework of circular bioeconomy models in diverse industrial and regional contexts?" This chapter aims to rectify the identified scientific and practical shortcomings by a comprehensive examination of machine learning-enabled predictive maintenance, automated waste classification, and product life cycle optimization systems. It provides a unified paradigm demonstrating how data intelligence may promote circularity, reduce biowaste, and improve decision-making for future researchers, businesses, and policymakers. This chapter delineates a definitive pathway for sustainable technological transformations, ensuring that the circular bioeconomy evolves into an essential environmental paradigm and a viable economic and governance framework for the 21st century.

Figure 1. The Ellen MacArthur "butterfly" circular-economy model Smart waste management (Fritsche & Iriarte, 2021)

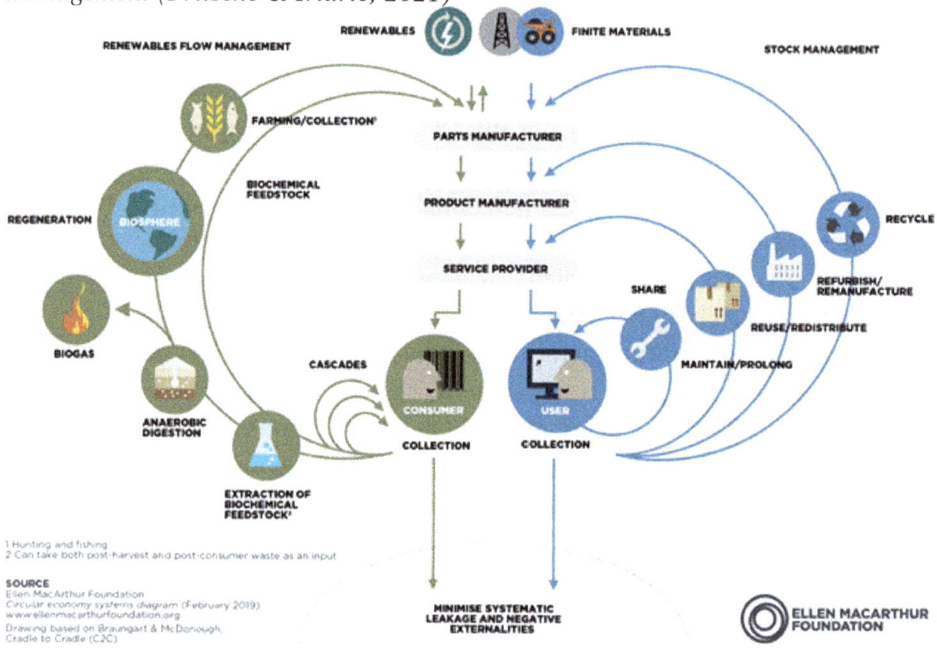

Supply chain optimization: This means designing supply chains that *slow, narrow, and close* material loops by using renewable biological feedstocks and recycling residues back into production (Fritsche & Iriarte, 2021). Tan and Lamers note that a "sustainable bioeconomy will require a sustainable supply chain, including sustainable biomass feedstock production and logistics" (Fritsche & Iriarte, 2021). Thus, supply chain optimization in this context involves coordinating forward (production and distribution) and reverse (collection and reuse) flows so that biomass and bioproducts circulate continuously between industry and the biosphere.

Figure 2. Circular bioeconomy components

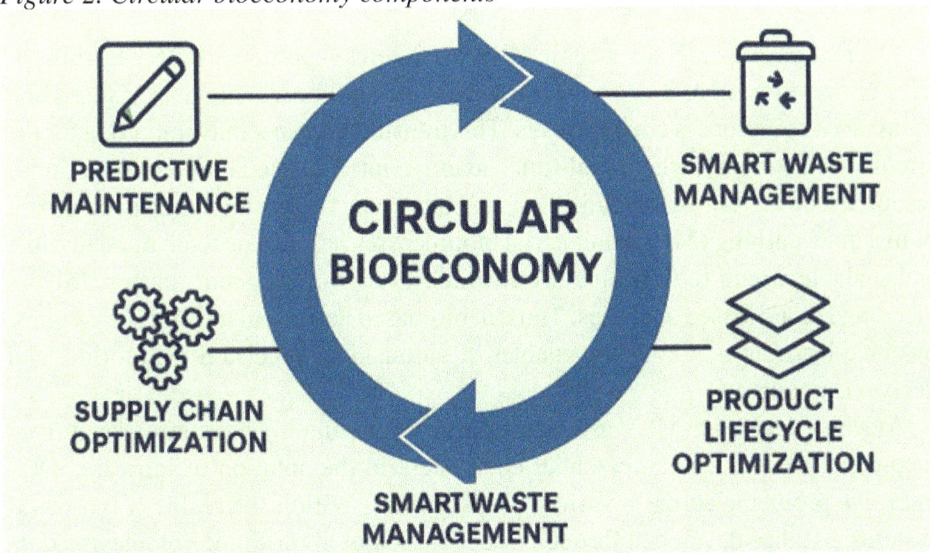

1.2 The Role of Digital Technologies in Sustainability

In the run to achieve Sustainable Development, scientists have enabled the use of different technologies in the field. Technologies such as the Internet of Things (IoT), cloud computing, big data analytics, blockchain, and artificial intelligence (AI)—including machine learning—are redefining how industries monitor, manage, and optimize their processes. In the framework of sustainability, these digital tools facilitate circular resource flows, encourage responsible production and consumption, and lessen environmental footprints. Our projects are more innovative, transparent, and resource-efficient thanks to these technologies.

These digital technologies help close the gap between our projects' and industries' operational viability and environmental goals. Also, these assist in compliance with environmental regulations, and contribute to circular economy strategies by identifying waste-to-value conversion opportunities. As bioeconomy sectors grow more complex, the integration of digital tools becomes indispensable in achieving sustainability targets, especially under the evolving paradigms of climate resilience and decarbonization. This integration and the importance of integration is explained in the next section.

1.3 Importance of Machine Learning in Modern Bioeconomy

Over the past decade, advances in ML architectures—particularly deep learning—have allowed for more nuanced interpretation of nonlinear biological systems and multivariate bioprocess environments. This transition is especially important for the circular bioeconomy, where real-time, adaptive intelligence is needed to optimise resource recovery, biomass utilisation, and bioproduct generation. The deployment of machine learning (ML) in industrial bioprocesses has also become more feasible and scalable due to the growing affordability of high-throughput sensors, IoT devices, and cloud-based analytics. Thus, in bio-based and circular economy systems, machine learning is now a key enabler of automation, precision monitoring, and decision support.

Machine learning (ML), as a subset of artificial intelligence, has grown from theoretical curiosity to an essential component in the solution of intricate, data-intensive problems across a variety of disciplines. Within the realm of bio-based systems, ML has developed through a coevolution of algorithmic complexity, data availability, and computing power. Early uses of ML in biology and biotechnology were primarily concerned with predictive modeling problems, such as prediction of protein structure and genome annotation. With the emergence of systems biology and -omics technologies, ML has become more useful in the integration of disparate data sets, the identification of hidden patterns, and the facilitation of real-time decision-making.

Figure 3. Evolution of machine learning in bio-based systems

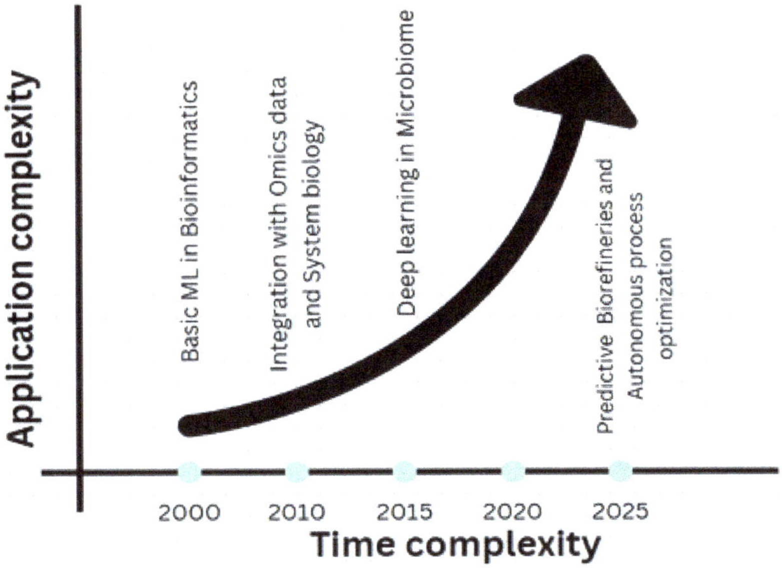

2. FOUNDATIONS OF CIRCULAR BIOECONOMY

The circular bioeconomy is basically a smarter, greener way of doing things compared to the old-school "take, make, toss" method. So, instead of gobbling up resources and spitting out mountains of waste, the focus here is on looping stuff back into the system—think recycling, but on steroids, and with biology in the mix. Bottom line: you take the leftovers (like plant scraps or food waste), give them a second life (bio-based plastics or clean energy), and try really hard not to trash the planet while you're at it. Behind the scenes, there's a lot of geeky science—like omics and bioinformatics—helping fine-tune all these bio-based processes, tweaking genes and data to squeeze out as much value as possible. Basically, it's the ultimate "waste not, want not" upgrade, just with more lab coats and less landfill drama. These foundations provide the conceptual and technological basis for implementing circularity across diverse bio-industrial sectors.

2.1 Principles: Regeneration, Resource Efficiency, Closed-loop Systems

Circular Bioeconomy ought to minimize the depletion of resources (for example, phosphate rock, fossil fuels or soils), encourage regenerative practices (for example, restoring fish stocks), prevent the loss of natural resources (for example, carbon, nutrients and water) and stimulate the reuse and recycling of inevitable by-products, losses or wastes in a way that adds the highest possible value to the system. (Befort N, 2020)

The European Commission (EC) defines the bioeconomy as "encompassing the production of renewable biological resources and the conservation of these resources and waste streams into value added products, such as food, feed, biobased products and bioenergy" (European Commission, COM 2012, p. 9)

2.1.1 Regeneration

Regeneration is all about patching up what we've trashed, but it goes further—it's about making things actually better than before. Not like the old school "take-what-you-can-get" method where nature gets steamrolled. Nope. This is about boosting soil life, letting plants and critters do their thing, and jamming more carbon back in the ground where it belongs. In the world of bioeconomy, this means you're not just mindlessly churning out crops—you're weaving farms and forests into a bigger, healthier system. We're talking growing stuff smarter, using waste in clever ways (think turning yesterday's muck into tomorrow's miracle product), and bringing new life to land that's been beat up. Regenerative farming isn't just a source of raw materials; honestly, it's like giving Mother Nature a spa day and some real respect for a change.

2.1.2 Resource Efficiency

Resource efficiency is an important component of the sustainability model, where inputs such as water, nutrients, and energy are being used to maximum effect to provide highest output with minimal environmental costs. In circular bioeconomy, this is being enabled by technologies such as precision fermentation, enzymatic catalysis, and process intensification, which find expression in terms of higher yield per unit biomass. Additionally, integration of side-stream valorization—conversion of side-streams into secondary feedstocks or biochemicals—is critical to maximizing the utilizable fraction of bio-resources.

2.1.3 Closed-loop Systems

Closed-loop systems? They're kinda like that friend who never wastes anything—seriously, they find a use for every last scrap. Instead of the usual "use it once and dump it" approach (which, let's be honest, is basically how most industries roll), closed-loop setups keep things spinning around. Leftovers—solid, liquid, whatever—don't get tossed; they get re-used, reimagined, or straight-up transformed. Think about turning kitchen scraps into biogas to heat your shower, or ripping apart wood waste and coaxing it into useful sugars and chemicals. Pulling this off isn't just guesswork, either—it takes a wild mix of skills: you need your bioengineers, sustainability nerds with their endless spreadsheets (hello, LCA), and people who know how to make industries play nice together. It's a whole ecosystem of resourcefulness.

2.2 Bio-based Materials, Bioenergy, and Biorefineries

Bio-based products, bioenergy, and biorefineries are the technology pillars of the circular bioeconomy. They are designed to replace fossil-based energy and products with renewable, biological substitutes. Bio-based products provide sustainable industry solutions through being renewable and frequently biodegradable. Bioenergy uses organic waste and biomass to generate clean energy, minimizing carbon emissions and loop closure. Biorefineries combine these methods, converting mixed biomass into a cascade of high-value products—from fuels to chemicals—utilizing each component to the maximum extent. They all demonstrate how biological innovation can power sustainable, circular growth.

2.2.1 Bio-based Materials

Bio-based materials are the foundation of the circular bioeconomy, providing renewable alternatives to products based on fossil fuels. Composed of biomass elements such as starch, cellulose, lignin, chitin, and proteins, they are applied in packaging, building, textiles, and even in high-performance composites. Developments in synthetic biology and polymer science have enabled the development of biodegradable plastics, such as polylactic acid and polyhydroxyalkanoates, and functional bio-coatings, on the basis of decreased reliance on petrochemical resources and improved end-of-life circularity through composting or enzymatic depolymerization.

2.2.2 Bioenergy

Bioenergy is an evolving renewable energy industry, including bioethanol, biodiesel, biogas, and advanced biofuels. Bioenergy enables the transformation of organic matter into heat, electricity, and transport fuels using biological or thermochemical conversions. Though the first-generation biofuels are essential, they create food-versus-fuel problems; hence, attention is now centered on second- and third-generation biofuels produced from lignocellulosic residues and algae, respectively. Bioenergy contribution to circular systems allows for decentralized energy generation and nutrient capture, particularly when integrated with waste management strategies.

2.2.3 Biorefineries

Alright, let's break it down — biorefineries are basically the cool, eco-friendly cousins of oil refineries, except they're all about turning plants and random waste into useful stuff instead of, you know, fossil fuels. Picture a giant smoothie blender, except way, way fancier. They've got all these tricks up their sleeve: smashing things up, cooking 'em with chemicals, unleashing enzymes, or letting microbes go wild, all to carve up biomass into a pile of goodies. We're talking about everything from biofuels (hello, greener road trips) and eco-friendly chemicals to supplements and plant-based fertilizers. And get this: the smart ones set up their factories to squeeze out every last useful drop, so barely anything goes to waste. Those are the real MVPs. Lately, there's a hot trend — hybrid biorefineries. Basically, they mix up techniques, say, starting with intense heating (gasification), then shifting gears and letting microbes finish the job through fermentation. Why? So they can chew through all sorts of random stuff: trashed veggies, factory leftovers, even seaweed. Sounds futuristic, but it's already happening.

2.3 Bioinformatics and Omics in Circular Bioprocessing

The advent of bioinformatics and omics technologies, including transcriptomics, proteomics, metabolomics, and fluxomics, has revolutionized the design and optimization of circular bioprocesses in a very significant manner. These approaches allow for the comprehensive comprehension of biological systems at various scales, ranging from metabolic pathways to ecosystem processes, thereby directing the design of efficient and dynamic bioprocessing systems.

2.3.1 Genomics and Metabolic Engineering

The application of high-throughput sequencing and genome annotation can allow for the detection of both native and genetically engineered microbial strains to efficiently valorize waste material or produce desirable bio-based products. The integration of genome-scale metabolic models (GEMs) with flux balance analysis (FBA) improves the ability to predict metabolic fluxes and detect putative bottlenecks to facilitate the strategic planning of strains for improving yield and tolerance in biorefineries.

2.3.2 Metabolomics and Process Optimization

Metabolic profiling is a discipline that gives valuable information on the intracellular and extracellular metabolite dynamics and is extremely important for the identification of metabolic abnormalities and the optimization of fermentation parameters. When integrated with process analytical technologies (PAT), this data could be employed in machine learning models for predictive modeling and real-time control of bioprocesses, improving stability and minimizing downtime.

2.3.3 Bioinformatics Platforms and Data Integration

Circular bioeconomy networks produce wide and heterogeneous data sets, which require strong bioinformatics platforms for integration and visualization. KEGG, MetaCyc, and STRING tools facilitate the reconstruction of metabolic pathways, whereas multi-omics integrative platforms allow for cross-scale correlations. Systems-level analyses by these tools facilitate precision biomanufacturing, scalability of processes, and adaptive decision-making under dynamic feedstock conditions.

2.3.4 Synthetic Biology and Omics-informed Design

Synthetic biology, directed by omics information, allows the design of novel biosynthetic routes and microbial consortia for circular uses. For example, consortia of engineered cellulolytic and solventogenic microbes can convert lignocellulosic biomass to butanol or organic acids directly. Besides, omics-driven design improves resilience in stress situations usually found in waste valorization, like pH fluctuation, inhibitor exposure, or nutrient deprivation.

These are the techniques and tools that have their background in biology and bioinformatics. The integrative tools from AIML are discussed in the next section. Those give us an idea and overview about how AIML helps in a sustainable and developmental way for the environment.

3. OVERVIEW OF MACHINE LEARNING TECHNIQUES

Machine learning (ML) is a pivotal technology in modern bioeconomy applications, offering powerful tools to analyze complex, large-scale biological datasets. ML techniques can be broadly classified into three main categories: supervised learning, unsupervised learning, and reinforcement learning.

3.1 Supervised, Unsupervised, and Reinforcement Learning

Supervised learning methods, such as regression and classification models, are widely applied in bioeconomic problems in which there are labeled datasets, i.e., datasets with known labels, for instance, predicting the yield of bio-based products or distinguishing among different types of biomass based on spectral data. Such methods are well proven to be extremely useful where there are strong correlations between the input features (e.g., biomass structure and environmental conditions) and output variables (e.g., the amount or quality of bioproducts). (Sofian et al., 2024).

On the other hand, unsupervised learning comes in handy when learning patterns in the absence of defined outcomes in data sets. Clustering approaches such as k-means and hierarchical clustering enable the grouping of similar biological entities or the identification of unforeseen biological mechanisms. Principal component analysis (PCA) and other dimensionality reduction techniques are used for extracting the most important features in high-dimensional omics data sets, thus enabling easier analysis of biological systems and bioprocesses. Such techniques are crucial in dealing with heterogeneous, unstructured data such as those derived from microbial communities or environmental sampling. (Tsui et al., 2023)

Reinforcement learning (RL) is a sophisticated type of machine learning (ML) that is increasingly being applied to improving real-time decision-making in bioprocesses. At the bioeconomic scale, RL algorithms can be applied to adaptive control systems that entail optimizing bioreactor parameters (temperature, pH, and nutrient concentrations) for optimal product output. These systems learn to improve their performance on a continuous basis by integrating feedback from the environment within which they are operating, thereby being very well-suited to dynamic and changing bioeconomic contexts. (Matheri et al., 2024)

3.2 Feature Selection, Dimensionality Reduction, and Model Evaluation

The precision of machine learning algorithms is largely a measure of the quality and relevance of input features. Feature selection is the act of selecting the most informative variables from raw data sets, which is imperative in bioeconomy usage where omics and sensor data are high-dimensional and noisy. Techniques employed to reduce redundancy and enhance the model's generalizability include recursive feature elimination, mutual information ranking, and LASSO regressionMeanwhile, stuff like PCA, t-SNE, and autoencoders are lifesavers when you're drowning in data with way too many dimensions. They sort of squish all that wild, complex info into something way less overwhelming—makes your computer happier and your eyes stop glazing over when you try to visualize it. Super handy for things like sifting through metagenomics spaghetti or making sense of spectral fingerprints (which, let's be real, usually look like alien code). Model performance is often evaluated using metrics like precision-recall, F1-score, R2 score, mean squared error (MSE), and area under the ROC curve (AUC-ROC), depending on the type of prediction task. Cross-validation methods, such as bootstrapping and k-fold validation, are used to assess the generalisability of the model across various data subsets and avoid overfitting. Careful assessment and feature transparency are essential for practical implementation in bioeconomic systems where model interpretability is just as significant as accuracy.

3.3 Deep Learning and Hybrid Models in Bioprocesses

A subset of machine learning known as "deep learning" is distinguished by multilayered neural networks that can model intricate, nonlinear relationships in sizable datasets. In the circular bioeconomy, both structured and unstructured data, such as biomass images, time-series data from bioreactors, and genomic sequences, are analysed using deep learning models like convolutional neural networks (CNNs), recurrent neural networks (RNNs), and long short-term memory (LSTM) networks. While RNNs and LSTMs are well-suited for forecasting dynamic process parameters in fermentation or anaerobic digestion systems, CNNs are especially helpful for image-based biomass quality assessment or pathogen detection in bioresource systems. In order to capitalise on the advantages of both data-driven and knowledge-based paradigms, hybrid modelling approaches—which combine machine learning with mechanistic or kinetic models—are becoming more popular than standalone models. For instance, hybrid models are able to more accurately model complex biochemical transformations by combining neural networks with mass balance equations. Particularly in bioprocess optimization and simulation scenarios, these methods provide improved extrapolation capabilities and predictive power. Deep learning's incorporation into bioprocess engineering processes is opening the door to circular bioeconomic systems that are more intelligent, self-sufficient, and scalable. (Matthew et al., 2020–2021)

3.4 Transformative Models: Reimagining Intelligence for a Circular Bioeconomy

In the fields of artificial intelligence and machine learning, transformative models—also known as transformers—represent a significant advancement. Transformer architectures are made to comprehend intricate, contextual relationships across whole data sequences, in contrast to traditional models that depend on fixed input-output structures or localised feature extraction. Transformer models were initially created for language processing tasks like text generation and translation, but because of their exceptional capacity to handle large amounts of diverse data quickly, they have quickly emerged as the cornerstone of contemporary deep learning.

The self-attention mechanism, which is the foundation of a transformative model, enables the model to assess each element's relevance in relation to every other element in an input sequence. Because of their unique design, transformers are able to capture complex patterns and long-range dependencies in data, which are essential when working with biological systems, environmental factors, and circular supply chains. Transformers provide parallel processing, increased scalability, and enhanced performance on large-scale, unstructured datasets compared to previous models such as recurrent neural networks (RNNs) or convolutional neural networks (CNNs).

Because transformative models can represent complexity across several levels of biological, industrial, and environmental systems, they are relevant to the circular bioeconomy. An integrated understanding of resource flows, microbial dynamics, metabolic processes, and the life cycle stages of bio-based products is necessary for the circular bioeconomy. From supply chain logistics and land-use data to genomic sequences and process engineering parameters, each of these domains produces high-dimensional and frequently noisy data. This variety of data can be ingested by transformative models, which can then reveal significant patterns that would otherwise go undetected.

A transformer model trained on multi-omics datasets, for example, might be able to pinpoint metabolic bottlenecks or recommend enzyme candidates to improve biomass conversion in bioprocess optimization. Transformers can recommend reuse pathways for forestry or agricultural residues in industrial symbiosis by analysing sensor data, textual reports, and material flow datasets. Furthermore, these models can help with the mining of scientific publications, legislation documents, and sustainability reports in order to synthesise insights and support evidence-based decisions in the design of policies and the planning of circular systems.

Figure 4. Transformer architecture (Vasvani et al., 2017)

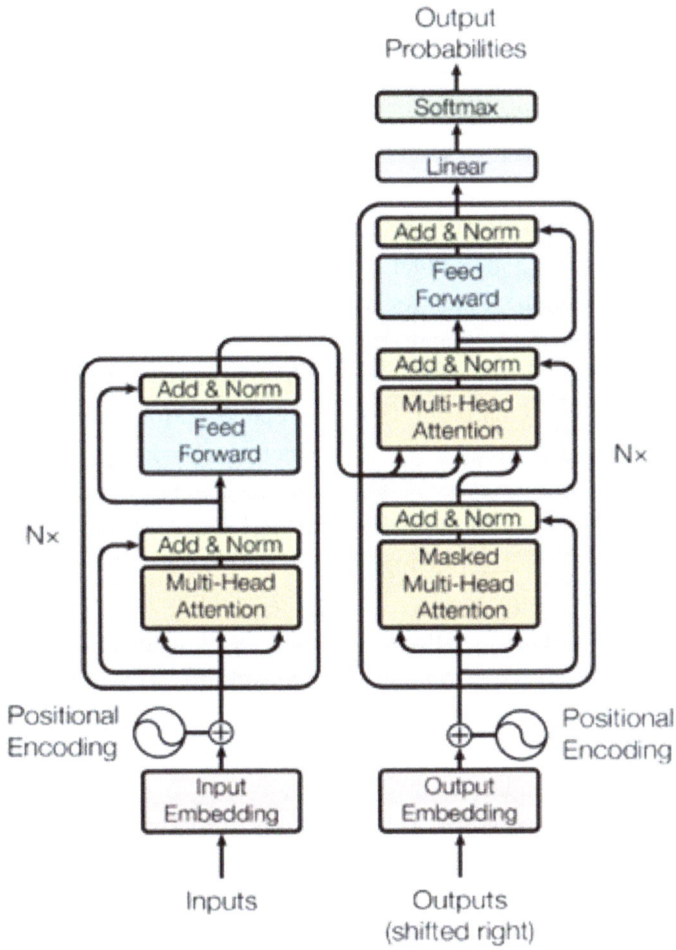

Another transformative feature is their transfer learning capability, which allows models trained on one type of data or task to be adapted for others with minimal retraining. This is especially useful in the circular bioeconomy, where data heterogeneity is high and standardized datasets are limited. A single transformer model could, for example, be pre-trained on large public environmental data and fine-tuned to predict circular potential in region-specific biomass streams or identify emerging biotechnological trends. (Amatrian et al., 2023)

3.5 Graph Neural Networks: Understanding Complex Systems for a Regenerative Future

A class of deep learning models called Graph Neural Networks (GNNs) was created especially to handle and learn from graph-structured data. Since graphs are fundamentally mathematical structures made up of nodes, or entities, and edges, or relationships, they are well suited to modelling interconnected systems, including supply chains, metabolic networks, molecular structures, and ecosystems. Because GNNs can learn from both individual elements and the structural context that connects them, they are uniquely positioned to interpret such relational data.

The complex dependencies and spatial relationships found in biological and environmental systems are frequently missed by traditional machine learning techniques, which usually rely on fixed, flat data representations. GNNs, on the other hand, use message-passing mechanisms in which every node gathers data from its neighbours and modifies its state in response to this local context. GNNs gradually construct enriched representations that encode both local and global patterns in the data by using several message-passing layers.

The circular bioeconomy is significantly impacted by this contextual learning ability. Modelling the flow of materials, energy, and information across networks is becoming more and more crucial as we work towards a systems-level redesign of biological and industrial processes. GNNs can be used to map circular resource flows in industrial or agricultural symbiosis systems, predict the biodegradability of molecules, or even simulate metabolic pathways.

For example, by treating atoms as nodes and bonds as edges, GNNs can predict molecular properties in the development of bio-based materials, which could lead to the discovery of new bioplastics or waste-degrading enzymes. Similar to this, knowledge graphs enhanced with GNNs can be used in waste valorisation to pinpoint underutilised biomass streams and propose potential bioconversion pathways that link them to downstream products or microbial consortia.

GNNs are developing to handle temporal and dynamic graphs in addition to static systems, which opens up possibilities for modelling how ecosystems change over time, how carbon cycles change, or how microbial communities within bioreactors vary. These time-aware models are particularly helpful for predicting the outcomes of interventions like changing a soil microbiome or introducing a new fermentation pathway.

Furthermore, GNNs' interpretability and transferability increase their usefulness in planning and policy. The insights produced are more transparent and actionable since their structure resembles systems that are easy for humans to understand, such as supply chains or metabolic networks. Researchers can visualise which nodes or subgraphs have an impact on decisions using tools like GNNExplainer, which promotes transparency and confidence in decision-making processes. (Corse et al., 2024)

4. ML TOOLS AND FRAMEWORKS USED IN BIOECONOMIC APPLICATIONS

A robust ecosystem of tools and frameworks designed for data collection, preprocessing, model development, and deployment makes it easier to apply machine learning in the circular bioeconomy. Libraries like scikit-learn, TensorFlow, PyTorch, and Keras are available on well-known open-source platforms like Python and R, facilitating the quick development and deployment of machine learning models. While TensorFlow and PyTorch support sophisticated deep learning architectures with GPU acceleration, Scikit-learn is especially helpful for traditional machine learning algorithms and preprocessing pipelines. (Matheri et. al., 2024).

Domain-specific tools such as Bioconductor (an R-based program) and Orange (a visual programming tool) are frequently used in bioinformatics and systems biology to integrate biological data with machine learning models. Tools like Plotly, Seaborn, and Matplotlib are essential for data visualisation and interpretation because they help identify patterns and trends in high-dimensional datasets. Additionally, AutoML frameworks like Google AutoML and H2O.ai are becoming more and more useful, particularly for biotechnology novice users who need automated model selection and hyperparameter tuning. Researchers and practitioners in the bioeconomy can now access advanced analytics thanks to the availability of cloud-based machine learning platforms (such as Google Colab and Azure ML Studio), which also facilitate scalable, collaborative model training. These tools serve as the technological foundation for ML-driven innovation in industrial ecology and sustainable bioprocesses (Mathew et al., 2021).

5. ML APPLICATIONS IN CIRCULAR BIOECONOMY

In the circular bioeconomy, where resource efficiency and sustainability are crucial to the development and optimisation of bio-based processes, machine learning is turning out to be a crucial tool. Classification and characterisation of biomass is one important application area. (Gado, 2020)

5.1 Biomass Classification and Characterization

In order to identify the best feedstocks for bioenergy or bioproducts, machine learning models are used to evaluate complicated datasets from various biomass types. More accurate and effective bioprocessing is made possible by the use of machine learning (ML) algorithms to process spectroscopic data, such as near-infrared (NIR) or Raman spectra, and classify biomass materials according to chemical composition, moisture content, and other factors. Spectral data is one example. (Leavy et. al., 2024).

5.2 Waste Stream Prediction and Optimization

ML techniques are essential for recognising and using waste as a resource in the field of waste stream prediction and optimisation. Machine learning algorithms can forecast waste generation patterns by combining data from multiple sources (such as sensors and supply chain data), which makes it possible to design closed-loop systems that convert waste into useful bio-based products. For example, ML models can forecast the potential conversion of agricultural or industrial waste into biofuels, bioplastics, or biofertilizers, reducing landfill dependence and advancing resource recovery strategies in the circular bioeconomy.

5.3 Intelligent Bioprocess Monitoring and Control

Intelligent bioprocess monitoring and control is another area where ML techniques provide significant value. Machine learning models can optimise conditions to maximise product yield and minimise resource consumption by analysing real-time data from fermentation systems and bioreactors. Algorithms can forecast equipment failures, identify process irregularities, and suggest changes to parameters like pH, temperature, and nutrient supply. In addition to increasing process efficiency, these systems lower operating expenses and waste production, which helps to further sustainability objectives.

5.4 Bio Product Yield Prediction and Process Optimization

ML models that use both historical and current process data help predict bioproduct yield and optimise processes. Biotechnologists can improve processes and boost product outputs by using predictive models to estimate the yield of bio-based products under different operating conditions. To increase yields while using fewer resources, researchers can optimise microbial strains, nutrient media, and fermentation times by using machine learning (ML) models that forecast the effectiveness of microbial fermentation processes.

5.5 Supply Chain Management and Lifecycle Assessment (LCA)

Machine learning is used in the field of supply chain management and lifecycle assessment (LCA) to model and optimise bio-based supply chains, guaranteeing effective resource use and waste minimisation. From sourcing to processing and distribution, ML algorithms can monitor the movement of raw materials through bio-based industries, evaluating the environmental effects at every turn. ML-powered life cycle assessments shed light on the sustainability of bioeconomic operations by pinpointing areas that require improvement in terms of material efficiency, energy consumption, and greenhouse gas emissions.

5.6 Predictive Maintenance in Biorefineries and Green Infrastructure

Finally, machine learning has shown great promise in the field of predictive maintenance in biorefineries and green infrastructure. Machine learning models can forecast probable failures, suggest maintenance plans, and avoid unscheduled downtime by evaluating sensor data from infrastructure and machinery. This keeps biorefineries running continuously, reducing interruptions to the production of bio-based products and promoting the circular bioeconomy's sustainability objectives. (Sharma et al., 2023).

6. ADVANTAGES OF ML IN CIRCULAR BIOECONOMY

The circular bioeconomy's objectives are directly aligned with machine learning's benefits, which include increased productivity, decreased resource waste, and the ability to implement closed-loop systems. ML models make it possible to accurately forecast biomass availability, product demand, and equipment failures by revealing hidden patterns in large, complex, and frequently non-linear datasets, such as those produced by agricultural sensors, supply chains, and waste management streams. Across all bio-based industrial processes, this predictive capability minimises overproduction, promotes more effective resource allocation, and cuts downtime. Additionally, by continuously learning from system feedback and adjusting to changing conditions, machine learning algorithms enable real-time logistics, process control, and material recovery optimisation. Higher rates of material recovery and upcycling are made possible by ML's assistance in the highly precise classification and sorting of bio-waste in waste valorisation.Strategically, ML connects operational intelligence with long-term sustainability goals by providing stakeholders with data-driven insights for life cycle assessment, circular design, and policy planning. All of these benefits put machine learning in a key position to support resilient, scalable, and regenerative systems in the circular bioeconomy.

Table 1. Comparison between traditional and ML-enabled approaches

Aspect	Traditional Circular Bioeconomy	ML-Enabled Circular Bioeconomy
Decision-making approach	Rule-based, expert-driven	Data-driven, adaptive, and autonomous
Resource forecasting	Manual estimation of statistical models	Predictive analytics using time-series ML (e.g., LSTM, ARIMA-RNN hybrids)
Process optimization	Static optimization or linear programming	Real-time optimization via reinforcement learning, neural networks, and genetic algorithms
Waste classification and sorting	Manual or basic automation	Computer vision and deep learning for smart waste segregation and material identification
Supply chain visibility	Fragmented, spreadsheet-based	Integrated with IoT sensors and ML for dynamic routing, traceability, and anomaly detection
Maintenance of bioprocesses	Scheduled or reactive maintenance	Predictive maintenance using supervised learning (e.g., SVMs, random forests)
Life Cycle assessment	Post-process evaluation using static data	Dynamic life cycle impact prediction using multivariate ML models
Scalability	Limited due to complexity and lack of automation	Highly scalable due to automation, real-time insights, and adaptive learning capabilities
Feedback integration	Slow or manual incorporation of user and environmental feedback	Continuous learning and adaptive feedback loops via online learning algorithms
Innovation support	Dependent on expert intuition and long development cycles	Accelerated through pattern recognition, generative design, and model-informed experimentation

7. CHALLENGES AND LIMITATIONS

While machine learning (ML) has demonstrated significant potential in advancing the circular bioeconomy, its integration into real-world biological systems presents numerous challenges. These challenges span technical, operational, skills, ethical, and societal domains. Addressing them systematically is crucial for realizing the full potential of ML-driven sustainable solutions.

Table 2. Potential solutions for challenges

Challenges	Description	Potential Solutions
Data Availability and Standardization	Limited, noisy, and non-standardized biological datasets	Open-access repositories, data augmentation, standard protocols
Model Interpretability and Trust	Black-box nature of complex models hinders acceptance	Explainable AI methods (SHAP, LIME), interpretable models
Integration with Bioprocess Pipelines	Legacy systems not designed for real-time ML applications	IoT upgrades, cloud-edge computing, interdisciplinary training
Ethical, Legal, and Social Issues (ELSI)	Data privacy, fairness, and societal impacts of ML	Ethical guidelines, participatory design, policy frameworks

7.1 Data Availability, Quality, and Standardization

One of the foremost challenges in applying machine learning to circular bioeconomy processes is the scarcity and heterogeneity of high-quality datasets. Biological systems are inherently complex, and data derived from them, such as biomass properties, bioconversion efficiencies, and environmental variables are often noisy, incomplete, or inconsistently measured. Small datasets are particularly problematic in bio-based industries, where experimental replication is costly and time-consuming.

Furthermore, the interoperability of datasets across various labs, industries, and geographical areas is hampered by the lack of standardisation in measurement units, metadata annotations, and data collection protocols. This makes it harder to train ML models that are generalisable and puts up obstacles to collaborative, large-scale analytics. Furthermore, confidentiality agreements frequently prevent access to sensitive industrial data, such as supply chain logistics or proprietary bioprocess parameters, which restricts open innovation.

Initiatives supporting data sharing frameworks, standardised protocols, and open-access repositories designed for the bioeconomy are desperately needed to get past these obstacles. The constraints imposed by small or unbalanced datasets can also be lessened with the use of transfer learning, data augmentation methods, and synthetic data generation.

7.2 Interpretability and Trust in ML Models

The interpretability of models is another significant barrier to using ML in the circular bioeconomy. Many high-performing algorithms, particularly deep learning models, function as “black boxes”; they make accurate predictions but don't reveal much about the decision-making process. It is not only desirable but also essential to comprehend the logic behind predictions in bio-based applications where safety, regulatory compliance, and environmental impact are of utmost importance.

Trust between stakeholders, such as environmental scientists, bioprocess engineers, regulators, and policymakers, is hampered by interpretability issues. It becomes challenging to reproduce experiments, validate results, and meet certification requirements in the absence of transparent models.

To close this gap, new approaches like interpretable model architectures (e.g., decision trees, generalised additive models), feature attribution techniques (e.g., SHAP, LIME), and explainable artificial intelligence (XAI) are being investigated more and more. In real-world situations, it is still difficult to strike a balance between model complexity, performance, and transparency.

7.3 Integration with Existing Bioprocess Pipelines

There are significant organisational and technical challenges in integrating machine learning models into current bioprocessing infrastructures. Real-time data collection, feedback loops, and machine learning-based optimization were not considered in the design of conventional bioprocess systems. Significant expenditures in sensors, automation hardware, and data management platforms are necessary for retrofitting such systems.

There is also a skills gap: employees in traditional bio-based industries frequently lack knowledge of how to deploy ML models or data science, which can result in resistance or less-than-ideal implementation. Multidisciplinary teams that can bridge the knowledge of biology, engineering, and computation are necessary for seamless integration.

The real-time operationalisation of machine learning models presents another technical challenge, as performance may be impacted by latency, data security, and computational limitations. Real-time, scalable, and reliable machine learning applications in industrial bioprocesses are becoming possible with the help of edge computing and hybrid architectures (cloud-edge solutions). Organisations must make investments in training, organisational change management, and cross-sector cooperation in addition to technology to guarantee successful integration.

7.4 Ethical, Legal, and Social Considerations (ELSI)

There are a number of social, legal, and ethical issues that need to be carefully considered when implementing machine learning technologies in the bioeconomy. Data privacy concerns are crucial, particularly when genetic, agricultural, or supply chain data are involved. Protecting the rights of individuals and communities requires that data use adhere to laws like the General Data Protection Regulation (GDPR).

From an ethical perspective, decision-making automation in bioeconomy sectors may result in unforeseen outcomes like labour displacement, algorithmic bias, or resource monopolisation. For instance, if not applied fairly, ML-driven predictive pricing in biomass markets may put smallholder farmers at a disadvantage.

Perceptions of benefit-sharing, transparency, and trustworthiness all have an impact on how socially ML technologies are accepted. Therefore, to promote responsible innovation, inclusive governance frameworks, participatory design procedures, and stakeholder engagement are required.

Environmental justice concerns also need to be taken into account: Inequalities or environmental burdens on vulnerable communities must not be reinforced by ML models. Planning and carrying out ML projects should routinely include ethical frameworks and impact analyses specific to the bioeconomy.

Figure 5. Challenges of machine learning in circular bioeconomy

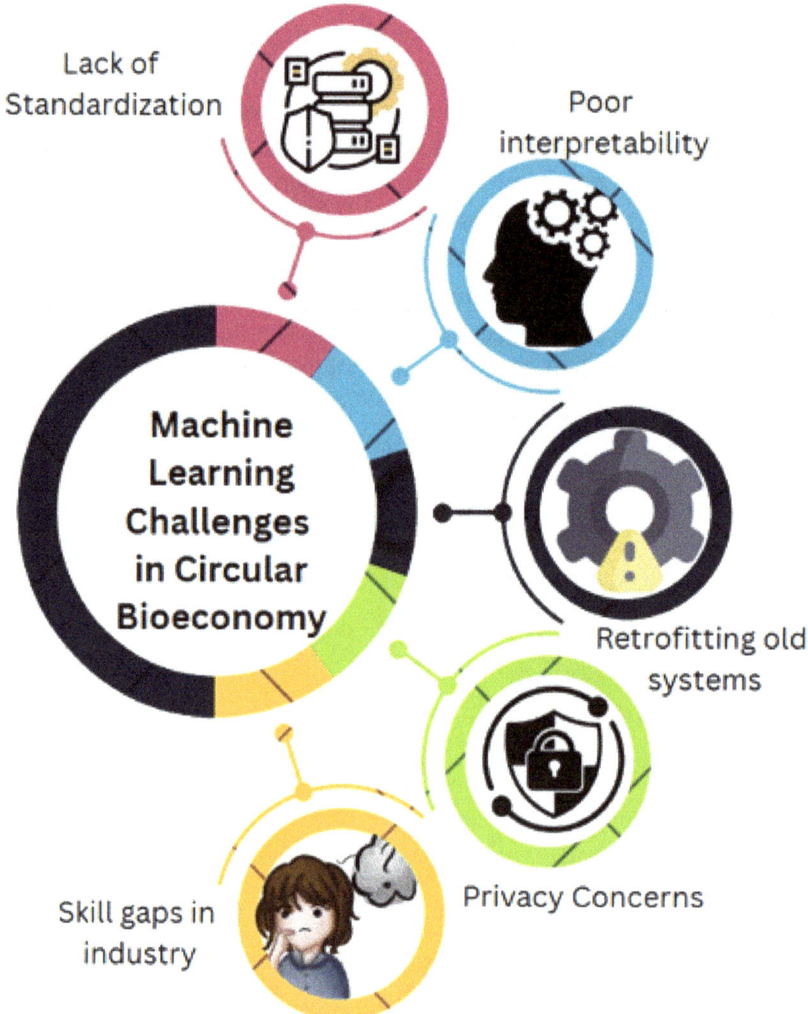

8. CASE STUDIES AND SUCCESS STORIES

This section offers a number of real-world case studies that demonstrate the efficient application of machine learning in frameworks related to the circular bioeconomy. The successful integration of predictive analytics, smart sensing, supply chain optimisation, and closed-loop systems is demonstrated by these examples, which cover a variety of industries such as bioplastics, bioenergy, food waste valorisation, and agriculture. Every case sheds light on the technology strategy, implementation tactics, and quantifiable results in terms of efficiency, sustainability, and circularity. When taken as a whole, these studies confirm the revolutionary potential of machine learning in actual industrial ecosystems while also pointing out obstacles and chances for further expansion.

Case Study 1: Integration of CE principles in Manufacturing companies which improved environmental performances and resource efficiencies.

A case study was presented by Lindgreen, Dewulf, and Valverde (2019) to examine how circular economy (CE) concepts can be effectively embedded within the operational framework of a real-world manufacturing firm. This study is a well-established illustration of how circular principles—such as lowering reliance on virgin raw materials, minimising waste generation, and increasing process efficiency—can be converted into actionable steps backed by measurable data, as industries throughout Europe start to match their strategies with sustainability goals. The heavy manufacturing company in question implemented a number of process changes to enhance resource efficiency and overall environmental performance, offering a useful benchmark for sectors transitioning to circular models.

The study used a mixed-approaches strategy that combined qualitative stakeholder engagement through semi-structured interviews with quantitative tools like Material Flow Analysis (MFA) and Life Cycle Assessment (LCA). MFA was utilized to systematically track the flow of materials within the production system, identifying input quantities, process losses, reuse loops, and waste outputs. The MFA framework followed the mass balance principle:

This allowed the authors to quantify the improvements in material handling and efficiency resulting from circular interventions. In addition, the LCA offered a comprehensive assessment of the production system's environmental effects. The study estimated midpoint environmental indicators, specifically Global Warming Potential (GWP) and Cumulative Energy Demand (CED), using SimaPro software integrated with the ReCiPe 2016 impact assessment method in accordance with ISO 14040/44 standards. With an emphasis on upstream resource extraction all the way to the factory gate, where the finished product is produced, the system boundaries were established from cradle to gate.

A number of adjustments to organisational procedures and physical processes were part of the circular interventions that were put into place. First, the dependence on virgin raw materials was decreased by institutionalising the reuse of internal production scrap and non-conforming material. Second, by trading by-products with nearby plants to use as raw material substitutes, the company practiced industrial symbiosis. This promoted local industrial cooperation in addition to lowering the amount of waste dumped in landfills. Additionally, by recirculating process water through filtration and reuse, the plant implemented closed-loop water systems, which reduce freshwater intake. Last but not least, waste heat was collected and repurposed by installing energy recovery systems, which subsequently reintegrated it into thermal processes.

These interventions had a significant impact that was assessed over a two-year period. Because of internal reuse and more effective sourcing, the company reported a 25% reduction in the use of virgin materials. Increased recycling and by-product exchange helped to support a 30% decrease in waste disposal, especially landfill contributions. Additionally, both thermal energy recovery and energy efficiency initiatives contributed to a 15% decrease in overall energy consumption. According to LCA results, these material improvements resulted in noticeable environmental benefits. Both the cumulative energy demand and the global warming potential (CO_2-equivalent emissions per unit of product) decreased by 17% and 22%, respectively, suggesting a much lighter environmental burden on each manufactured product.

In addition to focussing on technology and process metrics, the study also examined organisational dynamics and found that management support and internal culture were critical to the success of these circular measures. The authors discovered through interviews that maintaining circular practices required leadership participation, employee training, and the use of digital monitoring tools. Internal feedback loops, like regular sustainability performance reviews and participatory decision-making processes, played a crucial role in ensuring that the interventions were not only accepted but also improved upon over time.

Despite concentrating on a traditional manufacturing company, the case has important implications for the circular bioeconomy. The tactics employed, especially waste valorisation, process optimisation, and material reuse, are equally applicable to bio-based industries where environmental concerns and resource limitations are crucial. The study shows that businesses can make well-informed, fact-based decisions that balance environmental objectives with financial performance by combining organisational change with analytical tools like MFA and LCA.

This case illustrates how industries can shift from linear, extractive systems to regenerative ones in the larger framework of the circular bioeconomy. It supports the notion that circularity is more than just a theoretical framework; rather, it is a collection of practical tactics that, with the correct resources and assistance, can produce quantifiable gains in operational and environmental results.

Case Study 2: Leveraging Web Mining and NLP to Map Germany's Bioeconomy Landscape

Designing place-based strategies for sustainable development requires an understanding of the locations and methods of operation of bioeconomy businesses. However, it is still very difficult to track these companies using traditional industrial classifications. Because the bioeconomy encompasses both high-tech fields like biotechnology and bio-pharmaceuticals as well as more established ones like agriculture and forestry, traditional datasets frequently fall short in capturing its multifaceted and cross-sectoral character.

Researchers Lukas Kriesch and Sebastian Losacker (2024) created a unique, data-driven methodology to map bioeconomy firms throughout Germany in response to these constraints. Their method analysed firm-level website content by combining web mining with sophisticated natural language processing (NLP). They extracted and processed text from the websites of more than 678,000 businesses using the CommonCrawl dataset. They classified 142,949 businesses as belonging to the bioeconomy after identifying businesses engaged in bio-based economic activities through semantic search using a Sentence-BERT model that had already been trained. 13,554 of these were identified as high-tech companies with a strong presence in industries driven by innovation, such as biotechnology.

Different spatial patterns were identified by the geographic analysis. Rural areas were home to the majority of businesses operating in traditional bioeconomy sectors, such as those associated with forestry, agriculture, or biomass processing. This spatial alignment was particularly noticeable in areas where firm localisation is heavily influenced by the availability of natural resources, such as Cloppenburg and Südliche Weinstraße.

On the other hand, bioeconomy businesses that were involved in high-tech, sophisticated operations were more prevalent in cities.Cities like Heidelberg, Jena, and Munich became well-known centres thanks to their robust institutional networks, talent pools, and research infrastructure. These trends are reminiscent of traditional agglomeration effects and show how bio-based industries are becoming more complex and innovative.

Additionally, the study used topic modelling to investigate focus areas at the firm level and connected these findings with regional land-use data. According to this analysis, bioeconomy activities frequently co-locate with pertinent resource bases; for example, there are more wood-related businesses in areas with significant forest cover.

This example shows how digital techniques can improve our comprehension of the spatial dynamics of the bioeconomy. The study offers a reproducible framework for identifying bio-based economic activity at a fine, firm-level scale by utilising publicly accessible web data and going beyond traditional statistics. It also emphasises the need of customised policy approaches that reflect the variety of the bioeconomy, which has dual character based on traditional, resource-dependent sectors and emergent, knowledge-intensive industries.

Publically available and a great tool for academics and legislators trying to assist regional transitions towards more sustainable and circular economic systems is the dataset produced by this study.

(Lukas and Losacker, 2024)

Case Study 3: Modeling Algae–Bacteria Consortia for Wastewater Treatment Using Machine Learning Approaches (Del et. al., 2019)

In the journey toward a circular bioeconomy, integrating environmental sustainability with industrial biotechnology requires sophisticated modeling of biological systems—especially those capable of waste valorization.One outstanding example is the 2019 Del Rio-Chanona et al. study on optimising an algae–bacteria consortium-based wastewater treatment system with cutting-edge machine learning methods. Using limited and sometimes lacking datasets—a typical difficulty in real-world bioeconomic systems—the goal was to replicate dynamic biological behaviour under different environmental conditions.

Known for their complimentary roles in removing nitrogen, phosphorous, and carbon from synthetic wastewater, the researchers chose a mutualistic system comprising Chlorella vulgaris (a green microalga) and Bacillus subtilis (a bacterium). Under both high and low nutrient environments, these species were grown both individually and simultaneously. Bioreactors simulating industrial treatment environments comprised the experimental setup, and the resulting data included nutrient depletion over time and biomass growth.

Two approaches were used to model this intricate biosystem: data-driven models utilising artificial neural networks (ANNs) and Gaussian process (GP) regression, as well as traditional kinetic modelling (based on mechanistic equations such as Monod and Luedeking–Piret). When simulating simpler bacterial systems, kinetic models did fairly well; however, because of the high complexity and nonlinear interactions between light, nutrients, and microbial growth, they had trouble with algal and consortium dynamics. Furthermore, when applied outside of the particular experimental conditions for which they were calibrated, their predictive accuracy dramatically decreased.

In contrast, machine learning models—particularly GPs—demonstrated strong adaptability and predictive performance, even when trained on sparse datasets. GPs, in particular, provided not just accurate forecasts but also uncertainty quantification, which is crucial for process control in sensitive biosystems. The study highlighted that GP models required far fewer training data than ANNs (3 artificial datasets versus 50–100), making them ideal for data-limited bioprocesses, which are common in circular bioeconomy settings.

The case also delved into modeling interactions between algae and bacteria, revealing insights into mutualistic dynamics that enhanced nitrate removal. Interestingly, although neither ANN nor GP could learn previously unseen biological mechanisms (since the consortium data was excluded from training), GP-based simulations closely mirrored experimental results. This alignment implies that when machine learning models are robustly trained on well-designed single-strain datasets, they can approximate emergent behaviours even in the absence of explicit training on complex consortia.

In addition to proving that machine learning techniques are sometimes better than conventional physical models, this study also showed how applicable they are to the goals of the circular bioeconomy. More broadly, it demonstrated how data-driven modelling can help with the design of low-impact, effective bioprocesses that convert waste into resources, bringing us one step closer to a regenerative industrial paradigm.

Case Study 4: In Biorefineries and Bio-based Plants

In order to increase equipment reliability and decrease downtime, a number of biofuel and pulp production facilities in the USA, Brazil, and Europe have deployed advanced predictive maintenance (PdM) systems that use wireless IoT sensors and cloud-based analytics. ABB AbilityTM Smart Sensors, battery-operated MCM-100 devices, were installed on bearing housings at a Commonwealth Agri-Energy ethanol refinery in Kentucky, USA, to continuously monitor temperature and vibration. Through a Bluetooth gateway, these sensors send data to the ABB cloud, where predictive analytics detect bearing wear and notify operators prior to equipment failures. A significant producer of corn ethanol and biodiesel in Mato Grosso, Brazil, implemented LoRaWAN gateways and Dynamox HF vibration sensors, installing roughly 95 sensors throughout 50 vital assets at its Lucas do Rio Verde facility. With the help of machine learning analysis of the data on Dynamox's SaaS platform, the business is able to prevent numerous faults and reap quantifiable benefits, such as cost savings of about $78,000, avoided downtime of 12 hours, and a 48-hour faster maintenance response. Leading European producers of wood and pulp, including Valmet and ABB, have implemented comparable PdM technologies in their mills. They use cloud analytics in conjunction with vibration and acoustic sensors to keep an eye on parts like dryers and pumps. Double-digit decreases in unplanned outages have resulted from these implementations, though precise numbers are still confidential. These digital PdM systems are a prime example of the expanding use of smart sensing and analytics to maximise process efficiency and industrial dependability in all regions.

Case Study 5: In Bioenergy (Waste-to-Energy & Biogas)

Predictive maintenance (PdM) systems that use smart sensors and AI analytics are greatly increasing operational reliability and efficiency in a variety of industries, such as waste-to-energy, biogas, and food/bioprocessing. ABB Smart Sensors were installed on powertrain motors, bearings, and pumps at a sizable waste-to-energy (WtE) facility in Germany located at Industriepark Höchst, close to Frankfurt. These sensors gather information about temperature, vibration, motor speed, and power consumption, which is then sent to the ABB AbilityTM cloud platform via a gateway or mobile devices. On-demand maintenance scheduling is made possible by machine learning models that are integrated with the plant's SAP system to forecast equipment condition and failure risk. By replacing fossil fuels in downstream processes, this change has increased the amount of renewable steam and electricity produced to the industrial park, reduced unplanned outages, and prolonged asset lifespans. Similarly, operators of commercial biogas plants are using AI platforms like bioGASMAS, a software as a service tool that analyses methane flow, feed composition, and other production data, to find inefficiencies and forecast less-than-ideal fermentation conditions. This optimisation boosts methane yields, extends full-load operating hours by roughly 5%, and lowers emergency repair expenses by an estimated €50,000 per year. The system also includes a predictive maintenance module that monitors plant hardware health and sends mobile alerts to operators. In the food and bioprocessing sector, PdM adoption is growing as well; for instance, a major sugar processing mill in Asia deployed Nanoprecise IoT sensors and machine learning to monitor mixers and mills, achieving over eight hours of downtime savings through early fault detection. These applications typically rely on multi-sensor packages (including vibration and current monitoring) integrated with cloud-based analytics to ensure equipment reliability in complex bio-based manufacturing environments.

9. FUTURE DIRECTIONS FOR ML IN CIRCULAR BIOECONOMY

The developments in computing power, data accessibility, and the urgent need for sustainable development around the world, the nexus between machine learning and the circular bioeconomy is set to grow quickly. The digital foundation of intelligent bio-based industries will soon be formed by integrated AI ecosystems that combine ML, IoT, blockchain, and edge computing. In industries like waste valorisation, bio-manufacturing, bio-plastics, and agriculture, these systems will facilitate autonomous decision-making, real-time optimisation, and predictive life cycle modelling.

The creation of ethical and explainable machine learning models that adhere to circular principles will be the next big thing, guaranteeing stakeholder trust, transparency, and alignment with sustainability objectives. Additionally, collaborative model training across decentralised bioeconomy actors will be possible thanks to federated learning and privacy-preserving AI techniques, all without sacrificing data security. This will improve the generalisability and robustness of the models.

Digital twins of biorefineries and bioresource systems represent another new avenue in which machine learning (ML) will accurately model, forecast, and optimise operations, lowering experimental costs and facilitating quicker innovation cycles. These systems could help create new biomaterials and circular product systems that are both functional and regenerative by design when combined with generative machine learning models.

Socioeconomically speaking, machine learning will also be essential for policy modelling, carbon accounting, and incentive optimisation, directing circular transitions on a regional, national, and international level. Interoperable data platforms will enable multi-stakeholder collaboration as sustainability and data governance standards advance, enabling circularity to be traced, audited, and verified.

In conclusion, machine learning is a key component of the circular bioeconomy's future, which is not only biological and regenerative but also intelligent, automated, and resilient.

9.1 Digital Twins and ML-Augmented Circular Systems

Digital twins (DTs) – dynamic virtual replicas of physical assets – are poised to become cornerstones of next-generation circular bioeconomic systems. By continuously ingesting data on material flows and system performance, DTs enable closed-loop optimization across complex facilities such as biorefineries, agricultural supply chains or waste-treatment networks. Coupling DTs with machine learning greatly amplifies their power: recent studies note that integrating ML models into DT frameworks yields much more accurate predictions and optimization. For example, Tahmasebinia *et al.* (2023) report that a solar-farm DT achieves superior energy- and cost-savings when enhanced with predictive ML algorithms. Similarly, case studies of manufacturing systems have shown that DT-driven decision tools allow technicians to virtually inspect equipment in real time – "eliminating the necessity for physical access" and enabling condition-based maintenance. Other work has demonstrated "intelligent redesign" of used products via DT simulations: computer models iterate through design options to maximize reuse and remanufacturing outcomes. In the circular bioeconomy, one can imagine vast DT networks – from farms to factories to recycling centers – that share learning across a lifecycle. These ML-augmented DTs would continuously adapt process parameters (e.g. bioprocess yields or material sorting rules) in response to real-time sensor data, closing loops with minimal waste. Of course, this vision requires robust data infrastructure: as noted in the Catena-X automotive project, DT ecosystems need common standards and data models to avoid "data scattering" and to allow trusted end-to-end tracking. Developing such interoperable, secure platforms will be a key research and policy task to make DT-based circular systems practical.

9.2 Federated Learning and Decentralized Data Architectures

Circular bioeconomy applications will increasingly rely on distributed data sources – from family farms and bioreactors to consumer IoT – making federated learning (FL) and decentralized architectures highly relevant. In federated learning, each node (e.g. a farm, factory or municipality) trains an ML model locally and only shares model updates, so raw data never leaves its source. This is a powerful approach when data privacy, ownership or bandwidth are concerns. For instance, FL has been shown to be "essential for improving agricultural management and smart agriculture" by enabling analytics without compromising confidentiality. Recent reviews emphasize that FL "emerges as a promising solution" for collaborative modeling in agriculture precisely because it allows training across decentralized data sources "without sharing raw data". In practice, a network of biorefineries or recycling centers could use a federated scheme to jointly improve predictive models (for sorting efficiency or feedstock yields) while keeping proprietary data in-house. Edge-computing and lightweight aggregation protocols will be important here: local devices can pre-train models on-site (e.g. on a farm edge server) and only transmit compressed updates to a central server, reducing communication load. However, decentralized learning also poses challenges: agricultural and process data tend to be heterogeneous and unbalanced, and rural sites may have limited connectivity. Overcoming these hurdles may require new algorithmic techniques (e.g. hierarchical FL, differential privacy, or blockchain-based orchestration) tailored to the bioeconomy's characteristics. If successful, federated frameworks will allow multi-stakeholder circular networks (farmers, food processors, recyclers, regulators) to share intelligence – improving overall resource efficiency – without sacrificing data sovereignty.

9.3 Integration with Synthetic Biology and Genomic Engineering

Synthetic biology and genomic engineering are emerging frontiers that will deeply intertwine with ML to shape a circular bioeconomy. Engineered organisms can become "cellular machines" that convert waste streams into valuable bio-products, and ML is the key to designing them. In this bio-digital partnership, biotechnologists can exploit DNA synthesis and high-throughput experimentation to generate large labeled datasets, while ML/DL algorithms sift through these data to identify optimal genetic designs. As one review observes, synthetic biology can produce "large data sets for training models… and ML/DL models can be employed to inform design (for example, by generating new parts…)". In other words, automated biofoundries and learning algorithms form a closed loop: ML guides the Design–Build–Test–Learn (DBTL) cycle and reduces costly trial-and-error. This synergy has already begun to bear fruit: ML-driven tools now suggest synthetic gene circuits for tasks like pollutant degradation or biofuel production, accelerating what was once purely artisanal design. Indeed, ML has "come to light as a promising option to speed up the progress in synthetic biology design" by discovering hidden patterns in complex biological data. The practical implications are vast: one can envision tailor-made microbes engineered to produce biodegradable plastics or to bioremediate agricultural runoff, with ML continually refining their performance. Analysts note that synthetic biology could "reinforce the shift towards greener, less wasteful circular economies," as engineered microbes churn out bio-based chemicals and biodegradable materials to replace fossil-derived counterparts. Of course, integrating genomic engineering into industry raises important biosafety and ethical questions. Research must therefore pair these technological advances with robust safety-by-design practices and governance frameworks. But as genomic editing (e.g. CRISPR) becomes more precise and AI models more predictive, the combination promises to expand the circular economy's toolkit – from CO_2-fixing algae farms to plants engineered for nutrient-efficient recycling – fundamentally reshaping how biological resources are reused.

9.4 Policy Implications and Interdisciplinary Collaboration

Recent research has placed higher importance on using sustainable logistics and supply chain approaches to improve organizational and social performance, particularly in developing economies. For example, Kant and Ashuro (2025) examined the impact of eco-logistics practices on organizational performance in Ethiopia, noting there is a significant mediation impact of micro and small enterprise (MSE) competitiveness to enhance the sustainability-performance relationship. In addition,

Kant, Niguse, Terefe, and Adula (2025) explored trends and innovation regarding social sustainability in manufacturing supply chains, and the evolving consumer behavior trends in the Horn of Africa that have changed sustainable production and consumption. Moreover, Kant, Adula, and Alemu (2025) examined the effects of green supply chain management (GSCM) practices on firm performance, and the empirical role of green innovation as a mediating factor relating environmental responsibility to firm performance. Overall, these studies emphasize the growing importance of eco-innovation, consumer-driven sustainability, and green logistics strategies to achieve performance outcomes, improved efficiency, and social benefits for the environment in developing economies. All of these technical advances will only succeed within supportive policy and collaborative contexts. Governments and institutions must adapt: setting standards for data sharing, crafting incentives for circular design (such as extended producer responsibility or bio-preferred procurement), and funding infrastructure for smart bioindustrial networks. Encouragingly, recent frameworks suggest that AI can even aid policy makers themselves. For example, AI-driven simulations can analyze economic, environmental and social data "to predict the outcomes of policy changes" and identify the most effective regulatory approaches in the circular bioeconomy. In practice, a policymaker could use such tools to compare scenarios (e.g. tax shifts or material regulations) before implementation. At the same time, caution is warranted: several commentators warn that without conscious guidance, AI could inadvertently reinforce linear-economic biases. As one industry analysis notes, many "AI-driven optimisation tools are designed for traditional linear economies that prioritize cost reduction… rather than circularity" – meaning they may favor short-term throughput and virgin materials over recycling unless restrained for circular goals. This underscores the need for policy guardrails (e.g. algorithmic audits, circularity metrics in AI training) and for educating developers about sustainability objectives. Crucially, this is not a challenge for technologists alone: realizing an AI-powered circular bioeconomy will require interdisciplinary effort. Initiatives like the UK's NICER programme and various international consortia exemplify how bringing together computer scientists, biologists, engineers, economists and social scientists can break silos and accelerate innovation. As one recent review aptly concludes, only through "collaboration between environmental science, biotechnology, data science, and social sciences" can the full potential of AI for the circular bioeconomy be unlocked. In summary, the road ahead blends cutting-edge ML and biological engineering with forward-thinking policy and broad collaboration – a holistic endeavor toward a truly regenerative, AI-enabled bioeconomy.

REFERENCES

ABB. (2021, October 7). *Waste-to-energy plant reduces reactive maintenance and improves energy output using smart sensors*. https://new.abb.com/news/detail/63887/waste-to-energy-plant-reduces-reactive-maintenance-and-improves-energy-output-using-smart-sensors

Befort, N. (2020). Going beyond definitions to understand tensions within the bioeconomy: The contribution of socio technical regimes to contested fields. *Technological Forecasting and Social Change*, *153*, 119923. DOI: 10.1016/j.techfore.2020.119923

Bioenergy News. (2023, July 17). *Ground-breaking biogas plant software can save producers €50,000 each year*. https://www.bioenergy-news.com/news/ground-breaking-biogas-plant-software-can-save-producers-e50000-each-year/

Del Rio-Chanona, E. A., Cong, X., Bradford, E., Zhang, D., & Jing, K. (2019). Review of advanced physical and data-driven models for dynamic bioprocess simulation: Case study of algae–bacteria consortium wastewater treatment. *Biotechnology and Bioengineering*, *116*(2), 342–353. DOI: 10.1002/bit.26881

European Commission. (2012). *Innovating for sustainable growth: A bioeconomy for Europe* (No. SWD(2012) 11 final). Brussels: European Commission.

Fritsche, U. R., & Iriarte, L. (2021). Sustainability criteria and indicators for the bio-based economy in Europe: State of play and way forward. *Frontiers in Sustainability*, *2*, 701509. Advance online publication. DOI: 10.3389/frsus.2021.701509

. Gado, J. E. (2020). *Machine learning and bioinformatic insights into key enzymes for a bio-based circular economy*. [Unpublished manuscript].

Kant, S., Adula, M., & Alemu, G. M. (2025). Effect of Green Supply Chain Management Practice on Firm Performance With Mediation of Green Innovation in Ethiopia. In *Eco-Logistics and Sustainable Supply Chain Innovations* (pp. 61–84). IGI Global.

Kant, S., & Ashuro, T. (2025). Effect of Eco-Logistics Practices on Organizational Performance With Mediating Role of MSE Competitiveness in Ethiopia. In *Eco-Logistics and Sustainable Supply Chain Innovations* (pp. 39–60). IGI Global.

. Kant, S., Niguse, T., Terefe, A., & Adula, M. (2025). *Emerging Trends and Innovations: Effect on Social Sustainability in Manufacturing Supply Chains by Shifts in Consumer Behavior in the Horn of Africa. Enhancing Social Sustainability in Manufacturing Supply Chains*, 135–162. IGI Global.

Kriesch, L., & Losacker, S. (2024). Bioeconomy firms and where to find them. *REGION*, *11*(1), 55–78. DOI: 10.18335/region.v11i1.523

Leavy, S., Allegretti, G., Presotto, E., Montoya, M. A., & Talamini, E. (2024). Measuring the bioeconomy economically: Exploring the connections between concepts, methods, data, indicators and their limitations. *Sustainability (Basel)*, *16*(20), 8727. DOI: 10.3390/su16208727

Matheri, A. N., Sithole, Z. B., & Mohamed, B. (2024). Data-driven circular economy of biowaste to bioenergy with conventional prediction modelling and machine learning. *Circular Economy and Sustainability*, *4*(2), 929–950. DOI: 10.1007/s43615-023-00329-3

Mathew, A., Amudha, P., & Sivakumari, S. (2021). Deep learning techniques: An overview. In *Advanced Machine Learning Technologies and Applications: Proceedings of AMLTA 2020* (pp. 599–608). Springer. https://doi.org/DOI: 10.1007/978-3-030-67280-2_49

Sharma, V., Tsai, M. L., Chen, C. W., Sun, P. P., Nargotra, P., & Dong, C. D. (2023). Advances in machine learning technology for sustainable biofuel production systems in lignocellulosic biorefineries. *The Science of the Total Environment*, *886*, 163972. DOI: 10.1016/j.scitotenv.2023.163972

Sofian, B. A., Aiman, A. D., Sun, X., Gupta, V. K., Berenjian, A., Xia, A., Ma, Z., & Show, P. L. (2024). Advances, synergy, and perspectives of machine learning and biobased polymers for energy, fuels, and biochemicals for a sustainable future. *Energy & Fuels*, *38*(3), 1593–1617. DOI: 10.1021/acs.energyfuels.3c03842

Tan, E. C. D., & Lamers, P. (2021). *Circular Bioeconomy Concepts- a perspective* (Vol. 2). Sec. Circular Economy.

Tsui, T. H., van Loosdrecht, M. C., Dai, Y., & Tong, Y. W. (2023). Machine learning and circular bioeconomy: Building new resource efficiency from diverse waste streams. *Bioresource Technology*, *369*, 128445. DOI: 10.1016/j.biortech.2022.128445

Ubando, A. T., Felix, C. B., & Chen, W.-H. (2020). Biorefineries in circular bioeconomy: A comprehensive review. *Bioresource Technology*, *299*, 122585. DOI: 10.1016/j.biortech.2019.122585

Chapter 9
Future of Energy Innovation With AI and Industry 6.0:
Green Hydrogen, the Next Frontier in Clean Energy Innovation, Technology, and Green Taxes

Bhupinder Singh
https://orcid.org/0009-0006-4779-2553
Sharda University, India

Saurabh Chandra
https://orcid.org/0000-0003-4172-9968
Bennett University, Greater Noida, India

Kittisak Wongmahesak
https://orcid.org/0009-0000-2129-4691
North Bangkok University, Thailand

Arunima Shastri
https://orcid.org/0000-0002-6260-1253
Christ University, Bangalore, India

ABSTRACT

Green hydrogen produced via renewable powered electrolysis, is seen as a key solution on the clean energy technology landscape as the world transitions to sustainable energy systems powered by wind, solar, and similar technologies. Being

DOI: 10.4018/979-8-3373-9923-2.ch009

the cleanest form of hydrogen, it has enormous potential to decarbonize hard-to-abate sectors such as heavy industry, aviation, and shipping. Green hydrogen production, storage, and distribution are undergoing advancements accelerated by the convergence of artificial intelligence (AI) and Industry 6.0 technologies. Such smart grids powered by Industry 6.0 support seamless integration of hydrogen into existing energy infrastructures, while AI-driven predictive analytics optimize energy consumption during electrolysis, boost efficiency, and reduce operational costs. The possibilities for a more sustainable energy landscape through the merging of innovative technologies including AI, Industry 6.0 and hydrogen offer us a cleaner, smarter, and more resilient future.

1. INTRODUCTION

Green hydrogen is not just an energy source; it is also a key to sustainable industrial transformation and achieving global carbon neutrality goals (Hasan et al., 2024) (Jin et al., 2024). With the ambition of stimulating the adoption of green hydrogen and innovation on the energy front, as well as attracting investment to the private sector, countries around the world are also resorting to green taxes and green incentives (Martini et al., 2024) (Satheesh & Shukla, 2024). Such fiscal measures will not only work as incentives for industries to cut carbon emissions but will also create an economic ecosystem that favours sustainable energy transitions. AI-based monitoring systems also enhance transparency and environmental compliance for effective taxation and regulatory enforcement (Vacchi et al., 2024). The scalability and cost-competitiveness of green hydrogen remains a key challenge but ongoing research, development, and policy support are driving technological breakthroughs and economies of scale. An international green hydrogen economy must be forged through alliance between governments, industries and research centers (Sarkar et al., 2024).

The combustion of fossil fuels releases greenhouse gases (GHGs) into the atmosphere, and climate change is among the most urgent global issues of our time. The climate crisis is evidenced by the dichotomy of higher natural disasters like fires, floods, or hurricanes turning their backs on the planet and warming global temperatures and landscape destruction, alerting us to explore the urgency of hoping for new forms of energy that can provide any economic sustainability without emitting $CO2$ and with minimum interaction with the ecosystem. The energy transition is a key toolkit in the fighting against climate change because it changes how we produce, store, and use energy. This can be achieved by improving the efficiency, scalability, and integration of renewable energy systems into existing infrastructure, as technologies like solar, wind, and hydro have already shown that it is feasible to reduce the reliance on fossil fuels, but we need new, better systems to make it the norm (Ghobakhloo et al., 2024).

1.1 Importance of Energy Innovation in Addressing Climate Change

Renewable energy sources can also lead to an increase in energy innovation by creating smart grids and decentralized energy systems that are more resilient and flexible in the face of challenges. In contrast to conventional energy grids which depend on centralized production and long-distance transmission smart grids use digital technologies, artificial intelligence (AI) and real-time data analytics to maximize energy efficiency. This shift allows bad demand-side management to reduce energy waste and peak load pressure, but it also enables the integration of various energy sources. For example, predictive maintenance powered by AI can greatly increase the longevity and efficacy of renewable energy systems, optimizing operational costs and performance energy output.

Innovation in energy goes beyond renewables generation to include energy storage and efficiency improvements. This innovation across battery technology, hydrogen fuel cells and carbon capture and storage (CCS) solutions are vital to achieve a seamless transition to a low-carbon economy. Phenomenon extends air conditioners at night until summer to turn on more garden solar, and bulk energy storage on the order of solid-state batteries and pumped hydro storage helps mitigate the variance of solar and wind power (Gamberini & Pluchino, 2024). By improving energy efficiency in various domains, energy efficiency technologies help lessen overall energy consumption and carbon emissions. The role of governments, corporations, and research institutions in catalyzing energy innovation cannot be understated. These may include carbon pricing mechanisms, subscriptions for clean energy technologies, and international partnerships for research and development that catalyze the spread of energy solutions that are sustainable. Since then, the Paris Agreement and the Sustainable Development Goals (SDGs) have further highlighted the role of energy transition as a key pathway to achieve limit of global warming to below 1.5°C. Thus, ongoing energy sector investment and innovation are essential to address climate change and to help design a sustainable and resilient global economy.

2. AI AND INDUSTRY 6.0 IN ENERGY INNOVATION

If Industry 4.0 brought smart factories and digital transformation, Industry 6.0 brings self-learning systems and autonomous decision-making along with the full-blown adoption of AI-driven analytics. In energy, it transitions us from centralized fossil fuel-based systems to decentralized, AI-powered renewable energy networks.A better-integrated, adaptive energy grid with cyber-physical systems (CPS), Internet of Things (IoT), and AI capabilities. Cyberphysical systems (CPS) are state-of-the-art data technologies that provide real-time synchronization between the physical energy grid and digital control systems for improved efficiency, security, and adaptability. AI-driven analytics systems process the enormous amounts of data collected from AIOT sensors in solar panels, wind farms, and hydrogen plants to help organizations optimize their energy distribution and consumption.

Smart grids play a crucial role in Industry 6.0 energy transformation supporting a decentralized and autonomous energy management system. When you build algorithms you can predict the patterns of energy demand or load and make optimised decisions based on that. This is a peer-to-peer (P2P) energy trading platform that enables producer-consumer to trade and share surplus renewable energy in a more efficient manner. The decentralized configuration increases energy resilience, lessening dependence on centralized coal/gas/petrol power plants while facilitating the transition to a greener and more sustainable energy ecosystem.

2.1 AI-Driven Innovations in Energy Sector: AI in Predictive Analytics for Energy Efficiency

Utilizing AI machine-generated predictive analytics, energy efficiency is being transformed through prediction of consumption, identification of inefficiencies, and making contingency plans and recommendations. AI models assess history and real-time data from industries, homes, and freaking grids so they can cut down on energy consumption and reduce both operational costs and carbon footprints (Martín-Gómez et al., 2024). Smart buildings, for instance, utilize AI algorithms to regulate heating, cooling, and lighting in a way that prevents the wastage of excess energy. Fluctuations in energy demand and supply present major challenges, especially in renewable energy sources, which are intermittent in nature, such as solar and wind. Some companies use machine learning (ML) models that use weather forecasts, the conditions of the grid, and historical data to predict supply-demand mismatches. This enables energy companies to tap excess energy during high-production periods and unleash it during peak-demand hours. Based on data until October 2023, your mileage may vary and what becomes the norm for the percent of energy delivered changing as technology advances and integration is upgraded.

Hydrogen is a potential source of clean energy, but in order to maximize efficiency and cost-effectiveness, its production and storage must be exacting. In hydrogen electrolysis, AI can optimize the goals by controlling other parameters like pressure and temperature, as well as electricity input, aiming to give maximum production of hydrogen, and minimize energy losses. In storage, AI algorithms evaluate safety risks, identify leaks, and optimize distribution routes, help make hydrogen a competitive substitute for fossil fuels. The energy landscape of Industry 6.0 has also been shaped by AI-driven innovations that improve the scalability and affordability of green hydrogen solutions (Doluweera, 2024).

2.2 The Digital Twin Concept in Energy Systems

Using AI and IoT to create a virtual digital twin of physical energy assets such as a hydrogen plant. Monitoring critical parameters such as atmospheric pressure, temperature, and flow rates help organizations detect inefficiencies, predict failure, and improve the decision-making process. The use of these AI-driven virtual models helps in scenario testing and risk assessment, enhancing the overall resilience of the energy system while minimizing downtimes. The core goal of predictive maintenance is to reduce unexpected failure rates, thereby minimizing downtime and maximizing energy infrastructure longevity. Combining this with data feeds, AI-integrated digital twins process historical and live sensor data to identify potential faults before they become large breakdowns.

This reduces repair expenses and improves operational efficiency and energy security. AI also aids in planning these prognostics since, in many cases, the preventive maintenance schedule should be prepared so that there is minimum disruption of power supply and overall grid stability (Rane et al., 2024). Digital twins offer great potential to optimize hydrogen storage and transportation through enhancing simulation capabilities in the range of conditions an H2 storage system encounters, validating safety measures, and qualifying storage degradation over time. This strengthens energy reliability and enables the integration of hydrogen into smart grids in the future.

Figure 1. Points on AI-driven innovations in energy sector

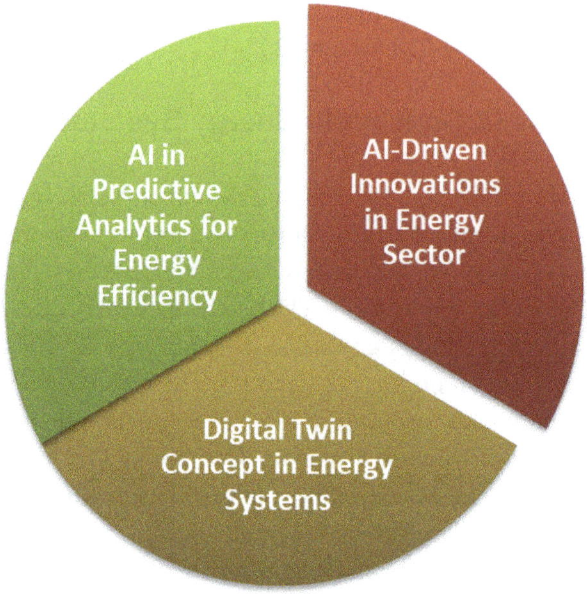

3. GREEN HYDROGEN: THE NEXT FRONTIER IN CLEAN ENERGY: TECHNOLOGICAL ADVANCES IN GREEN HYDROGEN PRODUCTION

Green hydrogen has become a key enabler to decarbonise advanced sectors like transportation, manufacturing and power generation as the world moves to a more sustainable energy future. Grey or blue hydrogen is produced from fossil fuels and emits CO_2, while green hydrogen is produced using renewable energy sources like solar, wind, or hydropower. Its viability is contingent on technological breakthroughs that improve efficiency, lower costs, and allow for production at the scale necessary to satisfy world energy needs. Accelerated in recent years by advances in electrolysis, AI-powered optimization and novel storage solutions, green hydrogen has become a linchpin of clean energy strategies across the globe.

The continuous improvements by millions of dollars are increasing every year in every domain we speak, which intangible technology like electrolysis or electrolysis technology might be one of the most important breakthroughs in green hydrogen production as it uses electricity to split water molecules into hydrogen and oxygen

(Sharma & Gupta, 2024). Conventional alkaline electrolyzers have been extensively utilized because of their low cost, but they suffer from issues in efficiency and flexibility. Proton Exchange Membrane (PEM) electrolyzers are far superior than this by providing higher current densities and quicker adjustments to fluctuating renewable power inputs. Solid oxide electrolyzer cells (SOECs) have emerged as a promising technology due to their ability to operate at high temperatures, allowing them to harness waste heat from other industrial processes to increase efficiency. These advancements in electrolysis improve the energy conversion process and facilitate seamless integration with renewable energy grids, providing a steady and scalable supply of green hydrogen.

Artificial intelligence (AI) and machine learning (ML) are storming the green hydrolysis production field by optimizing diverse aspects of the electrolysis process. Leveraging AI-driven models that analyze vast amounts of data from changes in energy input to operational and environmental parameters these systems enhance electrolysis performance on demand. This allows for predictive energy usage, reducing wasted energy and improving efficiency, as well as increasing the longevity of the electrolyzer components (Valeriya et al., 2024). AI is also essential in demand forecasting, which allows hydrogen producers to adjust production to match market demand and avoid wasting oversupply. Leveraging AI not only enhances cost-effectiveness but also strengthens the reliability of green hydrogen as an eco-friendly energy carrier. The major steps forward in green hydrogen technology have been the development of low-cost catalysts, leading to a decreased dependence on rare and expensive materials like platinum and iridium. Researchers have been looking at alternative catalyst materials, such as nickel, cobalt and iron-based compounds that can achieve similar efficiency at a fraction of the cost.

Catalytic performance has also been augmented by nanotechnology through larger surface area and faster reaction kinetics. Development of these next-gen catalysts is vital to improve the viability of electrolysis, which will boost the commercialization of green hydrogen. The storage and transportation of green hydrogen are one of the most dictating factors of its implementation, however, several developments in hydrogen storage technologies are working to resolve these concerns. Currently, hydrogen gas is compressed at really high pressure or liquefied at extremely low temperatures, both approaches needing a great deal of power input. New solid-state hydrogen storage technologies using metal hydrides and porous materials are emerging as promising methods by allowing safe and voluminous storage of hydrogen at lower pressures. Research on ammonia-based hydrogen carriers has accelerated as ammonia (NH_3) can store hydrogen in a stable form and most easily transport before converting back to hydrogen at point of use. These storage advances make hydrogen a more viable energy commodity worldwide.

3.1 Storage and Transportation of Green Hydrogen

There has also been a remarkable improvement in integrating green hydrogen with renewable energy systems and smart grids. Hydrogen can serve as an energy buffer, taking in excess electricity from wind and solar farms in times of high production and low demand, and sending it back to the grid when consumption peaks. The ability of gas to adapt significantly improves grid stability and helps mitigate the intermittency problems of renewables (Atiku et al., 2024). There are also hybrid systems that integrate hydrogen, battery storage, and pump hydroelectric energy solutions to improve the distribution and efficiency of energy. These advancements make green hydrogen one of the main enablers of a completely renewable energy system. It remain glued to high-temperature green hydrogen reactors, which are enabling decarbonization in industrial processes e.g. steel, ammonia, chemicals and are already commercial. These processes have traditionally been reliant upon fossil fuels, resulting in substantial carbon emissions. However, using hydrogen, a clean reducing agent, industries can be decarbonized at a high efficiency level and hence significantly lower their carbon footprint. To ensure the viability of industrial hydrogen applications, companies are increasingly dedicating their efforts to pilot projects and large-scale hydrogen hubs that can usher in a sustainable industrial revolution.

Government policies and partnerships with other countries are also fast-tracking green hydrogen innovation. Germany, Japan, and Australia, among other countries, have set ambitious hydrogen strategies, devoting significant investment to research, infrastructure, and commercialization (Ramírez-Márquez et al., 2024). The European Union's Hydrogen Strategy for a Climate-Neutral Europe and the U.S. Department of Energy's Hydrogen Shot Initiative, both seek to drive down the cost of green hydrogen production to less than $2 per kilogram over the next decade. These initiatives help drive innovation, trigger private-sector investments, and support the creation of a global hydrogen economy.

3.2 Hydrogen Economy and Industrial Applications

While green hydrogen technology is moving forward quickly, it still faces challenges, such as developing adequate infrastructure and regulatory frameworks, as well as achieving cost competitiveness. Scaling requires a huge build out of electrolyzer manufacturing, hydrogen refueling stations, and pipeline networks. Moreover, hydrogen vehicles and fuel cells are only viable in practice with continued improvements in efficiency and cost. Continued research, collaboration, and policy support will be crucial in addressing these challenges and enable green hydrogen to achieve its full potential as the next frontier in clean energy.

Green hydrogen is a key factor in the global clean energy transition empowered by tech innovations pushing its scalability, efficiency, and affordability. Sectors across the board are developing actualities that witness the early adoption of electrolysis, AI procedures, catalyst production and storage (Dacre et al., 2024). With ongoing investments in green hydrogen from governments, industries, and researchers, it will hopefully become a game changer for decarbonisation, energy sovereignty, and a greener future. Leveraging these technologies, the world can fully realize the potential of green hydrogen as an affordable, reliable, and clean energy source for generations to come.

4. GREEN HYDROGEN AND ENERGY MARKET TRANSFORMATION: ASSIMILATION OF GREEN HYDROGEN IN SMART ENERGY GRIDS

Green hydrogen in smart energy grids are reshaping the global energy landscape; global energy transition to a sustainable, resilient and the decentralized Energy Systems. Green hydrogen is set to become a critical enabler of carbon neutral energy solutions, with the ability to bridge the intermittence gaps of renewables like solar and wind as the world moves away from our fossil fuel addiction. Smart grids, enabled with artificial intelligence (AI), the Internet of Things (IoT), and advanced data analytics, offer perfect infrastructure for efficient optimization of green hydrogen generation, storage, and consumption. The integration of these diverse energy sources contributes to a transformative shift in energy systems towards more interconnected models that promote both grid resilience and flexibility, thus creating new economic opportunities and discourses in energy markets and policy worldwide (Ghobakhloo et al., 2024).

Integrating green hydrogen with smart energy grids comes with a major benefit the renewable nature of green hydrogen can act as an energy buffer, thus overcoming renewables' erratic nature. Because renewable energy only generates energy when it is sunny or windy, it can often produce more energy than is demanded, leading to curtailment and wasted energy. Efficient hydrogen production and storage can be achieved by tapping into excess electricity to run electrolyzers. This is referred to as Power-to-Hydrogen (P2H), and it allows for surplus renewable energy to be harnessed rather than wasted and, instead, converted into a storable and transportable fuel (Narkhede et al., 2024). When energy demand increases or renewable output drops, the hydrogen can be converted back into electricity using fuel cells or hydrogen turbines, providing balance to the grid. For a fully renewable energy grid, dynamic load balancing is vital so that the power generation can follow the unpredictable flow of weather.

Smart energy grids powered by AI and IoT are transforming the process of assimilating green hydrogen by facilitating real-time energy management. AI-driven predictive analytics can identify when and where hydrogen production should occur based on electricity prices, weather forecasts, and grid demand. This also helps ensure that hydrogen is being produced when electricity is at its cheapest and used when demand is highest by using machine learning algorithms to assess historical energy consumption behaviours and forecast peak demand times. Furthermore, IoT sensors offer real-time data regarding grid conditions, hydrogen storage levels, and system efficiency, allowing paired algorithms to make automatic decisions that reduce operational costs and enhance energy utilization through the process.

Apart from grid stability, the integration of green hydrogen into smart grids is giving rise to the establishment of hydrogen-based microgrids, especially in remote and off-grid areas. Conventional power infrastructure often fails to reach in isolated communities, islands, and disaster-prone regions, leading to energy insecurity (Mourtzis & Angelopoulos, 2024). Hydrogen microgrids running on locally produced green hydrogen, are one way to achieve energy independence and sustainability. These microgrids, which combine electrolyzers, hydrogen storage units, and fuel cells with smart control systems, enable communities to generate, store, and distribute electricity independently of external grids. Hydrogen microgrids, being decentralized, are better able to ensure an establishment can withstand power disruptions or power shortages, freeing it from being at the mercy of a larger centralized turbine or gas plant down the road, which is in line with building democracy through decentralization of the energy economy.

Green hydrogen is transforming the industrial and transportation sectors, generating new demand streams in the energy market. Industries like steel production, cement manufacturing, and chemical processing have long depended on fossil fuels, releasing enormous quantities of carbon dioxide (Lo et al., 2024). Integrating hydrogen in smart grids would provide these industries with a clean hydrogen alternative to natural gas or coal, which drastically reduces emissions. Smart grid-connected electrolyzers produce hydrogen for industrial applications at private- and public-sector megahubs, which governments and corporations are investing in. Such transition is accelerating the decarbonization of heavy industries, consistent with global climate objectives and sustainability commitments.

In the transportation space, hydrogen (H2)-fuel cell electric vehicles (FCEVs) have been increasingly marketed as a complement to battery electric vehicles (BEVs). Hydrogen refueling station deployment can benefit from smart grids, enabling a robust and sustainable hydrogen supply chain. AI can allow the decentralisation and real-time usage of all hydrogen as a fuel-cell vehicle, allowing for on demand hydrogen, even for longer trips where refueling will be needed along the way. This seamless integration with smart grids makes hydrogen a pillar for building a green mobility ecosystem and cleaner cities, helping to remove the need for oil-based fuels.

On the economic front, the integration of green hydrogen with smart grids is altering energy market dynamics, impacting pricing structures, investment patterns, and regulatory frameworks. Energy markets have historically been characterized by fossil fuel pricing volatility, geopolitical tensions, and centralized energy production (Kannan et al., 2024). Green hydrogen empowers a decentralized, localized energy model, insulating against more global supply chain shocks and price swings. The rise of hydrogen trading markets is providing new investment opportunities by opening up possibilities for countries to export and import green hydrogen depending on varying production surplus and demand. The evolving hydrogen certification processes, along with carbon credit frameworks, are providing additional incentives for green hydrogen adoption, prompting industries to shift to cleaner alternatives while leveraging carbon offsetting.

Also, government policies and international collaborations are critical to accelerating the integration of green hydrogen into smart grids. Germany, Japan, and the United States are among the countries that have established ambitious hydrogen strategies, with significant investment in hydrogen production infrastructure, research and development, and regulatory frameworks. The European Union's Hydrogen Backbone Initiative is proposing a cross-border hydrogen pipeline network to link production hubs with demand centers (Rane et al., 2024). The drive of hydrogen at a national scale is also evident in the public–private partnerships emerging around large-scale hydrogen projects. These policy measures are driving market transformation, stimulating innovation, and paving the way for green hydrogen's economic role in energy systems in the long run.

Even though green hydrogen and smart grid integration have huge potential, cost competitiveness, infrastructure development, and energy conversion efficiency present challenges. Electrolysis technology is improving but still needs to lower costs to be competitive with conventional fossil-fuel-based hydrogen production processes. Hydrogen refueling stations and pipeline networks must be established, a reverse of the current energy route, and fuel cell technology must be developed to be able to generate more energy. A magnificent market as green hydrogen has the potential to transform the energy market.

Smart grids are already incorporating AI, IoT, and advanced data analytics to address these challenges and could ultimately play a key role in ensuring the hydrogen economy can produce, store, and distribute hydrogen in a manner that complements renewable energy supply and creates new business prospects. At the same time, the rollout of hydrogen-based microgrids, the decarbonization of heavy industry, and the emergence of hydrogen-fueled transport all contribute to transforming the market landscape, making green hydrogen a critical pillar of the clean energy transition (Piron et al., 2024). Together, this collaboration will ensure that green hydrogen becomes a fundamental element of the energy mix, enabling global energy markets to thrive while also sustaining future generations.

5. GREEN TAXES AND REGULATORY FRAMEWORKS

Carbon taxes which charge emitters directly based on the quantity of carbon dioxide (CO_2) released into the atmosphere, are one of the first and most widely adopted green tax policies. They make fossil fuels more expensive to utilize, thereby providing industries with an incentive to fund renewable energy, energy-saving technology, and carbon capture. Other countries, such as Sweden and Canada, already have carbon tax systems in place, and researchers found that well-designed policies could be effective at cutting emissions while boosting economic growth.

The second type of policy, the cap-and-trade system, is a more explicit regulatory mechanism; it establishes an emissions limit across industries but lets companies purchase and trade carbon credits. This market driven mechanism has helped to achieve high-cost reduction in emissions, in its own, way by incentivising innovative low-carbon technologies. But green taxes and regulatory frameworks are also key in addressing environmental challenges. These policies aim to internalize the environmental costs of industrial activity and encourage enterprises and consumers to switch to greener alternatives (Ciucu-Durnoi et al., 2024). Green taxes impose a cost on carbon emissions, resource depletion, and environmental degradation, thereby encouraging investment in cleaner technologies and shifting consumption patterns towards more sustainable alternatives. At the same time, strong regulatory frameworks create legal templates for sectors to operate within and encourage decarbonization.

Green taxes go beyond carbon pricing to include taxes on plastic waste, water usage and air pollution. Several governments tax single-use plastic, which incentivizes businesses to transition to biodegradable or recyclable alternatives. In drier areas, taxes on water consumption additionally incentivize users to consume responsibly or invest in technologies that reduce demand on the system. Pollution taxes on industrial emissions e.g.: nitrogen oxides (NO_X) and sulfur dioxide (SO_2) are also important because the funds the government collects from such taxes will provide companies and firms incentives to produce cleaner materials, thus decreasing environmental and health risks related to air pollution.

Green taxes are often complemented by regulatory frameworks that set legally binding environmental metrics. However, governments around the world implement renewable energy mandates, emission reduction targets, and corporate sustainability reporting requirements to ensure businesses are held accountable with regards to their environmental impact. To give one example, Europe's Green Deal sets stringent targets to hit carbon neutrality by the year 2050 and tasks industry to move toward greener energy and sustainability (Ghobakhloo et al., 2024). Likewise, environmental impact assessments (EIAs) must be conducted in several jurisdictions to ensure new projects meet sustainability criteria.

Green taxes and regulatory frameworks will only work well in an environment of policy coherence, enforcement mechanisms, and global collaboration. Ineffective enforcement can result in tax evasion and regulatory loopholes that undermine environmental objectives. Some of those include uneven environmental regulations between nations that can lead to "carbon leakage" as companies move to places with less stringent rules. To counteract this, international cooperation in the form of the Paris Agreement and cross-border carbon pricing systems are key to establishing a level playing field for the sustainable expansion of the global economy. Green taxes and regulatory frameworks are an important piece of a larger strategy to combat climate change and environmental destruction. Combining financial incentives with rigorous legal metrics will effectively nudge policymakers to accelerate the transition to a more sustainable, resilient global economy (Katari et al., 2024).

5.1. Green Taxes: The Role in Transition to Energy

Green taxes are based on the concept of pay to play the more you use fossil fuels, the more you have to pay to use them, and the less you want to rely on them, the more you want to invest in cleaner alternatives. Such taxes serve as a deterrent by penalising activities detrimental to the environment and encouraging industries and the end consumers to pivot to clean energy alternatives. This would align economic and environmental goals by generating a market-based price for carbon emissions through green taxes embedded in national and international energy policies.

5.2 Fossil Fuel Taxation and Carbon Pricing

Carbon pricing and fossil fuel taxation are some of the most effective mechanisms for cutting greenhouse gas (GHG) emissions and driving the transition to renewable energy. Carbon taxes themselves apply a direct cost to using carbon dioxide (CO_2), effectively making fossil fuel-based production of energy less economically attractive, while incentivizing cleaner options, such as wind, solar, and hydrogen. Countries like Sweden, Canada, and Germany have successfully embraced carbon taxes, resulting in substantial emission reduction without sacrificing economic growth (Bhat & Parvez, 2024). The other primary sharing approach is the cap-and-trade system, where industries buy and sell allowances to emit carbon to a regulated market. This system sets a cap on overall emissions, which guarantees that emission reductions take place where it is cheapest to do so. Besides, fossil fuel subsidies that keep coal, oil, and gas prices very low are being eliminated in various countries, which will also promote the transition of energy. Raising fossil fuel taxes, together with spending on sustainable infrastructure, lowers the cost of renewables, speeding up the transition to a low-carbon economy.

5.3 Hydrogen Subsidies and Tax Credits

Governments around the world are introducing subsidies, tax credits and financial incentives to bring the price down, encouraging green hydrogen to become commercially viable (Zhen & Yao, 2024). Green hydrogen created from renewable energy using electrolysis is still energy and infrastructure-intensive, making it costly. But targeted tax exemptions and subsidies can close this gaping hole, rendering hydrogen a more attractive energy carrier. This includes the U.S. Inflation Reduction Act (IRA) of 2022, which established significant tax credits for clean hydrogen production with payments of up to $3 per kilogram of hydrogen to producers depending on carbon intensity.

The European Union's proposal for a Green Deal comes with funding mechanisms to help scale up hydrogen projects, and countries including Japan and South Korea have offered up direct financial incentives to increase the adoption of hydrogen fuel cells. These initiatives include the establishment of public-private partnerships (PPPs), which are crucial in enhancing the scale of hydrogen production and infrastructure, with governments co-investing in hydrogen refueling stations, electrolyzer manufacturing, and transportation networks (Bliznina, 2024). These subsidies and tax breaks are intended to help green hydrogen compete with fossil fuels, making its way into sectors such as transportation, industrial heating and power generation. Such policies pave the way to a hydrogen-powered future lowering production costs and driving demand in the market.

5.4 Domestic Policies for Green Hydrogen Development

To speed up their decarbonization path and heated ambitions of carbon neutrality, governments across the globe are embracing all-encompassing hydrogen strategies. They are based on a set of strategies around R&D, infrastructure development, regulatory incentives and international collaboration for making hydrogen one of the most important players in future energy systems (Bakator et al., 2024). European Union (EU) Hydrogen Strategy is at the forefront of global hydrogen growth, with a target of producing 10 million tonnes of renewable hydrogen by 2030 and constructing a hydrogen backbone linking Europe's supply and demand centers. The U.S. has taken bold action under the Bipartisan Infrastructure Law and Inflation Reduction

Act, committing more than $9.5 billion for clean hydrogen hubs and tax credits. The Hydrogen Shot Initiative from the U.S. Department of Energy (DOE) seeks goal of lowering hydrogen production costs to $1 per kilogram by 2031 to make hydrogen a viable commercial replacement for fossil fuels.

China, the world's top hydrogen producer, is directing significant investments toward green hydrogen pilot projects and has set a goal of establishing 50 hydrogen refueling stations by 2025. The government is also backing state-owned enterprises (SOEs) to ramp up hydrogen production from renewables. Japan, which has been a leader in utilizing hydrogen in fuel cells, has a highly ambitious Basic Hydrogen Strategy; the country aims to reach hydrogen demand of 3 million tonnes by the year 2030 and a long-term hydrogen economy (Santos et al., 2024). Japan's government is actively engaged in R&D support for hydrogen fuel cells, ammonia co-firing and large-scale hydrogen import.

6. INCENTIVES FOR HYDROGEN GENERATION AND UTILIZATION

To foist industry uptake, numerous countries are supplying low-interest loans, feed-in tariffs and duty breaks for hydrogen-powered transport and industrial processes. Other factors supporting the global hydrogen market expansion include the establishment of international hydrogen trade agreements between countries like Australia and Japan and Germany. Together these will help secure a position for hydrogen as a mainstream part of the global energy system. In addition to financial support, regulatory incentives are important drivers of hydrogen adoption (Ikram et al., 2024). Governments are developing compulsory hydrogen blending targets, emissions reduction mandates and certification schemes to facilitate the integration of green hydrogen into existing energy networks. The EU's Renewable Energy Directive (RED II) requires hydrogen quotas in transportation and industrial applications, and the U.S. Clean Hydrogen Standard provides clear rules on the production of green hydrogen.

AI is not a stranger to regulatory compliance and carbon accounting, rather it brings with it new ways to effect compliance by automating narrow and repetitive compliance functions, improving efficiency, accuracy, and transparency within regulatory disclosures including emissions disclosures. AI-fueled tools are used by corporations and agencies to track carbon emissions, monitor regulatory requirements, and enhance sustainability initiatives.

6.1 Artificial Intelligence for Carbon Footprint Tracking

Data analytics, machine learning, and blockchain in AI-powered platforms allow companies to compute their carbon footprints in real time. This systems interpret energy consumption patterns, monitor emissions throughout supply chains, and reveal opportunities for emissions reductions. Utilizing AI paired with IoT sensors and satellite monitoring would allow organizations to receive accurate and verifiable carbon accounting metrics that comply with global emissions standards. AI models can forecast CO_2 emissions linked to industrial processes, optimize the energy consumption of buildings, and improve the effectiveness of carbon offset initiatives (Barata & Kayser, 2024). AI is being used more and more to evaluate the performance of companies in terms of their environmental impact and whether or not they are meeting Environmental, Social, and Governance (ESG) standards, by organizations such as the Carbon Disclosure Project (CDP) and various corporate sustainability initiatives.

6.2 Regulatory Compliance Management and Automated Reporting

AI-based compliance systems can accelerate the regulatory side of reporting behind your organization by automating data collection, risk assessment, and even documentation processing. Leveraging the power of natural language processing (NLP), these systems analyze regulatory developments, ensuring that organizations remain up to date with changing environmental legislation (Rajumesh, 2024). This way AI can help to reduce penalties and legal disputes in compliance. With AI applications for sustainability, authorities and regulatory bodies can monitor emissions in real-time, enforce carbon pricing policies and can drive autonomy in green taxing implementations. AI also aids in climate risk modeling, where policymakers can create adaptive regulatory frameworks for a sustainable future (Rumayor et al., 2024). Leveraging AI in regulatory compliance and carbon accounting helps businesses and governments be more efficient, accurate and accountable in their sustainability efforts, all of which serve to accelerate the low-carbon, AI-enabled energy ecosystem.

7. CONCLUSION FUTURE SCOPE

As green hydrogen emerges as a key component of the clean energy transition, its future will depend on sustained technological innovation, international agreements, and Industry 6.0-driven creativity. AI, automation and smart energy ecosystems will be key to scaling production, optimizing energy efficiency, and delivering economic viability. Policy-makers need to ensure international cooperation, harmonised regulation and strong financial rewards are in place to create the incentive and leverage both AI and Industry 6.0 to stimulate innovation and integration to realise a hydrogen powered future. AI is the technology that will help to revolutionize green hydrogen production by optimizing electrolyzer design, enhancing efficiency, and increasing operational stability. Predictive maintenance powered by Artificial Intelligence cuts down on downtime, and machine learning models that optimize energy needs in hydrogen electrolysis further increases potential for H2 energy generation. Proactive hydrogen market intelligence powered by big data and beneath clouds data-based insights combining information from production, storage, distribution, and consumption will allow near real-time, demand-fold track forecasting of the hydrogen economy. AI also enables smart grid integration by balancing energy bursts for a smooth hydrogen transition.

Granular pricing would create a robust incentive for the first-movers in the green hydrogen market through a unified global policy framework. This will require governments to develop standardized guidelines for hydrogen production, storage, and trade of hydrogen products to achieve market consistency. This cross-border agreement, will complement coordinated investments from public and private sectors which will contribute to the development of the infrastructures needed for hydrogen trading internationally. Carbon credits, tax benefits and subsidies will drive industry adoption and reduce costs. The convergence of the latest automation, AI, and robotics technologies in Industry 6.0 will help kickstart green hydrogen ecosystems by establishing self-optimizing energy systems and smart "green hydrogen" refueling stations. The latest hydrogen fuel cells will allow next-generation efficiencies when paired with nanomaterial-based electrolyzers and therefore at a larger scale. By driving industrial development through combining AI, IoT and cyber-physical systems, Industry 6.0 will create a smart, robust and sustainable energy future with AI - providing the prospect of hydrogen-powered global economies.

REFERENCES

Atiku, S. O., Jeremiah, A., Semente, E., & Boateng, F. (Eds.). (2024). *Eco-Innovation and Sustainable Development in Industry 5.0*. IGI Global. DOI: 10.4018/979-8-3693-2219-2

Bakator, M., Ćoćkalo, D., Makitan, V., Stanisavljev, S., & Nikolić, M. (2024). The three pillars of tomorrow: How Marketing 5.0 builds on Industry 5.0 and impacts Society 5.0? *Heliyon*, *10*(17), e36543. DOI: 10.1016/j.heliyon.2024.e36543 PMID: 39281657

Barata, J., & Kayser, I. (2024). How will the digital twin shape the future of industry 5.0? *Technovation*, *134*, 103025. DOI: 10.1016/j.technovation.2024.103025

. Bhat, F. A., & Parvez, S. (2024). Emerging Challenges in the Sustainable Manufacturing System: From Industry 4.0 to Industry 5.0. *Journal of The Institution of Engineers (India): Series C*, 1-15.

Bliznina, N. (2024). *Redefining Economic Growth: the Review of Industry 4.0 and Industry 5.0 Progress*. Green and Low-Carbon Economy.

Ciucu-Durnoi, A. N., Delcea, C., Stănescu, A., Teodorescu, C. A., & Vargas, V. M. (2024). Beyond Industry 4.0: Tracing the Path to Industry 5.0 through Bibliometric Analysis. *Sustainability (Basel)*, *16*(12), 5251. DOI: 10.3390/su16125251

Dacre, N., Yan, J., Frei, R., Al-Mhdawi, M. K. S., & Dong, H. (2024). Advancing sustainable manufacturing: A systematic exploration of industry 5.0 supply chains for sustainability, human-centricity, and resilience. *Production Planning and Control*, •••, 1–30.

. Doluweera, L. K. (2024). Industry 5.0 Technologies for Supply Chain Management through Triple Bottom Line Approach in Companies of Sri Lanka for Economic Growth and Socio-Environmental Protection.

Gamberini, L., & Pluchino, P. (2024). Industry 5.0: A comprehensive insight into the future of work, social sustainability, sustainable development, and career. *Australian Journal of Career Development*, *33*(1), 5–14. DOI: 10.1177/10384162241231118

Ghobakhloo, M., Fathi, M., Iranmanesh, M., Vilkas, M., Grybauskas, A., & Amran, A. (2024). Generative artificial intelligence in manufacturing: Opportunities for actualizing Industry 5.0 sustainability goals. *Journal of Manufacturing Technology Management*, *35*(9), 94–121. DOI: 10.1108/JMTM-12-2023-0530

Ghobakhloo, M., Iranmanesh, M., Fathi, M., Rejeb, A., Foroughi, B., & Nikbin, D. (2024). Beyond Industry 4.0: A systematic review of Industry 5.0 technologies and implications for social, environmental and economic sustainability. *Asia-Pacific Journal of Business Administration.*

Ghobakhloo, M., Mahdiraji, H. A., Iranmanesh, M., & Jafari-Sadeghi, V. (2024). From Industry 4.0 digital manufacturing to Industry 5.0 digital society: A roadmap toward human-centric, sustainable, and resilient production. *Information Systems Frontiers*, •••, 1–33. DOI: 10.1007/s10796-024-10476-z

Hasan, M. R., Khan, M. A., & Wuest, T. (2024). Towards Industry 5.0: A Systematic Literature Review on Sustainable and Green Composite Materials Supply Chains. *arXiv preprint arXiv:2402.06100.*

Ikram, L., Afaf, D., & Latifa, E. (2024, May). Beyond Industry 5.0: Tracing the Past, Present, and Future of Digital Industrial Transformations. In *2024 4th International Conference on Innovative Research in Applied Science, Engineering and Technology (IRASET)* (pp. 1-7). IEEE.

Jin, Q., Chen, H., & Hu, F. (2024). Proposal of Industry 5.0-Enabled Sustainability of Product–Service Systems and Its Quantitative Multi-Criteria Decision-Making Method. *Processes (Basel, Switzerland)*, *12*(3), 473. DOI: 10.3390/pr12030473

Kannan, D., Amiri, A. S., Shaayesteh, M. T., Nasr, A. K., & Mina, H. (2024). Unveiling barriers to the integration of blockchain-based circular economy and Industry 5.0 in manufacturing industries: A strategic prioritization approach. *Business Strategy and the Environment*, *33*(8), 7855–7886. DOI: 10.1002/bse.3886

Katari, V., Goyal, S., Nigam, V., Jana, M., Maitra, A., Sharma, H., & Sahu, K. K. (2024). A Confluence of Emerging Technologies Like IoT, Edge & Cloud Computing, Blockchain, Industry 4.0 & 5.0, AI & ML toward the Realization of Eco-Friendly Supercapacitors. In *Eco-Friendly Supercapacitors: Design and Future Perspectives in Sustainable and Green Energy Storage Devices* (pp. 163-204). American Chemical Society.

Lo, H. W., Chan, H. W., Lin, J. W., & Lin, S. W. (2024). Evaluating the interrelationships of industrial 5.0 development factors using an integration approach of Fermatean Fuzzy Logic. *Journal of Operations Intelligence*, *2*(1), 95–113. DOI: 10.31181/jopi21202416

Martín-Gómez, A. M., Agote-Garrido, A., & Lama-Ruiz, J. R. (2024). A Framework for Sustainable Manufacturing: Integrating Industry 4.0 Technologies with Industry 5.0 Values. *Sustainability (Basel)*, *16*(4), 1364. DOI: 10.3390/su16041364

Martini, B., Bellisario, D., & Coletti, P. (2024). Human-centered and sustainable artificial intelligence in industry 5.0: Challenges and perspectives. *Sustainability (Basel), 16*(13), 5448. DOI: 10.3390/su16135448

. Mourtzis, D., & Angelopoulos, J. (2024). Challenges and Opportunities for the Design and Development of Intelligent, Sustainable and Resilient Personalized Product-Service Systems Towards Industry 5.0. *Data-Driven Decision Making for Product Service Systems*, 27-62.

Narkhede, G. B., Pasi, B. N., Rajhans, N., & Kulkarni, A. (2024). Industry 5.0 and sustainable manufacturing: A systematic literature review. *Benchmarking*.

Piron, M., Wu, J., Fedele, A., & Manzardo, A. (2024). Industry 4.0 and life cycle assessment: Evaluation of the technology applications as an asset for the life cycle inventory. *The Science of the Total Environment, 916*, 170263. DOI: 10.1016/j.scitotenv.2024.170263 PMID: 38253101

Rajumesh, S. (2024). Promoting sustainable and human-centric industry 5.0: A thematic analysis of emerging research topics and opportunities. *Journal of Business and Socio-economic Development, 4*(2), 111–126. DOI: 10.1108/JBSED-10-2022-0116

Ramírez-Márquez, C., Posadas-Paredes, T., Raya-Tapia, A. Y., & Ponce-Ortega, J. M. (2024). Natural Resource Optimization and Sustainability in Society 5.0: A Comprehensive Review. *Resources, 13*(2), 19. DOI: 10.3390/resources13020019

Rane, N., Kaya, Ö., & Rane, J. (2024). Digital Twins for Industry 4.0, 5.0, and Society 5.0. *Available at SSRN* 4918575. DOI: 10.2139/ssrn.4918575

Rane, N. L., Kaya, Ö., & Rane, J. (2024). *Artificial Intelligence, Machine Learning, and Deep Learning for Sustainable Industry 5.0*. Deep Science Publishing.

Rumayor, M., Margallo, M., Pinedo, J., & Albo, J. (2024). Learning by Doing using the Life Cycle Assessment tool: LCA Projects in collaboration with industries. *Education for Chemical Engineers, 48*, 44–52. DOI: 10.1016/j.ece.2024.05.002

Santos, B., Costa, R. L. C., & Santos, L. (2024). Cybersecurity in Industry 5.0: Open Challenges and Future Directions. *arXiv preprint arXiv:2410.09538*. DOI: 10.1109/PST62714.2024.10788065

Sarkar, B. D., Shardeo, V., Dwivedi, A., & Pamucar, D. (2024). Digital transition from industry 4.0 to industry 5.0 in smart manufacturing: A framework for sustainable future. *Technology in Society, 78*, 102649. DOI: 10.1016/j.techsoc.2024.102649

Satheesh, S., & Shukla, K. (2024). Industry 5.0, Quality of Life, and Sustainable Adaptation to Climate Change: Challenges and the Transformational Way Forward. In *Quality of Life and Climate Change: Impacts, Sustainable Adaptation, and Social-Ecological Resilience* (pp. 200-219). IGI Global.

Sharma, R., & Gupta, H. (2024). Leveraging cognitive digital twins in industry 5.0 for achieving sustainable development goal 9: An exploration of inclusive and sustainable industrialization strategies. *Journal of Cleaner Production*, *448*, 141364. DOI: 10.1016/j.jclepro.2024.141364

Vacchi, M., Siligardi, C., & Settembre-Blundo, D. (2024). Driving manufacturing companies toward industry 5.0: A strategic framework for process technological sustainability assessment (P-TSA). *Sustainability (Basel)*, *16*(2), 695. DOI: 10.3390/su16020695

Valeriya, G., Kirola, M., Gupta, M., Bharathi, P., & Acharya, P. (2024). Evaluating the Impact of AI-Based Sustainability Measures in Industry 5.0: A Longitudinal Study. In *BIO Web of Conferences* (Vol. 86, p. 01058). EDP Sciences.

Zhen, Z., & Yao, Y. (2024). The confluence of digital twin and blockchan technologies in Industry 5.0: Transforming supply chain management for innovation and sustainability. *Journal of the Knowledge Economy*, *16*(1), 1–27. DOI: 10.1007/s13132-024-02151-0

Chapter 10

Integrating Bioeconomy Into Education, Vocational Training, and Research Capacity Building

Ketan Sarvakar
https://orcid.org/0000-0003-4486-0224
Ganpat University, India

Dolly Prajapati
https://orcid.org/0009-0005-9112-0554
Ganpat University, India

ABSTRACT

This chapter highlights the role of education and capacity building in promoting global bionomically, which integrates ecological and economic principles of stability. This underlines the inclusion of bioeconomic standards in education to develop competent experts. Multi -colored fields such as ecological economy, environmental science and biotechnology are important for developing a skilled workforce. Important strategies include sustainable courses, bioinizing and special courses in renewable energy, and decisions of best practices from large institutions. Vocational education, especially for indigenous communities, is important for coordinating traditional skills with green economy. The chapter promotes progress in accurate agriculture, biotechnology and renewable energy through academic government cooperation. International cooperation is necessary to remove loss of biodiversity

DOI: 10.4018/979-8-3373-9923-2.ch010

and climate challenges. Governments should establish side rivers and public-private partnerships. It is important to achieve stability and balance organic, economic and social flexibility.

1 INTRODUCTION

The bioeconomy, which combines economic and ecological ideas, is now essential to solving the world's sustainability problems. It highlights how renewable biological resources can be used sustainably in fields including biotechnology, renewable energy, and agriculture(Ivar Virgin and E. Jane Morris, 2017). As the need for sustainable solutions increases, bioeconomy education and capacity building are crucial for giving professionals the know-how to spur innovation in these fields. In order to facilitate the shift to a sustainable, bio-based economy, this chapter evaluates the need for qualified professionals worldwide and the need to incorporate bioeconomy ideas into education at all levels.

1.1 Defining Bioeconomy Education and Capacity Building

An interdisciplinary approach known as "bioeconomy schooling" consists of ecological principles, sustainability, and bio-based total innovations into educational and career education packages. Its most important aim is to offer college students the records and capabilities they want to without a doubt impact critical fields like forestry, biotechnology, renewable energy, and agriculture. (Hamid et al., 2024) The goal is to broaden a new generation of professionals who can pressure change in companies that depend on biological resources that can be replenished and who understand the need for sustainable aid control. In both advanced and rising nations, this schooling cultivates a subculture of environmental stewardship and lays the groundwork for destiny professions in sustainable practices.

To assist bioeconomic growth, capability construction is just as important as education. It involves bolstering the technological, medical, and infrastructure capacities required to successfully observe bioeconomic strategies. Building ability guarantees that companies, governments, and corporations have the resources and know-how needed to enforce and enlarge sustainable technologies, like bio-primarily based production strategies, renewable energy systems, and sustainable farming strategies. This process is important for making certain that the team of workers has the technological understanding and realistic competencies to use bioeconomy concepts in real-world settings, in addition to expert them.

Incorporating bioeconomy concepts into school curricula is ultimately a crucial tactic for creating a workforce capable of handling sustainability issues on a global scale. (Bejinaru et al., 2018) In areas like biodiversity upkeep, beneficial resource conservation, and climate trade mitigation, this approach ensures that future generations can be ready to spearhead advances. In addition to fostering prolonged-time period economic and environmental resilience, societies can develop educated personnel able to spearhead the shift to a greater sustainable and bio-based monetary device via incorporating bioeconomy education into primary, secondary, and higher training structures similar to vocational schooling applications.

Figure 1. Bioeconomy education framework

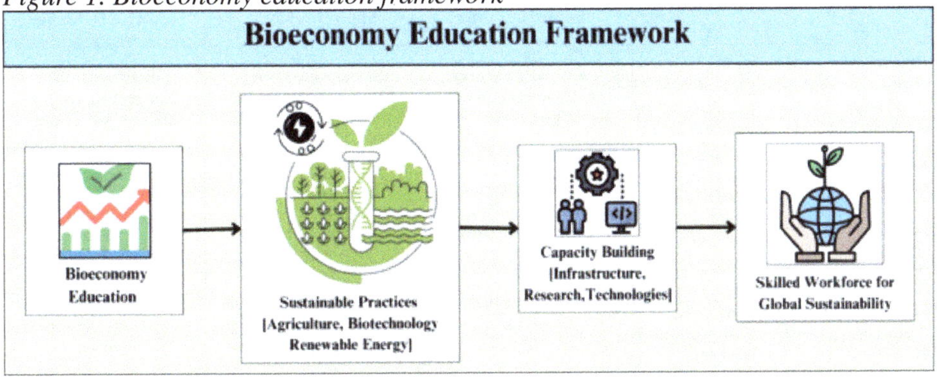

Figure 1 shows A model called the Bioeconomy Education Framework lists the important factors required for powerful bioeconomy schooling. It has a strong emphasis on increasing capacity through studies, generation improvement, and infrastructure, as well as integrating sustainable practices in biotechnology, renewable energy, and agriculture. The last objective is to enlarge employees with the vital capabilities to assist global sustainability.

1.2 Global Need for Education in Bioeconomy

The want for bioeconomy education is growing speedy because the globe deals with urgent problems like biodiversity loss, aid depletion, and climate alternate. (Faulkner et al., 2024) (Attal-Juncqua et al., 2024) These international concerns necessitate a group of workers that is familiar with bioeconomic concepts and may promote sustainable innovation in several industries. By getting ready professionals to address those issues through tendencies in biotechnology, sustainable agriculture, and renewable electricity, bioeconomy training promotes a balanced method for each economic and environmental development.

The need for bioeconomy education is developing rapidly due to the fact the globe faces pressing issues like biodiversity loss, resource depletion, and weather alternate. These international issues necessitate personnel who know bioeconomic principles and might sell sustainable innovation in a range of industries. By making ready professionals to address those problems through trends in biotechnology, sustainable agriculture, and renewable strength, bioeconomy training promotes a balanced method for each monetary and environmental development.

Table 1. The role of bioeconomy education in addressing global challenges

The Role of Bioeconomy Education in Addressing Global Challenges				
Global Challenge	**Bioeconomy Education Contribution**	**Impacted Sectors**	**Skills Developed**	**Expected Outcomes**
Climate change (Faulkner et al., 2024)	- Training in renewable energy technologies, carbon capture, and green policy	- Renewable energy, environmental policy, green tech	- Sustainable energy solution, knowledge of climate policy analysis	- Emissions with little carbon, energy infection for renewal
Resource Depletion (Attal-Juncqua et al., 2024)	- Education on sustainable resource management, circular economy practices	- Agriculture, Manufacturing, Waste Management	- Resource-efficient farming, waste recycling, sustainable production	- Efficient resource use, reduced environmental footprint
Biodiversity Loss (Hamid et al., 2024)	- Fostering innovation in biodiversity conservation, sustainable land use	- Biotechnology, Conservation, Agriculture	- Ecosystem management, biodiversity monitoring, conservation strategies	- Preservation of ecosystems, restoration of biodiversity
Economic Growth (Pubule et al., 2020)	- Development of green jobs, entrepreneurship in bio-based industries	- Biotechnology, Bio-manufacturing, Green Finance	- Bio-business skills, project management, innovation management	- Creation of green jobs, economic growth through bio-based industries
Social Well-being (Bößner et al., 2021)	- Promoting public health through biotechnology and sustainable agriculture	- Healthcare, Agriculture, Public Health	- Public health education, sustainable agriculture, biotechnology research	- Improved public health, sustainable food systems

Table 1 indicates the multifaceted function of bioeconomy education in addressing international challenges which include weather change, useful resource depletion, and biodiversity loss. It highlights how education in bioeconomy contributes to sectors like renewable energy, agriculture, and biotechnology, by using developing abilities in sustainable aid control, green technology, and conservation strategies. The table emphasizes the anticipated results of such education, together with reduced carbon emissions, green aid use, biodiversity maintenance, and the advent of inexperienced jobs, all of which help the transition to a sustainable and resilient destiny.

1.3 The Evolution of the Bioeconomy Concept

The term bioeconomy has emerged through various intellectual and industrial traditions rather than as a simple, uniform paradigm. Early antecedents can be traced to the circular bioeconomy movement in the 1920s and 1930s in the United

States, which promoted industrial use of agricultural surpluses to create biobased materials such as plastic, fibers, and fuel an early vision of a resource-effective bio-based industry (see the historical origin of a resource, biblical resource resource is a resource-effective resource resource, which is a resource-effective, which is a resource-effective, which is a resource-life resource-effective resource-effective, (Look at the historical. And sustainability SE) Scientific, Cambridge University Press, (Lewandowski, 2017)). The concept of bioeconomy was later promoted by Nicolas Georgescu-Roegen (1971), who offered an ecological explanation based on the Entropy Act and planetary limits for growth. His vision emphasized that thermodynamic realities limit economic processes and that real sustainability requires respecting the Earth's Biophysical Boundaries.

Since the beginning of the 2000s, political frameworks such as the EU knowledge-based bioeconomy (KBBE) and the OECD's bioeconomist strategy, entered the concept of biotechnology, innovation, and industrial competitiveness ((Carvache-Franco et al., 2022), (Lewandowski, 2017)). It marked an ideological shift from ecology-based restraint to technical economic expansion. (Vogt & Frankenreiter, 2022)These historical paths reveal a sustained tension: Is the bioeconomy a means of dealing with human activity within ecological boundaries, or a new phase of industrial development under the “green” label? Recognizing this duality is important for developing bioeconomy training that prepares students to critically evaluate competing models for sustainability and development. While the bioeconomy offers a way to sustainable use of resources, it also risks accelerating organic degradation if not critically controlled. The term “utilization of nature” should therefore be interpreted as the careful, conscious and regenerating use of biological systems instead of ineffective exploitation.(Bastos Lima & Palme, 2022) Bioeconomy education will help future professionals understand this double potential - that the bioeconomy can either improve or undermine biodiversity, depending on design, governance and ethical choices. Including this perspective at the beginning of the discussion, the chapter corresponds to the broader theme of balancing innovation with ecological integrity. Indigenous peoples and local communities have practiced sustainable use of resources through land management, cyclical production systems and societies management for centuries. These traditional bioeconomies provide vivid examples of flexibility and balance between ecology,(Ecology, 1999) economy and cultural principles that modern bioeconomy strategies can learn to ensure inclusion and long-term sustainability.

2 INTEGRATING BIOECONOMY PRINCIPLES INTO ACADEMIC CURRICULA

The incorporation of bioeconomy concepts into academic applications is critical to growing a staff ready to address the global issues of useful resource control, sustainability, and weather trade. (Pubule et al., 2020) The multi-disciplinary area of bioeconomy includes industries like biotechnology, sustainable agriculture, renewable energy, and circular economic system ideas. To provide college students with a thorough knowledge of ecological systems, environmental rules, bio-based totally technology, and the monetary ramifications of the use of bioresources, curricula ought to be created. Institutions guarantee that destiny leaders in industries inclusive of biotechnology, electricity, and agriculture can spur innovation at the same time as upholding social justice and environmental duty by using doing.

Academic packages must inspire multidisciplinary cooperation, important questioning, and problem-solving because these are crucial for handling tough bioeconomy issues. (Zou et al., 2024) Educational establishments can provide students with a whole know-how of how to deal with troubles like biodiversity loss, useful aid depletion, and waste management with the useful resource of integrating sustainability ideas into engineering, economics, biology, and other conventional topics. Students also can gain the actual international experience and realistic abilities essential to regional bioeconomy strategies in exercising cooperative efforts with agencies, governmental groups, and non-governmental groups

2.1 Curriculum Design for Sustainable Bioeconomy Education

A curriculum for teaching about the sustainable bioeconomy wants to be designed using an interdisciplinary method that incorporates expertise from distinct domains to offer college students a complete understanding of the bioeconomy. Important guides like ecology serve as the idea for this because they educate university college students on how ecosystems artwork and the way to control herbal sources sustainably. (Unito et al., 2020)(Abo-Khalil, 2024)Understanding ecosystems is crucial to developing bio-primarily based businesses that use renewable resources without harming the surroundings. To create a sustainable bioeconomy, decisions of conservation, land use, and natural useful resource control require a radical expertise of ecological ideas.

Economics, which focuses on the financial implications of sustainability and bio-based companies, is essential to bioeconomy education. Understanding the economic models that promote sustainable growth, such the circular economy, which minimizes waste and resource use, is part of this(Priefer et al., 2017). Economics also looks at how bioeconomy projects affect labor markets, regional development, and global markets more broadly. In order to assess the economic feasibility of bio-based technologies, the cost-benefit analysis of environmental laws, and the role of innovation in promoting economic growth while preserving ecological balance, students should be prepared. Students who comprehend policy frameworks and economic incentives can also better support the incorporation of bioeconomy ideas into public and private sector decision-making.

To promote innovation in sustainable practices, biotechnology must be incorporated into bioeconomy courses. From biofuels and bioplastics to agricultural breakthroughs that increase food security and lessen environmental impacts, biotechnology is a major force behind the bio-based industries(Sacchi et al., 2021). Students who receive biotechnology training gain the technical know-how required to create and implement innovative solutions that support sustainable business practices in a variety of industries. In a similar vein, teaching pupils the fundamentals of long-term ecological health requires taking sustainability and environmental science courses. Students who possess this knowledge are more equipped to build bio-based solutions that benefit society and the environment, as well as to comprehend the significance of preserving biodiversity, cutting pollution, and addressing climate change. By include these topics in the curriculum, educational establishments guarantee that students are not only well-versed in their professions but also equipped to take the lead in creating the sustainable bioeconomy of the future.

Table 2. Key interdisciplinary subjects in bioeconomy curriculum

Key Interdisciplinary Subjects in Bioeconomy Curriculum		
Subject	**Description**	**Relevance to Bioeconomy**
Ecology (Aguilar et al., 2019)	- Study of ecosystem, biodiversity, and natural resource management including the relationship between organisms and their environment.	- The dynamics of the ecosystem, the effect of human activities on biodiversity, and a basic topic to contribute to resource production to natural systems. It is important to continuously manage natural resources and ensure that bioeconomic ecological boundaries are operated within.
Economics (Urmetzer et al., 2018)	- Focus on status, resource distribution, market dynamics, biobased industries, and financial aspects of cost-profit analysis.	- The key to assessing the economic viability of bioeconomic practice as the scalability of biphobia-based technologies and the economic effects of durable resource management. Students gain a better understanding of market-operated incentives that support bioeconomic solutions because to this.
Biotechnology (Urmetzer et al., 2020)	- Innovations include innovations in biological technologies such as genetic technology, fermentation processes, biopsy, biofuels, and bioplastics.	- It is necessary to promote bio-based industries. Biotechnology enables the development of permanent products (biofuels, bioplastics) and technologies that reduce the dependence on fossil fuels, help reduce climate change, and support permanent agriculture and industrial practice.

continued on following page

Table 2. Continued

Key Interdisciplinary Subjects in Bioeconomy Curriculum		
Subject	**Description**	**Relevance to Bioeconomy**
Sustainability (Venkatesan, 2020)	- Encompasses the principles, practices, and methodologies for achieving long-term ecological health, including sustainable development, renewable energy, and carbon-neutral solutions.	- Offers a core understanding of how human activities can be balanced with environmental preservation. Sustainability education ensures that bioeconomy practices do not deplete or degrade resources, but rather maintain or improve ecological systems for future generations.
Environmental Science (Araripe & Zuin Zeidler, 2024)	- Focuses on scientific studies of environmental processes, pollution control, climate change, and the role of human activities in environmental loss.	- The environment provides the scientific knowledge required to develop lasting solutions. It is necessary to ensure that bioeconomic practice reduces pollution, prevents destruction of residences, and combat climate change, corresponding to extensive goals for environmental protection and ecological health.

Table 2: Important Multidisciplinary Topics in the Bioeconomy The curriculum offers a precis of the essential subjects that underpin education inside the bioeconomy. To broaden and manipulate sustainable bio-primarily based organizations, technologies, and answers, it emphasizes the significance of fields consisting of ecology, economics, biotechnology, sustainability, and environmental science.

Strengthening biological diversity knowledge in curriculum design.

In addition to listing "Ecology" as a subject, bioeconomy -learning plans should include important scientific and political concepts that operationalize sustainable utilization of biodiversity, for example:

- Valuation of ecosystem services: Techniques for measuring the benefits of non-market advantages in healthy ecosystems pollination, carbon storage, the Earth's fertility and water regulation that these values inform about land use and industrial decisions.
- Conservation Biology: Principles of maintaining species, genetic and habitat diversity while developing biobased industries.
- Restorative practice: Methods for designing bioeconomic activities (eg Agro-Forestry, Bio Mediation) that actively regenerating degraded ecosystems.
- Nature-based Solutions (NBS): An approach to integrate bioeconomics strategies with climate adaptation and biological diversity goals, according to the EU-Celac NBS framework(Latin American & Platform, 2023).

Including these modules develops biological diversity knowledge, ensuring that graduates can evaluate trade -offs between innovation and ecological integrity and design biobased solutions that improve rather than drain natural capital.

Illustrative example Ecuador's deforestation -free bioeconomy Ecuador has used a national strategy to promote high value, deforestation -free agricultural exports such as cocoa and coffee that combines revenue generation with forest conservation.

This model shows how economic incentives can strengthen biodiversity conservation when politics combines certification, education and local innovation.(Economic Cooperation & (BMZ), 2023) Such examples can be used as teaching in case studies in bioeconomy programs to highlight sustainable, sector -specific best practice. Curriculum design must move beyond a purely scientific and technical focus to integrate traditional ecological knowledge (TEK) and perspectives from the social sciences and humanities. To use indigenous peoples' approaches to land management,(Chanza & De Wit, 2016) ethics and resource sharing promotes intercultural dialogue and mutual respect between Western science and local knowledge, and helps students understand different sustainability routes.

2.2 Approaches to Curriculum Integration

Approaches to curriculum integration emphasize the need to easily incorporate bioeconomy principles into modern instructional packages. To do this, bioeconomy issues have to be incorporated into everyday curricula in diverse fields, inclusive of engineering, environmental technology, and economics. This will ensure that scholars collect an intensive awareness of biotechnology's place in the bioeconomy, sustainable aid management, and the importance of fusing environmental worries with technical and monetary advancement. (Bößner et al., 2021) Students will gain unique expertise and competencies to at once promote bioeconomy innovation if specialist publications in topics like bioengineering, environmental economics, and sustainable agriculture are provided. With an emphasis on vital bioeconomy domains consisting of green production, sustainable agriculture, and renewable electricity, these publications will provide college students the know-how to propel destiny trends in these fields.

A new technology of specialists who're professional in growing sustainable solutions for urgent international issues can be produced using academic establishments via encouraging a multidisciplinary technique, to better prepare college students for the complex, move-zone difficulties they'll come upon in the bioeconomy. (Castilla-Polo et al., 2020) Incorporating bioeconomy concepts into curricula necessitates a calculated, revolutionary approach that modifies present instructional frameworks to fulfill the demands of a changing, bio-based economic system. Through this aggregate, future leaders can be organized with the recognize-how to support sustainable improvement across industries, innovate, and effectively manage herbal assets.

Figure 2. Steps for integrating bioeconomy principles into academic curriculum

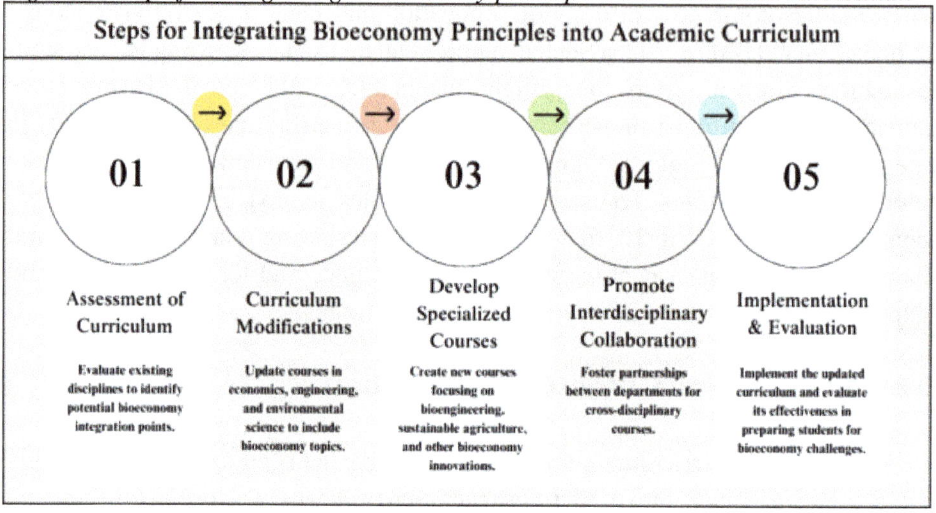

A 5-step process for integrating bioeconomy principles into educational curriculum is proven in Figure 2. Assessing modern guides to find areas for integration is step one. The subsequent step is to add bioeconomy elements to already-current courses in associated fields. Creating specialized publications focused on breakthroughs in the bioeconomy is the next section. The method promotes departmental interdisciplinary cooperation to increase an intensive understanding. Lastly, the changed curriculum's efficacy in getting ready college students for the issues of the bioeconomy is ensured by way of its implementation and evaluation.

2.3 Integrating ELSI into Bioeconomy Education

A sustainable bioeconomy must be technologically sound and socially responsible. Consequently, bioeconomic curricula should integrate ethical, legal and social implications (ELSI) in courses and training paths. Core content should include bioethics, environmental law and politics, intellectual property and access/distribution sharing, risk assessment and biosecurity/biosecurity, and science communication and public commitment. The frontier technologies quoted in this chapter (for example, gene editing, bioinformatics, precision agriculture) can cause unintended effects on ecosystems, equity and management if implemented without assessment.(Stilgoe et al., 2013) The installation of Elsi prepares graduates to practice responsible research and innovation (RRI) - pending injuries, engaging stakeholders early and coordinating innovation with the public interest.

Proposed learning outcomes include the ability to (i) evaluate trade-offs by using case law and policy tools, (ii) carry out stakeholder mapping and consent/ engagement planning, (iii) Apply fair/open science and data protection principles to biodata, and (IV) justify technology choices.

2.4 Context-Specific Approaches to Bioeconomy Education

The bioeconomy is not monolithic; It reflects regional resources, political goals and industrial routes. A single global template risks misalignment with local realities. (Juvančič & Van Leeuwen, 2021) Education strategies should therefore be context -specific while maintaining shared sustainability principles.

- EU (EU): Emphasis of circularity, advanced bio-refinery and prices of agricultural/forestry residues within regional smart experts (JRC mapping of regional bioeconomics strategies).
- USA (USA): Strong R&D management with instruments on the demand side (such as USDA BioPreferred® procurement) to create markets for certified biobased products.
- Emerging regions (such as LAC/Asia/Africa): Prioritize sustainable agriculture, preservation of biodiversity and social companies, often integrates nature -based solutions and rural development.

Curriculum design should therefore be located with: (i) case studies and policy tool sets; (ii) value chain laboratories around regional raw materials (eg agro-residues, algae, forestry); (iii) Entrepreneurship studios related to local procurement or certification schemes; and (iv) community engagement projects with indigenous peoples/local knowledge holders.

2.5 Developing Metrics for Evaluating Bioeconomy Education

In order to go beyond descriptive proposals, programs should use multidimensional evaluation that reflects the interdisciplinary and ethical extent of the bioeconomy(Daystar et al., 2021). Suggested indicators:

I. System-thinking integration across all courses (rubrics/portfolios showing interdisciplinary synthesis).
II. ELSI competence (demonstrates RRI principles in structured reflection, political summaries or technical alternatives).

III. Innovation and corporate results (student/alumni start-ups, Community Bio-Center Prize, Open Science, Patents With Safety).
IV. Regional adjustment (Capstone projects that have been mapped to local/regional bioeconomy strategies; stakeholder support).
V. Biodiversity and climate knowledge (ability to calculate/argue for ecosystem service weighing; NBS adjustment).
VI. Partnerships and placements (Industry/Public/NGO Co-SuperVision; Internship Conversion Rate).
VII. Equity and inclusion (participation from under -represented sectors/communities; distribution sharing mechanisms).

3 VOCATIONAL TRAINING FOR BIOECONOMY PRACTICES

This section makes a specialty of the essential position that vocational education may also play in offering people with the sensible competencies they want to take part in bioeconomy practices. It highlights business collaboration, talks approximately how to create schooling applications that meet the needs of sustainable bioeconomy sectors, and appears at how crucial it's miles to combine Indigenous and neighborhood know-how into bioeconomy practices.

3.1 Building Skills for Sustainable Bioeconomy Practices

Vocational schooling packages want to emphasize realistic, hands-on studying in vital areas collectively with waste control, biotechnology, renewable electricity, and sustainable agriculture so that you can increase expert employees that would help the bioeconomy. (Apostolopoulos et al., 2023)(Hinderer et al., 2021) The bioeconomy is predicated upon these sectors because of the truth they foster innovation, boom productiveness, and decrease environmental consequences. To reduce environmental damage and grow crop yields, sustainable agriculture training desires to cope with techniques that include natural farming, agroforestry, and using bio-primarily based inputs. Vocational training in renewable strength must equip human beings with the talents important to plot, put in force, and manage renewable energy structures like sun, wind, and bioenergy all of which might be vital for the shift far from fossil fuels. Training in waste control is similarly crucial, with an emphasis on technology that contributes to useful resource conservation and landfill trash reduction, which includes composting, recycling, and waste-to-power systems.

Programs for vocational schooling ought to adapt to the converting desires of the green economy. Vocational education needs to adapt to the growing emphasis on sustainability in companies. (Watkinson et al., 2012) This entails integrating current domain names consisting of green building technology, which deals with developing environmentally pleasant, strength-green systems, and sustainable manufacturing, which stresses minimum waste and electricity-efficient production strategies. To extend the existence cycle of materials, packages ought to additionally sell re-source reuse, recycling, and regeneration, all of which are tenets of the circular economic system. Vocational training seasoned-grams make certain that people can satisfy business needs and contribute to a sustainable destiny by focusing on these increasing sectors.

Table 3. Vocational training for sustainable bioeconomy

Vocational Training for Sustainable Bioeconomy			
Key Area	**Focus Areas**	**Skills Developed**	**Sectors Addressed**
Sustainable Agriculture (Socaciu, 2014)	- Organic farming techniques - Agroforestry systems - Use of bio-based inputs (e.g., biofertilizers, biopesticides) - Soil health management	- Proficiency in eco-friendly crop production methods - Expertise in agroecological practices and resource-efficient farming - Understanding of sustainable land management practices	- Agriculture, - Food Security, - Environmental Conservation, - Rural Development
Renewable Energy (Wohlgemuth et al., 2021)	- Solar and wind energy technologies - Bioenergy systems (e.g., biogas, biomass energy) - Smart grid integration and energy storage solutions	- Hands-on installation, operation, and maintenance of renewable energy systems - Technical expertise in renewable technologies - Knowledge in energy efficiency and storage systems	- Energy Sector, - Green Technology, - Climate Change Mitigation, - Renewable Energy
Biotechnology (Onpraphai et al., 2021)	- Genetic modification of crops and livestock - Bio-based chemical production - Bioprocess engineering (e.g., fermentation technologies)	- Expertise in biotechnological applications for agriculture, medicine, and industry - Innovation in bio-manufacturing and bioprocess design - Advanced skills in the development of bio-based products	- Biotechnology, - Pharmaceuticals, - Sustainable Agriculture, - Bio-manufacturing
Waste Management (Hariram et al., 2023)	- Waste-to-energy technologies - Composting and bioremediation - Circular economy practices (e.g., material recycling, resource recovery)	- Skills in waste reduction and resource recovery - Knowledge in environmental impact assessments and sustainable disposal - Expertise in creating zero-waste strategies and recycling technologies	- Waste Management, - Circular Economy, - Environmental Protection, - Resource Reco

Key vocational schooling disciplines which can be vital for developing competencies in sustainable bioeconomy activities are indexed in Table 3. It addresses subjects like waste control, biotechnology, renewable energy, and sustainable agriculture. In addition to outlining the precise abilities obtained in those domain names, the table highlights attention regions which include waste-to-energy systems, biotechnological packages, renewable energy technology, and environmentally pleasant farming.

This program prepares personnel to contribute to a sustainable and environmentally conscious economy, assembly the needs of the developing inexperienced sectors.

3.2 Building Skills for Sustainable Bioeconomy Practices

The status quo of sturdy partnerships amongst educational establishments, groups, and government agencies is essential to ensuring that education is in step with industrial demands. Through this partnership, education applications are created that don't forget the real-world necessities of the bioeconomy industry. (Mian et al., 2020) Through industry engagement, academic institutions may also encompass the most modern technology in their curriculum, making sure that scholars analyze modern-day and applicable competencies. The development of specialised training applications and courses that cater to the wishes of particular industries, along with biotechnology, sustainable agriculture, and renewable strength, is likewise made viable by way of industry input.

To put together college students for professions within the real bioeconomy, instructional packages ought to consist of realistic knowledge. Internships, on-the-task education, and projects that let students put their theoretical knowledge to use in actual-international conditions can assist obtain this. By bridging this hollow among schooling and enterprise company, graduates need to have the capabilities vital to manual the expansion of the bioeconomy, facilitating a more seamless transition from school to art work and inspiring innovation within the area.

3.3 Empowering Local Communities and Indigenous Knowledge

The importance of social companies equipped with resources and abilities, especially in rural and development areas, is important for performing permanent practices that emphasize economically at this stage. Especially the training programs designed for local communities can focus on subjects such as biological diversity security, nature assistance management, and sustainable agriculture, which supports them in implementing inexperienced practices that still their living standards standard beautifies. (Tleuken et al., 2022) These applications inspire lengthy-time period sustainability and boom local resilience to environmental issues, permitting these communities to play a crucial element inside the inexperienced financial system.

Incorporating indigenous know-how into bioeconomic fashions is crucial to growing long-term answers that honor lifestyle and the environment. Indigenous businesses have a long time of enjoying biodiversity conservation, ecological stability, and resource management. (Al-Kuwari et al., 2021) By acknowledging and utilizing this understanding, bioeconomic fashions can turn out to be more efficient, culturally applicable, and bendy. This partnership fosters a greater comprehensive method to sustainability by assisting the integration of conventional ecological know-how into present-day bioeconomy frameworks and bolstering environmental conservation tasks. Instead of "strengthening" communities from the outside, initiatives should support indigenous peoples and local groups to lead their own education, business development and policy commitment.(UNESCO, 2021) This co-development approach ensures that knowledge, innovation and economic value remain in local communities, while strengthening ecological and cultural integrity.

4 BUILDING CAPACITY IN RESEARCH AND TECHNOLOGY FOR GLOBAL SUSTAINABILITY

This segment focuses on the important role of research and technology in promoting global bi-economic and fetal-NG permanent practices. This underlines the need to strengthen research ability, promote international cooperation to promote technical infrastructure and fulfill stability goals.

4.1 Strengthening Research Capacity for Bioeconomy Innovations

Strengthening research capacity is fundamental to promoting bioeconomic innovations and promoting permanent practice in different fields. Bio-operated solutions require advanced research in areas such as biotechnology, synthetic biology, and ecological economy. (Cookey et al., 2023) These sectors offer important medical foundations for growing everlasting technologies, growing aid efficiency, and decreasing environmental influences. For example, biotechnology enables the improvement of environmentally friendly biobased products, even as artificial biology opens new paths for the manufacturing of permanent biofuels and biodegradable substances.

Research collaboration is important when it comes to the use of bioeconomic reforms. The partnership between educational installations, industry and authorities creates a dynamic ecosystem where ideas can be translated into practical answers. Academia brings advanced research and theoretical knowledge, while entering the Enterprise Intelligent Package and the Real Function, and the officer's body policy assistance and investment we do. (Alliance of Bioversity International and CIAT; Senior International Law and Policy Advisor ; CARICOM, 2024) This collaboration accelerates the development and commercialization of permanent technologies and ensures that they can be the hand, scalable and a type of area.

Table 4. Key elements in strengthening research capacity for bioeconomy innovations

Key Elements in Strengthening Research Capacity for Bioeconomy Innovations		
Focus Area	**Description**	**Examples of Application**
Biotechnology (João, 2021)	- Development of bio-based, environmentally friendly products.	- Bio-based plastics, - Biofuels, - Biodegradable packaging materials.
Synthetic Biology (Vuorio et al., 2024)	- Engineering biological systems for sustainable solutions.	- Creation of bioengineered crops, - Sustainable biofuels, - Microbial solutions for pollution cleanup.
Ecological Economics (Pascoli et al., 2022)	- Analysis of economic impacts of sustainability and resource management.	- Valuation of ecosystem services, - Development of circular economy models, - Sustainable resource pricing.
Academia-Industry-Government Collaboration (Issa et al., 2019)	- Partnerships leveraging research, application, and policy to foster innovation.	- University-industry R&D, - Government funding for bioeconomy projects, - Public-private technology hubs.
Technology Commercialization (Grzyb, 2017)	- Transitioning research into scalable, market-ready solutions.	- Commercial bioenergy technologies, - Genetically modified organisms (GMOs) for agriculture.

The essential components required to promote bioeconomic research and innovation have been postponed in Table 4: The most important elements to strengthen the research ability of bioeconomic innovations. This underlines the importance of specially produced areas in the study that promote resource efficiency and durable solutions such as biotechnology, synthetic biology, and ecological economy. The table also emphasizes the value of cooperation between the government, business, and academics showing how their common knowledge promotes innovation, helps with the commercialization of technologies, and successfully deals with questions about global stability with success. Together, these factors open the door for signs and scalable bioeconomy development.

4.2 Advancing Technological Capacity in Bioeconomy Sectors

It is important to pursue technical capacity for growth and success in bio-based industries, such as renewable energy, permanent agriculture, and biotechnology. The construction of a strong technical infrastructure enables the development of innovations that promote stability by increasing productivity. (Lewandowski, 2017) This includes sufficient investments in research and development (R&D) to promote the presentation of new, effective technologies that reduce environmental impact and increase the efficiency of bioconomic practice. As the world moves toward more durable systems, technological innovations in bioconomic fields are in front of this change. Emerging technologies which include CRISPR, bioinformatics, and accurate cultivation deliver revolution in bioeconomically by way of providing progressive solutions to persistent demanding situations. (García-Feijoo et al., 2020) The CRIS-

PR technique permits more correct genetic modifications, mainly to the increase of crops that are more bendy, effective, and proof against pests and sicknesses, thus decreasing the need for harmful chemical substances. Bio-information plays an important role in the analysis and management of biological data, which enables better insight into biological processes and improves the efficiency of biotechnology applications. These techniques not only have an opportunity to improve bio-based industries but have also played an important role in meeting global stability goals. By increasing efficiency, reducing waste, and adaptation of resource use, they contribute significantly to reducing carbon footprints in agricultural and industrial areas. To ensure that such techniques are much to used the bio-economic exercise matches global environmental goals and promotes a permanent future for future generations.

Table 5. Key technologies advancing the bioeconomy

Key Technologies Advancing the Bioeconomy			
Technology	**Primary Application**	**Benefits**	**Role in Sustainability**
CRISPR Gene Editing (Jiménez Aliaga et al., 2023)	- Developing drought-resistant crops, improving livestock, and producing bio-based materials.	- Enhances agricultural productivity, reduces reliance on chemical fertilizers, and increases yield.	- Promotes food security and reduces environmental impacts of conventional farming practices.
Bioinformatics (Giannoccaro et al., 2021)	- Analyzing biological data, genome sequencing, and drug discovery.	- Accelerates R&D in biotechnology and medicine, enabling precise and efficient innovation.	- Facilitates personalized medicine and efficient use of biological resources.
Precision Farming (Wei et al., 2022)	- Utilizing IoT, drones, and AI for efficient resource management in agriculture.	- Reduces resource waste, increases efficiency, and improves crop quality.	- Lowers carbon emissions, conserves water, and minimizes pesticide use.
Renewable Energy Tech (Stegmann et al., 2020)	- Bioenergy production, solar and wind power integration, and energy-efficient systems.	- Diversifies energy sources, reduces fossil fuel dependence, and creates sustainable energy cycles.	- Drives low-carbon energy transitions, reducing the overall carbon footprint.
Biotechnological Tools (Pink et al., 2024)	- Developing enzymes, bioplastics, and biofuels for industrial use.	- Boosts eco-friendly production, reduces reliance on petrochemicals, and opens new market sectors.	- Encourages adoption of greener industrial processes and circular economy models.
Advanced Waste Management (Kalnbalkite et al., 2022)	- Recycling, composting, and bio-conversion technologies for resource recovery.	- Converts waste into bioenergy, fertilizers, or other useful products, reducing landfill usage.	- Drives circular economy practices and minimizes environmental pollution.

CRISPR, bioinformatics, procedural agriculture, renewable energy systems, and biotechnological tools are some of the most important technologies that are pursued economically, which are highlighted in Table 5. The use, profit, and contribution of each technique for global stability are described in detail. According to global stability goals and environmental protection initiatives, they work together as a strong, resource -and environmentally friendly biobase.

4.3 Global Research Collaboration for Sustainable Practices

Global research collaboration plays an important role in promoting bioconomic innovations and addressing some of the world's most pressure environmental challenges. (Loizides et al., 2019) Promotes participation in countries, and enables international knowledge of research collaboration, expertise, and exchange of technologies, such as climate change, loss of biodiversity, and lack of resources to deal with questions. This affiliated effort allows land to gather its resources, now different approaches, and benefit from each other's strength to develop innovative, durable solutions that can be used globally.

Such cooperation leads to the creation of new technologies, practices, and strategies that can continue Global Biokum. (Zhang et al., 2020) By sharing the best practices, countries can use the most effective solutions and scale them to fit their contexts. This exchange of knowledge is important to accelerate the development of continuously competent technologies and practices that address global challenges. In addition, global research participation enables adaptation of guidelines and regulations and ensures that the nation works in concert to create a harmonious, bio-economically-operated approach to stability.

5 POLICY AND SUPPORT FOR BIOECONOMY EDUCATION

The important role of promoting education and capacity building in promoting institutional structures, management and policy sports is investigated in this section. This emphasizes how the authorities, the organization and the partnership can continue the workforce and bio-economic education.

5.1 Government and Institutional Roles in Promoting Bioeconomy Education

From K-12 to higher education, implementation of guidelines that promote bio-related subjects in the curriculum in all level, an important step in progress in biographical education (de Jong et al., 2021) is. These policies help to raise awareness and durable growth, which highlights the value of stability and promises of biotechnology, agriculture and renewable energy. Through the integration of bioeconomic principles in the course, governments can cultivate a new generation of students who are aware of and eager to work in this expanded industry. Governments should establish and maintain effective regulatory structures that encourage supporters and Bio-Economic Research and Development (R&D). (Lewandowski, 2017) These figures are necessary for the expansion of research processes, financing protection, and innovation reimbursement. Rules work to establish an environment that is adapted to creative research in addition to guaranteeing the R&D operation's moral and environmental standards. By balancing between stability and innovation, the authorities can help organizations promote bioeconomic redemption and ongoing development worldwide.

Table 6. Government and institutional roles in promoting bioeconomy education

Government and Institutional Roles in Promoting Bioeconomy Education		
Area	**Government Role**	**Institutional Role**
Policy Support (Takala et al., 2019)	- Implement policies to integrate bioeconomy topics into curricula at all education levels.	- Design and integrate bioeconomy-focused courses and educational programs.
Curriculum Development (Al-Kuwari et al., 2021)	- Develop national/regional frameworks for bioeconomy education.	- Develop specialized programs and degrees in bioeconomy research and innovation.
Funding & Resources (Tatar et al., 2023)	- Provide grants and funding for bioeconomy-related research projects and education.	- Secure external funding for bioeconomy research, development, and educational activities.
Regulatory Frameworks for R&D (de Almeida Barbosa Franco et al., 2024)	- Establish sustainable bioeconomy research guidelines and regulations.	- Ensure institutional research complies with environmental and ethical standards.
Public Awareness & Engagement (Banka Beograd, 2020)	- Promote campaigns for public awareness on bioeconomy careers and sustainability.	- Organize workshops, seminars, and events to engage students and researchers in the bioeconomy field.

Table 6 shows how institutions and authorities work together to promote biodynamic education. To encourage bioeconomic research and education, the authorities should develop policies, allocate funds, and install regulatory structures. In response, educational institutions create customized courses, create biodynamic initiatives, get more money, and plan public-seeking events to raise awareness. The development of a competent working group capable of promoting permanent bioeconomic solutions depends on the coordination of institutional and authorities.

5.2 Public-Private Partnerships for Training and Capacity Building

Public-Private Partnership (PPP) plays an important role in increasing bioeconomic education and research. Collaboration between the public and private sectors brings together both sides. (Vuojärvi et al., 2024) The private sector forms funding, competence, and vocational training opportunities that are necessary to equip the workforce with the skills required for bioeconomically. This participation ensures that educational programs are combined with industrial requirements, students gain relevant skills, and increase employment in areas such as biotechnology, renewable energy, and permanent agriculture. Successful examples of bioeconomic public-private participation include collaboration, where companies collaborate with universities and research institutes to share research and provide students with knowledge and internships or training. This participation not only promotes innovation but also has commercialization of new bioconomic technologies.

6 CHALLENGES AND OPPORTUNITIES IN BIOECONOMY EDUCATION AND CAPACITY BUILDING

The main obstacles to implementing bioeconomic education are investigated in this section, including inadequate wealth, old infrastructure and false to replace traditional education methods. (Hurst et al., 2019) It also discusses the challenges in the countryside and poor countries facing, which lacks the resources and capacity required to implement bioeconomic instructions. Despite these obstacles, there are many development opportunities, including resource exchange and the possibility of international cooperation in best practice.

6.1 Key Challenges in Implementing Bioeconomy Education

There are many important obstacles in the way of implementing bioeconomic education. Lack of funding is one of the biggest challenges that limit training programs, research projects, and construction of essential infrastructure.(Wydra, 2019) Economic obstacles often prevent educational institutions from updating courses or the inclusion of new courses related to bi-economic issues. In addition, many academic structures are bulky with the old infrastructure, making it hard to apply cutting-edge technologies and studies techniques. Another crucial task is resistance to trade in the traditional instructional structure, that could slow down the integration of interdisciplinary topics as economically inside the set-up route. The implementation of bioconomic education also presents more challenges for rural and poor countries. These areas often lack the facilities and resources required to support bioeconomic efforts, as well as to qualified teachers who are knowledgeable about these subjects. As a result, these areas have trouble developing a long-lasting two-economic workforce.

6.2 Opportunities for Growth and Expansion in Bioeconomy Education

There are many opportunities for development and expansion on bioeconomic education, despite the difficulties of bringing it into practice. (Marquez et al., 2023) Global cooperation is an important opportunity for nations and organizations to exchange resources, research and best practices that expand the knowledge body on bioeconomically globally. This participation can also help countries with limited resources to develop their potential, making bioeconomic education more widely accessible worldwide. Strong educational overview can lead to information and expertise that can be more easily shared for this world cooperation. There are many opportunities for bioeconomic research and education due to the expansion of the world around the world towards a green economy. (Núñez-Sánchez & Valente, 2023) There is an increasing demand from qualified workers in many fields, including biotechnology, durable agriculture and renewable energy, as the globe moves toward more environmentally friendly methods. Because of this requirement, educational programs require a pressure that can give people the opportunity and information to contribute to these subjects. Because bio -economic education is in line with global stability goals and increases the demand for experts in green industries, it has a bright future.

Table 7. Opportunities for growth and expansion in bioeconomy education

Opportunities for Growth and Expansion in Bioeconomy Education		
Opportunity Area	**Details**	**Impact/Outcome**
Global Collaboration (Marquez et al., 2023)	- Collaborative efforts between countries and institutions to share best practices, research, and resources. - Formation of international partnerships for capacity building in resource-limited regions.	- Strengthens global bioeconomy knowledge base. - Enhances accessibility and equity in bioeconomy education worldwide.
Green Economy Shift (Núñez-Sánchez & Valente, 2023)	- Rapid growth in demand for professionals in sectors like renewable energy, sustainable agriculture, and biotechnology. - Increased focus on sustainable development and eco-friendly industries.	- Creation of new educational programs to meet sector demands. - Supports the transition to a greener, more sustainable global economy.
Future Prospects (Wydra, 2019)	- Growing focus on bioeconomy-related research, education, and innovation. - Expansion of curriculum in response to sustainability goals and environmental challenges.	- Increased global career opportunities for graduates. - Boosts innovation in green technologies and sustainable practices.
Global Accessibility (Vuojärvi et al., 2024)	- Expansion of bioeconomy education programs across the globe, including developing regions. - Enhanced availability of resources for online education and distance learning in bioeconomy fields.	- Provides equitable access to bioeconomy education worldwide. - Bridges the knowledge gap in underrepresented regions.

Given worldwide access, opportunity, international cooperation, and change towards a green economy, Table 7 prepared a significant moment for the development of bioeconomic education. This emphasizes the potential benefits of global collaboration in education, increasing experts' demand for permanent positions and increasing the importance of bioeconomic research.

7 RECOMMENDATIONS FOR FUTURE EDUCATION AND CAPACITY BUILDING INITIATIVES

The section on proposals for future educational and capacity development projects provides a strategy for increasing biosonomic education worldwide, and emphasizes the integration of bioconomic principles into national, regional and international curricula and educational policies. (Warnants Promotor, 2012) This underlines the need for interdisciplinary collaboration between teachers, corporate officials and legislators to mix effective courses with practical applications. In addition, expansion of learning platforms online is considered an important strategy to increase access to bioeconomic education, especially in neglected areas, ensuring global coverage.

7.1 Strategic Development of Bioeconomy Education

The necessity of incorporating bioeconomic concepts and educational policy courses at the national, regional, and international levels is emphasized by the strategic development of bio-economic education. (Výbošt'ok et al., 2022) Many educational topics are related to two economic subjects to ensure that students in a variety of fields, including science, engineering, politics, and economics, have a thorough understanding of the permanent practice and the biobed industries where we work. It ought to be covered under discipline.

A coordinated effort is necessary to submit these bioeconomic concepts in existing educational overviews, which promote a comprehensive approach to education. This integration should include both theoretical knowledge and practical applications, students must equip the skills required to operate innovation and stability in industries such as agricultural culture, biotechnology, and renewable energy. In addition, there should be part of extensive educational reforms that prefer stability and environmental management. The purpose of working for a long time with increasing demand from professionals in the two-economic sector must be coordinated with educational systems. By entering bi-economic education at courses all over the world, institutes can create a skilled working group that is ready to handle the global stability challenges we are facing today.

7.2 Promoting Interdisciplinary Education and Collaboration

To build effective bio-economic initiatives, reputable education and collaboration must be encouraged. To guarantee that bioeconomic programs are professionally demanding and practically useful, it emphasizes the need for collaboration between teachers, business leaders, and MLA -er. (Högfeldt et al., 2019) This participation makes it possible to develop a course that meets the requirements of the BI economic industry and the education system and guarantees that students are ready for their future employment.

This kind of collaboration is required to combine theoretical knowledge with real-world experience. While teachers impart fundamental educational knowledge, professional experts offer insight into challenges in the newest technologies, trends, and bioeconomic issues. Decision makers can back policies that encourage collaboration between academia and business to guarantee that bioeconomic initiatives stay in line with real-world needs. (Adeoye et al., 2024) This interdisciplinary approach requires the necessary theoretical knowledge and practical skills in bioeconomic fields including permanent agriculture, biotechnology and renewable energy.

7.3 Expanding Online Learning and Global Outreach

Online learning and the growth of global search demonstrate how digital platforms are expanding to enable access to bi-economic education worldwide. Bioeconomic education can now be used to increase reliance on online resources for a wide audience, including marginalized and poor people who typically do not have easy access to traditional educational institutions. (Giurca et al., 2022) This technique becomes more accessible to information and helps individuals join the state -art subjects in development areas. The use of online teaching materials and courses guarantees that learning opportunities are not limited to physical space and allow bioeconomic knowledge sharing in many geographical regions.

Educational institutions may also offer pinnacle-notch, adaptable learning options that meet the needs of college students globally, no matter their monetary or physical obstacles, through using digital systems. Additionally, increasing bioeconomy education via virtual structures promotes potential building and worldwide engagement in sustainable practices. (Ocampo-López et al., 2023) Because on line getting to know fills the space and affords a method of producing educated workforce in bioeconomy sectors, that is especially critical for regions with constrained get right of entry to standard academic establishments.

8 CONCLUSION

It is an important first step to promote sustainable development worldwide. We provide the next generation with the information and abilities that they need to inspire innovation, handle environmental issues, and use permanent business practices by integrating these ideas into educational institutions. By bridging the difference between education and industry expectations, corporate training guarantees that practical application corresponds to the theoretical foundation. In addition to preparing professionals and students to handle modern bioeconomic entanglements, this integration helps create flexible and resource-related economies worldwide. These initiatives are even stronger by enabling institutions and communities to embrace innovative solutions for stability problems and increase research and technical capacity. The exchange of ideas and best practices is possible by strengthening research infrastructure and encouraging borders, which speeds up the achievement of global stability goals. To operate and guarantee systemic changes such as bio-economic principles act as a basis for permanent practice for future generations, a comprehensive strategy that includes education, vocational training, and research capacity building is finally necessary. This chapter now presents bioeconomy bioferees as a continuum of risks and opportunities. Education, research and professional training must prepare students to handle this duality by developing biobased innovations that restore ecosystems instead of destroying them. By incorporating biological diversity, conservation principles and nature -based solutions (NBS) in bioeconomy training, the framework corresponds to the book's central theme for "responsible utilization of biodiversity" for long -term planetary sustainability. This belt approach makes bioeconomy learning an engine for ecological resistance, and ensures that innovation, politics and capacity building work together to maintain both human progress and natural systems.

REFERENCES

Abo-Khalil, A. G. (2024). Integrating sustainability into higher education challenges and opportunities for universities worldwide. *Heliyon, 10*(9), e29946. Advance online publication. DOI: 10.1016/j.heliyon.2024.e29946 PMID: 38707336

Adeoye, S. O., Batarseh, F., Brown, A. M., & Kaufman, E. K. (2024). UNDERSTANDING THE LANDSCAPE OF CYBERBIOSECURITY FOR INTEGRATIVE EDUCATIONAL PROGRAMMING. In *Journal of the ASABE* (Vol. 67, Issue 1, pp. 207–217). American Society of Agricultural and Biological Engineers. DOI: 10.13031/ja.15739

Aguilar, A., Twardowski, T., & Wohlgemuth, R. (2019). Bioeconomy for Sustainable Development. In *Biotechnology Journal* (Vol. 14, Issue 8). Wiley-VCH Verlag. DOI: 10.1002/biot.201800638

Al-Kuwari, M. M., Al-Fagih, L., & Koç, M. (2021). Asking the right questions for sustainable development goals: Performance assessment approaches for the Qatar education system. *Sustainability (Basel), 13*(7), 3883. Advance online publication. DOI: 10.3390/su13073883

Alliance of Bioversity International and CIAT, & the Senior International Law and Policy Advisor. CARICOM. (2024). *management, technical and scientific cooperation and technology Capacity Building Related to Multilateral Environmental.* https://ssrn.com/abstract=4834159

Apostolopoulos, N., Kakouris, A., Liargovas, P., Borisov, P., Radev, T., Apostolopoulos, S., Daskou, S., & Anastasopoulou, E. (2023). Just Transition Policies, Power Plant Workers and Green Entrepreneurs in Greece, Cyprus and Bulgaria: Can Education and Retraining Meet the Challenge? *Sustainability (Basel), 15*(23), 16307. Advance online publication. DOI: 10.3390/su152316307

Araripe, E., & Zuin Zeidler, V. G. (2024). Advancing sustainable chemistry education: Insights from real-world case studies. *Current Research in Green and Sustainable Chemistry, 9*, 100436. Advance online publication. DOI: 10.1016/j.crgsc.2024.100436

Attal-Juncqua, A., Getz, J., Morhard, R., & Gronvall, G. K. (2024). Integrating safety, security, sustainability, and social responsibility principles into the U.S. bioeconomy. *MSphere, 9*(5), e00084-24. Advance online publication. DOI: 10.1128/msphere.00084-24 PMID: 38687115

Banka Beograd, A. A. (2020). *Časopis Društva ekonomista Beograda (Osnovano 1932.g.).*

Bastos Lima, M. G., & Palme, U. (2022). The Bioeconomy–Biodiversity Nexus: Enhancing or Undermining Nature's Contributions to People? *Conservation*, *2*(1), 7–25. DOI: 10.3390/conservation2010002

Bejinaru, R., Hapenciuc, C. V., Condratov, I., & Stanciu, P. (2018). The University role in developing the human capital for a sustainable bioeconomy. *Amfiteatru Economic*, *20*(49), 583–598. DOI: 10.24818/EA/2018/49/583

Bößner, S., Johnson, F. X., & Shawoo, Z. (2021). Governing the bioeconomy: What role for international institutions? *Sustainability (Basel)*, *13*(1), 1–24. DOI: 10.3390/su13010286

Carvache-Franco, M., Orden-Mejía, M., Carvache-Franco, W., del Carmen Lapo, M., & Carvache-Franco, O. (2022). Gastronomy Motivations as Predictors of Satisfaction at Coastal Destinations. *Sustainability (Basel)*, *14*(18), 11437. Advance online publication. DOI: 10.3390/su141811437

Castilla-Polo, F., Ruiz-Rodríguez, M. C., Moreno, A., Licerán-Gutiérrez, A., de la Fuente, M. C., Rufián, E. C., & Cano-Rodríguez, M. (2020). Classroom learning and the perception of social responsibility amongst graduate students of management accounting. *Sustainability (Basel)*, *12*(17), 7093. Advance online publication. DOI: 10.3390/su12177093

Chanza, N., & De Wit, A. (2016). Enhancing climate governance through indigenous knowledge: Case in sustainability science. *South African Journal of Science*, *112*(3–4), 7. Advance online publication. DOI: 10.17159/sajs.2016/20140286

Cookey, P. E., Peter-Cookey, M. A., Richard, I. U., & Brdanovic, D. (2023). Multi-Level Perceptions on Higher Education Development for Sanitation and Hygiene Management in Nigeria. *Hygiene*, *3*(4), 465–491. DOI: 10.3390/hygiene3040035

Daystar, J., Handfield, R., Golden, J. S., McConnell, E., & Pascual-Gonzalez, J. (2021). An economic impact analysis of the US biobased products industry. *Industrial Biotechnology (New Rochelle, N.Y.)*, *17*(5), 259–270. DOI: 10.1089/ind.2021.29263.jda

de Almeida Barbosa Franco, J., Franco, A.Junior, Battistelle, R. A. G., & Bezerra, B. S. (2024). Dynamic Capabilities: Unveiling Key Resources for Environmental Sustainability and Economic Sustainability, and Corporate Social Responsibility towards Sustainable Development Goals. *Resources*, *13*(2), 22. Advance online publication. DOI: 10.3390/resources13020022 de Jong, W., Huang, K., Zhuo, Y., Kleine, M., Wang, G., Liu, W., & Xu, G. (2021). A comparison of forestry continuing education academic degree programs. *Forests*, *12*(7), 824. Advance online publication. DOI: 10.3390/f12070824

Ecology, S. (1999). *Traditional ecological knowledge and resource management*. Taylor and Francis.

Economic Cooperation, F. M. (BMZ), D. (2023). Protecting the Environment – Ecuador Priority Area. In *BMZ – German Federal Ministry for Economic Cooperation and Development*.

Faulkner, J. P., Murphy, E., & Scott, M. (2024). Downscaling EU bioeconomy policy for national implementation. *Cleaner and Circular Bioeconomy*, *9*, 100121. Advance online publication. DOI: 10.1016/j.clcb.2024.100121

García-Feijoo, M., Eizaguirre, A., & Rica-Aspiunza, A. (2020). Systematic review of sustainable-development-goal deployment in business schools. *Sustainability (Basel)*, *12*(1), 440. Advance online publication. DOI: 10.3390/su12010440

Giannoccaro, I., Ceccarelli, G., & Fraccascia, L. (2021). Features of the Higher Education for the Circular Economy: The Case of Italy. *Sustainability (Basel)*, *13*(20), 11338. Advance online publication. DOI: 10.3390/su132011338

Giurca, A., Nichiforel, L., Stăncioiu, P. T., Drăgoi, M., & Dima, D. P. (2022). Unlocking Romania's Forest-Based Bioeconomy Potential: Knowledge-Action-Gaps and the Way Forward. *Land (Basel)*, *11*(11), 2001. Advance online publication. DOI: 10.3390/land11112001

Grzyb, K. (2017). B. E. A. C. F. and I. Minor. (2017). *Title: Bioenergy Education: A Curriculum Framework and Interdisciplinary Minor*.

Hamid, N. A., Rasul, M. S., & Kamaruzaman, F. M. (2024). Circular Economy and Sustainable Technology in Technical and Vocational Education and Training: A Bibliometric Analysis. *International Journal of Learning. Teaching and Educational Research*, *23*(9), 141–160. DOI: 10.26803/ijlter.23.9.8

Hariram, N. P., Mekha, K. B., Suganthan, V., & Sudhakar, K. (2023). Sustainalism: An Integrated Socio-Economic-Environmental Model to Address Sustainable Development and Sustainability. *Sustainability (Basel)*, *15*(13), 10682. Advance online publication. DOI: 10.3390/su151310682

Hinderer, S., Brändle, L., & Kuckertz, A. (2021). Transition to a sustainable bioeconomy. *Sustainability (Basel)*, *13*(15), 8232. Advance online publication. DOI: 10.3390/su13158232

Högfeldt, A. K., Rosén, A., Mwase, C., Lantz, A., Gumaelius, L., Shayo, E., Lujara, S., & Mvungi, N. (2019). Mutual capacity building through north-south collaboration using challenge-driven education. *Sustainability (Basel), 11*(24), 7236. Advance online publication. DOI: 10.3390/su11247236

Hurst, G. A., Slootweg, J. C., Balu, A. M., Climent-Bellido, M. S., Gomera, A., Gomez, P., Luque, R., Mammino, L., Spanevello, R. A., Saito, K., & Ibanez, J. G. (2019). International Perspectives on Green and Sustainable Chemistry Education via Systems Thinking. *Journal of Chemical Education, 96*(12), 2794–2804. DOI: 10.1021/acs.jchemed.9b00341

Issa, I., Delbrück, S., & Hamm, U. (2019). Bioeconomy from experts' perspectives – Results of a global expert survey. In *PLoS ONE* (Vol. 14, Issue 5). Public Library of Science. DOI: 10.1371/journal.pone.0215917

Ivar Virgin and E. Jane Morris. (2017). *Creating Sustainable Bioeconomies*. www.routledge.com/series/RSEE

Jiménez Aliaga, R., De los Ríos-Carmenado, I., Huamán Cristóbal, A. E., Aliaga Balbín, H., & Marroquín Heros, A. M. (2023). Competencies and Capabilities for the Management of Sustainable Rural Development Projects in the Value Chain: Perception from Small and Medium-Sized Business Agents in Jauja, Peru. *Sustainability (Basel), 15*(21), 15580. Advance online publication. DOI: 10.3390/su152115580

João, E. (2021). *Outcome of the summer school for teachers interested in developing bioeconomy curricula 2 Document information Project name: BE-Rural Project title: Bio-based strategies and roadmaps for enhanced rural and regional development in the EU Internal peer review: Ludmila Metzova, Martin Stoyanov (BIA)*. https://be-rural.eu/.

Juvančič, L., & Van Leeuwen, M. (2021). *Unleashing regional bioeconomy potential: the BioEconomy Regional Strategy Toolkit.*, http://www.berst.eu/RegionalPartners.aspx

Kalnbalkite, A., Pubule, J., & Blumberga, D. (2022). Education for Advancing the Implementation of the Green Deal Goals for Bioeconomy. *Environmental and Climate Technologies, 26*(1), 75–83. DOI: 10.2478/rtuect-2022-0007

Latin American, E. U. – C., & Platform, C. S. (EU-C. (2023). Bioeconomy and Nature-Based Solutions. In *EU-CELAC Platform*.

Lewandowski, I. (2017). Bioeconomy: Shaping the transition to a sustainable, biobased economy. In *Bioeconomy: Shaping the Transition to a Sustainable, Biobased Economy*. Springer International Publishing., DOI: 10.1007/978-3-319-68152-8

Loizides, M. I., Loizidou, X. I., Orthodoxou, D. L., & Petsa, D. (2019). Circular bioeconomy in action: Collection and recycling of domestic used cooking oil through a social, reverse logistics system. *Recycling*, *4*(2), 16. Advance online publication. DOI: 10.3390/recycling4020016

Marquez, R., Barrios, N., Vera, R., Mendez, M. E., Tolosa, L., Zambrano, F., & Li, Y. (2023). *A Perspective on The Synergistic Potential of Artificial Intelligence and Product-Based Learning Strategies in Biobased Materials Education*. https://doi .org/DOI: 10.21203/rs.3.rs-2711749/v1

Mian, S. H., Salah, B., Ameen, W., Moiduddin, K., & Alkhalefah, H. (2020). Adapting universities for sustainability education in industry 4.0: Channel of challenges and opportunities. *Sustainability (Basel)*, *12*(15), 6100. Advance online publication. DOI: 10.3390/su12156100

Núñez-Sánchez, S., & Valente, M. J. (2023). Sustainable Development Goals and Climate Change in Spanish Technology Disciplines' Curricula: From LOMCE to LOMLOE. *Sustainability (Basel)*, *15*(13), 10301. Advance online publication. DOI: 10.3390/su151310301

Ocampo-López, C., Muñoz-Blandón, O., Rendón-Castrillón, L., & Ramírez-Carmona, M. (2023). Post-Digital Learning for Rural Development: A Case Study of Open Biotec MOOCs in Colombia. *Future Internet*, *15*(4), 141. Advance online publication. DOI: 10.3390/fi15040141

Onpraphai, T., Jintrawet, A., Keoboualapha, B., Khuenjai, S., Guo, R., Wang, J., & Fan, J. (2021). Sustaining biomaterials in bioeconomy: Roles of education and learning in mekong river basin. *Forests*, *12*(12), 1670. Advance online publication. DOI: 10.3390/f12121670

Pascoli, D. U., Aui, A., Frank, J., Therasme, O., Dixon, K., Gustafson, R., Kelly, B., Volk, T. A., & Wright, M. M. (2022). The US bioeconomy at the intersection of technology, policy, and education. *Biofuels, Bioproducts & Biorefining*, *16*(1), 9–26. DOI: 10.1002/bbb.2302

Pink, M., Kiełbasa, B., Tamáš, V., Pereira, F. M. D. S. M., Santamarta, J. C., Cruz Pérez, N., Rodríguez-Alcántara, J. S., & Luty, L. (2024). Perception and awareness of the bioeconomy: An empirical study of chosen European academia. *International Journal of Sustainability in Higher Education*, *25*(6), 1137–1155. DOI: 10.1108/IJSHE-01-2023-0002

Priefer, C., Jörissen, J., & Frör, O. (2017). Pathways to shape the bioeconomy. In *Resources* (Vol. 6, Issue 1). Molecular Diversity Preservation International Publishing (MDPI). DOI: 10.3390/resources6010010

Pubule, J., Blumberga, A., Rozakis, S., Vecina, A., Kalnbalkite, A., & Blumberga, D. (2020). Education for advancing the implementation of the bioeconomy goals: An analysis of MASTER study programmes in bioeconomy. *Environmental and Climate Technologies, 24*(2), 149–159. DOI: 10.2478/rtuect-2020-0062

Sacchi, S., Lotti, M., & Branduardi, P. (2021). Education for a biobased economy: Integrating life and social sciences in flexible short courses accessible from different backgrounds. *New Biotechnology, 60*, 72–75. DOI: 10.1016/j.nbt.2020.10.002 PMID: 33039695

Socaciu, C. (2014). Bioeconomy and green economy: European strategies, action plans and impact on life quality. *Bulletin of University of Agricultural Sciences and Veterinary Medicine Cluj-Napoca. Food Science and Technology, 71*(1), 1. www.biofuelstp.eu/. DOI: 10.15835/buasvmcn-fst:10121

Stegmann, P., Londo, M., & Junginger, M. (2020). The circular bioeconomy: Its elements and role in European bioeconomy clusters. In *Resources, Conservation and Recycling: X* (Vol. 6). Elsevier B.V. DOI: 10.1016/j.rcrx.2019.100029

Stilgoe, J., Owen, R., & Macnaghten, P. (2013). Developing a framework for responsible innovation. *Research Policy, 42*(9), 1568–1580. DOI: 10.1016/j.respol.2013.05.008

Takala, T., Tikkanen, J., Haapala, A., Pitkänen, S., Torssonen, P., Valkeavirta, R., & Pöykkö, T. (2019). Shaping the concept of bioeconomy in participatory projects – An example from the post-graduate education in Finland. *Journal of Cleaner Production, 221*, 176–188. DOI: 10.1016/j.jclepro.2019.02.007

Tatar, M., Khrapunenko, M., Henahan, R. K., & Asser, A. (2023). Engaging Citizens in the Bioeconomy: Insights from the Co-Creation and Co-Design in the Development of the Serious Bioeconomy Game "Mission BioHero.". *Sustainability (Basel), 15*(18), 13364. Advance online publication. DOI: 10.3390/su151813364

Tleuken, A., Tokazhanov, G., Jemal, K. M., Shaimakhanov, R., Sovetbek, M., & Karaca, F. (2022). Legislative, Institutional, Industrial and Governmental Involvement in Circular Economy in Central Asia: A Systematic Review. In *Sustainability (Switzerland)* (Vol. 14, Issue 13). MDPI. DOI: 10.3390/su14138064

UNESCO. (2021). Local and Indigenous Knowledge Systems (LINKS) Programme. In *UNESCO*.

Unito, W., Sanna, F., & Fenrich, D. (2020). *Addressing the current and Future skIll needs for sustainability, digitalization and the bio-Economy in agricuLture: European skills agenDa and Strategy D1.1: Stakeholders strategic plans and analysis report Document description Work package title Skills needs identification Status* Partner responsible Author(s).*

Urmetzer, S., Lask, J., Vargas-Carpintero, R., & Pyka, A. (2020). Learning to change: Transformative knowledge for building a sustainable bioeconomy. *Ecological Economics*, *167*, 106435. Advance online publication. DOI: 10.1016/j.ecolecon.2019.106435

Urmetzer, S., Schlaile, M. P., Bogner, K. B., Mueller, M., & Pyka, A. (2018). Exploring the dedicated knowledge base of a transformation towards a sustainable bioeconomy. *Sustainability (Basel)*, *10*(6), 1694. Advance online publication. DOI: 10.3390/su10061694

Venkatesan, M. (2020). The Role of Culture and Moral Responsibility in Facilitating a Sustainable Bioeconomy. In *Sustainable Bioeconomy: Pathways to Sustainable Development Goals* (pp. 11–33). Springer Singapore. DOI: 10.1007/978-981-15-7321-7_2

Vogt, M., & Frankenreiter, I. (2022). Bioeconomy: The Innovative Twin of Sustainability. *Sustainability (Basel)*, *14*(22), 14924. Advance online publication. DOI: 10.3390/su142214924

Vuojärvi, H., Vartiainen, H., Eriksson, M., Ratinen, I., Saramäki, K., Torssonen, P., Vanninen, P., & Pöllänen, S. (2024). Boundaries and boundary crossing in a multidisciplinary online higher education course on forest bioeconomy. *Teaching in Higher Education*, *29*(5), 1197–1214. DOI: 10.1080/13562517.2022.2122791

Vuorio, E., Pernaa, J., & Aksela, M. (2024). Lessons for Sustainable Science Education: A Study on Chemists' Use of Systems Thinking across Ecological, Economic, and Social Domains. *Education Sciences*, *14*(7), 741. Advance online publication. DOI: 10.3390/educsci14070741

Výbošťok, J., Navrátilová, L., Dobšinská, Z., Dúbravská, B., Giertliová, B., Aláč, P., Suja, M., & Šálka, J. (2022). Bioeconomy perception by students of different study programs - study from Slovakia. *Central European Forestry Journal*, *68*(2), 91–100. DOI: 10.2478/forj-2021-0025

Warnants Promotor, T. (2012). *Bachelor's thesis supply and students' views on online international studies in the eu in english at a higher education level related to bioeconomy, renewable energy and circular economy.*

Watkinson, I. I., Bridgwater, A. V., & Luxmore, C. (2012). Advanced education and training in bioenergy in Europe. *Biomass and Bioenergy*, *38*, 128–143. DOI: 10.1016/j.biombioe.2011.06.038

Wei, X., Luo, J., Pu, A., Liu, Q., Zhang, L., Wu, S., Long, Y., Leng, Y., Dong, Z., & Wan, X. (2022). From Biotechnology to Bioeconomy: A Review of Development Dynamics and Pathways. In *Sustainability (Switzerland)* (Vol. 14, Issue 16). MDPI. DOI: 10.3390/su141610413

Wohlgemuth, R., Twardowski, T., & Aguilar, A. (2021). Bioeconomy moving forward step by step – A global journey. *New Biotechnology*, *61*, 22–28. DOI: 10.1016/j.nbt.2020.11.006 PMID: 33197617

Wydra, S. (2019). Value chains for industrial biotechnology in the bioeconomy-innovation system analysis. *Sustainability (Basel)*, *11*(8), 2435. Advance online publication. DOI: 10.3390/su11082435

Zhang, T., Shaikh, Z. A., Yumashev, A. V., & Chład, M. (2020). Applied model of E-learning in the framework of education for sustainable development. *Sustainability (Basel)*, *12*(16), 6420. Advance online publication. DOI: 10.3390/su12166420

Zou, J., Su, S., Wang, F., & Chen, X. (2024). Navigating the Changing Landscape of Agricultural Economics Education: Lessons for China and Beyond. *Pakistan Journal of Agricultural Sciences*, *61*(3), 703–713. DOI: 10.21162/PAKJAS/24.36

Chapter 11

The Contribution of a Touristic Destination's Soundscape to a Holistic Approach to Sustainability

Christina Alavanou
https://orcid.org/0009-0008-9997-322X
University of the Aegean, Greece

Panoraia Poulaki
https://orcid.org/0000-0002-2226-1557
University of the Aegean, Greece

ABSTRACT

This research examines the role of soundscape in sustainable tourism and its potential to enhance Greece's appeal as a leading destination for eco-friendly travel. Soundscape, consisting of natural, cultural, and social sounds, plays a significant role in enriching the visitor experience, creating a relaxing atmosphere, and leaving lasting memories. In today's tourism industry, where sustainability is increasingly prioritized, the role of sensory experiences, including sound, in shaping travelers' perceptions has gained more recognition. Visitors seek destinations that offer more than just visual beauty—they also look for environments that nurture well-being, providing restorative and immersive experiences that are in harmony with nature.

DOI: 10.4018/979-8-3373-9923-2.ch011

INTRODUCTION

Soundscape plays a vital yet often underestimated role in sustainable development, blending the natural, cultural, and social auditory elements of a location into an engaging sensory experience. As the global tourism industry shifts toward sustainability, soundscape gains prominence in crafting distinctive and impactful travel experiences. This research focuses on the potential of soundscape to enhance sustainable tourism, with a particular emphasis on its capacity to strengthen Greece's reputation as a top destination for environmentally responsible travel. By exploring the interplay between natural and cultural sound elements, the research highlights how soundscapes can enhance travelers' connections to their environment.

Greece, renowned for its rich cultural heritage, stunning landscapes, and hospitality, offers an abundance of auditory experiences that can further elevate its tourism appeal. The country's diverse environments, from busy cities to peaceful island getaways, offer a chance to make soundscape a key part of sustainable tourism. By including soundscape in tourism planning, Greece can improve visitors' experiences while supporting the environment, preserving culture and benefiting local communities.

Through a comprehensive review of existing literature and primary data collection, the research identifies key factors that influence the auditory dimension of travel, including noise management and the impact of natural soundscape on mental and physical relaxation. By examining Greece's soundscape across varied geographical and cultural contexts, this research shows how auditory elements can be used to support sustainable tourism.

Policy recommendations and practical measures are proposed to enhance Greece's soundscape, ranging from reducing noise pollution in urban areas to promoting eco-friendly tourism practices. The findings underscore the potential of soundscape not only to enrich travel experiences but also to position Greece at a higher level in global sustainable tourism by offering travelers a harmonious blend of nature, culture, and serenity.

USEFULNESS AND ORIGINALITY OF THE RESEARCH

Alternative forms of tourism are grounded in sustainability and have emerged as a response to mass tourism. A principal characteristic of alternative tourism is the respect and protection of nature, the promotion of social values, and the enhancement of the local population's quality of life, as well as, among other aspects, physical and mental rejuvenation. According to the World Tourism Organization (UNWTO), sustainable tourism is defined as "tourism that fully takes into account the current and future economic, social, and environmental impacts, and responds to the needs of visitors, the industry, and the communities in host destinations."

The significance of this research lies in examining the contribution of soundscapes to a holistic approach to sustainability and the principles of sustainable development. It evaluates visitors' preferences while highlighting the important connection between a destination's unique soundscape and the quality of vacations, relaxation, recreation, and the authentic sense of hospitality. This is achieved by capturing sounds and images not only of nature but also of the local culture. The study reveals that the recording of sounds of nature, the local population, language, and other elements of a place's soundscape can instill in the visitor a desire to return, rewarding them for their unique experience—since each soundscape is inherently unique.

This research investigates how soundscape influences travel decisions, enhances visitor experiences, and promotes repeat visits to Greece. Through primary research, the study analyzes how soundscapes affect travel planning, experience evaluation, and perceptions of the acoustic environment. It also explores the relationship between everyday sounds, such as urban noise and work environments, and travelers' preferences, memories, and motivations, assessing their connection to the soundscape.

LITERATURE REVIEW

Definitions – Key Principles – Characteristics – Properties

The official definition of the term "soundscape," according to ISO 12913-1, was introduced in 2014, and it defines soundscape as: "the acoustic environment as perceived, experienced, or understood by one or more individuals."

The term was first used by graduate student Michael Southworth in 1969 in a scientific paper on the acoustic environment of cities. Specifically, the paper focused on the development of soundscape recording techniques, the study of sound quality and its interaction over time with the evolution of urban environments, the study of the characteristics of soundscapes as perceived by humans, experimental techniques for soundscape analysis and the relationship between urban sound design and the establishment of planning criteria.

In 1973, Canadian composer Murray Schafer, a professor at Simon Fraser University, published the recording *The Vancouver Soundscape* after three years of detailed study with a group of students on the degradation of Vancouver's soundscape. During this research, he examined the relationship between humans and the sounds of their environment and the changes occurring over time, coining the term "soundscape."

According to M. Schaffer, "the natural and artificial sounds of our environment constitute an acoustic landscape – a soundscape." Schaffer placed the study of soundscapes at the intersection of science, society, and the arts, investigating acoustics, psychoacoustics, the relationship between humans and sound, the influence of human behavior, and the creation of both real and imagined soundscapes.

In 1978, Schaffer and his colleague Barry Truax, a professor at Simon Fraser University, published the "World Soundscape Project," an international research initiative that examined Canada's acoustic ecology through soundscape studies, noise measurements, acoustic communication diagrams, psychoacoustics, and environmental acoustics.

This project led to numerous research studies globally on noise pollution and the documentation of soundscapes. In 1987, Barry Truax defined soundscape as "an environment of sound (or acoustic environment) with a focus on how it is perceived and understood by individuals or society."

For Bernie Krause, the soundscape consists of "signature sources," referring to the unique identity and quality of each sound and the amount of information it reveals, creating a distinct signature. Therefore, each soundscape is entirely different from any other. As indicated by Bernie Krause, each sound, no matter its source, has a unique acoustic signature. This signature contains valuable information that can be analyzed.

For Almo Farina (2014), the soundscape is defined as "the total sound energy produced in a landscape, resulting from three sound sources: biophony, geophony, and anthropophony." The combination of these sound sources is referred to as a "sonotope" environment, which can vary depending on weather conditions and the season.

The soundscape refers to the acoustic environment, including both natural sounds, like animal calls, and human-made sounds, such as music, speech, and industrial noises like machinery. (Ekmetsoglou, 2014)

Soundscape and Acoustic Environment While the concept of soundscape shares certain similarities with that of the acoustic environment, they are not identical. Schaffer differentiates between these two concepts. The acoustic environment, as he sees it, includes all auditory inputs, whereas the soundscape emerges from the ways humans engage with, connect to, and interact with this acoustic environment.

David Schwarz (1997) explains that listening involves understanding music's ideas, history, culture, and emotions. He notes that people hear and interpret sounds in different ways. These differences are shaped by their social and educational backgrounds.

Sound serves as how individuals connect with their surroundings. It is the mechanism that activates the body to awaken and is continuously engaged in daily life. According to psychologists, the sound environment also constitutes an individual's primary psychological space. Psychoanalyst Guy Rosolato (1986) asserts that the acoustic environment is intrinsically linked to all our auditory experiences.

According to the European Landscape Convention (Law 3827/2010), a landscape is defined as "an area, as perceived by people, whose character is the result of the action and interaction of natural and/or human factors." Rodaway (2002) further elaborates that the concept of "landscape" encompasses both elements of observation and analysis, thereby distancing the observer from a static representation.

A landscape may captivate through its aesthetic qualities, including the combination of vegetation and geomorphological features, its colors, and the dynamic changes it undergoes. It represents a synthesis of nature and human culture (cultural landscape), from which one can derive insights into customs, religious beliefs, traditions, daily life, and the overall way of life of the people inhabiting it.

Aural Characteristics - The significance of Sounds Similar to how an event has a duration (comprising a beginning, middle, and end) and occurs at a specific location, sound events take place within a distinct time and space. These sound events are generated by both living organisms and natural elements.

According to M. Schafer, the characteristics of the soundscape are shaped by keynote sounds, sound signals, and soundmarks. Each soundscape is composed of unique and original tones, forming a collective set of sound events. The tones are identified as sound signals.

Keynote sounds are the background noises of a place produced by geographical features and climatic conditions, such as animals, forests, and bodies of water. They shape the overall sound of the environment but are usually heard without us noticing.

Sound signals are subconsciously captured in our perception. For example, the sounds of bells and sirens, alarms, or conversations, standing out from the ambient soundscape. Soundmarks, on the other hand, represent the characteristic sounds of the area in which we live, comparable to landmarks in a landscape, which hold cultural or historical significance. A soundmark is a distinct sound event that uniquely characterizes a specific place. Through these soundmarks, an identity is created, giving a travel destination with a sense of distinctiveness and uniqueness. These sounds are representative of the local environment and are primarily perceived by the inhabitants of that region.

Marine and Terrestrial Soundscapes Humans are inherently connected to the sea. The sound of the sea and water is frequently used in music therapy, concentration exercises, relaxation, and well-being practices. Additionally, it evokes feelings of rest and carefree enjoyment—emotions that are often significant elements in the concept of vacation.

In Greece, the sound of the sea is a common companion during a trip. Due to the size of the islands, the variety of coastlines, and the country's diverse landscapes, the sound of the sea accompanies us from place to place. Among our memories, there is the sound of waves on beaches, the splash of waves hitting the bow of a ship, the flowing waters of a waterfall, and many others.

The sounds of rain and wind also have healing effects. The vocal variations of wind are numerous. Climate and geographical location are factors that alter a soundscape. Even a mountain in Crete, compared to the mountains of Pindus, will produce a different sound. The same applies to a mountain in a different country.

The wind can either hide or make other sounds louder. For example, the sound of a lone traveler's footsteps in the snow in a quiet part of Russia would stand out, while the sound of footsteps on the cobblestone streets of the medieval castle in Rhodes might be drowned out by a loud bang from shutters hitting the wall due to a strong wind.

The sound of birds is also a sound that positively influences human imagination, making it one of the most pleasant sounds to the human ear. When the life in a forest changes, its soundscape also changes. The noise from timber, the woodcutter's axe, and the sound of chainsaws cutting trees slowly sets off a chain reaction in the overall sound of the forest. Bernie Krause has spent years studying changes in soundscapes in forests. In his recordings, he observed and documented the changes (dissonance) over time and sometimes concluded that the intensity of bird and animal sounds had decreased by 50%.

Through the "Sounds of the Forest" website, created for the Timber Festival (a festival celebrating humanity's connection with trees), it is possible to listen to the different sounds of forests from around the world, including in Greece, such as on Samothrace, Mount Olympus, the Pindus National Park, Cephalonia, Karpenisi, Xanthi, and others. The site offers an immersive experience, allowing visitors to explore the natural soundscapes of these regions, further enhancing the understanding of how diverse and unique each forest environment can be. The auditory experience contributes to the appreciation of the forest's role in both environmental sustainability and cultural significance.

The sound of human interactions also defines the soundscape of a region and country. Northern cities are typically quieter, with winter being more silent, reducing human activity sounds in parks and squares. Moreover, snow absorbs sound. In Mediterranean countries, human activity is more intense. We often hear human speech in municipal markets, playgrounds, restaurants and coffee shops, people talking in the neighborhood, conversations as passing by a house, people chatting while walking, young people socializing in a park, people having conversations in the bus stations or outside a bank, etc. The human voice reflects aspects of people's culture.

Sound walks are designed to observe sounds and the environment, gather information and connect people with the sounds of nature that they may have learned to ignore. For instance, in a tourist shopping mall, one can focus on the various languages spoken and try to recognize them. Westerkamp Hildegard, one of the founding members of the World Forum for Acoustic Ecology and a participant in the World Soundscape Project, contributes to the concept of sound walks: "Listen to our cities as indigenous people listen to their forests."

In urban planning, improving the acoustic identity of cities is an important goal. The UNISCPAPE (European Network of Universities dedicated to landscape studies and education according to the principles of the European Landscape Convention) emphasizes the importance of soundscapes for the need of a subjecting analysis of urban planning.

Studies on the sound of car traffic involve three key parameters: vehicle sound, vehicle count, and vehicle speed. According to the European Environment Agency (EEA 2020), although manufacturers are striving to reduce the noise levels produced by cars, their numbers will continue to rise, leading to a persistent negative trend in traffic sound levels.

The Concept of Noise - Acoustic Ecology Noise impacts human health, hearing, and mental well-being. These impacts are influenced by intensity, duration, and exposure time. According to Schafer, noise is characterized as an undesirable sound, while Robert Koch, in the early 20th century, presciently stated, "One day, mankind will combat noise with the same resolve it fights cholera and plague."

Noise is recognized as a contributor to the economic decline of regions, a matter with legal dimensions, and a significant public health risk. It is examined not only as an environmental challenge but also as a political issue (Truax, 1994). Truax (1994) suggested that sounds can be perceived as noise when the listening environment becomes too disrupted by acoustic masking, reducing harmony. For instance, the maximum permissible noise level in urban areas is 65 dB, the sound of birdsong averages 45 dB, and a car horn can reach 110 db.

Numerous studies on noise levels have been conducted since the 1960s. The overlap of soundscape elements may occur when noise intensity peaks, exceeding the auditory carrying capacity. However, individual perceptions and auditory responses to sound vary depending on listening habits, acoustic and psychoacoustic factors, as well as ethnographic characteristics.

Some musical genres have been associated to the idea of noise. Architect Le Corbusier, whose 17 works have been designated UNESCO World Heritage Sites, likened jazz music to noise. His urban planning philosophy emphasized the necessity of "sky, space, trees, steel, and concrete, in that order and hierarchy."

Acoustic ecology, also known as soundscape ecology, is a field that studies the relationship between people and the surrounding sounds. Pioneers like R. Murray Schafer, Barry Truax, and Hildegard Westerkamp developed this discipline to explore how soundscapes—the unique acoustic environments of an area—shape and reflect ecological, cultural, and social systems. The field highlights the importance of protecting soundscapes as essential for environmental health and human well-being.

A key idea in acoustic ecology is active listening. By paying attention to the sounds in an environment, individuals can better understand the natural processes and cultural identities connected to those sounds. This practice raises environmental awareness and encourages sustainable actions to reduce noise pollution, which is a growing problem in both natural and urban settings.

Noise pollution, defined as excessive or unwanted sound, can harm both ecosystems and human health. For wildlife, it disrupts communication, migration, and reproduction, while for humans, it can cause stress, sleep problems, and other health issues. The rapid increase in noise pollution also reduces the clarity of natural soundscapes, diminishing their quality.

Organizations like the Hellenic Society for Acoustic Ecology (HSAAE) and the World Forum for Acoustic Ecology (WFAE) work to address these challenges. In Greece, HSAAE collaborates with the Laboratory of Electroacoustic Music and Applications (LEMA) at the Ionian University. These groups research soundscapes, promote environmental listening, and develop strategies to protect the acoustic environment. Their activities include public education, soundscape composition, and advocating for integrating acoustic ecology into urban planning and tourism.

Protecting soundscapes through noise reduction, awareness campaigns, and policy-making supports healthier communities and preserves the cultural and ecological value of our surroundings. By embracing the principles of acoustic ecology, we can create more sustainable and harmonious environments.

CHARACTERISTICS AND PROPERTIES OF SOUND SOURCES

1) Origin of Sounds

In his 2015 book *Voices of the Wild*, Bernie Krause talks about a system he developed with Stuart Gage from Michigan State University to categorize the main sounds that make up a soundscape. They divided these sounds into three main types. These three types of sounds create the soundscape of an area. Understanding these sounds can help us learn more about the health of ecosystems and how human activity affects nature.

The first type is geophony, which includes non-living sounds made by the environment. Examples of this are the wind through trees, ocean waves, or thunder. The second type is biophony, which refers to sounds made by living creatures in the environment. This can include animal calls, birds singing, or insects buzzing. The third type is anthrophony, which refers to sounds made by humans. This includes noises like machines, traffic, and people talking.

As part of the World Soundscape Project, R. Murray Schafer and his team created a system called "families of sounds" to categorize the different types of sounds in the environment. This system, introduced in 1977, helps us understand the variety of sounds around us and how they impact our perception and experiences. By grouping sounds into categories, Schafer aimed to make it easier to study the soundscape and its effects on people.

The first category is natural sounds, which are sounds that occur in nature without any human involvement (wind blowing through trees, birds singing, rivers flowing, and animal sounds). Natural sounds are especially important in rural and natural areas, helping create a connection to the environment.

The second category is human sounds, which includes any sounds made by humans - talking, walking, laughing, and sounds from human activities like working or playing. Human sounds are most noticeable in cities, where they can mix with other sounds, sometimes making it hard to hear natural sounds.

Mechanical sounds is another category, which refers to sounds made by machines and technology, like the noise of vehicles, machinery, and electronic devices. As technology has advanced, mechanical sounds have become a common part of modern life, often contributing to noise pollution in cities.

Schafer also includes other categories like sounds and society, quiet and silence, and sounds as signals. Sounds and society focus on how sounds are used in social situations, such as music, rituals, or public announcements. Quiet and silence are also important, as moments of quiet provide rest and clarity. Finally, sounds as signals refer to sounds used to communicate important information, like alarms, sirens, or bells, which alert us to danger or other important events.

Schafer's system helps us understand the different types of sounds around us and how they affect our daily lives. By categorizing sounds, we can better appreciate how they shape our environment and well-being. This understanding is important for creating better urban spaces and preserving natural areas, ensuring that the soundscapes we experience are enjoyable and healthy.

2) Foreground and Background Sounds

Schafer distinguished between foreground (or surface) sounds and background sounds (keynotes), based on their importance as acoustic events. Foreground sounds are those that remain in our constant awareness. They are usually more prominent and capture our attention, such as a conversation, a bird singing, or the honking of a car horn. These sounds are dynamic and tend to stand out in each environment.

Background sounds, however, are present but not consistently noticed, even though they form an essential part of the acoustic environment. While they are still significant, they often fade into the background, such as the hum of an air conditioner, distant chatter, or traffic noise. Over time, background sounds have increased, especially in urban and industrial areas, as traffic and technological advancements have grown.

In Western cultures, which are predominantly visually oriented, people have become conditioned to overlook certain sounds, treating them as mere "background noise." This means that we may no longer pay much attention to these sounds, even though they play a vital role in shaping the surrounding atmosphere. While this can help us focus on more pressing auditory stimuli, it can also lead to a decreased awareness of our surroundings.

Ignoring background sounds, particularly noise pollution, can have negative effects on our well-being. It can contribute to stress, sleep disturbances, and even hearing loss over time, as we become desensitized to these ongoing environmental sounds. Therefore, Schafer's distinction highlights the balance between sounds that demand attention and those that quietly form the backdrop of our lives.

3) Hi-Fi and Lo-Fi Soundscapes **.** Soundscapes can be categorized into high fidelity (Hi-fi) and low fidelity (Lo-fi) soundscapes, as described by Schafer (1999) and Truax (1994). Hi-fi soundscapes are typically found in natural environments, like forests, mountains, or rural areas, where both nearby and distant sounds are clear and distinct. In these environments, sounds are sharp and easy to identify, offering a rich and detailed auditory experience.

The clarity of these soundscapes allows us to perceive the environment more fully. Hi-fi soundscapes are also more sensitive to changes in the weather, such as wind or rain, which can change the sounds we hear and enhance the interactive quality of the soundscape.

In contrast, Lo-fi soundscapes have lower sound quality. These environments often have noise, distortion, or other imperfections that make the sounds less clear. For example, urban areas, busy streets, or industrial zones typically have more background noise, like traffic or machinery, that can obscure individual sounds. Lo-fi soundscapes can feel rough or unpolished because of this constant background noise. In these environments, it is harder to focus on specific sounds or hear the finer details, as the noise tends to blend.

Schafer used these terms to show how we experience different sound environments. Hi-fi soundscapes are clearer and more distinct, while Lo-fi soundscapes are more chaotic and difficult to separate. This distinction helps explain why some environments feel peaceful and immersive, while others can feel overwhelming or cluttered with noise.

Social and Cultural Perceptions of Noise According to Pierre Schaeffer, the auditory process is a dynamic interaction between humans, reality, technology, and imagination. Unlike Murray Schafer, Schaeffer focuses on the environment created by sound itself, rather than its connection to the surrounding environment.

Schaeffer's approach to sound emphasizes how we experience and perceive sound, focusing on its qualities and the way it shapes our surroundings. He introduced the idea of “reduced listening,” which encourages listeners to focus on the sound itself, without considering its source. This allows for a deeper understanding of sound, as it becomes something to explore on its own, rather than just a signal or message. In spaces like archaeological museums, background sounds are often intentionally removed. This absence of sound can make even the smallest noises, like a visitor’s footsteps, stand out. While some people find this “silence” peaceful and calming, others may find it uncomfortable or even unsettling.

The lack of sound can evoke feelings of loneliness or isolation, which can negatively affect the visitor's experience. In social settings, silence can create awkwardness or tension. Research on silence in archaeological settings reveals mixed responses. Some visitors appreciate the quiet, finding it helps them focus and connect with the exhibits. Others feel that the lack of sound makes the space feel empty or disconnected, taking away from the experience. These differing reactions highlight the importance of considering how silence or background noise can influence how people engage with a space.

Soundscape and Culture Music serves as a universal code of communication, capable of uniting people and nationalities from all corners of the world. Each place has its unique sound. For example, the sound of the lyre is often associated with Crete. For instance, the lyre's music is frequently linked to Crete. Yet, hearing its melody in the United States could spark someone's interest in traveling to Greece.

Additionally, sounds reveal insights into daily life, human emotions, moments of joy and sorrow, challenges, and celebrations. Beyond festivities, sounds accompany interactions with the sacred and the divine. For example, listening to the sitar's melody might be associated with India, where the instrument plays a significant role in the country's religion and culture. Similarly, the imam chanting daily in Muslim countries forms part of the local soundscape, reflecting elements of daily life and religious practice.

Tourism showcases cultural activities through traditional settings, music, and theater, contributing to the preservation and revival of folklore (festivals, fairs, etc.). The music of a region often serves as a narrative tool, conveying aspects not only of its history but also of its folklore and culture. The influences of each country’s history on its musical evolution reveal its cultural and historical trajectory.

PEOPLE AND SOUNDSCAPE

1) Ways of Listening

According to Schwarz (1997), the ways of listening refer to the process of analyzing the philosophical, psychological, political, historical, and theoretical dimensions of music and sound. Schwarz argues that there are several distinct ways of listening, each offering a different approach to perceiving and interacting with sound. These include active, passive, critical, reflective, and empathetic listening. Each mode allows for varying levels of engagement and interpretation, with some listeners focusing deeply on the sound, while others might only engage with it peripherally or contextually.

Active listening involves a high level of focus and attention, where the listener engages fully with the sound, often analyzing its components and meaning. Passive listening, on the other hand, involves a more relaxed or involuntary listening experience, where the listener may be aware of the sound but does not actively engage with it. Critical listening goes further by involving judgment and evaluation, where the listener may critique the sound based on certain criteria. Reflective listening encourages the listener to think about how the sound makes them feel or what it makes them think. Lastly, empathetic listening involves understanding and connecting emotionally with the sound, often putting oneself in the position of the source or the creator of the sound.

Almo Farina (2014) suggests that these ways of listening can vary based on an individual's social and educational background, indicating that personal experiences and cultural context shape how people perceive and interpret sound. Farina emphasizes the importance of sound as a crucial element in modern communication and information processing, suggesting that it functions not only as a boundary for interaction but also as a means of engaging listeners on a deeper level. Sound is integral to how we process information and relate to our environment, offering a rich layer of meaning and emotional resonance.

Barry Truax (1994) categorizes listening into three types: background listening, alert listening, and searching listening. Background listening is passive, occurring when sound is present in the environment but not actively focused on, such as when music plays in the background of a café. Alert listening requires more attention, such as when a person hears a bus passing by on the street and needs to respond or interpret the sound. Finally, searching listening is fully engaged, where the listener focuses entirely on a specific sound, like listening for a referee's whistle during a soccer match. This type of listening demands the listener's full concentration and is often goal oriented.

These categories and methods of listening highlight the dynamic relationship between sound, perception, and context. The way we listen shapes how we interact with the world around us and the experiences we have. Each form of listening provides a unique opportunity to engage with sound in different environments, whether for understanding, enjoyment, or practical purposes. As sound becomes an increasingly important part of communication, especially in urban environments, these ways of listening allow individuals to process auditory information in diverse ways, adapting their listening habits to their surroundings and needs.

2) Psychoacoustics – Bioacoustics

Psychoacoustics is a branch of psychophysics and acoustics that studies the various ways in which individual auditory systems perceive soundscape. The way a person perceives a sound, including speech or music, may differ in intensity and timbre from another person's perception. Additionally, hearing limits are different for each organism. The human ear can distinguish approximately 1,400 frequencies and 280 distinct sound levels.

A key factor in perception is the suddenness of a sound and the frequency of exposure to it. For example, an elderly woman who has lived in a village for many years and visits her children in the city after a long time may be surprised by the honk of a car while walking along a busy street. In contrast, a long-time city resident is used to such sudden sounds, such as a bus horn, since they are frequent in their daily life. Therefore, auditory ability varies based on sound intensity, suddenness, and the listener's capacity to process sound.

Bioacoustics combines acoustics and biology, focusing on the study of sounds produced according to anatomical characteristics. It examines how organisms communicate through the understanding and production of sounds, with sound serving as a medium for transmitting information. For animals, their acoustic abilities are essential for communication and survival.

Organisms evolved with the necessity to produce and receive sounds. Some species share similarities in their acoustic communication, while others produce similar sounds. Another phenomenon observed in research is the change in voice tonality depending on the environment. Studies began around 1920, initiated by some ornithologists who recorded bird sounds. Shortly afterward, Ludwig Koch, while working at the BBC, recorded bird sounds in Great Britain and introduced the modern concept of "bioacoustics," which is also referred to as the "acoustic niche hypothesis".

In the 1980s, studies continued, and Koch, along with his colleague Ruth Happel, observed that, through the composition of a wild soundscape, each organism's evolution aimed to "be heard" at a specific frequency and time. A critical condition for an organism to be heard is that its sound does not overlap with other sound signals in the same time frame or acoustic space.

Studies on the interaction of sound sources continue today. Notably, recent studies have shown that birds in urban environments tend to alter their vocal cords (University of Urbino, Italy), and killer whales are impacted by ship noise (Krause, 2015).

3) Landscape Ecology

The European Landscape Convention (Law 3827/2010) defines landscape as "an area, as perceived by people, whose character is shaped by the interaction of natural and human factors." This definition emphasizes the dynamic relationship between the environment and human influence. In this context, landscape is more than just a visual scene; it is an interactive process that involves both observation and analysis (Rodaway, 2002).

Landscapes can be found in various forms, including urban areas, forests, and natural environments. They are shaped by a mix of factors such as industrial development, environmental conditions, living organisms (animals, plants, and other life forms), and non-living elements (soil, water, and climate). Each landscape can evoke different emotional or aesthetic responses based on these elements. The visual qualities, including the arrangement of vegetation, landforms, and colors, can also enhance its overall appeal.

Landscape ecology examines how landscapes function within a larger system, particularly focusing on human interaction with nature. A landscape reflects both natural processes and human activity, resulting in what is often called a "cultural landscape." Over time, human activities—such as agriculture, construction, and industrial development—have significantly influenced the appearance and function of these areas. Additionally, landscapes offer insights into cultural and societal practices, providing valuable information about people's ways of life, customs, and beliefs. By analyzing landscapes in this way, we gain a deeper understanding of how human culture and the environment shape one another.

Conclusions and Research *Methodological Approach* The methodological approach of the research is based on qualitative data analysis, aiming to study the role of soundscape in shaping the identity of tourist destinations in Greece. The focus is on evaluating the effects of sound on the tourism experience and the connection between soundscape and the strategic promotion of the tourist product. The research seeks to understand the role of soundscape in shaping the identity of tourist destinations in Greece, with an emphasis on assessing the impact of sound on the tourist experience and its relation to the tourist product.

The sample consists of tourists, Greek visitors, and students from music schools. The research was conducted on various islands and regions of Greece, with data collected through questionnaires distributed in both paper and electronic forms. The sample was selected based on participants' travel experience and their knowledge of soundscape.

The questionnaire includes both closed and open-ended questions, covering four main areas: demographic details, the relationship between soundscape and marketing/ branding, traveler preferences, and suggestions for improvement.

For the purposes of this quantitative research with purposive sampling, various methods of data summarization were employed. The analysis was conducted using descriptive statistics, variable correlation, and parametric tests, such as the Chi-square test and Spearman's correlation coefficient. Open-ended responses were grouped according to the literature and participants' experiences.

The aim of the analysis is to draw conclusions about the influence of soundscape on the tourism experience and tourists' preferences, as well as to identify ways to improve the Greek soundscape as a tool for tourism strategy.

Data Collection The research results were derived from three distinct groups. The first group consists of tourists who visited the islands of Kos, Rhodes, Kalymnos, and Nisyros. The second group is domestic tourists from various regions of Greece and the third group consists of students from music schools, who had a background or experience in music and were familiar with sound-related topics. The sample included tourists and music school students from Greece (69.7%), who were part of the second and third research groups.

The sample of the first group consisted of tourists from various countries, such as Belgium (1.5%), France (2.6%), Netherlands (8.7%), Germany (6.4%), Denmark (1.2%), The United States (0.9%), United Kingdom (0.9%), Finland (2.0%), Sweden (3.5%), Spain (0.6%), Italy (1.2%),

Regarding the gender distribution from the total sample of 343 people, 185 participants were women, and 158 were men. The 90.4% of the respondents were up to 55 years old, a demographic imbalance caused by the mobility challenges caused by the pandemic. As for their educational background of the responders: 48 were primary school graduates, 78 were middle school graduates, 57 were high school graduates, 42 were Vocational Training Insitute graduates (IEK), 60 were University/ College graduates and 58 were holders of a master's or doctoral degree.

FINDINGS FROM THE RESEARCH INQUIRES

Travel Planning, Evaluation of Travel Experience and of the Acoustic Environment

The conclusions drawn from the empirical research indicate that soundscapes significantly influence both travel planning and the evaluation of travel experiences. Travel planning is often initiated through personal research. Visitors who engage in independent research and occasionally consult travel agencies tend to prioritize the soundscape when selecting a travel destination.

These individuals often form expectations about the acoustic environment of a destination before their visit. They may be attracted to places that they associate with a specific set of sounds, whether it be the peaceful sounds of nature, the vibrancy of urban environments, or the lively atmosphere of tourist attractions. In contrast, visitors who rely heavily on advertisements to plan their trips are less likely to prioritize the soundscape in their decision-making process. This suggests that personal engagement in trip planning leads to a deeper appreciation or interest in the sensory experiences a destination offers.

When evaluating the travel experience, the most prominent memories visitors recall are often related to the landscape and entertainment activities. These elements significantly contribute to the overall impression and enjoyment of the trip. Additionally, travelers who frequently choose European destinations tend to associate their most vivid memories with personal interactions, such as conversations with locals or cultural exchanges.

These interpersonal experiences, along with the surrounding soundscape, create lasting impressions that influence the traveler's perception of the destination and overall satisfaction with the trip. Therefore, the acoustic environment, when considered a part of the travel experience, can have a profound impact on a visitor's memories and the emotional connections they form with a place.

Soundscape as a Criterion for Selecting a Travel Destination The results are derived from the research of the relationship between visitors who choose Europe as their destination and the variable related to their first memory when reminiscing about their vacation.

For tourists traveling to Europe, the most significant memories are associated with the landscape - nature, mountains, sea - and nightlife, with each accounting for 28.9% of responses. Culture and people ranked third (18.8%), followed by the acoustic environment and the overall atmosphere. The results show that the first vacation memory and the soundscape as a travel motivator are interdependent variables, meaning these two aspects are closely related.

For repeaters traveling frequently to Europe, the top memory (28.4%) is culture and people, followed by nightlife (21%) and the atmosphere and acoustic environment (19.8%). Responses from different countries showed interesting differences.

Visitors from Denmark and the United Kingdom most frequently remembered the human element (66.7%). Finnish tourists gave the same response (42.9%). Italian tourists primarily recalled entertainment (68.9%). Swedish visitors (50%) most vividly remembered the atmosphere, including the acoustic environment and visuals. Greek visitors identified entertainment (31.8%) and the landscape (30.5%) as their most prominent memories, followed by the atmosphere (16.7%) and people (16.3%).

In conclusion, for tourists traveling to Europe, the most prominent memories are linked to the landscape, such as nature, mountains, and the sea, as well as nightlife, with cultural elements and the acoustic environment following closely behind. These findings suggest that visitors' first memories are shaped by the sensory experiences associated with the destination.

Additionally, the study reveals that repeat visitors to Europe tend to prioritize culture and people as their top memories, highlighting the importance of human interaction in shaping memorable experiences. While some groups, like visitors from Denmark and the UK, recall the human element more often, others, such as Italian tourists, focus on entertainment. It is highlighted how both the environment and social experiences shape travel memories, with sound playing an important role in a destination's overall appeal. Understanding these factors can help improve destinations and make visitors more satisfied.

Overall, the research demonstrates that tourists' first memories of their vacations are deeply influenced by the environmental and social aspects of the destinations, including the acoustic qualities of the location that are shaping their travel experience. Landscapes, including nature, mountains, and the sea, along with nightlife, emerge as the most prominent memories for first-time visitors, while cultural elements and the acoustic environment also play pivotal roles.

Preferences for Shaping the Soundscape by type of Tourist Travelers who gather information about their travel destination through personal research are more likely to choose that destination. The data also show that visitors primarily obtain information through personal research (136 responses) and through friends or acquaintances who have visited the destination (113 responses). The next most common method was through travel agencies (66 responses), with travel guides (8 responses) and advertisements (6 responses) being the least common. Travelers who rely on personal research are more likely to choose a destination, with advice from friends or acquaintances also playing an important role. Independent travelers, particularly those visiting Greece, often recall the natural sounds of the environment as a key part of their trip.

Musical awareness also influences positive experiences, especially in museums and archaeological sites, where silence is appreciated more by individuals with a strong interest in music. Regarding the respondents' musical perception and their experience of silence in museums and archaeological sites, the results indicate a connection between higher musical perception and more positive feelings associated with silence in these spaces. The response "I like it" was the most common, while the neutral response, "sometimes I like silence, sometimes I do not," decreased as musical perception increased. It is also noteworthy that 46.3% of respondents stated that they "really like" the silence in museums and archaeological sites.

As daily life is shaped by various sounds associated with both the work environment and the urban surroundings, research has been conducted to examine the relationship between the work environment and perceptions of city sounds. Regarding the sounds of the city, 43.2% of respondents reported being disturbed. Specifically, 52.9% of individuals working in quiet environments, 47.7% working in acoustically balanced environments, 47.3% working in noisy environments, 43.5% working in relatively noisy environments, and 41.8% working in relatively quiet environments indicated being disturbed by urban sounds.

The findings of the study reveal a significant correlation between the work environment and the perception of city sounds. City sounds, however, pose challenges, with 43.2% of respondents reporting discomfort caused by urban noise. This discomfort is linked to the acoustic conditions of their work environments, underscoring the need for cities to improve their soundscapes for both residents and visitors. As highlighted, it is essential to continue conducting research on the urban environment and to enhance the acoustic identity of cities

When analyzing the relationship between age and vacation memories, the results show that younger age groups (under 18, 18-25 and 26-35 years old), most associated their memories with nightlife, followed by landscape (20%), people (15%), and atmosphere (10%). For the 26-35 age group, landscape and entertainment were the most common memories (32.1% each), with atmosphere following at 22.6%. Further analysis revealed that respondents under 18 years old primarily associated their memories with entertainment (60.2%), followed by human culture and presence (15.4%), nature and the landscape (13.8%), the environment and atmosphere (7.3%), and gastronomy (3.3%). In contrast, older age groups, 36-45 years old (50.8%) and 46-55 years old (41.7%), more often cited the landscape as their main memory. These findings reveal that different groups have unique travel priorities, which destinations can address to enhance visitor satisfaction.

Degree of the Soundscape's Response to Tourist Expectations. For the tourist islands, the soundscape met the expectations of tourists, with 72 positive responses, 101 answered "most of the time," 60 answered "a few times," and 57 answered negatively. Of the negative responses, 56% came from travelers who were informed about the destination through friends and acquaintances.

Regarding visitors to big cities the soundscape met the expectations of those who were informed about their travel destination through friends or acquaintances, with a rate of 43.0%.

The results for visitors who were informed through advertisements are notably different, with only 1.2% answering "yes," 4.3% stating "most of the time," and 3.0% responding "a few times." The highest percentage (63.8%) came from visitors who personally researched their travel destination, stating that the soundscape did not meet their expectations.

Based on the results, we can conclude that both the expectations of the soundscape of large cities and the method of informing about the travel destination are dependent. Similarly, the analysis of the expectations of the soundscape of small islands and the method of informing about the travel destination are dependent.

Methods for Enhancing the Soundscape of Greece According to the research's results, 37, 56.6% of the respondents believe that the soundscape of Greece can be improved, while 43.4% believe it cannot be improved. The most common response regarding the methods for enhancing it, that was given by 13.2% of respondents, was "green energy." The second response was "education," (9,9%) and the third response was "reducing machine noise." (6,6%) and following "personal awareness (6,1%).

Other responses include reducing noise pollution combined with natural sounds (5.2%), actions by municipalities (4.7%), promoting cultural heritage (3.8%), respecting nature and protecting flora and fauna (3.3%), incentives for decentralization (1.9%), and an equal percentage of responses related to live music in restaurants and taverns, gentle activities, and changing the culture in the workplace (1.4%).

Regarding the country of origin of the respondents, 100% of Danish visitors selected "personal awareness." The same response was given by 50% of Finnish respondents, 25% of UK visitors, 18.2% of Dutch visitors, and 3.3% of Greek visitors. Greek respondents also indicated that soundscape could be improved through green energy (17.5%) and education (11.0%). Similarly, 12.5% of Germans and 13% of Dutch respondents believe that education could improve the Greek soundscape.

Most respondents (56.6%) believe Greece's soundscape can be improved, with suggestions including green energy (13.2%), education (9.9%), and reducing machine noise (6.6%). Personal awareness was especially highlighted by Danish respondents, while Greeks emphasized green energy and education. Other ideas included reducing noise pollution, promoting cultural heritage, and municipal actions.

RESEARCH CONCLUSIONS

The research highlights the significant role that soundscape plays in the selection of travel destinations. In urban environments, many respondents described city sounds as disruptive, particularly individuals who work in noisy settings and seek peace and quiet during their leisure time. Additionally, visitors often preferred quieter atmospheres in places such as clubs, with those under 18 years of age expressing a desire for lower noise levels.

Furthermore, the study found that soundscape contributes to the creation of the desired atmosphere for visitors. Quiet, calming soundscapes were associated with positive emotional responses, while loud, chaotic environments were often viewed as less desirable. Visitors increasingly seek destinations that offer a balance between lively city life and peaceful, tranquil areas.

The study also found that music appreciation and knowledge positively contribute to the overall experience when visiting museums and archaeological sites. Visitors with an interest in or understanding of music reported a more engaging and enjoyable experience in these environments. Notably, the educational level of the visitor did not seem to influence their perception of the soundscape, suggesting that the quality of the auditory experience itself played a more significant role. Overall, respondents viewed the soundscape of museums and archaeological sites as tranquil, with many associating the calm atmosphere with a more focused and enriching experience.

In contrast, the soundscape in large cities often did not meet visitor expectations. Popular tourist destinations such as Athens, Crete, and Rhodes were perceived as overly noisy, which sometimes detracted from the visitor experience. However, the research suggests there is potential for improvement. How visitors receive information about the soundscape significantly influences their perception. Those who obtained information through personal networks or independent research tended to have a more favorable view of the sound environment.

To improve the soundscape experience, the research proposes a variety of strategies. These include enforcing noise regulations, raising awareness about the effects of noise pollution, and promoting eco-friendly practices. Additionally, urban planning efforts should aim to create quieter spaces and zones where visitors can escape the noise. Education and cultural promotion can further help enhance the visitor experience, while the encouragement of alternative forms of tourism, such as eco-tourism, may help reduce noise pollution and contribute to a more peaceful environment.

Implementing these strategies could result in a more enjoyable and sustainable experience for both tourists and local communities. Moreover, it would also promote a deeper connection between travelers and the destination they visit, fostering greater appreciation and respect for the local environment and its acoustic properties.

Policy Measures Specifically, the proposed legislative measures are categorized into compliance with existing laws and the establishment of new laws. Suggestions for ensuring compliance with current legislation include enforcing the decibel limits, particularly in nightclubs and bars, following quite hours, controlling and enforcing traffic regulations related to noisy vehicles and motorcycles, and ensuring mandatory emission testing for vehicles.

Regarding the establishment of new laws, proposals include legal measures for areas of natural beauty, museums, and historical centers. Additionally, the introduction of designated zones in tourist areas is suggested, with traffic restrictions and new legislation for forest protection zones.

Another proposal focuses on municipal actions, which should prioritize green energy, park improvements, localized studies, the protection of flora and fauna, the enhancement of natural elements in urban environments, and the creation of more pedestrian paths and bike lanes.

The reduction of noise pollution garnered numerous responses. Proposed measures to achieve this include reducing traffic, minimizing car use, promoting public transportation and electric vehicles, applying soundproof asphalt, enhancing building sound insulation, reducing industrial machinery noise, and altering workplace culture.

In terms of noise management, it is recommended to increase natural sounds and reduce mechanical ones, as outlined in M. Schafer's World Soundscape Project. Education and awareness programs could help increase attention to the sounds produced in each area, raising understanding of the significance and value of the local soundscape.

Another suggestion from the primary research is decentralization and offering incentives for decentralization, combined with promoting small islands and remote areas by highlighting the uniqueness of each location. In terms of cultural activities, recommended measures include promoting traditional arts and music, establishing live music performances in taverns, restaurants, and bars to counter the rise of commercialized music toward industrialized music, promoting Greek customs and traditions, and increasing cultural events throughout Greece.

Finally, the role of alternative forms of tourism and the promotion of sustainable activities is emphasized. Mass tourism on islands such as Kos has caused noticeable changes in the soundscape, particularly due to the promotion of the destination as a nightlife center and a low-cost destination. Supporting businesses, such as agrotourism units, is a key incentive for creating new enterprises and maintaining existing ones. Other businesses that could help improve the soundscape and reduce noise pollution through subsidies include vehicle rental services, motorcycle rentals, and nightclubs.

REFERENCES

Ekmetsoglou, I. (2014). Education in acoustic ecology for children and youth with emphasis on aesthetic and ethical issues of electronically mediated sound. *3rd Acoustic Ecology Conference "Acoustic Ecology and Education,"* Athens, Greece.

Farina, A. (2014). *Soundscape ecology: Principles, patterns, methods, and applications*. Springer Science & Business Media. DOI: 10.1007/978-94-007-7374-5

Krause, B. (2015). *Voices of the wild: Animal songs, human din, and the call to save natural soundscapes*. Yale University Press.

Rodaway, P. (2002). *Sensuous geographies: Body, sense and place*. Routledge. DOI: 10.4324/9780203082546

Schafer, R. M. (1999). *Soundscape: Our sonic environment and the tuning of the world*. Inner Traditions Bear & Company.

Schwarz, D. (1997). *Listening objects: Music, psychoanalysis, culture*. Duke University Press.

Schwarz, D. (1997). *The sense of sound: Aesthetic and cultural aspects of sound*. Oxford University Press.

Truax, B. (1994). The inner and outer complexity of music. *Perspectives of New Music*, *32*(1), 176–193. DOI: 10.2307/833161

KEY TERMS AND DEFINITIONS

Acoustic Ecology: The study of how sound affects humans and the environment. It looks at how both natural and man-made sounds influence well-being and how soundscapes can be designed for a healthier environment.

Auditory Perception: The way in which people hear and interpret sounds. In tourism, this refers to how travelers perceive and react to the sounds of a destination, influencing their enjoyment and overall experience.

Bioacoustics: The study of sound in living organisms, including humans. In tourism, it refers to how natural sounds influence travelers' experiences and well-being.

Noise Pollution: Unwanted or harmful sounds that disturb the environment or people's activities. This includes sounds from cities, transportation, and industry, which can negatively affect travelers' experiences.

Psychoacoustics: The study of how people perceive sound and how it impacts their emotions, behavior, and memory. It explores how different sounds shape travel experiences.

Soundscape: The combination of natural, cultural, and social sounds that make up the environment of a place. It affects how people experience and feel about a location, including sounds of nature, local culture, and urban noise.

Sustainable Tourism: Tourism that respects the environment, local communities, and culture. It aims to minimize negative impacts and promote long-term ecological balance, often through eco-friendly transportation and practices like agritourism.

Urban Soundscapes: The collection of sounds within urban environments, including street noise, traffic, and human activity. It affects how people perceive a city and influences their experience as a destination.

Compilation of References

Abad-Segura, E., Fuente, A. B. D. L., Gonzâlez-Zamar, M. D., & Belmonte-Ureña, L. J. (2020). Effects of circular economy policies on the environment and sustainable growth: Worldwide research. *Sustainability (Basel)*, *12*(14), 5792. DOI: 10.3390/su12145792

ABB. (2021, October 7). *Waste-to-energy plant reduces reactive maintenance and improves energy output using smart sensors.* https://new.abb.com/news/detail/63887/waste-to-energy-plant-reduces-reactive-maintenance-and-improves-energy-output-using-smart-sensors

Abo-Khalil, A. G. (2024). Integrating sustainability into higher education challenges and opportunities for universities worldwide. *Heliyon*, *10*(9), e29946. Advance online publication. DOI: 10.1016/j.heliyon.2024.e29946 PMID: 38707336

Achuthan, K., & Khobragade, S. (2025). Content dynamics and emotional engagement in online zero waste communities: A longitudinal study. *Cities (London, England)*, *165*, 106119. DOI: 10.1016/j.cities.2025.106119

Adami, L., & Schiavon, M. (2021). From circular economy to circular ecology: A review on the solution of environmental problems through circular waste management approaches. *Sustainability (Basel)*, *13*(2), 925. DOI: 10.3390/su13020925

Adeoye, S. O., Batarseh, F., Brown, A. M., & Kaufman, E. K. (2024). UNDERSTANDING THE LANDSCAPE OF CYBERBIOSECURITY FOR INTEGRATIVE EDUCATIONAL PROGRAMMING. In *Journal of the ASABE* (Vol. 67, Issue 1, pp. 207–217). American Society of Agricultural and Biological Engineers. DOI: 10.13031/ja.15739

Aditi, & Singh, R. (2022). Eco-friendly post-harvest technologies of banana: A review. The Pharma Innovation Journal, 11(7), 4375–4381.

Agarwal, S., Agarwal, A., Sharma, G. L., Kothari, H., & Maloo, S. R. (2023, August). Organic Farming Issues and Challenges: Application of ICT. In *International conference on WorldS4* (pp. 189-204). Singapore: Springer Nature Singapore.

Agencia, S. I. N. C. (2021). *El sistema alimentario mundial genera el 34% de las emisiones de gases de efecto invernadero*. https://www.agenciasinc.es

Agricultural and Processed Food Products Export Development Authority (APEDA). (2023–2024). *Organic products in India.* https://apeda.gov.in/apedawebsite/organic/Organic_Products.htm

Agricultural and Processed Food Products Export Development Authority (APEDA). (2025). *Organic products in India.* https://www.apeda.gov.in/OrganicProducts

Aguilar, A., Twardowski, T., & Wohlgemuth, R. (2019). Bioeconomy for Sustainable Development. In *Biotechnology Journal* (Vol. 14, Issue 8). Wiley-VCH Verlag. DOI: 10.1002/biot.201800638

Akram, M. W., Akram, N., Hongshu, W., & Mehmood, A. (2019). An assessment of economic viability of organic farming in Pakistan. *Custos E Agronegocio Line*, *15*(1), 141–169.

Ali, E. B., Shayanmehr, S., Radmehr, R., Bayitse, R., & Agbozo, E. (2024). Investigating environmental quality among G20 nations: The impacts of environmental goods and low-carbon technologies in mitigating environmental degradation. *Geoscience Frontiers*, *15*(1), 1–14. DOI: 10.1016/j.gsf.2023.101695

Al-Kuwari, M. M., Al-Fagih, L., & Koç, M. (2021). Asking the right questions for sustainable development goals: Performance assessment approaches for the Qatar education system. *Sustainability (Basel)*, *13*(7), 3883. Advance online publication. DOI: 10.3390/su13073883

Alliance of Bioversity International and CIAT, & the Senior International Law and Policy Advisor. CARICOM. (2024). *management, technical and scientific cooperation and technology Capacity Building Related to Multilateral Environmental*. https://ssrn.com/abstract=4834159

Almansour, M., & Akrami, M. (2024). Towards Zero Waste: An In-Depth Analysis of National Policies, Strategies, and Case Studies in Waste Minimisation. *Sustainability (Basel)*, *16*(22), 10105. DOI: 10.3390/su162210105

Al-Romeedy, B. S., Emam, M. E., & Tyagi, P. K. (2025). Exploring Waste Reduction Potential in Rural Tourism: What Solutions Can Be Implemented? In *Solid Waste Management for Rural Regions* (pp. 193-214). IGI Global Scientific Publishing.

Altieri, M. A., & Nicholls, C. I. (2017). Agroecology: A brief account of its origins and currents of thought in Latin America. *Agroecology and Sustainable Food Systems*, *41*(3–4), 231–237. DOI: 10.1080/21683565.2017.1287147

Altieri, M. A., & Nicholls, C. I. (2020). *Agroecología: Bases científicas para una agricultura sustentable*. CLACSO.

Al-Wahaibi, A., Osman, A. I., Al-Muhtaseb, A. A. H., Alqaisi, O., Baawain, M., Fawzy, S., & Rooney, D. W. (2020). Techno-economic evaluation of biogas production from food waste via anaerobic digestion. *Scientific Reports*, *10*(1), 15719. DOI: 10.1038/s41598-020-72897-5

Apostolopoulos, N., Kakouris, A., Liargovas, P., Borisov, P., Radev, T., Apostolopoulos, S., Daskou, S., & Anastasopoulou, E. (2023). Just Transition Policies, Power Plant Workers and Green Entrepreneurs in Greece, Cyprus and Bulgaria: Can Education and Retraining Meet the Challenge? *Sustainability (Basel)*, *15*(23), 16307. Advance online publication. DOI: 10.3390/su152316307

Araripe, E., & Zuin Zeidler, V. G. (2024). Advancing sustainable chemistry education: Insights from real-world case studies. *Current Research in Green and Sustainable Chemistry*, *9*, 100436. Advance online publication. DOI: 10.1016/j.crgsc.2024.100436

Ardolino, F., Cardamone, G. F., Parrillo, F., & Arena, U. (2021). Biogas-to-biomethane upgrading: A comparative review and assessment in a life cycle perspective. *Renewable & Sustainable Energy Reviews*, *139*, 110588. DOI: 10.1016/j.rser.2020.110588

Arfanuzzaman, M., & Rahman, A. A. (2017). Sustainable water demand management in face of rapid urbanization and ground water depletion for social-ecological resilience building. *Global Ecology and Conservation*, *10*(1), 9–22. DOI: 10.1016/j.gecco.2017.01.005

Arora, M., Gupta, S., & Mittal, A. (2024). Qualitative Insights Into Harvesting Sustainability: The Role of Organic Agriculture in Advancing Sustainable Development Goals. In *The Emerald Handbook of Tourism Economics and Sustainable Development* (pp. 41-62). Emerald Publishing Limited.

Aryal, J. P., Rahut, D. B., Sonobe, T., Tortajada, C., & Chhay, P. (2024). Water resource management in agricultural for achieving food and water security in Asia. *International Journal of Water Resources Development*, *40*(3), 319–322. DOI: 10.1080/07900627.2024.2332222

Ashton, W. S., Fratini, C. F., Isenhour, C., & Krueger, R. (2022). Justice, equity and the circular economy: Introduction to the special double issue. *Local Environment*, *27*(10-11), 1173–1181. DOI: 10.1080/13549839.2022.2118247

Aslam, W., Shahzad Noor, R., Ullah, S., & Chen, H. (2020). Comparative economic analysis of crop yield under organic and conventional farming systems in Punjab, Pakistan. *Asian Journal of Agriculture and Biology*, *8*(2), 113–118. DOI: 10.35495/ajab.2020.02.093

Atiku, S. O., Jeremiah, A., Semente, E., & Boateng, F. (Eds.). (2024). *Eco-Innovation and Sustainable Development in Industry 5.0.* IGI Global. DOI: 10.4018/979-8-3693-2219-2

Attal-Juncqua, A., Getz, J., Morhard, R., & Gronvall, G. K. (2024). Integrating safety, security, sustainability, and social responsibility principles into the U.S. bioeconomy. *MSphere*, *9*(5), e00084-24. Advance online publication. DOI: 10.1128/msphere.00084-24 PMID: 38687115

Awan, U., & Sroufe, R. (2022). Sustainability in the circular economy: Insights and dynamics of designing circular business models. *Applied Sciences (Basel, Switzerland)*, *12*(3), 1521. DOI: 10.3390/app12031521

Awasthi, A. K., Cheela, V. S., D'Adamo, I., Iacovidou, E., Islam, M. R., Johnson, M., & Li, J. (2021). Zero waste approach towards a sustainable waste management. *Resources. Environmental Sustainability*, *3*, 100014.

Ayadi, M., Fersi, C., Mahjoub, B., Ben Salah, I., & Touati, F. (2025). Vertical Constructed Wetlands Integrated with Biochar: A Green Nature-Based Solution for Wastewater Treatment. *Chemistry Africa*, *8*(2), 607–618. DOI: 10.1007/s42250-024-01149-0

Azam, I., Guo, Y., & Naseer, M. M. (2024). The sustainability challenge and social benefits of industrialisation in NICs. *Resources Policy*, *103*(1), 1–12. DOI: 10.1016/j.resourpol.2025.105541

Azam, M. S., & Ponnam, A. (2024). Disparity in Agri-Marketing Challenges in India: Organic vs. Conventional Food Producers. *Journal of International Food & Agribusiness Marketing*, *36*(5), 870–898. DOI: 10.1080/08974438.2023.2228783

Azam, M. S., Shaheen, M., & Narbariya, S. (2019). Marketing challenges and organic farming in India—Does farm size matter? *International Journal of Nonprofit and Voluntary Sector Marketing*, *24*(4), e1654. DOI: 10.1002/nvsm.1654

Baba-Nalikant, M., Syed-Mohamad, S. M., Husin, M. H., Abdullah, N. A., Mohamad Saleh, M. S., & Abdul Rahim, A. (2023). A zero-waste campus framework: Perceptions and practices of university campus community in Malaysia. *Recycling*, *8*(1), 21. DOI: 10.3390/recycling8010021

Bakator, M., Ćoćkalo, D., Makitan, V., Stanisavljev, S., & Nikolić, M. (2024). The three pillars of tomorrow: How Marketing 5.0 builds on Industry 5.0 and impacts Society 5.0? *Heliyon, 10*(17), e36543. DOI: 10.1016/j.heliyon.2024.e36543 PMID: 39281657

Banka Beograd, A. A. (2020). *Časopis Društva ekonomista Beograda (Osnovano 1932.g.).*

Baralla, G., Pinna, A., Tonelli, R., & Marchesi, M. (2023). Waste management: A comprehensive state of the art about the rise of blockchain technology. *Computers in Industry, 145*, 103812. DOI: 10.1016/j.compind.2022.103812

Barata, J., & Kayser, I. (2024). How will the digital twin shape the future of industry 5.0? *Technovation, 134*, 103025. DOI: 10.1016/j.technovation.2024.103025

Barros, M. V., Salvador, R., do Prado, G. F., de Francisco, A. C., & Piekarski, C. M. (2021). Circular economy as a driver to sustainable businesses. *Cleaner Environmental Systems, 2*, 100006. DOI: 10.1016/j.cesys.2020.100006

Basso, B., Jones, J. W., Antle, J., Martinez-Feria, R. A., & Verma, B. (2021). Enabling circularity in grain production systems with novel technologies and policy. *Agricultural Systems, 193*, 103244. DOI: 10.1016/j.agsy.2021.103244

Bastos Lima, M. G., & Palme, U. (2022). The Bioeconomy–Biodiversity Nexus: Enhancing or Undermining Nature's Contributions to People? *Conservation, 2*(1), 7–25. DOI: 10.3390/conservation2010002

Befort, N. (2020). Going beyond definitions to understand tensions within the bioeconomy: The contribution of socio technical regimes to contested fields. *Technological Forecasting and Social Change, 153*, 119923. DOI: 10.1016/j.techfore.2020.119923

Begum, Y. A., Kumari, S., Jain, S. K., & Garg, M. C. (2024). A review on waste biomass-to-energy: Integrated thermochemical and biochemical conversion for resource recovery. *Environmental Science. Advances, 3*(9), 1197–1216. DOI: 10.1039/D4VA00109E

Behera, K. K., Alam, A., Vats, S., Sharma, H. P., & Sharma, V. (2012). Organic farming history and techniques. *Agroecology and strategies for climate change*, (pp.287-328).

Bejinaru, R., Hapenciuc, C. V., Condratov, I., & Stanciu, P. (2018). The University role in developing the human capital for a sustainable bioeconomy. *Amfiteatru Economic, 20*(49), 583–598. DOI: 10.24818/EA/2018/49/583

Bernardo, M., Lapa, N., Fonseca, I., & Esteves, I. A. (2021). Biomass valorization to produce porous carbons: Applications in CO2 capture and biogas upgrading to biomethane—a mini-review. *Frontiers in Energy Research*, *9*, 625188. DOI: 10.3389/fenrg.2021.625188

Bioenergy News. (2023, July 17). *Ground-breaking biogas plant software can save producers €50,000 each year*. https://www.bioenergy-news.com/news/ground-breaking-biogas-plant-software-can-save-producers-e50000-each-year/

Biswas, J. K., Mondal, B., Priyadarshini, P., Abhilash, P. C., Biswas, S., & Bhatnagar, A. (2022). Formulation of water sustainability index for India as a performance gauge for realizing the United Nations Sustainable Development Goal 6. *Ambio*, *51*(6), 1569–1587. DOI: 10.1007/s13280-021-01680-1 PMID: 34932186

Biswas, S., Ali, M. N., Goswami, R., & Chakraborty, S. (2014). Soil health sustainability and organic farming: A review. *Journal of Food Agriculture and Environment*, *12*(3-4), 237–243.

Bliznina, N. (2024). *Redefining Economic Growth: the Review of Industry 4.0 and Industry 5.0 Progress*. Green and Low-Carbon Economy.

Booker, J. F., & Trees, W. S. (2021). Implications of water scarcity for water productivity and farm labor. *Water (Basel)*, *12*(1), 1–20. DOI: 10.3390/w12010308

Borah, S. K., Dutta, C., Pal, D., Sarkar, S., & Sethi, L. N. (2025). Harnessing Artificial Intelligence in Agriculture for a Sustainable Future. 1:95-120. ISBN: 978-93-5860-467-2

Borah, S. K., Pal, D., Sarkar, S., & Sethi, L. N. (2025). AI-Powered Drones for Sustainable Agriculture and Precision Farming. In Sadiq, S., Ahmad, M., Karunakaran, N., & Atapattu, A. (Eds.), *Advancing Global Food Security With Agriculture 4.0 and 5.0* (pp. 69–98). IGI Global Scientific Publishing. DOI: 10.4018/979-8-3693-9964-4.ch004

Bößncr, S., Johnson, F. X., & Shawoo, Z. (2021). Governing the bioeconomy: What role for international institutions? *Sustainability (Basel)*, *13*(1), 1–24. DOI: 10.3390/su13010286

Bottazzi, P., Seck, S. M., Niang, M., & Moser, S. (2023). Beyond motivations: A framework unraveling the systemic barriers to organic farming adoption in northern Senegal. *Journal of Rural Studies*, *104*, 103158. DOI: 10.1016/j.jrurstud.2023.103158

Braden, J. B., & van Lerland, E. C. (1999). Balancing: The economic approach to sustainable water management. *Water Science and Technology*, *39*(5), 17–23. DOI: 10.2166/wst.1999.0217

Brévault, T., & Bouyer, J. (2014). From integrated to system-wide pest management: Challenges for sustainable agriculture. *Outlooks on Pest Management*, *25*(3), 212–213. DOI: 10.1564/v25_jun_05

Buvaneshwaran, M., Radhakrishnan, M., & Natarajan, V. (2023). Influence of ultrasound-assisted extraction techniques on the valorization of agro-based industrial organic waste–A review. *Journal of Food Process Engineering*, *46*(6), e14012. DOI: 10.1111/jfpe.14012

Cao, L., Wang, J., Xiang, S., Huang, Z., Ruan, R., & Liu, Y. (2019). Nutrient removal from digested swine wastewater by combining ammonia stripping with struvite precipitation. *Environmental Science and Pollution Research International*, *26*(7), 6725–6734. DOI: 10.1007/s11356-019-04153-x PMID: 30632036

Cao, X., Williams, P. N., Zhan, Y., Coughlin, S. A., McGrath, J. W., Chin, J. P., & Xu, Y. (2023). Municipal solid waste compost: Global trends and biogeochemical cycling. *Soil & Environmental Health*, *1*(4), 100038. DOI: 10.1016/j.seh.2023.100038

Carvache-Franco, M., Orden-Mejía, M., Carvache-Franco, W., del Carmen Lapo, M., & Carvache-Franco, O. (2022). Gastronomy Motivations as Predictors of Satisfaction at Coastal Destinations. *Sustainability (Basel)*, *14*(18), 11437. Advance online publication. DOI: 10.3390/su141811437

Castilla-Polo, F., Ruiz-Rodríguez, M. C., Moreno, A., Licerán-Gutiérrez, A., de la Fuente, M. C., Rufián, E. C., & Cano-Rodríguez, M. (2020). Classroom learning and the perception of social responsibility amongst graduate students of management accounting. *Sustainability (Basel)*, *12*(17), 7093. Advance online publication. DOI: 10.3390/su12177093

Castro, L. M., Calvas, B., & Knoke, T. (2015). Ecuadorian banana farms should consider organic banana with low price risks in their land-use portfolios. *PLoS One*, *10*(3), e0120384. DOI: 10.1371/journal.pone.0120384

Chang, M., Li, F., Lin, S., Zhang, J., & Shi, H. (2024). How is agricultural water efficiency affected by digital economy? Insights from China. *Water Policy*, *26*(1), 1–17. DOI: 10.2166/wp.2023.168

Chang, S. H. (2020). Utilization of green organic solvents in solvent extraction and liquid membrane for sustainable wastewater treatment and resource recovery—A review. *Environmental Science and Pollution Research International*, *27*(26), 32371–32388. DOI: 10.1007/s11356-020-09639-7 PMID: 32533493

Chanza, N., & De Wit, A. (2016). Enhancing climate governance through indigenous knowledge: Case in sustainability science. *South African Journal of Science, 112*(3–4), 7. Advance online publication. DOI: 10.17159/sajs.2016/20140286

Chen, C. C., & Pao, H. T. (2024). Cicular economy and ecological footprint: A disaggregated analysis for the EU. *Ecological Indicators, 160*, 111809. DOI: 10.1016/j.ecolind.2024.111809

Chen, W. M., & Kim, H. (2019). Circular economy and energy transition: A nexus focusing on the non-energy use of fuels. *Energy & Environment, 30*(4), 586–600. DOI: 10.1177/0958305X19845759

Chia, S. L. (2021). The optimization algorithms for artificial intelligence in sustainable river water quality management can be obtained from http://eprints.utar.edu.my/4067

Chopra, R., Agrawal, A., Sharma, G. D., Kallmuenzer, A., & Vasa, L. (2024). Uncovering the organizational, environmental, and socio-economic sustainability of digitization: Evidence from existing research. *Review of Managerial Science, 18*(1), 685–709. DOI: 10.1007/s11846-023-00637-w

Chu, Z., Li, Q., Zhou, A., Zhang, W., Huang, W. C., & Wang, J. (2023). Strategy formulation path towards zero-waste of municipal solid waste: A case study from Shanghai. *Journal of Cleaner Production, 418*, 138091. DOI: 10.1016/j.jclepro.2023.138091

Ciucu-Durnoi, A. N., Delcea, C., Stănescu, A., Teodorescu, C. A., & Vargas, V. M. (2024). Beyond Industry 4.0: Tracing the Path to Industry 5.0 through Bibliometric Analysis. *Sustainability (Basel), 16*(12), 5251. DOI: 10.3390/su16125251

Clark, S. (2020). Organic farming and climate change: The need for innovation. *Sustainability (Basel), 12*(17), 7012. DOI: 10.3390/su12177012

Clune, T. (2021). Conceptualising policy for sustainable agriculture development. *Australian Journal of Public Administration, 80*(3), 493–509. DOI: 10.1111/1467-8500.12436

Cobîrzan N, Muntean R, Thalmaier G, Felseghi RA. Recycling of Mining Waste in the Production of Masonry Units. *Materials (Basel)*. 2022;15(2):594. Published 2022 Jan 13.

Coelho, J. P., Filipe, R. M., Robalo, M. P., & Stateva, R. P. (2018). Recovering value from organic waste materials: Supercritical fluid extraction of oil from industrial grape seeds. *The Journal of Supercritical Fluids, 141*, 68–77. DOI: 10.1016/j.supflu.2017.12.008

Comin, L. C., Aguiar, C. C., Sehnem, S., Yusliza, M.-Y., Cazella, C. F., & Julkovski, D. J. (2020). Sustainable business models: A literature review. *Benchmarking*, *27*(7), 2028–2047. DOI: 10.1108/BIJ-12-2018-0384

Compoli, J. S., Junior, P. N. A., Kodama, T. K., Nagano, M. S., & Burnquist, H. L. (2024). G20 countries' progress on the 7th SDG under circular economy DEA model. *Environmental Science & Policy*, *160*(1), 1–15. DOI: 10.1016/j.envsci.2024.103839

Cookey, P. E., Peter-Cookey, M. A., Richard, I. U., & Brdanovic, D. (2023). Multi-Level Perceptions on Higher Education Development for Sanitation and Hygiene Management in Nigeria. *Hygiene*, *3*(4), 465–491. DOI: 10.3390/hygiene3040035

Coraggio, J. L. (2011). *Economía social y solidaria: El trabajo antes que el capital.* Ediciones Abya Yala.

Cosgrove, W. J., & Loucks, D. P. (2015). Water management: Current and future challenges and research directions. *Water Resources Research*, *51*(1), 4823–4839. DOI: 10.1002/2014WR016869

Coulis, M., Sauvadet, M., Falk, A., Prochasson, A., Tsoukas, L., Gervais, L., & Guillermet, C. (2022, August). Multidisciplinary assessment of two organic banana production systems in Martinique. In *XXXI International Horticultural Congress (IHC2022): XII International Symposium on Banana: Celebrating Banana Organic 1367* (pp. 35-46).

Dacre, N., Yan, J., Frei, R., Al-Mhdawi, M. K. S., & Dong, H. (2024). Advancing sustainable manufacturing: A systematic exploration of industry 5.0 supply chains for sustainability, human-centricity, and resilience. *Production Planning and Control*, •••, 1–30.

Daystar, J., Handfield, R., Golden, J. S., McConnell, E., & Pascual-Gonzalez, J. (2021). An economic impact analysis of the US biobased products industry. *Industrial Biotechnology (New Rochelle, N.Y.)*, *17*(5), 259–270. DOI: 10.1089/ind.2021.29263.jda

de Almeida Barbosa Franco, J., Franco, A.Junior, Battistelle, R. A. G., & Bezerra, B. S. (2024). Dynamic Capabilities: Unveiling Key Resources for Environmental Sustainability and Economic Sustainability, and Corporate Social Responsibility towards Sustainable Development Goals. *Resources*, *13*(2), 22. Advance online publication. DOI: 10.3390/resources13020022

De Angelis, R. (2018). *Business models in the circular economy: Concepts, examples and theory*. Springer. DOI: 10.1007/978-3-319-75127-6 de Jong, W., Huang, K., Zhuo, Y., Kleine, M., Wang, G., Liu, W., & Xu, G. (2021). A comparison of forestry continuing education academic degree programs. *Forests*, *12*(7), 824. Advance online publication. DOI: 10.3390/f12070824

De Ponti, T., Rijk, B., & Van Ittersum, M. K. (2012). The crop yield gap between organic and conventional agriculture. *Agricultural Systems*, *108*, 1–9. DOI: 10.1016/j.agsy.2011.12.004

Del Rio-Chanona, E. A., Cong, X., Bradford, E., Zhang, D., & Jing, K. (2019). Review of advanced physical and data-driven models for dynamic bioprocess simulation: Case study of algae–bacteria consortium wastewater treatment. *Biotechnology and Bioengineering*, *116*(2), 342–353. DOI: 10.1002/bit.26881

Deng, S., & Chang, J. (2025). Application of biochar as an innovative substrate in constructed wetlands/biofilters for wastewater treatment: Performance and ecological benefits. In *Emerging Developments in Constructed Wetlands* (pp. 595–628). Elsevier. DOI: 10.1016/B978-0-443-14078-5.00025-8

Deutsche Gesellschaft für Internationale Zusammenarbeit. (2019). *Solar-powered irrigation systems: A farmer's guide*. https://www.giz.de/en/downloads/giz2019-en-solar-powered-irrigation.pdf

Dhanya, D., Kumar, S. S., Thilagavathy, A., Prasad, D., & Boopathi, S. (2023). Data Analytics and Artificial Intelligence in the Circular Economy: Case Studies. In *Intelligent Engineering Applications and Applied Sciences for Sustainability* (pp. 40–58). IGI Global.

Dhole KS, Bahadure S, Bandre GR, Noman O. Navigating Challenges in Biomedical Waste Management in India: A Narrative Review. *Cureus*. 2024;16(3):e55409. Published 2024 Mar 2. DOI: 10.7759/cureus.55409

Dimitri, C., & Effland, A. (2020). From farming to food systems: The evolution of US agricultural production and policy into the 21st century. *Renewable Agriculture and Food Systems*, *35*(4), 391–406. DOI: 10.1017/S1742170518000522

Dixit, A., Suvadarshini, P., & Pagare, D. V. (2024). Analysis of barriers to organic farming adoption in developing countries: A grey-DEMATEL and ISM approach. *Journal of Agribusiness in Developing and Emerging Economies*, *14*(3), 470–495. DOI: 10.1108/JADEE-06-2022-0111

Dong, L., Liu, Z., & Bian, Y. (2021). Match circular economy and urban sustainability: Re-investigating circular economy under sustainable development goals (SDGs). *Circular Economy and Sustainability*, *1*(1), 243–256. DOI: 10.1007/s43615-021-00032-1

Dube, P. I., Olorunfemi, O. D., & Nyawo, P. H. (2025). Perception and Utilisation of Organic Farming Practices among Smallholder Farmers: Evidence from a Micro-Level Survey in Ehlanzeni District South Africa. *South African Journal of Agricultural Extension*, *53*(1), 169–192. DOI: 10.17159/2413-3221/2025/v53n1a18444

Ecology, S. (1999). *Traditional ecological knowledge and resource management*. Taylor and Francis.

Economic Cooperation, F. M. (BMZ), D. (2023). Protecting the Environment – Ecuador Priority Area. In *BMZ – German Federal Ministry for Economic Cooperation and Development*.

Egbo, O. P., Ezeaku, H. C., Okolo, V. O., Anisiuba, C. A., Ibe, G., Okeke, O. M., & Igwe, P. A. (2022). Enhancing agricultural and industrial productivity through freshwater withdrawals and management: Implications for the BRICS countries. *Environment, Development and Sustainability*, *25*(1), 3771–3799. DOI: 10.1007/s10668-022-02202-z

Ekmetsoglou, I. (2014). Education in acoustic ecology for children and youth with emphasis on aesthetic and ethical issues of electronically mediated sound. *3rd Acoustic Ecology Conference "Acoustic Ecology and Education,"* Athens, Greece.

Elia, V., Gnoni, M. G., & Tornese, F. (2017). Measuring circular economy strategies through index methods: A critical analysis. *Journal of Cleaner Production*, *142*(1), 2741–2751. DOI: 10.1016/j.jclepro.2016.10.196

Ellen MacArthur Foundation. (2019). *Cities and circular economy for food*. https://ellenmacarthurfoundation.org/cities-and-circular-economy-for-food

Ellen MacArthur Foundation. (2019). *Completing the picture: How the circular economy tackles climate change*. https://ellenmacarthurfoundation.org/completing-the-picture-climate-change

Ellen MacArthur Foundation. (2021). *The new plastics economy global commitment*. https://ellenmacarthurfoundation.org

Elvin, E., & Wibowo, A. (2024). Forecasting water quality through machine learning and hyperparameter optimization. *Indonesian Journal of Electrical Engineering and Computer Science*, *33*(1), 496–506. DOI: 10.11591/ijeecs.v33.i1.pp496-506

Ember - Yearly Electricity Data. (2023). Ember - European Electricity Review (2022);Energy Institute - Statistical Review of World Energy. (2023) – with major processing by Our World in Data. https://ember-energy.org/latest-insights/european-electricity-review-2022/

Esguerra, E. B., & Rolle, R. (2018). Post-harvest management of banana for quality and safety assurance: Guidance for horticultural supply chain stakeholders. Food and Agriculture Organization of the United Nations.

Eti, H. S. (2025). The Effects of Perceptions of Economic Sustainability and Barriers on Organic Farming Implementation. *Sustainability (Basel)*, *17*(2), 786. DOI: 10.3390/su17020786

European Biogas Association. (2023). *Biogas: Fit for the future.* https://www.europeanbiogas.eu

European Bioplastics. (2022). *Bioplastics market data 2022.* https://www.european-bioplastics.org/market

European Commission. (2012). *Innovating for sustainable growth: A bioeconomy for Europe* (No. SWD(2012) 11 final). Brussels: European Commission.

Expósito, A., & Cebollero, E. D. (2025). How the digital revolution is reshaping water management and policy: A focus on Spain. *Utilities Policy*, *96*(1), 1–9. DOI: 10.1016/j.jup.2025.102020

Ezeudu, O. B., & Ezeudu, T. S. (2019). Implementation of circular economy principles in industrial solid waste management: Case studies from a developing economy (Nigeria). *Recycling*, *4*(4), 42–57. DOI: 10.3390/recycling4040042

Fang, B., Yu, J., Chen, Z., Osman, A. I., Farghali, M., Ihara, I., Hamza, E. H., Rooney, D. W., & Yap, P.-S. (2023). Artificial intelligence for waste management in smart cities: A review. *Environmental Chemistry Letters*, *21*(4), 1959–1989. DOI: 10.1007/s10311-023-01604-3

FAO & IFOAM. (2020). *Bioinsumos: Herramientas clave para la sostenibilidad de la agricultura.* https://www.fao.org/3/ca6797es/ca6797es.pdf

FAO, & OECD. (2021). Water and agriculture. an issues note produces for the G20 Presidency of the Kingdom of Saudi Arabia. Rome. https://openknowledge.fao.org/server/api/core/bitstreams/a6d0e4b9-ce9b-4688-be37-bf06952fa6b4/content

FAO. (2014). *The state of food and agriculture: Innovation in family farming.* https://www.fao.org/3/i4040e/i4040e.pdf

FAO. (2019). *El estado de la agricultura y la alimentación en el mundo.* https://www.fao.org/3/ca6030es/ca6030es.pdf

FAO. (2020). *Emissions due to agriculture.* https://www.fao.org/3/ca1334en/ca1334en.pdf

FAO. (2021). *The state of food and agriculture 2021: Making agrifood systems more resilient to shocks and stresses*. https://www.fao.org/publications/sofa/2021

FAO. (2022). *Food systems and climate change*. https://www.fao.org/climate-change

Farina, A. (2014). *Soundscape ecology: Principles, patterns, methods, and applications*. Springer Science & Business Media. DOI: 10.1007/978-94-007-7374-5

Farzana, S. Z., Paudyal, D. R., Chadalavada, S., & Alam, J. (2024). Decision Support Framework for Water Quality Management in Reservoirs Integrating Artificial Intelligence and Statistical Approaches. *Water (Basel)*, *16*(20), 2944. DOI: 10.3390/w16202944

Faulkner, J. P., Murphy, E., & Scott, M. (2024). Downscaling EU bioeconomy policy for national implementation. *Cleaner and Circular Bioeconomy*, *9*, 100121. Advance online publication. DOI: 10.1016/j.clcb.2024.100121

Feng, W., Mao, Y., & Chen, H. (2007). Study on development pattern of circular economy in chemical industry parks in China. *Modern Chemical Industry*, *27*(3), 7–17.

Ferasso, M., Beliaeva, T., Kraus, S., Clauss, T., & Ribeiro-Soriano, D. (2020). Circular economy business models: The state of research and avenues ahead. *Business Strategy and the Environment*, *29*(8), 3006–3024. DOI: 10.1002/bse.2554

Fiksel, J., Sanjay, P., & Raman, K. (2021). Steps toward a resilient circular economy in India. *Clean Technologies and Environmental Policy*, *23*(1), 203–218. DOI: 10.1007/s10098-020-01982-0

Fisher, P. (1989). Barriers to the adoption of organic farming in Canterbury (*Doctoral dissertation, Lincoln College, University of Canterbury*).

Flint, R. W. (2004). The sustainable development of water resources. *Water Resources Update*, *127*(1), 48–50.

Food and Agriculture Organization of the United Nations (FAO). (2017). Water for sustainable food and agriculture: a report produced for the G20 presidency of Germany. [Online]. https://openknowledge.fao.org/server/api/core/bitstreams/b48cb758-48bc-4dc5-a508-e5a0d61fb365/content

Food, E. I. T. (2023). *The future of sustainable food systems in Europe*. https://www.eitfood.eu

Forster, D., Andres, C., Verma, R., Zundel, C., Messmer, M. M., & Mäder, P. (2013). Yield and economic performance of organic and conventional cotton-based farming systems–results from a field trial in India. *PLoS One*, *8*(12), e81039. DOI: 10.1371/journal.pone.0081039

Francis, M. R., Nagarajan, G., Sarkar, R., Mohan, V. R., Kang, G., & Balraj, V. (2015). Perception of drinking water safety and factors influencing acceptance and sustainability of a water quality intervention in rural southern India. *BMC Public Health*, *15*(731), 1–9. DOI: 10.1186/s12889-015-1974-0 PMID: 26223687

Fritsche, U. R., & Iriarte, L. (2021). Sustainability criteria and indicators for the bio-based economy in Europe: State of play and way forward. *Frontiers in Sustainability*, *2*, 701509. Advance online publication. DOI: 10.3389/frsus.2021.701509

Gallego-Schmid, A., Chen, H. M., Sharmina, M., & Mendoza, J. M. F. (2020). Links between circular economy and climate change mitigation in the built environment. *Journal of Cleaner Production*, *260*, 121115. DOI: 10.1016/j.jclepro.2020.121115

Gamage, A., Gangahagedara, R., Gamage, J., Jayasinghe, N., Kodikara, N., Suraweera, P., & Merah, O. (2023). Role of organic farming for achieving sustainability in agriculture. *Farming System*, *1*(1), 100005. DOI: 10.1016/j.farsys.2023.100005

Gamberini, L., & Pluchino, P. (2024). Industry 5.0: A comprehensive insight into the future of work, social sustainability, sustainable development, and career. *Australian Journal of Career Development*, *33*(1), 5–14. DOI: 10.1177/10384162241231118

Ganthavee, V., & Trzcinski, A. P. (2024). Artificial intelligence and machine learning for the optimization of pharmaceutical wastewater treatment systems: A review. *Environmental Chemistry Letters*, *22*(5), 2293–2318. Advance online publication. DOI: 10.1007/s10311-024-01748-w

Gao, M., Li, S., Zou, H., Wen, F., Cai, A., Zhu, R., Tian, W., Shi, D., Chai, H., & Gu, L. (2021). Aged landfill leachate enhances anaerobic digestion of waste activated sludge. *Journal of Environmental Management*, *293*, 112853. DOI: 10.1016/j.jenvman.2021.112853 PMID: 34044237

García-Feijoo, M., Eizaguirre, A., & Rica-Aspiunza, A. (2020). Systematic review of sustainable-development-goal deployment in business schools. *Sustainability (Basel)*, *12*(1), 440. Advance online publication. DOI: 10.3390/su12010440

Gardossi, L., Philp, J., Fava, F., Winickoff, D., D'Aprile, L., Dell'Anno, B., Marvik, O. J., & Lenzi, A. (2023). Bioeconomy national strategies in the G20 and OECD countries: Sharing experiences and comparing existing policies. *EFB Bioeconomy Journal*, *3*, 100053. DOI: 10.1016/j.bioeco.2023.100053

Garg, A., Raut, R. D., Kumar, M., Zhang, C., & Ghokhale, R. (2025). Does the circular economy transition aid to carbon neutrality? Examining net-zero policy and stakeholder impact from the environmental justice viewpoint. *Journal of Cleaner Production, 491*, 144851. DOI: 10.1016/j.jclepro.2025.144851

Geissdoerfer, M., Morioka, S. N., de Carvalho, M. M., & Evans, S. (2018). Business models and supply chains for the circular economy. *Journal of Cleaner Production, 190*, 712–721. DOI: 10.1016/j.jclepro.2018.04.159

Getahun, S., Kefale, H., & Gelaye, Y. (2024, October 9). Application of Precision Agriculture Technologies for Sustainable Crop Production and Environmental Sustainability: A Systematic Review. *TheScientificWorldJournal, 2024*(1), 2126734. DOI: 10.1155/2024/2126734 PMID: 39421732

Ghobakhloo, M., Fathi, M., Iranmanesh, M., Vilkas, M., Grybauskas, A., & Amran, A. (2024). Generative artificial intelligence in manufacturing: Opportunities for actualizing Industry 5.0 sustainability goals. *Journal of Manufacturing Technology Management, 35*(9), 94–121. DOI: 10.1108/JMTM-12-2023-0530

Ghobakhloo, M., Iranmanesh, M., Fathi, M., Rejeb, A., Foroughi, B., & Nikbin, D. (2024). Beyond Industry 4.0: A systematic review of Industry 5.0 technologies and implications for social, environmental and economic sustainability. *Asia-Pacific Journal of Business Administration.*

Ghobakhloo, M., Mahdiraji, H. A., Iranmanesh, M., & Jafari-Sadeghi, V. (2024). From Industry 4.0 digital manufacturing to Industry 5.0 digital society: A roadmap toward human-centric, sustainable, and resilient production. *Information Systems Frontiers*, •••, 1–33. DOI: 10.1007/s10796-024-10476-z

Ghosh, A., Kumar, S., & Das, J. (2023). Impact of leachate and landfill gas on the ecosystem and health: Research trends and the way forward towards sustainability. *Journal of Environmental Management, 336*, 117708. DOI: 10.1016/j.jenvman.2023.117708 PMID: 36913859

Ghosh, D., Adhikary, S., & Sau, S. (2023). *AI-Based Smart Water Quality Monitoring and Wastewater Management*. IGI Global., DOI: 10.4018/979-8-3693-1194-3.ch007

Ghosh, D., Siddique Md, A., & Pal, D. (2024). *AI driven approach for Precision Agriculture in the Book 'AI in Agriculture for Sustainable and Economic Management*. Taylor and Francis.

Giannoccaro, I., Ceccarelli, G., & Fraccascia, L. (2021). Features of the Higher Education for the Circular Economy: The Case of Italy. *Sustainability (Basel), 13*(20), 11338. Advance online publication. DOI: 10.3390/su132011338

Gignarta, T. S., Borojo, D. G., & Guan, Z. (2024). The impacts of economic policy uncertainties on agriculture export. *Cogent Economics & Finance*, *12*(1), 2382359. DOI: 10.1080/23322039.2024.2382359

Giurca, A., Nichiforel, L., Stăncioiu, P. T., Drăgoi, M., & Dima, D. P. (2022). Unlocking Romania's Forest-Based Bioeconomy Potential: Knowledge-Action-Gaps and the Way Forward. *Land (Basel)*, *11*(11), 2001. Advance online publication. DOI: 10.3390/land11112001

Gliessman, S. R. (2016). *Agroecology: The ecology of sustainable food systems* (3rd ed.). CRC Press.

Global Carbon Budget. (2023). Population based on various sources (2023) [Online]. OurWorldInData.org/co2-and-greenhouse-gas-emissions

Global Waste Management Outlook. 2024. UNEP - UN Environment Programme. https://www.unep.org/resources/global-waste-management-outlook-2024

Golubev, G. N. (1983). Economic activity, water resources and the environment: A challenge for hydrology. *Hydrological Sciences Journal*, *28*(1), 57–75. DOI: 10.1080/02626668309491143

Goncharova, Y. K., Kharitonov, E. M., Ochkas, N. A., Gapishko, N. I., & Neschadim, H. H. (2020). Features of rice (Oryza sativa L.) varieties for organic farming in connection with marker assisted breeding. *Selskokhozyaistvennaya Biologiya*, *55*(5), 847–860. DOI: 10.15389/agrobiology.2020.5.847eng

González de Molina, M., & Toledo, V. M. (2014). *The social metabolism: A socio-ecological theory of historical change*. Springer., DOI: 10.1007/978-3-319-06358-4

Gopinath, K. A., Venkatesh, G., Manjunath, M., Jayalakshmi, M., Prasad, T. V., Rajkumar, B., & Singh, V. K. (2023). Impact of organic and integrated production systems on yield and seed quality of rainfed crops and on soil properties. *Frontiers in Nutrition*, *10*, 1127970. DOI: 10.3389/fnut.2023.1127970

Goswami, K., & Bisht, P. S. (2017). The role of water resources in socio-economic development. *International Journal for Research in Applied Science and Engineering Technology*, *5*(12), 669–1674.

Green, T., Gourdain, E., Hirschy, G., Sine, M., Geyer, M., Laun, N., & de Jong, J. R. (2022). Farming system perspective. In *Handbook digital farming: digital transformation for sustainable agriculture* (pp. 277–339). Springer Berlin Heidelberg. DOI: 10.1007/978-3-662-64378-5_5

Gross, T., Breitenmoser, L., Kumar, S., Ehrensperger, A., Wintgens, T., & Hugi, C. (2021). Anaerobic digestion of biowaste in Indian municipalities: Effects on energy, fertilizers, water and the local environment. *Resources, Conservation and Recycling*, *170*, 105569. DOI: 10.1016/j.resconrec.2021.105569

Grzyb, K. (2017). B. E. A. C. F. and I. Minor. (2017). *Title: Bioenergy Education: A Curriculum Framework and Interdisciplinary Minor.*

Gupta, Y., Barrett, B., & Vlachos, D. G. (2024). Understanding microwave-assisted extraction of phenolic compounds from diverse food waste feedstocks. *Chemical Engineering and Processing*, *203*, 109870. DOI: 10.1016/j.cep.2024.109870

Guthman, J. H. (2000). *Agrarian dreams? The paradox of organic farming in California*. University of California.

Hajam, Y. A., Kumar, R., & Kumar, A. (2023). Environmental waste management strategies and vermi transformation for sustainable development. *Environmental Challenges*, *13*, 100747. DOI: 10.1016/j.envc.2023.100747

Hajirad, I. (2025). Role of Artificial Intelligence in Improving Water Resource Management: From Demand Forecasting to Waste Reduction and Water Crisis Mitigation. *Nutrition and Food Processing*, *8*(5), 01–05. https://doi.org/.DOI: 10.31579/2637-8914/305

Hale, S. E., Folde, M. S., Melby, U. H., Sjødahl, E. U., Smebye, A. B., & Oen, A. M. (2021). From landfills to landscapes—Nature-based solutions for water management taking into account legacy contamination. *Integrated Environmental Assessment and Management*, *18*(1), 99–107. DOI: 10.1002/ieam.4467 PMID: 34019725

Hamdan, A., Panda, S., Jain, M. S., Raj, V., & Mathew, S. (2025). Assessing Municipal solid Waste in Indian Smart Cities: A Path towards Waste-to-Energy. *Heliyon*, *e42770*(February), e42770. DOI: 10.1016/j.heliyon.2025.e42770

Hamid, N. A., Rasul, M. S., & Kamaruzaman, F. M. (2024). Circular Economy and Sustainable Technology in Technical and Vocational Education and Training: A Bibliometric Analysis. *International Journal of Learning. Teaching and Educational Research*, *23*(9), 141–160. DOI: 10.26803/ijlter.23.9.8

Haq, R., & Shafique, S. (2009). Impact of water management on agricultural production. *Asian Journal of Agriculture and Development*, *6*(2), 1–10. DOI: 10.37801/ajad2009.6.2.5

Harikaran, M., Boopathi, S., Gokulakannan, S., & Poonguzhali, M. (2023). Study on the Source of E-Waste Management and Disposal Methods. In *Sustainable Approaches and Strategies for E-Waste Management and Utilization* (pp. 39–60). IGI Global. DOI: 10.4018/978-1-6684-7573-7.ch003

Hariram, N. P., Mekha, K. B., Suganthan, V., & Sudhakar, K. (2023). Sustainalism: An Integrated Socio-Economic-Environmental Model to Address Sustainable Development and Sustainability. *Sustainability (Basel)*, *15*(13), 10682. Advance online publication. DOI: 10.3390/su151310682

Hasan, M. R., Khan, M. A., & Wuest, T. (2024). Towards Industry 5.0: A Systematic Literature Review on Sustainable and Green Composite Materials Supply Chains. *arXiv preprint arXiv:2402.06100*.

Heintz, H. T. (2004). Applying the concept of sustainability to water resources management. *Water Resources Update*, *127*(1), 6–10.

Hinderer, S., Brändle, L., & Kuckertz, A. (2021). Transition to a sustainable bioeconomy. *Sustainability (Basel)*, *13*(15), 8232. Advance online publication. DOI: 10.3390/su13158232

HLPE. (2013). *Investing in smallholder agriculture for food security*. High Level Panel of Experts on Food Security and Nutrition. https://www.fao.org/3/i2953e/i2953e.pdf

Högfeldt, A. K., Rosén, A., Mwase, C., Lantz, A., Gumaelius, L., Shayo, E., Lujara, S., & Mvungi, N. (2019). Mutual capacity building through north-south collaboration using challenge-driven education. *Sustainability (Basel)*, *11*(24), 7236. Advance online publication. DOI: 10.3390/su11247236

Höglund, L. (1999). Household demand for water in Sweden with implications of a potential tax on water use. *Water Resources Research*, *35*(12), 3853–3863. DOI: 10.1029/1999WR900219

Home, R., Indermuehle, A., Tschanz, A., Ries, E., & Stolze, M. (2019). Factors in the decision by Swiss farmers to convert to organic farming. *Renewable Agriculture and Food Systems*, *34*(6), 571–581. DOI: 10.1017/S1742170518000121

Howard, A., & Moubray, J. (1940). The book of the quarter: 1an agricultural testament. *African Affairs*, *39*(CLVII), 367–375. DOI: 10.1093/oxfordjournals.afraf.a101058

Huang, Y., & Fan, L. (1993). Artificial intelligence for waste minimization in the process industry. *Computers in Industry*, *22*(2), 117–128. DOI: 10.1016/0166-3615(93)90059-A

Huang, Y., Huang, X., Xie, M., Cheng, W., & Shu, Q. (2021). A study on the effects of regional differences on agricultural water resource utilization efficiency using super-efficiency SBM model. *Scientific Reports, 11*(1), 1–18. DOI: 10.1038/s41598-021-89293-2 PMID: 33976285

Hurst, G. A., Slootweg, J. C., Balu, A. M., Climent-Bellido, M. S., Gomera, A., Gomez, P., Luque, R., Mammino, L., Spanevello, R. A., Saito, K., & Ibanez, J. G. (2019). International Perspectives on Green and Sustainable Chemistry Education via Systems Thinking. *Journal of Chemical Education, 96*(12), 2794–2804. DOI: 10.1021/acs.jchemed.9b00341

Hussain, Z., Babe, M., Saravanan, S., Srimathy, G., Roopa, H., & Boopathi, S. (2023). Optimizing Biomass-to-Biofuel Conversion: IoT and AI Integration for Enhanced Efficiency and Sustainability. In *Circular Economy Implementation for Sustainability in the Built Environment* (pp. 191–214). IGI Global.

Ibro, M. K., Ancha, V. R., Lemma, D. B., & Pohl, M. (2024). Enhancing Biodegradability of Coffee Husk and Water Hyacinth Using Food Waste: Synergistic and Kinetic Evaluation Under Co-digestion. *BioEnergy Research, 17*(3), 1953–1970. DOI: 10.1007/s12155-024-10750-7

IEA, IRENA, UNSD, World Bank, WHO. (2023). Tracking SDG 7: The Energy Progress Report. World Bank, Washington DC. https://trackingsdg7.esmap.org/time

Ikram, L., Afaf, D., & Latifa, E. (2024, May). Beyond Industry 5.0: Tracing the Past, Present, and Future of Digital Industrial Transformations. In *2024 4th International Conference on Innovative Research in Applied Science, Engineering and Technology (IRASET)* (pp. 1-7). IEEE.

Indian Council of Agricultural Research. (2013). Post-harvest management and value-addition. In DARE/ICAR Annual Report 2012–13 (pp. 68–73). ICAR.

Ingle, R. B., Swathi, S., Mahendran, G., Senthil, T., Muralidharan, N., & Boopathi, S. (2023). Sustainability and Optimization of Green and Lean Manufacturing Processes Using Machine Learning Techniques. In *Circular Economy Implementation for Sustainability in the Built Environment* (pp. 261–285). IGI Global. DOI: 10.4018/978-1-6684-8238-4.ch012

Ingrao, C., Strippoli, R., Lagioia, G., & Huisingh, D. (2023). Water scarcity in agriculture: An overview of causes, impacts and approaches for reducing the risk. *Heliyon, 9*(8), 1–16. DOI: 10.1016/j.heliyon.2023.e18507 PMID: 37534016

International Centre for Environment Audit and Sustainable Development (iCED), Jaipur, India, The Energy and Resources Institute (TERI), New Delhi. Municipal Solid Waste Management in India-A Compendium Report. International Centre for Environment Audit and Sustainable Development (iCED). Published 2022. Accessed March 27, 2025.

IPBES. (2019). *Global assessment report on biodiversity and ecosystem services*. https://ipbes.net/global-assessment

IPCC. (2019). *Climate change and land: An IPCC special report on climate change, desertification, land degradation, sustainable land management, food security, and greenhouse gas fluxes in terrestrial ecosystems*. https://www.ipcc.ch/srccl/

IRENA. (2023). *Renewable Capacity Statistics 2023; & IRENA (2023), Renewable Energy Statistics 2023*. The International Renewable Energy Agency.

Ischia, G., & Fiori, L. (2021). Hydrothermal carbonization of organic waste and biomass: A review on process, reactor, and plant modeling. *Waste and Biomass Valorization*, *12*(6), 2797–2824. DOI: 10.1007/s12649-020-01255-3

Ishaq, M., Ghouse, G., Fernandez-Gonzalez, R., Puime-Guillen, F., Tandir, N., & Santos de Oliveira, H. M. (2022). From fossil energy to renewable energy: Why is circular economy needed in the energy transition? *Frontiers in Environmental Science*, *10*, 941791. DOI: 10.3389/fenvs.2022.941791

Issa, I., Delbrück, S., & Hamm, U. (2019). Bioeconomy from experts' perspectives – Results of a global expert survey. In *PLoS ONE* (Vol. 14, Issue 5). Public Library of Science. DOI: 10.1371/journal.pone.0215917

Ivar Virgin and E. Jane Morris. (2017). *Creating Sustainable Bioeconomies*. www .routledge.com/series/RSEE

Janardhana, K., Singh, V., Singh, S. N., Babu, T. R., Bano, S., & Boopathi, S. (2023). Utilization Process for Electronic Waste in Eco-Friendly Concrete: Experimental Study. In *Sustainable Approaches and Strategies for E-Waste Management and Utilization* (pp. 204–223). IGI Global.

Jeyaseeli, P., Jeyamangalam, F., Selvaraj, S., & Vella, D. S. (2021). Investigation of physico-chemical, physical properties and moisture content studies of soil using organic amendment. *Agricultural Technology (Thailand)*, *17*(3), 855–870.

Jiang, P., Zhang, L., You, S., Van Fan, Y., Tan, R. R., Klemeš, J. J., & You, F. (2023). Blockchain technology applications in waste management: Overview, challenges and opportunities. *Journal of Cleaner Production*, *421*, 138466. DOI: 10.1016/j. jclepro.2023.138466

Jiang, X., Zhao, Y., & Yan, J. (2022). Disposal technology and new progress for dioxins and heavy metals in fly ash from municipal solid waste incineration: A critical review. *Environmental Pollution*, *311*, 119878. DOI: 10.1016/j.envpol.2022.119878 PMID: 35944780

Jiménez Aliaga, R., De los Ríos-Carmenado, I., Huamán Cristóbal, A. E., Aliaga Balbín, H., & Marroquín Heros, A. M. (2023). Competencies and Capabilities for the Management of Sustainable Rural Development Projects in the Value Chain: Perception from Small and Medium-Sized Business Agents in Jauja, Peru. *Sustainability (Basel)*, *15*(21), 15580. Advance online publication. DOI: 10.3390/su152115580

Jimenez, M., Van der Veken, L., Neirynck, H., Rodríguez, H., Ruiz, O., & Swennen, R. (2007). Organic banana production in Ecuador: Its implications on black Sigatoka development and plant–soil nutritional status. *Renewable Agriculture and Food Systems*, *22*(4), 297–306. DOI: 10.1017/S1742170507001895

Jin, Q., Chen, H., & Hu, F. (2024). Proposal of Industry 5.0-Enabled Sustainability of Product–Service Systems and Its Quantitative Multi-Criteria Decision-Making Method. *Processes (Basel, Switzerland)*, *12*(3), 473. DOI: 10.3390/pr12030473

João, E. (2021). *Outcome of the summer school for teachers interested in developing bioeconomy curricula 2 Document information Project name: BE-Rural Project title: Bio-based strategies and roadmaps for enhanced rural and regional development in the EU Internal peer review: Ludmila Metzova, Martin Stoyanov (BIA)*. https://be-rural.eu/.

John, J., Varkey, M. S., Podder, R. S., Sensarma, N., Selvi, M., Santhosh Kumar, S. V. N., & Kannan, A. (2022). Smart prediction and monitoring of waste disposal system using IoT and cloud for IoT based smart cities. *Wireless Personal Communications*, *122*(1), 243–275. DOI: 10.1007/s11277-021-08897-z

Juvančič, L., & Van Leeuwen, M. (2021). *Unleashing regional bioeconomy potential: the BioEconomy Regional Strategy Toolkit.*, http://www.berst.eu/RegionalPartners.aspx

Kala, K., & Bolia, N. B. (2024). Empowering the informal sector in urban waste management: Towards a comprehensive waste management policy for India. *Environmental Development*, *49*, 100968. DOI: 10.1016/j.envdev.2024.100968

Kalmykova, Y., Sadagopan, M., & Rosado, L. (2018). Circular economy–From review of theories and practices to development of implementation tools. *Resources, Conservation and Recycling*, *135*(1), 190–201. DOI: 10.1016/j.resconrec.2017.10.034

Kalnbalkite, A., Pubule, J., & Blumberga, D. (2022). Education for Advancing the Implementation of the Green Deal Goals for Bioeconomy. *Environmental and Climate Technologies*, *26*(1), 75–83. DOI: 10.2478/rtuect-2022-0007

Kamilaris, A., Kartakoullis, A., & Prenafeta-Boldú, F. X. (2017). A review on the practice of big data analysis in agriculture. *Computers and Electronics in Agriculture*, *143*, 23–37. DOI: 10.1016/j.compag.2017.09.037

Kamyab, H., SaberiKamarposhti, M., Hashim, H., & Yusuf, M. (2024). Carbon dynamics in agricultural greenhouse gas emissions and removals: A comprehensive review. *Carbon Letters*, *34*(1), 265–289. DOI: 10.1007/s42823-023-00647-4

Kannan, D., Amiri, A. S., Shaayesteh, M. T., Nasr, A. K., & Mina, H. (2024). Unveiling barriers to the integration of blockchain-based circular economy and Industry 5.0 in manufacturing industries: A strategic prioritization approach. *Business Strategy and the Environment*, *33*(8), 7855–7886. DOI: 10.1002/bse.3886

Kant, S., Adula, M., & Alemu, G. M. (2025). Effect of Green Supply Chain Management Practice on Firm Performance With Mediation of Green Innovation in Ethiopia. In *Eco-Logistics and Sustainable Supply Chain Innovations* (pp. 61–84). IGI Global.

Kareem, A., Farooqi, Z. U. R., Kalsom, A., Mohy-Ud-Din, W., Hussain, M. M., Raza, M., & Khursheed, M. M. (2022). Organic farming for sustainable soil use, management, food production and climate change mitigation. *Sustainable agriculture: technical progressions and transitions*, 39-59.

Katari, V., Goyal, S., Nigam, V., Jana, M., Maitra, A., Sharma, H., & Sahu, K. K. (2024). A Confluence of Emerging Technologies Like IoT, Edge & Cloud Computing, Blockchain, Industry 4.0 & 5.0, AI & ML toward the Realization of Eco-Friendly Supercapacitors. In *Eco-Friendly Supercapacitors: Design and Future Perspectives in Sustainable and Green Energy Storage Devices* (pp. 163-204). American Chemical Society.

Katko, T. S., & Hukka, J. J. (2015). Social and economic importance of water services in the build environment: Need for more structural thinking. *Procedia Economics and Finance*, *21*(1), 217–223. DOI: 10.1016/S2212-5671(15)00170-7

Khalifa, A. A., Ibrahim, A. J., Amhamed, A. I., & El-Naas, M. H. (2022). Accelerating the transition to a circular economy for net-zero emissions by 2050: A systematic review. *Sustainability (Basel)*, *14*(18), 11656. DOI: 10.3390/su141811656

Khan, H., & Khan, I. U. (2012). From growth to sustainable development in developing countries: A conceptual framework. *Environment and Ecology*, *3*(1), 23–31.

Khan, S. A. R., Ponce, P., Thomas, G., Yu, Z., Al-Ahmadi, M. S., & Tanveer, M. (2021). Digital technologies, circular economy practices and environmental policies in the era of COVID-19. *Sustainability (Basel), 13*(22), 12790. DOI: 10.3390/su132212790

Khunt, R. S., Makadia, J. J., & Varasani, J. V. (2022). Review on prospects and constraints of organic production in India: A new paradigm in agricultural production. *Indian Journal of Economics and Development, 18*(4), 958–964.

Kibria, M. G., Masuk, N. I., Safayet, R., Nguyen, H. Q., & Mourshed, M. (2023). Plastic Waste: Challenges and Opportunities to Mitigate Pollution and Effective Management. *International Journal of Environmental Research, 17*(1), 20. DOI: 10.1007/s41742-023-00507-z PMID: 36711426

Kim, H. (2018). Economic and environmental implications of the recent energy transition on South Korea's electricity sector. *Energy & Environment, 29*(5), 752–769. DOI: 10.1177/0958305X18759177

King, F. H. (2004). Farmers of forty centuries: Organic farming in China, Korea, and Japan. *Courier Corporation.*

Kishore, A. R., Niveditha, K., Uriti, A., Anilkumar, C., Sarabu, A., & Prasanna, K. V. L. (2023, December). An in-depth Analysis of the Elements Shaping Organic Farmers: A Systematic Review. In *2023 International Conference on Energy, Materials and Communication Engineering (ICEMCE)* (pp. 1-5). IEEE. DOI: 10.1109/ICEMCE57940.2023.10434263

Koshariya, A. K., Khatoon, S., Marathe, A. M., Suba, G. M., Baral, D., & Boopathi, S. (2023). Agricultural Waste Management Systems Using Artificial Intelligence Techniques. In *AI-Enabled Social Robotics in Human Care Services* (pp. 236–258). IGI Global. DOI: 10.4018/978-1-6684-8171-4.ch009

Krause, B. (2015). *Voices of the wild: Animal songs, human din, and the call to save natural soundscapes*. Yale University Press.

Kriesch, L., & Losacker, S. (2024). Bioeconomy firms and where to find them. *REGION, 11*(1), 55–78. DOI: 10.18335/region.v11i1.523

Kumar, D. J. P., Mishra, R. K., Chinnam, S., Binnal, P., & Dwivedi, N. (2024). A comprehensive study on anaerobic digestion of organic solid waste: A review on configurations, operating parameters, techno-economic analysis and current trends. *Biotechnology Notes, 5*, 33–49. DOI: 10.1016/j.biotno.2024.02.001 PMID: 39660169

Kumar, R., Gupta, G., Hussain, A., Rani, A., Thapliyal, A., Gunsola, D., & Mitra, D. (2025). Pioneering zero-waste technologies utilization and its framework on sustainable management: International, national and state level. *Discover Applied Sciences*, *7*(3), 224. DOI: 10.1007/s42452-025-06693-z

Kuwornu, J. K., Oduro, E., Amegashie, D. P., Fening, K. O., Yangyouru, M., MacCarthy, D. S., & Datta, A. (2018). Cost-benefit analysis of conventional and integrated crop management for vegetable production. *International Journal of Vegetable Science*, *24*(6), 597–611. DOI: 10.1080/19315260.2018.1457585

La Vía Campesina. (2019). *Declaration of the rights of peasants and other people working in rural areas*. https://viacampesina.org/en/declaration-of-the-rights-of-peasants/

Lado, C. (1997). Socio-economic factors influencing sustainable water supply in Botswana. *GeoJournal*, *41*(1), 43–53. DOI: 10.1023/A:1006844220546 PMID: 12348506

Lahti, T., Wincent, J., & Parida, V. (2018). A definition and theoretical review of the circular economy, value creation, and sustainable business models: Where are we now and where should research move in the future? *Sustainability (Basel)*, *10*(8), 2799. DOI: 10.3390/su10082799

Lampkin, N. (1990). *Organic Farming Farming Press Books and Videos*. Ipswitch.

Lant, C. (2004). Water resources sustainability: An ecological economics perspective. *Water Resources Update*, *127*(2), 20–30.

Latin American, E. U. – C., & Platform, C. S. (EU-C. (2023). Bioeconomy and Nature-Based Solutions. In *EU-CELAC Platform*.

Laumann, F., & Tambo, T. (2018). Enterprise architecture for a facilitated transformation from a linear to a circular economy. *Sustainability (Basel)*, *10*(11), 3882. DOI: 10.3390/su10113882

Leavy, S., Allegretti, G., Presotto, E., Montoya, M. A., & Talamini, E. (2024). Measuring the bioeconomy economically: Exploring the connections between concepts, methods, data, indicators and their limitations. *Sustainability (Basel)*, *16*(20), 8727. DOI: 10.3390/su16208727

Lee, M. E., Steiman, M. W., & Angelo, S. K. S. (2021). Biogas digestate as a renewable fertilizer: Effects of digestate application on crop growth and nutrient composition. *Renewable Agriculture and Food Systems*, *36*(2), 173–181. DOI: 10.1017/S1742170520000186

Lemke, S., Smith, N., Thiim, C., & Stump, K. (2024). Drivers and barriers to adoption of regenerative agriculture: Cases studies on lessons learned from organic. *International Journal of Agricultural Sustainability*, *22*(1), 2324216. DOI: 10.1080/14735903.2024.2324216

Leontief, W. (1991). The economy as a circular flow. *Structural Change and Economic Dynamics*, *2*(1), 181–212. DOI: 10.1016/0954-349X(91)90012-H

Lewandowski, I. (2017). Bioeconomy: Shaping the transition to a sustainable, biobased economy. In *Bioeconomy: Shaping the Transition to a Sustainable, Biobased Economy*. Springer International Publishing., DOI: 10.1007/978-3-319-68152-8

Lewandowski, M. (2016). Designing the business models for circular economy—Towards the conceptual framework. *Sustainability (Basel)*, *8*(1), 43. DOI: 10.3390/su8010043

Li, H., Spelman, D., & Sansalone, J. (2023). Coupling Computational Fluid Dynamics and Artificial Intelligence for Sustainable Urban Water Management and Treatment. *Environmental Sciences Proceedings*, *21*(1), 87.

Lima, P. A., Jesus, G. M., Ortiz, C. R., Frascareli, F. C., Souza, F. B., & Mariano, E. B. (2021). Sustainable development as freedom: Trends and opportunities for the circular economy in the human development literature. *Sustainability (Basel)*, *13*(23), 13407. DOI: 10.3390/su132313407

Lin, B. H., Smith, T. A., & Huang, C. L. (2008). Organic premiums of US fresh produce. *Renewable Agriculture and Food Systems*, *23*(3), 208–216. DOI: 10.1017/S1742170508002238

Lindamulla, L., Nanayakkara, N., Othman, M., Jinadasa, S., Herath, G., & Jegatheesan, V. (2022). Municipal solid waste landfill leachate characteristics and their treatment options in tropical countries. *Current Pollution Reports*, *8*(3), 273–287. DOI: 10.1007/s40726-022-00222-x

Li, Q., & Zhang, S. (2025). Impact of globalization and industrialization on ecological footprint: Do institutional quality and renewable energy matter? *Frontiers in Environmental Science*, *13*(1), 1–16. DOI: 10.3389/fenvs.2025.1535638

Lishma, N. P., Cherian, K. A., Louis, V., Sureshkumar, R., Kumar, P. N., Chandran, D., Pran, M., & Sharma, R. (2024). Integrated management of Fusarium wilt disease of banana in Kerala, India. *Vegetos*, *37*(1), 117–124. DOI: 10.1007/s42535-023-00576-7

Litterick, A. M., & Watson, C. A. (2016). *Organic Farming. Encylopedia of Applied Plant Sciences* (Vol. 3). Elsevier., DOI: 10.1016/B978-0-12-394807-6.00004-6

Lo, H. W., Chan, H. W., Lin, J. W., & Lin, S. W. (2024). Evaluating the interrelationships of industrial 5.0 development factors using an integration approach of Fermatean Fuzzy Logic. *Journal of Operations Intelligence*, *2*(1), 95–113. DOI: 10.31181/jopi21202416

Loizides, M. I., Loizidou, X. I., Orthodoxou, D. L., & Petsa, D. (2019). Circular bioeconomy in action: Collection and recycling of domestic used cooking oil through a social, reverse logistics system. *Recycling*, *4*(2), 16. Advance online publication. DOI: 10.3390/recycling4020016

Lorenz, K., & Lal, R. (2016). Environmental impact of organic agriculture. *Advances in Agronomy*, *139*, 99–152. DOI: 10.1016/bs.agron.2016.05.003

Lori, M., Symnaczik, S., Mäder, P., De Deyn, G., & Gattinger, A. (2017). Organic farming enhances soil microbial abundance and activity—A meta-analysis and meta-regression. *PLoS One*, *12*(7), e0180442. DOI: 10.1371/journal.pone.0180442

Lowe, M., Qin, R., & Mao, X. (2022). A Review on Machine Learning, Artificial Intelligence, and Smart Technology in Water Treatment and Monitoring. *Water (Basel)*, *14*(9), 1384. DOI: 10.3390/w14091384

Luczka, W., Smoluk-Sikorska, J., & Wojciechowska-Solis, J. (2024). Opportunities and Barriers to the Development of Organic Farming from the Perspective of Conventional Farms. *European Research Studies*, *27*(2), 607–619. DOI: 10.35808/ersj/3862

Luo, J., Dang, R., Lan, P., Hu, Y., & Yang, B. (2025). Urban-rural disparities in low-carbon policy intensity and residents' willingness to pay in environmental sustainability. *Cities (London, England)*, *159*, 105795. DOI: 10.1016/j.cities.2025.105795

Lynch, D. H., Halberg, N., & Bhatta, G. D. (2012). Environmental impacts of organic agriculture in temperate regions. *CABI Reviews*, 1-17.

MacArthur, E. (2013). Towards the circular economy, economic and business rationale for an accelerated transition. Ellen MacArthur Foundation: Cowes, UK, 1. https://www.ellenmacarthurfoundation.org/towards-the-circular-economy-vol-1-an-economic-and-business-rationale-for-an

Macarthur, E. L. L. E. N., & Heading, H. E. A. D. I. N. G. (2019). How the circular economy tackles climate change. *Ellen MacArthur Found*, 1(1), 1-71. https://www.ellenmacarthurfoundation.org/completing-the-picture

MacArthur, E., Zumwinkel, K., & Stuchtey, M. R. (2015). Growth within: a circular economy vision for a competitive Europe. *Ellen MacArthur Foundation*, 100. https://www.ellenmacarthurfoundation.org/growth-within-a-circular-economy-vision-for-a-competitive-europe

Maguluri, L. P., Ananth, J., Hariram, S., Geetha, C., Bhaskar, A., & Boopathi, S. (2023). Smart Vehicle-Emissions Monitoring System Using Internet of Things (IoT). In *Handbook of Research on Safe Disposal Methods of Municipal Solid Wastes for a Sustainable Environment* (pp. 191–211). IGI Global.

Majeed, M. T., & Luni, T. (2020). Renewable energy, circular economy indicators and environmental quality: A global evidence of 131 countries with heterogeneous income groups. [PJCSS]. *Pakistan Journal of Commerce and Social Sciences*, *14*(4), 866–912. https://www.econstor.eu/handle/10419/228728

Mamimin, C., Chanthong, S., Leamdum, C., O-Thong, S., & Prasertsan, P. (2021). Improvement of empty palm fruit bunches biodegradability and biogas production by integrating the straw mushroom cultivation as a pretreatment in the solid-state anaerobic digestion. *Bioresource Technology*, *319*, 124227. DOI: 10.1016/j.biortech.2020.124227 PMID: 33049444

Mamo, M., Kassa, H., Ingale, L., & Dondeyne, S. (2021). Evaluation of compost quality from municipal solid waste integrated with organic additive in Mizan–Aman town, Southwest Ethiopia. *BMC Chemistry*, *15*(1), 1–11. DOI: 10.1186/s13065-021-00770-1 PMID: 34281617

Marconi, P., & Rosa, L. (2023). Role of biomethane to offset natural gas. *Renewable & Sustainable Energy Reviews*, *187*, 113697. DOI: 10.1016/j.rser.2023.113697

Mariappan, S., Arumugam, S., Ponnusamy, J., Natesan, R., & Kumar, S. S. (2025). Next-generation natural farming practices for crop improvement. In *Next-Generation Strategies for Crop Improvement* (pp. 307–354). Springer., DOI: 10.1007/978-981-95-0309-4_11

Marquez, R., Barrios, N., Vera, R., Mendez, M. E., Tolosa, L., Zambrano, F., & Li, Y. (2023). *A Perspective on The Synergistic Potential of Artificial Intelligence and Product-Based Learning Strategies in Biobased Materials Education*. https://doi.org/DOI: 10.21203/rs.3.rs-2711749/v1

Martín, C., Zervakis, G. I., Xiong, S., Koutrotsios, G., & Strætkvern, K. O. (2023). Spent substrate from mushroom cultivation: Exploitation potential toward various applications and value-added products. *Bioengineered*, *14*(1), 2252138. DOI: 10.1080/21655979.2023.2252138 PMID: 37670430

Martín-Gómez, A. M., Agote-Garrido, A., & Lama-Ruiz, J. R. (2024). A Framework for Sustainable Manufacturing: Integrating Industry 4.0 Technologies with Industry 5.0 Values. *Sustainability (Basel), 16*(4), 1364. DOI: 10.3390/su16041364

Martini, B., Bellisario, D., & Coletti, P. (2024). Human-centered and sustainable artificial intelligence in industry 5.0: Challenges and perspectives. *Sustainability (Basel), 16*(13), 5448. DOI: 10.3390/su16135448

Mathaba, M., & Banza, J. (2024). A comprehensive review on artificial intelligence in water treatment for optimization. Clean water now and the future. *Journal of Environmental Science and Health. Part A, Toxic/Hazardous Substances & Environmental Engineering*, •••, 1–14. DOI: 10.1080/10934529.2024.2309102 PMID: 38293764

Matheri, A. N., Sithole, Z. B., & Mohamed, B. (2024). Data-driven circular economy of biowaste to bioenergy with conventional prediction modelling and machine learning. *Circular Economy and Sustainability, 4*(2), 929–950. DOI: 10.1007/s43615-023-00329-3

Mathew, A., Amudha, P., & Sivakumari, S. (2021). Deep learning techniques: An overview. In *Advanced Machine Learning Technologies and Applications: Proceedings of AMLTA 2020* (pp. 599–608). Springer. https://doi.org/DOI: 10.1007/978-3-030-67280-2_49

Meena, A. L., Karwal, M., Dutta, D., & Mishra, R. P. (2021). Composting: phases and factors responsible for efficient and improved composting. *Agriculture and Food: e-Newsletter, 1*, 85-90.

Mehmood, U., Tariq, S., Aslam, M. U., Agyekum, E. B., Uhunamure, S. E., Shale, K., Kamal, M., & Khan, M. F. (2023). Evaluating the impact of digitalization, renewable energy use, and technological innovation on load capacity factor in G8 nations. *Scientific Reports, 13*(1), 1–15. DOI: 10.1038/s41598-023-36373-0 PMID: 37277449

Mian, S. H., Salah, B., Ameen, W., Moiduddin, K., & Alkhalefah, H. (2020). Adapting universities for sustainability education in industry 4.0: Channel of challenges and opportunities. *Sustainability (Basel), 12*(15), 6100. Advance online publication. DOI: 10.3390/su12156100

Mishra, S., Chauhan, M. S., Sundaramurthy, S., Raj, V., Vishwakarma, A., & Niranjan, U. S. (2024). Waste to Wealth: A Philosophy of Zero Waste. In *From Waste to Wealth* (pp. 85–107). Springer Nature Singapore. DOI: 10.1007/978-981-99-7552-5_5

Mitra, S. K. (2008). Organic tropical and subtropical fruit production in India-prospects and challenges. In *IV International Symposium on Tropical and Subtropical Fruits 975* (pp. 303-307).

Mohanty, A., Venkateswaran, N., Ranjit, P., Tripathi, M. A., & Boopathi, S. (2023). Innovative Strategy for Profitable Automobile Industries: Working Capital Management. In *Handbook of Research on Designing Sustainable Supply Chains to Achieve a Circular Economy* (pp. 412–428). IGI Global.

Mollison, B. (1990). *Permaculture: A practical guide for a sustainable future.* Island Press.

Mongo, M., Laforest, V., Belaïd, F., & Tanguy, A. (2021). Assessment of the impact of the circular economy on CO2 emissions in Europe. *Journal of Innovation Economics & Management*, I107-29. https://shs.cairn.info/revue-journal-of-innovation-economics-2022-3-page-15?lang=en

Mpanga, I. K., Tronstad, R., Guo, J., LeBauer, D. S., & Idowu, O. J. (2021). On-farm land management strategies and production challenges in United States organic agricultural systems. *Current Research in Environmental Sustainability, 3*, 100097. DOI: 10.1016/j.crsust.2021.100097

Musah, A., & Yakubu, I. N. (2023). Exploring industrialization and environmental sustainability dynamics in Ghana: A fully modified least squares approach. *Technological Sustainability, 2*(2), 142–155. DOI: 10.1108/TECHS-06-2022-0028

Mutezo, G., & Mulopo, J. (2021). A review of Africa's transition from fossil fuels to renewable energy using circular economy principles. *Renewable & Sustainable Energy Reviews, 137*, 110609. DOI: 10.1016/j.rser.2020.110609

MYILSAMY SURESHKUMAR, V. R. P., S. BOOPATHI, M. SABAREESH. (2018). The improving Wear Resistance Properties of Molybdenum Alloy Under Cryogenic Treatment. *International Journal of Mechanical and Production Engineering Research and Development, 8*(7), 724–728.

Nandwani, D., & Nwosisi, S. (2016). Global trends in organic agriculture. *Organic farming for sustainable agriculture*, 1-35.

Narkhede, G. B., Pasi, B. N., Rajhans, N., & Kulkarni, A. (2024). Industry 5.0 and sustainable manufacturing: A systematic literature review. *Benchmarking.*

Nastase, M. (2013). Issues Regarding the Certification of Organic Vegetables in Romania. *Quality - Access to Success*, •••, 118–123.

National Footprint and Biocapacity Accounts. (2023). *GDP, International Financial Statistics (IFS); Population*. U.N. Food and Agriculture Organization.

Nguyen-Phung, H. T., & Le, H. (2024). Elderlywell-being amidst energy poverty: Exploring the health, social, and economic impacts in Vietnam. *Energy Research & Social Science*, *118*, 103762. DOI: 10.1016/j.erss.2024.103762

Niwalkar, A., Indorkar, T., Gupta, A., Anshul, A., Bherwani, H., Biniwale, R., & Kumar, R. (2023). Circular economy based approach for green energy transitions and climate change benefits. *Proceedings of the Indian National Science Academy. Part A, Physical Sciences*, *89*(1), 37–50. DOI: 10.1007/s43538-022-00137-7

Nmere, O. N., Abugu, J. O., Alio, F. C., & Anetoh, J. C. (2020). Influence of public relations' media public enlightenment campaign and community participation strategies on waste management. *Problems and Perspectives in Management*, *18*(1), 82. DOI: 10.21511/ppm.18(1).2020.08

Nordahl, S. L., Preble, C. V., Kirchstetter, T. W., & Scown, C. D. (2023). Greenhouse gas and air pollutant emissions from composting. *Environmental Science & Technology*, *57*(6), 2235–2247. DOI: 10.1021/acs.est.2c05846 PMID: 36719708

Núñez-Sánchez, S., & Valente, M. J. (2023). Sustainable Development Goals and Climate Change in Spanish Technology Disciplines' Curricula: From LOMCE to LOMLOE. *Sustainability (Basel)*, *15*(13), 10301. Advance online publication. DOI: 10.3390/su151310301

O'Connell, E. (2017). Towards Adaptation of Water Resource Systems to Climatic and Socio-Economic Change. *Water Resources Management*, *31*(1), 2965–2984. DOI: 10.1007/s11269-017-1734-2

Ocampo-López, C., Muñoz-Blandón, O., Rendón-Castrillón, L., & Ramírez-Carmona, M. (2023). Post-Digital Learning for Rural Development: A Case Study of Open Biotec MOOCs in Colombia. *Future Internet*, *15*(4), 141. Advance online publication. DOI: 10.3390/fi15040141

Okafor, C., Madu, C., Ajaero, C., Ibekwe, J., & Otunomo, F. (2021). Situating coupled circular economy and energy transition in an emerging economy. *AIMS Energy*, *9*(4), 651–675. DOI: 10.3934/energy.2021031

Onpraphai, T., Jintrawet, A., Keoboualapha, B., Khuenjai, S., Guo, R., Wang, J., & Fan, J. (2021). Sustaining biomaterials in bioeconomy: Roles of education and learning in mekong river basin. *Forests*, *12*(12), 1670. Advance online publication. DOI: 10.3390/f12121670

Ortiz, J. A., & Zamudio-García, V. M. (2025). Optimising Water Use Through Smart Models and Artificial Intelligence. In *Smart Water Technology for Sustainable Management in Modern Cities* (pp. 165–196). IGI Global Scientific Publishing. DOI: 10.4018/979-8-3693-8074-1.ch008

Ostermann, C. M., Nascimento, L. da S., Steinbruch, F. K., & Callegaro-de-Menezes, D. (2021). Drivers to implement the circular economy in born-sustainable business models: A case study in the fashion industry. *Revista de Gestão*, *28*(3), 223–240. DOI: 10.1108/REGE-03-2020-0017

Pajura, R. (2024). Composting municipal solid waste and animal manure in response to the current fertilizer crisis-a recent review. *The Science of the Total Environment*, *912*, 169221. DOI: 10.1016/j.scitotenv.2023.169221 PMID: 38101643

Pandey, P. R., Gupta, J. K., Narvariya, R. K., Meena, S. C., & Narwariya, D. (2019). Constraints faced by farmers in adoption of integrated farming system in Vindhyan Plateau of Madhya Pradesh. *Plant Archives*, *19*(2), 512–514.

Panghal, V., Singh, A., Arora, D., & Kumar, S. (2024). Biochar-modified constructed wetlands using Eclipta alba as a plant for sustainable rural wastewater treatment. *Environmental Science and Pollution Research International*, *31*(11), 17299–17310. DOI: 10.1007/s11356-024-32144-0 PMID: 38340301

Panneerselvam, P., Halberg, N., Vaarst, M., & Hermansen, J. E. (2012). Indian farmers' experience with and perceptions of organic farming. *Renewable Agriculture and Food Systems*, *27*(2), 157–169. DOI: 10.1017/S1742170511000238

Parthasarathy, P., Zuhara, S., Al-Ansari, T., & McKay, G. (2023). A review on catalytic CO2 pyrolysis of organic wastes to high-value products. *Fuel*, *335*, 127073. DOI: 10.1016/j.fuel.2022.127073

Pascoli, D. U., Aui, A., Frank, J., Therasme, O., Dixon, K., Gustafson, R., Kelly, B., Volk, T. A., & Wright, M. M. (2022). The US bioeconomy at the intersection of technology, policy, and education. *Biofuels, Bioproducts & Biorefining*, *16*(1), 9–26. DOI: 10.1002/bbb.2302

Patel, R. (2009). Food sovereignty. *The Journal of Peasant Studies*, *36*(3), 663–706. DOI: 10.1080/03066150903143079

PIB. (2023). Research unit, Press Information Bureau, Ministry of Information and Broad, Government of India. https://static.pib.gov.in/WriteReadData/specificdocs/documents/2023/may/doc2023517199601.pdf

Pieroni, M. P., McAloone, T. C., & Pigosso, D. C. (2019). Business model innovation for circular economy and sustainability: A review of approaches. *Journal of Cleaner Production, 215*, 198–216. DOI: 10.1016/j.jclepro.2019.01.036

Pink, M., Kiełbasa, B., Tamáš, V., Pereira, F. M. D. S. M., Santamarta, J. C., Cruz Pérez, N., Rodríguez-Alcántara, J. S., & Luty, L. (2024). Perception and awareness of the bioeconomy: An empirical study of chosen European academia. *International Journal of Sustainability in Higher Education, 25*(6), 1137–1155. DOI: 10.1108/IJSHE-01-2023-0002

Piron, M., Wu, J., Fedele, A., & Manzardo, A. (2024). Industry 4.0 and life cycle assessment: Evaluation of the technology applications as an asset for the life cycle inventory. *The Science of the Total Environment, 916*, 170263. DOI: 10.1016/j.scitotenv.2024.170263 PMID: 38253101

Poore, J., & Nemecek, T. (2018). Reducing food's environmental impacts through producers and consumers. *Science, 360*(6392), 987–992. DOI: 10.1126/science.aaq0216 PMID: 29853680

Priefer, C., Jörissen, J., & Frör, O. (2017). Pathways to shape the bioeconomy. In *Resources* (Vol. 6, Issue 1). Molecular Diversity Preservation International Publishing (MDPI). DOI: 10.3390/resources6010010

Pubule, J., Blumberga, A., Rozakis, S., Vecina, A., Kalnbalkite, A., & Blumberga, D. (2020). Education for advancing the implementation of the bioeconomy goals: An analysis of MASTER study programmes in bioeconomy. *Environmental and Climate Technologies, 24*(2), 149–159. DOI: 10.2478/rtuect-2020-0062

Purvis, B., Celebi, D., & Pansera, M. (2023). A framework for a responsible circular economy. *Journal of Cleaner Production, 400*, 136679. DOI: 10.1016/j.jclepro.2023.136679

Qi, S., Chen, Y., Wang, X., Yang, Y., Teng, J., & Wang, Y. (2024). Exploration and practice of "zero-waste city" in China. *Circular Economy, 3*(1), 100079. DOI: 10.1016/j.cec.2024.100079

Rahmaniah, H., Darma, R., Asrul, L., & Taufik, D. K. (2020, October). The potential of organic agriculture, soil structure and farmers income for inclusive agriculture sustainability: A review. [). IOP Publishing.]. *IOP Conference Series. Earth and Environmental Science, 575*(1), 012099. DOI: 10.1088/1755-1315/575/1/012099

Raj, T. (2019). Economic viability of organic farming in Himachal Pradesh: An empirical verification. *Indian Journal of Hill Farming, 32*(1).

Rajumesh, S. (2024). Promoting sustainable and human-centric industry 5.0: A thematic analysis of emerging research topics and opportunities. *Journal of Business and Socio-economic Development*, *4*(2), 111–126. DOI: 10.1108/JBSED-10-2022-0116

Ramírez-Márquez, C., Posadas-Paredes, T., Raya-Tapia, A. Y., & Ponce-Ortega, J. M. (2024). Natural Resource Optimization and Sustainability in Society 5.0: A Comprehensive Review. *Resources*, *13*(2), 19. DOI: 10.3390/resources13020019

Rane, N. L., Kaya, Ö., & Rane, J. (2024). *Artificial Intelligence, Machine Learning, and Deep Learning for Sustainable Industry 5.0*. Deep Science Publishing.

Rane, N., Kaya, Ö., & Rane, J. (2024). Digital Twins for Industry 4.0, 5.0, and Society 5.0. *Available at SSRN* 4918575. DOI: 10.2139/ssrn.4918575

Rani, G. M., Pathania, D., Umapathi, R., Rustagi, S., Huh, Y. S., Gupta, V. K., & Chaudhary, V. (2023). Agro-waste to sustainable energy: A green strategy of converting agricultural waste to nano-enabled energy applications. *The Science of the Total Environment*, *875*, 162667. DOI: 10.1016/j.scitotenv.2023.162667 PMID: 36894105

Rathore, P., & Sarmah, S. P. (2020). Economic, environmental and social optimization of solid waste management in the context of circular economy. *Computers & Industrial Engineering*, *145*, 10–22. DOI: 10.1016/j.cie.2020.106510

Rattanapan, C., & Ounsaneha, W. (2021). Water footprint assessment of Thai banana production. *International Journal of Environmental Science and Development*, Vol.12 (5), PP.151-156.

Raygoza-L., M. E., Orduño-Osuna, J. H., Trujillo-Hernández, G., & Murrieta-Rico, F. N. (2025). AI in public administration: Transformative opportunities for climate resilience and sustainable development. *Revista de Ciencia, Innovación y Tecnología*, *8*(2), Artículo e398. https://doi.org/DOI: 10.37636/recit.v8n2e398

Raygoza-Limón, M. E., Orduño-Osuna, J. H., Trujillo-Hernández, G., Bravo-Zanoguera, M. E., Amezquita Garcia, J. A., Ramírez-Hernández, L. R., Flores-Fuentes, W., Antúnez-García, J., & Murrieta-Rico, F. N. (2025). Supply chain management in renewable energy projects from a life cycle perspective: A review. *Applied Sciences (Basel, Switzerland)*, *15*(9), 5043. DOI: 10.3390/app15095043

Raźniewska, M. (2022). Compostable packaging waste management—Main barriers, reasons, and the potential directions for development. *Sustainability (Basel)*, *14*(7), 3748. DOI: 10.3390/su14073748

Reddy, A. A., Melts, I., Mohan, G., Rani, C. R., Pawar, V., Singh, V., Choubey, M., Vashishtha, T., Suresh, A., & Bhattarai, M. (2022). Economic impact of organic agriculture: Evidence from a Pan-India survey. *Sustainability (Basel)*, *14*(22), 15057. DOI: 10.3390/su142215057

Reeve, J. R., Hoagland, L. A., Villalba, J. J., Carr, P. M., Atucha, A., Cambardella, C., & Delate, K. (2016). Organic farming, soil health, and food quality: Considering possible links. *Advances in Agronomy*, *137*, 319–367. DOI: 10.1016/bs.agron.2015.12.003

Reganold, J. P., & Wachter, J. M. (2016). Organic agriculture in the twenty-first century. *Nature Plants*, *2*(2), 1–8. DOI: 10.1038/nplants.2015.221

Ribeiro, L. R., Oliveira, L. M. D., Silva, S. D. O., & Borges, A. L. (2012). Physical and chemical characterization of bananas produced in conventional and organic cultivation systems. *Revista Brasileira de Fruticultura*, *34*, 774–782. DOI: 10.1590/S0100-29452012000300017

Richards, M., & Sander, B. O. (2014). *Alternate wetting and drying in irrigated rice: Implementation guidance for policymakers and investors*. CGIAR Research Program on Climate Change, Agriculture and Food Security. https://cgspace.cgiar.org/handle/10568/35421

Ricono, C., Mony, C., Alignier, A., Aviron, S., Bertrand, C., Precigout, P. A., & Vandenkoornhuyse, P. (2024). Effect of organic farming on root microbiota, seed production and pathogen resistance in winter wheat fields. *Plants, People, Planet*.

Rios, P. C. S., Deen, T. A., Nagabhatla, N., & Ayala, G. (2018). Explaining water pricing through a water security lens. *Water (Basel)*, *10*(1173), 1–20.

Rockström, J., Steffen, W., Noone, K., Persson, Å., Chapin, F. S.III, Lambin, E., Lenton, T. M., Scheffer, M., Folke, C., Schellnhuber, H. J., Nykvist, B., de Wit, C. A., Hughes, T., van der Leeuw, S., Rodhe, H., Sörlin, S., Snyder, P. K., Costanza, R., Svedin, U., & Foley, J. A. (2017). A safe operating space for humanity. *Nature*, *461*(7263), 472–475. DOI: 10.1038/461472a PMID: 19779433

Rodale, J. I. (1945). Farming & gardening with composts. *Pay. dirt.*, 242.

Rodaway, P. (2002). *Sensuous geographies: Body, sense and place*. Routledge. DOI: 10.4324/9780203082546

Rolewicz-Kalińska, A., Lelicińska-Serafin, K., & Manczarski, P. (2020). The circular economy and organic fraction of municipal solid waste recycling strategies. *Energies*, *13*(17), 43–66. DOI: 10.3390/en13174366

Ruiz Medina, M. D., & Ruales, J. (2024). Post-harvest alternatives in banana cultivation. *Agronomy (Basel), 14*(9), 2109. DOI: 10.3390/agronomy14092109

Rumayor, M., Margallo, M., Pinedo, J., & Albo, J. (2024). Learning by Doing using the Life Cycle Assessment tool: LCA Projects in collaboration with industries. *Education for Chemical Engineers, 48*, 44–52. DOI: 10.1016/j.ece.2024.05.002

Saberi, S., Kouhizadeh, M., Sarkis, J., & Shen, L. (2019). Blockchain technology and its relationships to sustainable supply chain management. *International Journal of Production Research, 57*(7), 2117–2135. DOI: 10.1080/00207543.2018.1533261

Sacchi, S., Lotti, M., & Branduardi, P. (2021). Education for a biobased economy: Integrating life and social sciences in flexible short courses accessible from different backgrounds. *New Biotechnology, 60*, 72–75. DOI: 10.1016/j.nbt.2020.10.002 PMID: 33039695

Sahu, R. S., & Tiwari, M. (2024). Ensuring sustainable livelihoods and inclusive growth of Indian smallholder farmers through organic farming: A systematic literature review. *Socio-Ecological Practice Research, 6*(3), 1–15. DOI: 10.1007/s42532-024-00190-0

Santos, B., Costa, R. L. C., & Santos, L. (2024). Cybersecurity in Industry 5.0: Open Challenges and Future Directions. *arXiv preprint arXiv:2410.09538*. DOI: 10.1109/PST62714.2024.10788065

Sarkar, B. D., Shardeo, V., Dwivedi, A., & Pamucar, D. (2024). Digital transition from industry 4.0 to industry 5.0 in smart manufacturing: A framework for sustainable future. *Technology in Society, 78*, 102649. DOI: 10.1016/j.techsoc.2024.102649

Sarkar, B., Debnath, A., Chiu, A. S., & Ahmed, W. (2022). Circular economy-driven two-stage supply chain management for nullifying waste. *Journal of Cleaner Production, 339*, 130513. DOI: 10.1016/j.jclepro.2022.130513

Sarkar, S., Bayen, S., Samanta, S., & Pal, D. (2024). Spent Mushroom Substrate-Prospects and Challenges of Agrowaste management into sustainable solutions: A Review. *International Journal of Agriculture Environment and Biotechnology, 17*(04), 731–741.

Satheesh, S., & Shukla, K. (2024). Industry 5.0, Quality of Life, and Sustainable Adaptation to Climate Change: Challenges and the Transformational Way Forward. In *Quality of Life and Climate Change: Impacts, Sustainable Adaptation, and Social-Ecological Resilience* (pp. 200-219). IGI Global.

Schafer, R. M. (1999). *Soundscape: Our sonic environment and the tuning of the world*. Inner Traditions Bear & Company.

Schneeberger, W., Darnhofer, I., & Eder, M. (2002). Barriers to the adoption of organic farming by cash-crop producers in Austria. *American Journal of Alternative Agriculture, 17*(1), 24–31. DOI: 10.1079/AJAA20017

Schneider, M., & McMichael, P. (2011). Deepening, and repairing, the metabolic rift. *The Journal of Peasant Studies, 37*(3), 461–484. DOI: 10.1080/03066150.2010.494371 PMID: 20645448

Schnoor, J. L. (2010). *Water sustainability in a changing world.* National Water Research Institute.

Schröder, P. (2020). Promoting a just transition to an inclusive circular economy (pp. p-33). Royal Institute of International Affairs. https:/Promoting a just transition to an inclusive circular economy

Schroeder, P., Anggraeni, K., & Weber, U. (2019). The relevance of circular economy practices to the sustainable development goals. *Journal of Industrial Ecology, 23*(1), 77–95. DOI: 10.1111/jiec.12732

Schumann, F. R. (2020). Circular economy principles and small island tourism Guam's initiatives to transform from linear tourism to circular tourism. *Journal of Global Tourism Research, 5*(1), 13–20. DOI: 10.37020/jgtr.5.1_13

Schwarz, D. (1997). *Listening objects: Music, psychoanalysis, culture.* Duke University Press.

Schwarz, D. (1997). *The sense of sound: Aesthetic and cultural aspects of sound.* Oxford University Press.

Selvaraj, P. S., Periasamy, K., Suganya, K., Ramadass, K., Muthusamy, S., Ramesh, P., & Palanisami, T. (2022). Novel resources recovery from anaerobic digestates: Current trends and future perspectives. *Critical Reviews in Environmental Science and Technology, 52*(11), 1915–1999. DOI: 10.1080/10643389.2020.1864957

Sharma, H. B., Vanapalli, K. R., Samal, B., Cheela, V. S., Dubey, B. K., & Bhattacharya, J. (2021). Circular economy approach in solid waste management system to achieve UN-SDGs: Solutions for post-COVID recovery. *The Science of the Total Environment, 800*, 149605. DOI: 10.1016/j.scitotenv.2021.149605

Sharma, R., & Gupta, H. (2024). Leveraging cognitive digital twins in industry 5.0 for achieving sustainable development goal 9: An exploration of inclusive and sustainable industrialization strategies. *Journal of Cleaner Production, 448*, 141364. DOI: 10.1016/j.jclepro.2024.141364

Sharma, V., Tsai, M. L., Chen, C. W., Sun, P. P., Nargotra, P., & Dong, C. D. (2023). Advances in machine learning technology for sustainable biofuel production systems in lignocellulosic biorefineries. *The Science of the Total Environment*, *886*, 163972. DOI: 10.1016/j.scitotenv.2023.163972

Shenyoputro, K., & Jones, T. E. (2023). Reflections on a two-decade journey toward zero waste: A case study of Kamikatsu town, Japan. *Frontiers in Environmental Science*, *11*, 1171379. DOI: 10.3389/fenvs.2023.1171379

Shirur, M., Barh, A., & Annepu, S. K. (2021). Sustainable Production of Edible and Medicinal Mushrooms: Implications on Mushroom Consumption. In Hebsale Mallappa, V. K., & Shirur, M. (Eds.), *Climate Change and Resilient Food Systems* (pp. 315–346). Springer. DOI: 10.1007/978-981-33-4538-6_12

Shukla, P. R., Skeg, J., Buendia, E. C., Masson-Delmotte, V., Pörtner, H. O., Roberts, D. C., . . . Malley, J. (2019). Climate Change and Land: an IPCC special report on climate change, desertification, land degradation, sustainable land management, food security and greenhouse gas fluxes in terrestrial ecosystems. https://www.ipcc.ch/srccl/

Sikarwar, V. S., Pohořelý, M., Meers, E., Skoblia, S., Moško, J., & Jeremiáš, M. (2021). Potential of coupling anaerobic digestion with thermochemical technologies for waste valorization. *Fuel*, *294*, 120533. DOI: 10.1016/j.fuel.2021.120533

Simonne, A., Ozores-Hampton, M., Treadwell, D., & House, L. (2016). Organic and conventional produce in the US: Examining safety and quality, economic values, and consumer attitudes. *Horticulturae*, *2*(2), 5. DOI: 10.3390/horticulturae2020005

Singh, A., & Singh, R. (2022). Eco-friendly post-harvest technologies of banana: A review. The Pharma Innovation Journal, 11(7), 4375–4381. https://www.thepharmajournal.com/archives/2022/vol11issue7S/PartAI/SP-11-7-225-884

Singh, R., Solanki, C., & Bala, M. (2023). Post-harvest handling and value-addition of organic produce. *International Journal of Advanced Biochemistry Research*, *7*(2), 184–188. DOI: 10.33545/26174693.2023.v7.i2Sc.206

Sinkko, T., Sanyé-Mengual, E., Corrado, S., Giuntoli, J., & Sala, S. (2023). The EU Bioeconomy Footprint: Using life cycle assessment to monitor environmental impacts of the EU Bioeconomy. *Sustainable Production and Consumption*, *37*, 169–179. DOI: 10.1016/j.spc.2023.02.015

Socaciu, C. (2014). Bioeconomy and green economy: European strategies, action plans and impact on life quality. *Bulletin of University of Agricultural Sciences and Veterinary Medicine Cluj-Napoca. Food Science and Technology, 71*(1), 1. www.biofuelstp.eu/. DOI: 10.15835/buasvmcn-fst:10121

Sofian, B. A., Aiman, A. D., Sun, X., Gupta, V. K., Berenjian, A., Xia, A., Ma, Z., & Show, P. L. (2024). Advances, synergy, and perspectives of machine learning and biobased polymers for energy, fuels, and biochemicals for a sustainable future. *Energy & Fuels, 38*(3), 1593–1617. DOI: 10.1021/acs.energyfuels.3c03842

Soltani, S., Azadi, H., Mahmoudi, H., & Witlox, F. (2014). Organic agriculture in Iran: Farmers' barriers to and factors influencing adoption. *Renewable Agriculture and Food Systems, 29*(2), 126–134. DOI: 10.1017/S1742170513000069

Sondhi, N., & Vani, V. (2007). An empirical analysis of the organic retail market in the NCR. *Global Business Review, 8*(2), 283–302. DOI: 10.1177/097215090700800207

Song, S., Lim, J. W., Lee, J. T., Cheong, J. C., Hoy, S. H., Hu, Q., & Tong, Y. W. (2021). Food-waste anaerobic digestate as a fertilizer: The agronomic properties of untreated digestate and biochar-filtered digestate residue. *Waste Management (New York, N.Y.), 136*, 143–152. DOI: 10.1016/j.wasman.2021.10.011 PMID: 34666296

Soni, R., & Yadav, S. K. (2019). Prospects of organic farming as financial sustainable strategy in modern agriculture. *Soil fertility management for sustainable development*, 251-265.

Souza, A., Junior, C. K., Zarpellon, F. R., & da Veiga, C. P. (2024). Sustainable production and consumption: Assessing the economic viability of traditional and organic yerba mate cultivation. *Humanities & Social Sciences Communications, 11*(1), 1–16. DOI: 10.1057/s41599-024-04014-0

Stahel, W. R. (1982). The product life factor. an inquiry into the nature of sustainable societies: the role of the private sector (Series: 1982 Mitchell Prize study), NARC, 74-96. https://www.quebeccirculaire.org/data/sources/users/4/32217.pdf

Stegmann, P., Londo, M., & Junginger, M. (2020). The circular bioeconomy: Its elements and role in European bioeconomy clusters. In *Resources, Conservation and Recycling: X* (Vol. 6). Elsevier B.V. DOI: 10.1016/j.rcrx.2019.100029

Stilgoe, J., Owen, R., & Macnaghten, P. (2013). Developing a framework for responsible innovation. *Research Policy, 42*(9), 1568–1580. DOI: 10.1016/j.respol.2013.05.008

Stolze, M., & Lampkin, N. (2009). Policy for organic farming: Rationale and concepts. *Food Policy, 34*(3), 237–244. DOI: 10.1016/j.foodpol.2009.03.005

Suárez-Eiroa, B., Fernández, E., & Méndez, G. (2021). Integration of the circular economy paradigm under the just and safe operating space narrative: Twelve operational principles based on circularity, sustainability and resilience. *Journal of Cleaner Production*, *322*(1), 12–33. DOI: 10.1016/j.jclepro.2021.129071

Sun, L., Li, Z., Fujii, M., Hijioka, Y., & Fujita, T. (2018). Carbon footprint assessment for the waste management sector: A comparative analysis of China and Japan. *Frontiers in Energy*, *12*(3), 400–410. DOI: 10.1007/s11708-018-0565-z

Suresha, K. M., Joshi, H. G., & Joisa, J. (2025). Agri social entrepreneurship and rural transformation in Karnataka, India. *Discover Sustainability*, *6*(1), 994. Advance online publication. DOI: 10.1007/s43621-025-01886-3

Tahat, M., M., M. Alananbeh, K., A. Othman, Y., & I. Leskovar, D. (. (2020). Soil health and sustainable agriculture. *Sustainability*, *12*(12), 4859. DOI: 10.3390/su12124859

Takala, T., Tikkanen, J., Haapala, A., Pitkänen, S., Torssonen, P., Valkeavirta, R., & Pöykkö, T. (2019). Shaping the concept of bioeconomy in participatory projects – An example from the post-graduate education in Finland. *Journal of Cleaner Production*, *221*, 176–188. DOI: 10.1016/j.jclepro.2019.02.007

Tamil Nadu Policy Note. (2024). Agriculture Farmers welfare Department. Available at https://tnhorticulture.tn.gov.in/site_assets/site-pdfs/policy_note/AG-FW-Policy-Note-English-(2024-25).pdf. Accessed on 01.03.2025

Tan, E. C. D., & Lamers, P. (2021). *Circular Bioeconomy Concepts- a perspective* (Vol. 2). Sec. Circular Economy.

Tan, W. Y., & Abd Rahim, M. H. I. (2024). Potential of Implementing Artificial Intelligence (AI) for Reducing Waste at Construction Site. *Research in Management of Technology and Business*, *5*(1), 1559–1575.

Tatar, M., Khrapunenko, M., Henahan, R. K., & Asser, A. (2023). Engaging Citizens in the Bioeconomy: Insights from the Co-Creation and Co-Design in the Development of the Serious Bioeconomy Game "Mission BioHero.". *Sustainability (Basel)*, *15*(18), 13364. Advance online publication. DOI: 10.3390/su151813364

Tautges, N. E., Sullivan, T. S., Reardon, C. L., & Burke, I. C. (2016). Soil microbial diversity and activity linked to crop yield and quality in a dryland organic wheat production system. *Applied Soil Ecology*, *108*, 258–268. DOI: 10.1016/j.apsoil.2016.09.003

Taylor, P., Steenmans, K., & Steenmans, I. (2020). Blockchain technology for sustainable waste management. *Frontiers in Political Science, 2*, 590923. DOI: 10.3389/fpos.2020.590923

Thakur, N., Sharma, R., Roy, P., Kumar, S., Kumar, K., & Roy, T. N. (2024). Elucidating economic sustainability of organic vis-a-vis conventional vegetable production in North Western Himalayas. *Current Science (00113891)*, 127(10).

Thamarai, P., Deivayanai, V. C., Saravanan, A., Vickram, A. S., & Yaashikaa, P. R. (2024). Carbon mitigation in agriculture: Pioneering technologies for a sustainable food system. *Trends in Food Science & Technology, 147*, 104477. DOI: 10.1016/j.tifs.2024.104477

Tiwari, A. K. (2021). Comparative analysis of organic farming practices: Impacts on soil health, crop yield, and environmental sustainability. *Plant Science Archives, 1*(04).

Tiwari, S., Mohammed, K. S., Mentel, G., Majewski, S., & Shahzadi, I. (2023). Role of circular economy, energy transition, environmental policy stringency and supply chain pressure on CO2 emissions in emerging economies. *Geoscience Frontiers, 15*(3), 1–14. DOI: 10.1016/j.gsf.2023.101682

Tjamos, E. C., Papavizas, G. C., & Cook, R. J. (1992). *Biological control of plant diseases: Progress and challenges for the future*. Springer., DOI: 10.1007/978-1-4757-9468-7

Tleuken, A., Tokazhanov, G., Jemal, K. M., Shaimakhanov, R., Sovetbek, M., & Karaca, F. (2022). Legislative, Institutional, Industrial and Governmental Involvement in Circular Economy in Central Asia: A Systematic Review. In *Sustainability (Switzerland)* (Vol. 14, Issue 13). MDPI. DOI: 10.3390/su14138064

Toledo, V. M., & Barrera-Bassols, N. (2008). *La memoria biocultural: La importancia ecológica de las sabidurías tradicionales*. Icaria Editorial.

Torkaycsh, A. E., Rajaeifar, M. A., Rostom, M., Malmir, B., Yazdani, M., Suh, S., & Heidrich, O. (2022). Integrating life cycle assessment and multi criteria decision making for sustainable waste management: Key issues and recommendations for future studies. *Renewable & Sustainable Energy Reviews, 168*, 112819. DOI: 10.1016/j.rser.2022.112819

Toyosumi, I. D. S., Silva, T. S. M. D., Melo, D. M., Azevedo Neto, A. D. D., Soares, T. M., & Coelho Filho, M. A. (2021). Optimization of banana plantlets acclimatization by hydroponic cultivation. *Scientia Agrícola, 78*(suppl 1), e20200165. DOI: 10.1590/1678-992x-2020-0165

Truax, B. (1994). The inner and outer complexity of music. *Perspectives of New Music*, *32*(1), 176–193. DOI: 10.2307/833161

Tsironis, G., Daglis, T., & Tsagarakis, K. P. (2024). The circular economy through the prism of machine learning and the YouTube video media platform. *Journal of Environmental Management*, *368*, 121977. DOI: 10.1016/j.jenvman.2024.121977

Tsui, T. H., van Loosdrecht, M. C., Dai, Y., & Tong, Y. W. (2023). Machine learning and circular bioeconomy: Building new resource efficiency from diverse waste streams. *Bioresource Technology*, *369*, 128445. DOI: 10.1016/j.biortech.2022.128445

Tundisi, J. G. (2008). Water resources in the future: Problems and solutions. *Estudos Avançados*, *22*(63), 1–8. DOI: 10.1590/S0103-40142008000200002

Tunn, V. S., Bocken, N. M., van den Hende, E. A., & Schoormans, J. P. (2019). Business models for sustainable consumption in the circular economy: An expert study. *Journal of Cleaner Production*, *212*(1), 324–333. DOI: 10.1016/j.jclepro.2018.11.290

Ubando, A. T., Felix, C. B., & Chen, W.-H. (2020). Biorefineries in circular bioeconomy: A comprehensive review. *Bioresource Technology*, *299*, 122585. DOI: 10.1016/j.biortech.2019.122585

Uma, S., & Kumar, P. S. (2025). Organic Production of Fruits: Issues, Challenges, and Opportunities. *Advances in Agri-Food Systems*, *I*, 141–177. DOI: 10.1007/978-981-96-0759-4_9

Ume, C., & Bahta, Y. T. (2024). Policy support strategies for organic farming extensification in Nigeria. *Organic Agriculture*, *14*(3), 1–22. DOI: 10.1007/s13165-024-00467-4

UNESCO. (2021). *Education for sustainable development: A roadmap*. https://unesdoc.unesco.org/ark:/48223/pf0000374802

UNESCO. (2021). Local and Indigenous Knowledge Systems (LINKS) Programme. In *UNESCO*.

United Nations Environment Programme. (2020). *Preventing the next pandemic: Zoonotic diseases and how to break the chain of transmission*. https://www.unep.org/resources/report/preventing-future-zoonotic-disease-outbreaks

United Nations Environment Programme. (2021). *Food waste index report 2021*. https://www.unep.org/resources/report/unep-food-waste-index-report-2021

United Nations. (2022). *World population prospects 2022: Summary of results*. United Nations, Department of Economic and Social Affairs. https://www.un.org/development/desa/pd/content/world-population-prospects-20224

Unito, W., Sanna, F., & Fenrich, D. (2020). *Addressing the current and Future skIll needs for sustainability, digitalization and the bio-Economy in agricuLture: European skills agenDa and Strategy D1.1: Stakeholders strategic plans and analysis report Document description Work package title Skills needs identification Status* Partner responsible Author(s).*

University of California Vegetable Research and Information Center. (n.d.). Organic farming practices: Postharvest handling. University of California. Retrieved from http://postharvest.ucdavis.edu

Urmetzer, S., Lask, J., Vargas-Carpintero, R., & Pyka, A. (2020). Learning to change: Transformative knowledge for building a sustainable bioeconomy. *Ecological Economics*, *167*, 106435. Advance online publication. DOI: 10.1016/j.ecolecon.2019.106435

Urmetzer, S., Schlaile, M. P., Bogner, K. B., Mueller, M., & Pyka, A. (2018). Exploring the dedicated knowledge base of a transformation towards a sustainable bioeconomy. *Sustainability (Basel)*, *10*(6), 1694. Advance online publication. DOI: 10.3390/su10061694

Vacchi, M., Siligardi, C., & Settembre-Blundo, D. (2024). Driving manufacturing companies toward industry 5.0: A strategic framework for process technological sustainability assessment (P-TSA). *Sustainability (Basel)*, *16*(2), 695. DOI: 10.3390/su16020695

Valeriya, G., Kirola, M., Gupta, M., Bharathi, P., & Acharya, P. (2024). Evaluating the Impact of AI-Based Sustainability Measures in Industry 5.0: A Longitudinal Study. In *BIO Web of Conferences* (Vol. 86, p. 01058). EDP Sciences.

Vallgårda, A. F. (2018). The value of water – A valuation study of groundwater in Uppsala municipality. Sveriges lantbruksuniversitet Swedish University of Agricultural Sciences, http://stud.epsilon.slu.se

Varadharajan, C., Appling, A. P., Arora, B., Christianson, D. S., Hendrix, V., Kumar, V., Lima, A. R., Mueller, J., Oliver, S. K., Ombadi, M., Perciano, T., Sadler, J. M., Weierbach, H., Willard, J., Xu, Z., & Zwart, J. A. (2022). Is it possible to minimize the time required to identify the river water quality processes and to forecast its water quality employing machine learning and hyperparameter optimization? *Hydrological Processes*, *36*(4). Advance online publication. DOI: 10.1002/hyp.14565

Venkatesan, M. (2020). The Role of Culture and Moral Responsibility in Facilitating a Sustainable Bioeconomy. In *Sustainable Bioeconomy: Pathways to Sustainable Development Goals* (pp. 11–33). Springer Singapore. DOI: 10.1007/978-981-15-7321-7_2

Verma, R., Christiana, M. B. V., Maheswari, M., Srinivasan, V., Patro, P., Dari, S. S., & Boopathi, S. (2024). Intelligent Physarum Solver for Profit Maximization in Oligopolistic Supply Chain Networks. In *AI and Machine Learning Impacts in Intelligent Supply Chain* (pp. 156–179). IGI Global. DOI: 10.4018/979-8-3693-1347-3.ch011

Vijaya Lakshmi, V., Mishra, M., Kushwah, J. S., Shajahan, U. S., Mohanasundari, M., & Boopathi, S. (2024). Circular Economy Digital Practices for Ethical Dimensions and Policies for Digital Waste Management. In *Harnessing High-Performance Computing and AI for Environmental Sustainability* (pp. 166–193). IGI Global., DOI: 10.4018/979-8-3693-1794-5.ch008

Vinay Mehla, V. M., & Saroj Kumari, S. K. (2012). Organic farming for health and sustainability. *Annals of Agri Bio Research*, *17*(2), 120–124.

Vogt, M., & Frankenreiter, I. (2022). Bioeconomy: The Innovative Twin of Sustainability. *Sustainability (Basel)*, *14*(22), 14924. Advance online publication. DOI: 10.3390/su142214924

Vuojärvi, H., Vartiainen, H., Eriksson, M., Ratinen, I., Saramäki, K., Torssonen, P., Vanninen, P., & Pöllänen, S. (2024). Boundaries and boundary crossing in a multidisciplinary online higher education course on forest bioeconomy. *Teaching in Higher Education*, *29*(5), 1197–1214. DOI: 10.1080/13562517.2022.2122791

Vuorio, E., Pernaa, J., & Aksela, M. (2024). Lessons for Sustainable Science Education: A Study on Chemists' Use of Systems Thinking across Ecological, Economic, and Social Domains. *Education Sciences*, *14*(7), 741. Advance online publication. DOI: 10.3390/educsci14070741

Výbošt'ok, J., Navrátilová, L., Dobšinská, Z., Dúbravská, B., Giertliová, B., Aláč, P., Suja, M., & Šálka, J. (2022). Bioeconomy perception by students of different study programs - study from Slovakia. *Central European Forestry Journal*, *68*(2), 91–100. DOI: 10.2478/forj-2021-0025

Wang, A., Rauf, A., Ozturk, I., Wu, J., Zhao, X., & Du, H. (2024). The key to sustainability: In-depth investigation of environmental quality in G20 countries through the lens of renewable energy, economic complexity and geopolitical risk resilience. *Journal of Environmental Management*, *354*(1), 1–12. DOI: 10.1016/j.jenvman.2024.120045 PMID: 38232591

Wang, B., Wang, S., Li, G., Fu, L., Chen, H., Yin, M., & Chen, J. (2025). Reducing nitrogen fertilizer usage coupled with organic substitution improves soil quality and boosts tea yield and quality in tea plantations. *Journal of the Science of Food and Agriculture*, *105*(2), 1228–1238. DOI: 10.1002/jsfa.13913

Wang, C., Mahmood, H., & Khalid, S. (2024). Examining the impact of globalization and natural resources on environmental sustainability in G20 countries. *Scientific Reports*, *14*(1), 1–20. DOI: 10.1038/s41598-024-81613-6 PMID: 39730646

Wang, H., Xie, J., & Li, H. (2010). Water pricing with household surveys: A study of acceptability and willingness to pay in Chongqing, China. *China Economic Review*, *21*(1), 136–149. DOI: 10.1016/j.chieco.2009.12.001

Warnants Promotor, T. (2012). *Bachelor's thesis supply and students' views on online international studies in the eu in english at a higher education level related to bioeconomy, renewable energy and circular economy.*

Wastes | US EPA. US EPA. https://www.epa.gov/report-environment/wastes. Published July 8, 2024. Acessed on 28.03.2025.

Wastling, T., Charnley, F., & Moreno, M. (2018). Design for circular behaviour: Considering users in a circular economy. *Sustainability (Basel)*, *10*(6), 1743. DOI: 10.3390/su10061743

Watkinson, I. I., Bridgwater, A. V., & Luxmore, C. (2012). Advanced education and training in bioenergy in Europe. *Biomass and Bioenergy*, *38*, 128–143. DOI: 10.1016/j.biombioe.2011.06.038

Wei, X., Luo, J., Pu, A., Liu, Q., Zhang, L., Wu, S., Long, Y., Leng, Y., Dong, Z., & Wan, X. (2022). From Biotechnology to Bioeconomy: A Review of Development Dynamics and Pathways. In *Sustainability (Switzerland)* (Vol. 14, Issue 16). MDPI. DOI: 10.3390/su141610413

WHO. (2024). *Proportion of population with primary reliance on clean fuels and technologies for cooking (%).* [Online]. https://www.who.int/data/gho/data/indicators/indicator-details/GHO/gho-phe-primary-reliance-on-clean-fuels-and-technologies-proportion WHO/UNICEF (2023). [Online]. washdata.org.

WHO/UNICEF (2023). Joint Monitoring Programme (JMP) for Water Supply, Sanitation and Hygiene. washdata.org.

Wijesinghe, J., Botheju, S. M., Nallaperuma, B., & Kanuwana, N. (2023). Organic farming: the influence on soil health. *One Health: Human, Animal, and Environment Triad*, 185-197.

Willer, H., Trávníček, J., Meier, C., & Schlatter, B. (2021). The world of organic agriculture 2021-statistics and emerging trends.

Willer, H. J. T., & Schlatter, B. (Eds.). (2025). *The World of Organic Agriculture. Statistics and Emerging Trends 2025. Research Institute of Organic Agriculture FiBL*. Frick, and IFOAM – Organics International.

Witjes, S., & Lozano, R. (2016). Towards a more Circular Economy: Proposing a framework linking sustainable public procurement and sustainable business models. *Resources, Conservation and Recycling*, *112*, 37–44. DOI: 10.1016/j.resconrec.2016.04.015

Wohlgemuth, R., Twardowski, T., & Aguilar, A. (2021). Bioeconomy moving forward step by step – A global journey. *New Biotechnology*, *61*, 22–28. DOI: 10.1016/j.nbt.2020.11.006 PMID: 33197617

Wolfert, S., Ge, L., Verdouw, C., & Bogaardt, M.-J. (2017). Big data in smart farming – A review. *Agricultural Systems*, *153*, 69–80. DOI: 10.1016/j.agsy.2017.01.023

World Bank Group (WBG). (2025). Water is the foundation of a liveable planet. [Online]. https://www.worldbank.org/en/topic/water/overview

Wydra, S. (2019). Value chains for industrial biotechnology in the bioeconomy-innovation system analysis. *Sustainability (Basel)*, *11*(8), 2435. Advance online publication. DOI: 10.3390/su11082435

Xian, M. (2025). Impact of inclusive growth, environmental policy incentives, fintech and globalization on environmental sustainability in G20 countries. *Sustainability (Basel)*, *17*(1), 1–21. DOI: 10.3390/su17010050

Yaashikaa, P. R., Kumar, P. S., Nhung, T. C., Hemavathy, R. V., Jawahar, M. J., Neshaanthini, J. P., & Rangasamy, G. (2022). A review on landfill system for municipal solid wastes: Insight into leachate, gas emissions, environmental and economic analysis. *Chemosphere*, *309*, 136627. DOI: 10.1016/j.chemosphere.2022.136627 PMID: 36181852

Yang, M., Chen, L., Wang, J., Msigwa, G., Osman, A. I., Fawzy, S., Rooney, D. W., & Yap, P. S. (2023). Circular economy strategies for combating climate change and other environmental issues. *Environmental Chemistry Letters*, *21*(1), 55–80. DOI: 10.1007/s10311-022-01499-6

Yang, Y., Huang, S., & Wang, C. (2024). Public policies in support of organic agriculture in China. In *Organic Agriculture and Biodiversity in China* (pp. 65–81). Academic Press. DOI: 10.1016/B978-0-323-90602-9.00007-1

Yang, Y., Zhou, T., Cheng, M., Xie, M., Shi, N., Liu, T., & Li, B. (2024). Recent advances in organic waste pyrolysis and gasification in a CO2 environment to value-added products. *Journal of Environmental Management, 356*, 120666. DOI: 10.1016/j.jenvman.2024.120666 PMID: 38490005

Zhang, D. (2019). Application of blockchain technology in incentivizing efficient use of rural wastes: A case study on yitong system. *Energy Procedia, 158*, 6707–6714. DOI: 10.1016/j.egypro.2019.01.018

Zhang, T., Shaikh, Z. A., Yumashev, A. V., & Chład, M. (2020). Applied model of E-learning in the framework of education for sustainable development. *Sustainability (Basel), 12*(16), 6420. Advance online publication. DOI: 10.3390/su12166420

Zhao, L., Dai, T., Qiao, Z., Sun, P., Hao, J., & Yang, Y. (2020). Application of artificial intelligence to wastewater treatment: A bibliometric analysis and systematic review of technology, economy, management, and wastewater reuse. *Process Safety and Environmental Protection, 133*, 169–182. DOI: 10.1016/j.psep.2019.11.014

Zhao, X., Becker, G. C., Faweya, N., Rodriguez Correa, C., Yang, S., Xie, X., & Kruse, A. (2018). Fertilizer and activated carbon production by hydrothermal carbonization of digestate. *Biomass Conversion and Biorefinery, 8*(2), 423–436. DOI: 10.1007/s13399-017-0291-5

Zhen, Z., & Yao, Y. (2024). The confluence of digital twin and blockchan technologies in Industry 5.0: Transforming supply chain management for innovation and sustainability. *Journal of the Knowledge Economy, 16*(1), 1–27. DOI: 10.1007/s13132-024-02151-0

Zlati, M. L., Antohi, V. M., Ionescu, R. V., Iticescu, C., & Georgescu, L. P. (2024). Quantyfing the impact of the water security index on socio-economic development in EU27. *Socio-Economic Planning Sciences, 93*, 101912. DOI: 10.1016/j.seps.2024.101912

Zou, J., Su, S., Wang, F., & Chen, X. (2024). Navigating the Changing Landscape of Agricultural Economics Education: Lessons for China and Beyond. *Pakistan Journal of Agricultural Sciences, 61*(3), 703–713. DOI: 10.21162/PAKJAS/24.36

About the Contributors

Saurabh Agarwal is presently designated as a Research Professor in the Department of Computer Engineering at Yeungnam University, South Korea. He has a distinguished academic background with a Ph.D. in Computer Engineering from the University of Delhi, where his thesis focused on the design and analysis of image forensic techniques. Dr. Agarwal has accumulated extensive research and teaching experience, previously serving as a Postdoctoral Researcher at Andong National University and Kyungil University in South Korea. During his postdoctoral tenure, he led pioneering studies in image forgery detection utilizing advanced machine learning and deep learning techniques. Dr. Agarwal has held significant academic positions, including Associate Professor roles at Amity University and SRMSCET, Bareilly, India, where he instructed various computer science subjects, mentored students, and contributed to accreditation tasks. His academic contributions have been recognized with several prestigious awards, such as the Korean Research Fellowship and a Ph.D. fellowship from NSIT, Delhi. Notably, Infosys Technologies Limited highlighted his excellence in the Campus Connect Program. Dr. Agarwal's research interests encompass computer vision, image forensics, quantum computing, machine learning, and deep learning. He has published extensively, with numerous articles in high-impact international journals and conference proceedings. His recent publications include works on digital image steganalysis, forensic analysis, and image operator forensics, among others. In addition to his research, Dr Agarwal has actively participated in various training programs and workshops, including cloud computing, machine learning, and big data analytics. He has also contributed to the academic community as a reviewer for several prestigious journals and conferences. Dr Agarwal's academic qualifications include an M. Tech in Software Engineering from APJ AKTU, Lucknow, and a B.E. in Computer Science & Engineering from Barkatullah University, Bhopal. His extensive teaching experience spans over a decade, during which he has taught a wide range of subjects, mentored numerous students, and engaged in various administrative and examination duties. Dr. Agarwal has been instrumental in advancing the field of computer science through his innovative research and dedication to teaching. His work has significantly contributed to the understanding and development of image forensic techniques and machine-learning applications in digital forensics.

Lakshmi D is presently designated as a Senior Associate Professor in the School of Computing Science Engineering and Artificial Intelligence and Assistant Director, at the Centre for Innovation in Teaching & Learning (CITL) at VIT Bhopal. From 2016 to 2021 served as an Educational Research Officer, at Vishnu Educational Development and Innovation Centre (VEDIC) Shri Vishnu Educational Society, Hyderabad She has 26 years of teaching experience. She has addressed innumerable guest lectures, acted as a session chair, and was invited as a keynote speaker at several international conferences. She has conducted FDPs that cover approximately ~1,00,000 plus faculty members including JNTU, TEQIP, SERB, SWAYAM, DST, AICTE, MHRD, ATAL, ISTE, Madhya Pradesh Government-sponsored, MALVIYA MISSION TEACHER TRAINING, Central University of Gujarat and self-financed workshops across India as well as Misamis University, Philipines on Artificial Intelligence in Education: The Future and Futuristic Perspectives both theory and practical sessions. The other titles such as Modern Tools and Software in Teaching Learning Practices, Outcome Based Education, Scientific Educational Practices, Flipped Learning, Blended Learning, Activity Based Learning, Marching towards Quality and Excellence in Higher Educational Institutions, NEP 2022, Emotional Intelligence, Python Essential, Data Analytics, IoT, Machine Learning, Deep Learning, Cyber Security, AR/VR in Medicine, Architecture and Military Applications Instructional Strategies, Assessment techniques, Research Writing, etc. She has 20 international conference presentations, and 50 international journal papers and book chapters inclusive of SCOPUS & SCI. A total of 20 SCOPUS-indexed book chapters. A total of 24 patents are in various stages and 18 patents have been granted at both national and international levels. She was appointed as an external examiner for several Ph.D candidates at reputed universities. Under her supervision, one scholar has completed a Ph.D. at Annamalai University. One scholar is pursuing a Ph.D. right now at VIT Bhopal University. She has won two Best Paper awards at international conferences, one at the IEEE conference and another one at EAMMIS 2021 (First European, Asian, Middle Eastern North African Conference on Management & Information Systems). She received two awards in the year 2022 on the eve of Teacher's Day 1. Kamal Sharma Award of Academic Excellence - 2022 from Lexicon Group of Institutions, Pune for the Engaged Pedagogies. from the virtual ceremony. 2. Bharat Academic Excellence "UttamaAdyapika" Award from Braino Vision. She published a book on "Theory of Computation" in 2003, "Leading Education in the Age of Disruption" in 2021, and "Smart Cities: Disruptive

Technologies Driving the Force", in 2023. In the last three editions, she acted as a SPOC for KAVACH and the Smart India Hackathon. She has created 15 hours of the high-quality "Python Essentials" online course at VITyarthi Online Learning Platform. She has 9 SCOPUS Indexed book edits with three CRS Press, Taylor, and Francis, four IGI Global, and two IEEE Rivers.

***

Alavanou Christina (MSc) is a graduate in Tourism and Hospitality Business Management from the Department of Business Administration, TEI of Heraklion and holds a Master's degree in Strategic Management of Tourism and Hospitality Enterprises. Her academic interests lie in the intersection of tourism, culture, and sound, with a particular focus on sustainable tourism practices and their impact on visitor experiences.She has researched tourism impacts on society and the environment, visitor experiences in Greek museums and archaeological sites, tourism development in the South Aegean, tourism policy through Cabo Verde case studies, and ecotourism in Kalymnos. She has attended numerous seminars in the fields of tourism, music therapy, arts, and culture, which have broadened her interdisciplinary perspective on designing meaningful tourism experiences.

Saurabh Chandra is an accomplished legal scholar and currently serves as an Associate Professor & Assistant Dean at the School of Law, Bennett University, India. With a robust academic foundation, he earned his Bachelor of Arts and Bachelor of Laws (B.A. LL.B.) from the prestigious Aligarh Muslim University (A.M.U.). He further specialized in Business Laws, completing his Master of Laws (LL.M.) at the renowned National Law School of India University (NLSIU), Bangalore. Dr. Chandra's academic journey culminated in a Doctorate in Law (Ph.D.) from the esteemed National Law University (NLU) Delhi. In addition to his impressive legal education from some of India's most prestigious institutions, Dr. Saurabh Chandra also holds a master's degree in Management with specialization in Human Resources in Management and another in Journalism and Mass Communication. With 16 years of teaching experience, he has established himself as an expert in Business and Corporate Laws, with numerous publications to his credit. Dr. Saurabh Chandra is a distinguished expert in Business and Corporate Laws, with a profound understanding of the intricate legal frameworks that govern the business world. His expertise is complemented by a robust portfolio of scholarly publications, which underscores his commitment to advancing knowledge in his field. Throughout his career, Dr. Chandra has consistently produced high-impact research that addresses critical issues in Business and Corporate Law. His publications are widely recognized for their depth of analysis, innovative perspectives, and practical relevance. He has contributed extensively to leading journals, where his work has often set new standards for legal scholarship. His publications not only reflect his scholarly rigor but also his dedication to addressing contemporary challenges faced by businesses and policymakers. By bridging the gap between theoretical insights and real-world applications, Dr. Chandra's work serves as a valuable resource for academics, legal practitioners, and industry professionals alike. Dr. Chandra brings a wealth of experience in Academic Administration, having successfully held various key administrative positions. His diverse qualifications and extensive experience make him a distinguished figure in the academic and legal communities.

Meenakshi Gupta is working as an Associate Professor in the School of Economics, at Shri Mata Vaishno Devi University, Katra. She has teaching and research experience of almost 18 years. She has been a part of many academic and non- academic committees of the university since 2007. Her main areas of interest are Agricultural Economics, Environmental Economics and Development Economics. Her research work has been published in various national and international journals. She has contributed to various books also. She has also presented various articles at National and International Conferences. She is also awarded with many prestigious national and international awards. She is a life Member of Indian Economic Association, Indian Society of Agri- business and Management, Indian Society of Agricultural Economics, TIES, AERA, etc.

Bhim Jyoti has been working with V.C.S.G., UUHF, College of Forestry, Ranichauri, Tehri Garhwal, Uttarakhand, India as Assistant Professor of Seed and Technology. She received MSc in Seed and Technology from CCS University Meerut and PhD in Seed and Technology from G. B. Pant University of Agriculture, Pantnagar, Uttarakhand. She has published several research articles in the seed and technology, plant growth, seed vigour, genetic variability, Biotechnological approaches, climate change and agricultural productivity.

Sanjeev Kumar is currently working as an Assistant Professor at the Department of Economics, Hansraj College, University of Delhi. He has completed his PhD from the Department of Humanities and Social Sciences, Indian Institute of Technology Roorkee. He has published several research papers in reputed journals such as Asia Pacific Journal of Regional Science, Emerging Economy Studies, Decision, and Indian Journal of Industrial Relations. His major areas of interest lie in the fields of industrialisation and labour market dynamics, climate change and agricultural productivity.

M. Santhosh Kumar (Santhosh Kumar Muthusamy) received B.Tech degree in IT from LCR College of Engineering & Technology, Chennai affiliated to Anna

University in 2010. M.Tech Degree in CSE from Karpagam University, Coimbatore affiliated to Karpagam University in 2013. He is currently working toward the Ph.D. degree at the Department of Computer Science Engineering, Karpagam University, and Coimbatore. My research interests include Deep Learning, Cyber Security, Networks & Communication Internet of Things and Artificial Intelligence

Fabian N. Murrieta-Rico received B.Eng. and M.Eng. degrees from Instituto Tecnológico de Mexicali (ITM) in 2004 and 2013 respectively. In 2017, he received his PhD in Materials Physics at Centro de Investigación Científica y Educación Superior de Ensenada (CICESE). He has worked as an automation engineer, systems designer, as a university professor, and as postdoctoral researcher at Facultad de Ingeniería, Arquitectura y Diseño from Universidad Autónoma de Baja California (UABC) and at the Centro de Nanociencias y Nanotecnología from Universidad Nacional Autónoma de México (CNyN-UNAM), currently he works as professor at the Universidad Politécnica de Baja California. His research has been published in different journals and presented at international conferences since 2009. He has served as reviewer for different journals, some of them include IEEE Transactions on Industrial Electronics, IEEE Transactions on Instrumentation, Measurement and Sensor Review. His research interests are focused on the field of time and frequency metrology, the design of wireless sensor networks, automated systems and highly sensitive chemical detectors.

Shomini Parashar, Assistant Professor, Department of Biotechnology, IMS Engineering College Ghaziabad

Manas Kumar Pedi is an Assistant Professor and Assistant Controller of Examination at the School of Economics and Commerce, KIIT Deemed to be University. With an M.Phil. and Ph.D. in Economics from the Central University of Gujarat and a Postgraduate degree from Pondicherry University, he has four years of teaching experience, mentoring undergraduate, postgraduate, and doctoral students. His research interests include economic growth, human capital mobility, rural development, public policy, and agriculture, with work presented at national and international conferences and published in prestigious journals. His teaching expertise spans Microeconomics, Economic Growth and Development, Research Methodology, and the Indian Economy.

Panoraia Poulaki (BSc, MSc, PhD) is Laboratory Teaching Staff in Department of Economics and Management of Tourism of the University of the Aegean. She also teaches in MSc Programme in Strategic Management of Tourism Destinations and Hospitality Enterprises of the University of the Aegean. She holds a first degree in History and Archaeology from the National and Kapodistrian University of

Athens, Master of Science (MSc) in Planning, Management and Policy of Tourism from the University of the Aegean and a Doctor of Philosophy (PhD) in Tourism from the same University. She has written a book about the contribution of the Ottoman Monuments of Chios to the development of cultural tourism and she has published research papers in scientific journals and has presented her research work in international conferences. Her research interests focus on the development, planning and management of tourism, with emphasis on special and alternative forms of tourism.

Dolly Prajapati is a dynamic Assistant Professor and dedicated research scholar at Ganpat University, with a specialized focus in Machine Learning and Deep Learning. Her academic journey began with a Diploma in Computer Engineering, followed by a B.Tech and M.Tech from Ganpat University demonstrating a consistent trajectory of academic excellence and deep technical acumen. Her research is centered on developing intelligent, data-driven systems that address complex real-world problems. She is particularly passionate about advancing AI-driven models and bridging the gap between theoretical innovation and practical implementation in areas such as healthcare, smart systems, and automation. In her current role, she actively contributes to the academic ecosystem through teaching, mentorship, capstone project guidance, and collaborative research. She is committed to nurturing future engineers with a strong foundation in emerging technologies and real-world problem-solving. Known for her visionary thinking, technical depth, and commitment to innovation, Dolly aims to make meaningful contributions to the fields of Artificial Intelligence and Computer Science & Engineering both in academia and industry. Her mission is to inspire, innovate, and lead with purpose in the evolving technological landscape.

María E. Raygoza-L holds a Ph.D. in Chemistry and Energy from the Engineering Institute of the Universidad Autónoma de Baja California (UABC) and a Bachelor's degree in Industrial Engineering (Manufacturing specialization). She is a full-time professor and researcher at the Universidad Politécnica de Baja California (UPBC) and a subject professor at UABC in Energy Engineering and Renewable Energies. With extensive industry experience, her research focuses on renewable energy, energy efficiency, environmental assessment and management, energy management systems, and the integration of governance and public-policy instruments for sustainable development. She is also pursuing a second Bachelor's degree in Psychology, strengthening her interdisciplinary perspective on human factors and technology adoption in sustainability transitions.

Ketan Sarvakar is a highly skilled researcher and professor with a focus on artificial intelligence and computer science. Having worked in academia for more than 20 years, he is currently a professor at Ganpat University. Prof. Sarvakar has received the Staff Excellence Award for Outstanding Faculty and Researcher on several occasions. His extensive research has produced ten patents in the UK, Canada, Australia, and India, as well as more than fifty research papers in journals indexed in the Web of Science, Scopus, IEEE, and other databases covering facial emotion recognition, sentiment analysis, and machine learning. He actively participates in professional organizations and research initiatives, showcasing his creative contributions. Professor Sarvakar is a prominent and esteemed member of the academic community in his field. He was also a member of the IEEE Gujarat Section's Ex-COM in 2021 to 2024. In addition, he has reviewed articles for a number of international journals and served as a reviewer in a wide range of international journals.

Ajay Kumar Sharma, currently serving as Professor & Head at IMS Engineering College, Ghaziabad, brings over two decades of extensive experience in the realms of Teaching, Research, Training & Administration. Holding a Ph.D. in Biotechnology from BITS, Pilani, along with a Master's in Engineering (Biotechnology) and a Bachelor's in Pharmacy, Dr. Sharma's academic journey is distinguished by his commitment to excellence. Dr. Sharma's contributions extend beyond academia; he has successfully supervised Ph.D. & PG research projects, chaired interdisciplinary committees, and actively participated in NBA & NAAC core teams. Dr. Sharma has participated in/ organized more than 50 skill programs and published research papers in peer reviewed international journals. Dr. Sharma has travelled extensively across India for academia and industrial interaction and to foster opportunities for students. He is a life member of three Scientific and Cultural Societies and Association.

Arunima Shastri is a legal academic with a focus on the intersections of law, technology, and social justice. She holds an LL.M. in Corporate and Commercial Law from NLU Odisha and is currently completing her Ph.D. at Gujarat National Law University, where her research critically explores the interplay between intellectual property rights, visual art, deepfakes, and digital expression. Her teaching and research interests include intellectual property law, data privacy, blockchain regulation, and human rights law, with a particular emphasis on LGBTQ+ rights. Through her work, she bridges doctrinal legal analysis with contemporary technological and cultural developments, contributing to scholarship and curriculum development in emerging areas of law.

Ajay K. Singh is working as an Associate Professor (Research) in the Department of Humanities and Social Science, Graphic Era (Deemed to be University) Dehradun. He has worked as Assistant Professor (Economics) in the School of Liberal Arts & Management, DIT University Dehradun for 6 years. He did Post-Doctorate Research with EDI of India, Ahmedabad, Gujarat (India). He received MPhil (Economics) from DAVV Indore (India), and PhD (Economics) from IIT Indore (India. He has published several research papers in the diversified area such as climate change, agricultural productivity, assessment of food security; estimation of GFSI, development of environmental sustainability index (ESI) and its association with socio-economic indicators; measurement and determinants of entrepreneurship ecosystem, and dimension of sustainable development and its interlinkages with economic development.

Bhupinder Singh working as Professor at Sharda University, India. Also, Honorary Professor in University of South Wales UK and Santo Tomas University Tunja, Colombia. His areas of publications as Smart Healthcare, Medicines, fuzzy logics, artificial intelligence, robotics, machine learning, deep learning, federated learning, IoT, PV Glasses, metaverse and many more. He has 3 books, 139 paper publications, 163 paper presentations in international/national conferences and seminars, participated in more than 40 workshops/FDP's/QIP's, 25 courses from international universities of repute, organized more than 59 events with international and national academicians and industry people's, editor-in-chief and co-editor in journals, developed new courses. He has given talks at international universities, resource person in international conferences such as in Nanyang Technological University Singapore, Tashkent State University of Law Uzbekistan; KIMEP University Kazakhstan, All'ah meh Tabatabi University Iran, the Iranian Association of International Criminal law, Iran and Hague Center for International Law and Investment, The Netherlands, Northumbria University Newcastle UK,

Srinivasan Vasan is an Assistant Professor in the Department of Humanities and Social Sciences at Graphic Era (Deemed to be University), with 14 years of teaching and field expertise. He has served in the Ministry of Health and Family Welfare, as a Guest Faculty, and as a Mobilization Training Specialist with the State Government. Recently, he contributed to a tuberculosis project funded by GFATM and USAID. He has published 60 papers, with 20 more under peer review in UGC-CARE and SCOPUS journals.

Kittisak Wongmahesak lectures at North Bangkok University's Faculty of Political Science and directs the Association of Legal & Political Studies. He is also a Research Fellow at Shinawatra University in Thailand and Universiti Sultan

Zainal Abidin in Malaysia. His academic influence also extends to Indonesia, where he holds roles such as Adjunct Professor at Sekolah Tinggi Ilmu Administrasi Abdul Haris and various other Indonesian universities, including Universitas Muhammadiyah Sinjai, Makassar, and Sidenreng Rappang. He has served as a Full Professor of Public Administration at Huanghe Business School, Henan University of Economics and Law in China, and University of City Island, Cyprus. Furthermore, he was an Adjunct Researcher at Vietnam's Ton Duc Thang University and Duy Tan University. He holds a Ph.D. in Social Sciences alongside his M.A. and B.A. in Political Science from Kasetsart University, and obtained an M.B.A. and M.P.A. from Ramkhamhaeng University, alongside a B.Pol.Sc. in International Relations from Sukhothai Thammathirat Open University. His expertise covers Political Science, Public and Private Management, International Political Economy, and Social Research.

Index

A

B

C

D

T

V

W

www.ingramcontent.com/pod-product-compliance
Lightning Source LLC
LaVergne TN
LVHW080908300926
849162LV00003B/596